IAMBLICHUS
On the Pythagorean Way of Life
Text, Translation, and Notes

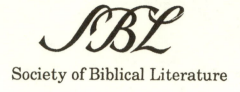

Society of Biblical Literature

TEXTS AND TRANSLATIONS
GRAECO-ROMAN RELIGION SERIES

edited by
Hans Dieter Betz
Edward N. O'Neill

Texts and Translations 29
Graeco-Roman Religion Series 11

IAMBLICHUS
On the Pythagorean Way of Life
Text, Translation, and Notes

Iamblichus
On the Pythagorean Way of Life
Text, Translation, and Notes

by
John Dillon
Jackson Hershbell

Scholars Press
Atlanta, Georgia

IAMBLICHUS
On the Pythagorean Way of Life
Text, Translation, and Notes

by
John Dillon
Jackson Hershbell

Library of Congress Cataloging-in-Publication Data

Iamblichus, ca. 250-ca. 330.
    [On the Pythagorean life. English & Greek]
    On the Pythagorean way of life / Iamblichus ; text, translation,
and notes by John Dillon, Jackson Hershbell.
    p. cm. — (Texts and translations ; 29. Graeco-Roman religion
series ; 11.)
    English and Greek text of: On the Pythagorean life.
    Includes bibliographical references and indexes.
    ISBN 1-55540-522-3 (alk. paper). —ISBN 1-55540-523-1 (pbk. :
alk. paper)
    1. Pythagoras and Pythagorean school—Early works to 1800.
2. Neoplatonism—Early works to 1800. I. Dillon, John M.
II. Hershbell, Jackson P., 1935- . III. Title. IV. Series: Texts
and translations ; no. 29. V. Series: Texts and translations.
Graeco-Roman religion series ; 11.
B669.0522E5 1990
182'.2—dc20   90-44149
                                  CIP

Printed in the United States of America
on acid-free paper

CONTENTS

v

PREFACE

Our work on Iamblichus' *De vita pythagorica* (hereafter *VP*) is the result of several years of a very pleasant collaboration. Much of it has been by correspondence, but we were also able to have productive meetings in Chicago, Dublin, and Minneapolis. Our translation is based on the text of L. Deubner, later emended by U. Klein (Stuttgart, 1975), and we are very grateful to the B. G. Teubner Verlag, Stuttgart, for its generous permission to reproduce the Deubner-Klein text. M. von Albrecht's excellent German translation, *Pythagoras: Legende, Lehre, Lebensgestaltung* (Zurich/Stuttgart, 1963), was often valuable for understanding some difficult passages. At the time we were working on *VP* the only English translation known to us was that of Thomas Taylor, *Iamblichus, Life of Pythagoras, or Pythagoric Life* (London, 1818) which has many faults, not surprising for the age in which it was undertaken. Since completion of our work, G. Clark's *Iamblichus: On the Pythagorean Life* (Liverpool, 1989) has appeared, a sometimes free rendering of the text which does not always reflect the ponderous style of Iamblichus.

We have not attempted a full commentary on the text and translation. Generally, notes indicate parallel passages both in Iamblichus' *VP,* and in other ancient authors, especially Porphyry and Diogenes Laertius. They also mention modern discussions of major issues, and provide alternate translations where there is ambiguity. Occasionally variant readings are adopted. The reader who desires more information should consult the primary and secondary sources cited in the notes, and in the select bibliography. Each sentence of Iamblichus' work probably deserves comment, but mindful of the shortness of life, we offer a text and translation designed for readers interested in studying this difficult but very important work for the history of Pythagoreanism, and for the philosophy and religion of the Graeco-Roman world.

Each chapter of *VP* is prefaced by the relevant portion of the κεφάλαια or summaries found at the beginning of Deubner's edition. These summaries, or chapter headings, may be by Iamblichus himself, and are certainly useful for better understanding the contents of the work. We have tried to be consistent in transliterating Greek proper names into their Latin forms, e.g. Ancaeus, not Ankaios, or Hippasus, not Hippasos. In the case of Greek place names, we generally use conventional forms, e.g. Samos, not Samus, Cnidos not Cnidus. Abbreviations used are in conformity with those found in *A Greek-English Lexicon* compiled by H. G. Liddell and R. Scott, ed. by H. S. Jones and R. McKenzie, Oxford, 1940. Several recurrent special terms such as *symbola* or *acusmata* are given in transliteration.

In the introduction, we deal with topics such as the growth of the legend of Pythagoras and the biographical tradition, the life and works of Iamblichus, and the structure and purpose of his *VP.* The problem of Iamblichus' sources is treated partly in the biographical tradition, and in the notes. It is further well discussed by W. Burkert, *Lore and Science in Ancient Pythagoreanism* (Cambridge, Mass. 1972) 98-105.

Our attempt to translate Iamblichus' *VP* began about 1980 when I was working on Plutarch and Pythagoreanism. I realized that help was needed, especially from someone knowledgeable about Iamblichus and Neoplatonism. That person whom I knew from previous collaboration, was John Dillon. His help with the translation, notes, and introduction has been invaluable, and so I think it only appropriate that our work appear as Dillon-Hershbell. He has worked very hard on the project, and I value his contributions to a work which might never have seen the light of day. Special thanks also are due to Hans Dieter Betz who has shown continuing interest in our project, and made many valuable suggestions for the improvement of this volume. The assistance of Edward O'Neil, co-editor of the Graeco-Roman Religion series, is also much appreciated. A final note of thanks is due to Ronald Hock who also made a number of corrections and suggestions. If we have shed some light on an important text for the history of Pythagoreanism, we shall be pleased indeed. Thanks are also due to Jon Solomon who helped in translating Iamblichus' discussion of Pythagorean musical theory (chap. 26); and to Mrs. Marlos Rudie who was much involved in typing the manuscript(s) before her retirement from the University of Minnesota, Mrs. Jan Philibert who continued Mrs. Rudie's work, and to Oliver Nicholson who most graciously offered to do the indices.

Last (but not least) of all, special thanks are due to Darwin Melnyk who has seen the manuscript through various stages of final production.

Jackson P. Hershbell,
Minneapolis, Minnesota, U.S.A.

John Dillon,
Dublin, Republic of Ireland

ABBREVIATIONS

AJP	*American Journal of Philology*
ANRW	*Aufstieg und Niedergang der Römischen Welt*
ARW	*Archiv für Religionswissenschaft*
CB	*Classical Bulletin*
D.-K.	H. Diels, ed. *Die Fragmente der Vorsokratiker.* Vols. I-III. 8th ed. (5th and subsequent editions revised by W. Kranz). Berlin: Weidmann, 1956.
GRBS	*Greek, Roman, and Byzantine Studies*
HTR	*Harvard Theological Review*
IDB	G. Buttrick, ed. *The Interpreter's Dictionary of the Bible,* Vols. I-IV. New York: Abingdon, 1962.
JHS	*Journal of Hellenic Studies*
LCL	*Loeb Classical Library*
LSJ	H. G. Liddell, R. Scott, H.S. Jones, *A Greek-English Lexicon.* Oxford: Clarendon, 1968.
OCD	N. G. L. Hammond and H. H. Scullard, eds. *The Oxford Classical Dictionary,* 2nd ed. Oxford: Clarendon, repr. 1984.
Philol.	*Philologus*
RAC	*Reallexikon für Antike und Christentum*
RE	*Realencyclopädie der classischen Altertumswissenschaft*
REA	*Revue des études anciennes*
REG	*Révue des études grecques*
RhM	*Rheinisches Museum*
SVF	*Stoicorum Veterum Fragmenta*
TAPA	*Transactions of the American Philological Association*
ZNW	*Zeitschrift für die neutestamentliche Wissenschaft*

INTRODUCTION

I. The Importance of Iamblichus' Treatise for
Graeco-Roman Philosophy and Religion

Iamblichus' *On the Pythagorean* (or *Pythagoric*) *Way of Life* is by far the longest, and most complex of the extant ancient works on Pythagoras, and it was originally an introduction to a ten volume study of Pythagoreanism entitled *A Compendium of Pythagorean Doctrine* (Συναγωγὴ τῶν Πυθαγορείων δογμάτων).[1] Unlike the accounts of Diogenes Laertius and Porphyry in which "dürre Daten" predominate, Iamblichus' *VP* is much more than a biography.[2] For example, chapters 2-7 focus on details of Pythagoras' early life and development, but in chapters 8-11 biographical information becomes subordinate to the speeches given by Pythagoras in Croton. In chapters 12-27 major portions of Pythagoras' teaching and way of life are presented, and chronology seems quite unimportant. The remaining chapters of *VP* concentrate on Pythagoras as the teacher of individual and political virtues. On the whole, *VP* is not a biography of Pythagoras, but a systematic presentation of the way of life and doctrines which he taught to his followers and other human beings.

In the preface to *VP* (chap. 1), Iamblichus draws attention to Pythagoreanism as the "divine philosophy," and throughout the work he treats Pythagoras as the divine man and thaumaturge whose soul was in close contact with Apollo.[3] Early on in chapters 2-4, he connects Pythagoras with the near east, e.g. Phoenicia and Babylonia, and with Egypt, lands often associated with a divine or holy man. Matthew, for example, describes how magi came from the east to honor Jesus' birth, and how the holy family went to Egypt. Indeed, it is not amiss to view *VP* as a "gos-

---

1. See the excellent study of B. D. Larsen, *Jamblique de Chalcis. Exégète et philosophe* (Aarhus, 1972). Chapter II is entitled the "Synagoge Pythagorica," 66-147, and *VP* is treated on pps. 80-98.

2. See M. von Albrecht, "Das Menschenbild in Iamblichs Darstellung der pythagoreischen Lebensform," *Antike und Abendland* 12 (1966) 52. As von Albrecht and others have noted, the title, Περὶ τοῦ Πυθαγορείου (or: -ικοῦ) βίου, clearly suggests that this is not a biography or life of Pythagoras.

3. See *VP* 2,7. According to von Albrecht, *Antike und Abendland* 12 (1966) 53: "von Anfang an wird also mit Entschiedenheit ein platonisch-heidnischer Spiritualismus vertreten, der deutlich der christlichen Auffassung von der Fleischwerdung des Gottessohnes, von der Erlösung auch des menschlichen Leibes, widerspricht." For a full account of the concept of the divine man in Graeco-Roman antiquity, see H.D. Betz, "Gottmensch II (Griechisch-römische Antike und Urchristentum)," *RAC* XII (1983) 234-312, especially 257-59 on Pythagoras.

1

pel" (see Thales' proclamation of "good news" at 2,12), and both Iamblichus' *VP*
and Porphyry's *Life of Pythagoras* have parallels to the Christian gospels.[4]

But while Iamblichus regards Pythagoras as the divine man, he also believes
that he is an embodiment or symbol of the contemplative or intellectual life, the
βίος θεωρητικός. According to Diogenes Laertius (8.1), Pythagoras was φιλομαθής,
and this characteristic is vividly portrayed by Iamblichus: Pythagoras is the
founder of philosophy who not only much advanced the mathematical and natural sciences, but also discovered harmonic ratios (chap. 26). Pythagoras is also an
exemplar of the active or practical life, the βίος πρακτικός, e.g. he liberated Italian
cities from tyranny (chap. 7), and was a leader in Croton's civic life (chap. 8 *et
passim*). Pythagoras also practiced and taught the virtues of justice, temperance
(or "sound-mindedness"), courage, and friendship (chaps. 30 ff.), and this latter
virtue is especially important since it unites different levels of being: gods, humans, and animals. Friendship also brings human beings together, and within an
individual it unites various parts of the body and soul, so that these function in
harmony. Pythagoras himself was a link or bond between the human (or mortal)
and the divine (see, for example, *VP* 28, 143 f.). In sum, Pythagoras is the wise
man par excellence who had close contact with divinity, and who exemplified the
contemplative and practical ways of life.

As von Albrecht observed in "Das Menschenbild in Iamblichs Darstellung der
pythagoreischen Lebensform," the *VP* is an important document for understanding the philosophical and religious thought of late antiquity.[5] In it Iamblichus presents a view of humanity in which weakness and dependence on the divine are
emphasized. At the beginning of *VP*, for example, Iamblichus states that understanding the "nobility and greatness" of Pythagoras' philosophy is a very slow pro-
cess, and the gods' assistance is necessary. One must summon their aid
(παρακαλεῖν), and follow their guidance (ἔπεσθαι). Given close connections between Platonism and Pythagoreanism, it is not surprising that *VP* begins with this
preface much influenced by *Timaeus* 27c. For Iamblichus the religious and ethical
are closely connected: the person who knows human limitations and trusts in the
gods, is σώφρων or "sound-minded." And later in *VP* (chap. 31) the virtue of σωφροσύνη receives extensive treatment. It is, of course, a virtue much discussed by
Plato, e.g. in the *Republic*, and in the *Charmides* (164d) where it is equated with
"self-knowledge" (γνῶθι σεαυτόν).[6] According to von Albrecht, Iamblichus' treatment brings together the themes of self-knowledge and piety (or reverence to the
gods), in an extraordinary way.[7] Among the signs of Pythagoras' piety were his be-

---

4. See p. 24 ff. of this introduction, and M. Hadas and M. Smith, *Heroes and Gods. Spiritual Biographies in Antiquity* (New York, 1965) 106-107.

5. Like Iamblichus' *De Mysteriis*, it may be a "Grundbuch der spätantiken Religion." See von
Albrecht who here quotes Nilsson's assessment of *De Mysteriis*, *Antike und Abendland* 12 (1966) 51
ff. See M. P. Nilsson, *Geschichte der griechischen Religion* II, 3rd ed. (Munich 1974) 447 ff.

lief in an immortal soul and a recognition that in past incarnations, he was Euphorbus, a hero of the Trojan war, who with Apollo's help, slew Patroclus. Pythagoras' soul also stood in very close contact with Apollo, and in both instances, self-knowledge is best understood as knowledge of one's immortal soul, a belief expressed in Plato's *Alcibiades* I (133c).[8] If von Albrecht is correct, "self-knowledge" appears on three levels in *VP.* 1) the metaphysical where humans are viewed in a hierarchical world order, and subject to divine powers; 2) the ethical which arises from the metaphysical emphasis on subordination to the divine, and leads to an evaluation of one's own bilities; and 3) the psychological level where self-knowledge results in knowledge ot ne's immortal soul.[9]

Contrary to those who have condemned *VP* for its prolixity, repetitiveness, or seeming lack of order, Iamblichus does have organizational principles: after Pythagoras' exoteric teaching (chaps. 7-11), there follows his esoteric teaching (chaps. 12-27), and the remaining chapters of *VP* seem to be mainly organized about the political, "cathartic," and theoretical virtues, a schema developed by Porphyry in his treatment of the virtues.[10] So, for example, Iamblichus twice discusses music (chap. 15 and chaps. 25-26), a repetition which does not mean a lack of order. If von Albrecht is correct, the first discussion of music in *VP* is in the context of the "cathartic" or "purificatory" virtues (see the heading to chap. 16); the second is in the context of the theoretical virtues. Moreover, as will be discussed in Pt. VI of our introduction, there is a protreptic purpose to *VP*, and the repetitions serve to reinforce important points, points especially intended for Iamblichus' own students.[11] Certainly he presents the Pythagorean way of life with great vividness and enthusiasm.

In conclusion, the *VP* is a very important work for the history of the Pythagoras legend, and for understanding Iamblichus' own Platonic beliefs in which philosophy and religion were closely connected. In composing *VP* as an introduction to a ten volume work on Pythagoreanism, Iamblichus used many earlier sources, e.g., Aristotle, Aristoxenus, Apollonius of Tyana, and Nicomachus of Gerasa, and it is thus a valuable source-book for the Pythagorean way of life. It is also a valuable summation of the ethical tradition of Greek philosophy, a tradition in which philosophy was not simply learning doctrines, but pursuing a whole way of life. *VP* thus reveals the interests and mind of a thinker who lived when another way of

---

6. For an excellent study of *sophrosyne* in Plato, see H. North, *Sophrosyne. Self-knowledge and Self-Restraint in Greek Literature* (Ithaca, 1966), especially 150-197. *Sophrosyne* in Neoplatonism and Neopythagoreanism is discussed on pps. 234-242.

7. See von Albrecht, *Antike und Abendland* 12 (1966) 57-58.

8. Iamblichus wrote a commentary on this work. See p. 22 of this introduction.

9. Von Albrecht, *Antike und Abendland* 12 (1966) 60-61.

10. Von Albrecht, *Antike und Abendland* 12 (1966), 55.

11. See p. 22 and pps. 28-29 of this introduction.

life, Christianity, was gaining converts, and supplanting the Hellenic values of the past. It is hoped that the remainder of this introduction to *VP* will further clarify its importance for understanding Graeco-Roman philosophy and religion.

II. The Legend of Pythagoras

Ancient authors interested in Pythagoras often viewed him from their own literary, philosophical, religious, or social perspectives, and, like their modern counterparts, were sometimes dependent on the fragmentary and inconsistent sources at their disposal. According to Porphyry, for example, Eudoxus of Cnidos claimed that Pythagoras was a vegetarian, and avoided cooks and hunters.[12] But, according to Diogenes Laertius, Aristoxenus reported that Pythagoras ate almost all kinds of meat, and abstained only from ploughing oxen and rams.[13] As F. Wehrli noted, Aristoxenus probably limited Pythagoras' abstention from eating meat to certain animals in order to repudiate superstition ("das Superstitiöse zu leugnen"), and gave economical-ethical reasons for the prohibition.[14] Many other discrepancies in the ancient reports about Pythagoras could be cited, and even the extant "biographies" by Diogenes Laertius, Porphyry, and Iamblichus, portray Pythagoras from different points of view. To be sure, Iamblichus relied on earlier sources as did Diogenes and Porphyry, but his use of these sources was for his own literary and philosophical purposes. Hence, before examining the biographical tradition and Iamblichus' own work, some consideration of the "legend" of Pythagoras seems appropriate. This legend has received extensive treatment in the twentieth century, especially by I. Lévy and W. Burkert.[15] Without attempting to duplicate their studies, or those of many other scholars, the following discussion is offered primarily as an introduction to Iamblichus' knowledge and use of sources for the Pythagoras legend. There are few references to Pythagoras (or his followers) before Aristotle and other fourth century B.C. writers. Heraclitus of Ephesus in the fifth century refers to Pythagoras' "learning of many things" with contempt (D.-K., B 40; cf. B 129).[16] Herodotus mentions Zalmoxis, a slave of Pythagoras, and his master who was "not the feeblest intellect of the Hellenes" (IV.95), and in II.81, he refers to a Pythagorean prohibition against burial in wool-

---

12. Porph. *VP* 7; μάγειροι could mean either "cooks" or "butchers."

13. D. L. 8. 20; on Diogenes Laertius' report, see A. Delatte, *La vie de Pythagore de Diogène Laërce* (New York, reprint 1979) 188-90. See also W. Burkert, *Lore and Science in Ancient Pythagoreanism*, trans. E. L. Minar, Jr. (Cambridge, Mass. 1972) 180-181, who deals briefly with the conflicting evidence, and believes that Aristoxenus was thinking of "theoretical" Pythagoreans who did eat meat.

14. F. Wehrli, *Die Schule des Aristoteles*, vol. II: *Aristoxenos* (Basel, 1945) 56.

15. I. Lévy, *Recherches sur les sources de la légende de Pythagore* (Paris, 1926), and *La Légende de Pythagore de Grèce en Palestine* (Paris, 1927). For Burkert, see n. 13 of this study. Burkert's bibliography is extremely useful for studies of Pythagoras and Pythagoreanism prior to 1972.

en clothing. Ion of Chios possibly doubts Pythagoras' status as a true intellectual or σοφός (Ion fr.4 = D. L. 1. 120). There may also be references to Pythagoras by the poet-philosophers, Xenophanes and Empedocles, whose verses connect him with belief in reincarnation.[17] Additional evidence about Pythagoras is not found in the remains of fifth century B.C. literature.

Beginning with Plato and his students in the fourth century B.C., the Pythagoras legend assumes greater dimensions: Plato briefly refers twice to Pythagoras and his followers (*R.* 530d and 600 a-b), but his few remarks on a "Pythagorean way of life," and his report that astronomy and harmony are "sister" sciences, have not prevented ancient and modern interpreters of Plato from discerning Pythagorean influence on many of his writings, especially the *Philebus* and *Timaeus*. The belief that Plato was indebted to Pythagoreans was expressed, for example, by Aristotle in his *Metaphysics* (987a 29 ff.). From the available evidence, some of Plato's students, notably Heraclides Ponticus, were drawn not only to Pythagoreanism, but to the person of Pythagoras. It was Heraclides who recounts Pythagoras' story of his previous incarnations: he was first Aethalides, Hermes' son, and received from his father the gift of remembering all, both in life and death; later he was Euphorbus, Hermotimus, Pyrrhus, a fisherman of Delos, and lastly, he became Pythagoras.[18] Attempts have been made to reconstruct Heraclides' *Abaris* which perhaps contained two important episodes: a) the meeting of the wonder-worker Abaris with Pythagoras, and b) a descent by Pythagoras to the underworld.[19] Although scholars are not agreed on a reconstruction of Heraclides' *Abaris*, or on his portrayal of Pythagoras in other works, there seems to be unanimity that Heraclides regarded Pythagoras as an unusual person to whom special powers were given.[20]

Aristotle, originally a student of Plato, wrote *On the Pythagoreans* (a work of the same title is ascribed to Heraclides)[21] in which he reported that the Crotoniates proclaimed Pythagoras as the Hyperborean Apollo, and depicted Pythagoras as

16. D.-K. refers to the Diels-Kranz collection of the fragments of early Greek philosophical works: H. Diels, *Die Fragmente der Vorsokratiker*, ed. W. Kranz. I, 8th ed. (Berlin, 1956). The Heraclitus fragments and other fifth century B.C. evidence on Pythagoras have often been discussed; see, for example, W.K.C. Guthrie, *A History of Greek Philosophy* I (Cambridge, 1962) 157-161, or G. S. Kirk, J. E. Raven, and M. Schofield, *The Presocratic Philosophers*, 2nd ed. (Cambridge, 1983) 216-222.

17. Xenophanes D.-K. B7. That Empedocles, D.-K. B 129, refers to Pythagoras is by no means certain. Burkert, *Lore and Science*, 127 remarks that some ancients thought that it referred to Parmenides right after stating that "Pythagoras appears as a superhuman figure" in Empedocles' verses.

18. See, Burkert, *Lore and Science*, 138-139, and more recently H. B. Gottschalk, *Heraclides of Pontus* (Oxford, 1980) 115-118, for a critical and readable account of Heraclides' *Abaris*.

19. See Burkert, *Lore and Science*, 103 n. 32. Gottschalk, *Heraclides*, 118 ff. is very critical of attempts to reconstruct Heraclides' *Abaris*.

20. *Ibid.* 114 ff.

the focus of wondrous events or deeds, e.g. the revelation of his golden thigh, a greeting by the river Casas, his prediction of a white bear in Caulonia, and his biting to death a poisonous snake in Etruria[22] Aristotle's *On the Pythagoreans* also dealt with Pythagoras' teachings, the *acusmata* or *symbola*, oral maxims or sayings, many of which are preserved in Iamblichus (e.g. *VP* 82-86), and other ancient authors.[23]

In his extant works, however, Aristotle never mentions Pythagoras by name, only Pythagoreans or "so-called Pythagoreans," and reports on Pythagoras by other fourth century authors are sparse.[24] Andron of Ephesus, for example, discussed Pythagoras in his *Tripous*, narrated three miracles similar to those in Aristotle's *On the Pythagoreans*, and believed that Pythagoras was Pherecydes' student.[25] Eratosthenes identified Pythagoras the philosopher with Pythagoras of Samos, an Olympic victor in 588 B.C. Lévy considered this report to be part of the "légende d'enfance" which grew about Pythagoras: even as a boy, he won an Olympic contest.[26]

Between Heraclides and authors of the first century A.D., there is almost an eclipse of "l'histoire fabuleuse" of Pythagoras, and although the miraculous aspects of this legend were not wholly forgotten, authors such as Aristoxenus, Dicaearchus, and Timaeus of Tauromenium were inclined to regard Pythagoras as a philosopher and moralist rather than as a divine person or wonder-worker.

III. The Biographical Tradition

It is with Aristoxenus, "the founder of literary biography,"[27] that the first life of Pythagoras appears. Aristoxenus' interest was not confined to Pythagoras himself: besides a *Life of Pythagoras* (or *About Pythagoras and his Followers*), some ancient writers refer to Aristoxenus' *Pythagorean Sayings* and *On the Pythagorean Way of Life*. From the remains of these works collected by F. Wehrli,[28] it seems that Aristoxenus regarded Pythagoras as a wise man free from anything superstitious or super-

21. The fragments of Aristotle's *On the Pythagoreans* are in *Aristotelis fragmenta*, ed. V. Rose (Leipzig, 1886) 153-164, and in *Aristotelis fragmenta selecta*, ed. W. D. Ross (Oxford, 1955) 129-143. See also J. A. Philip, "Aristotle's Monograph on the Pythagoreans," *TAPA* 94 (1963) 185-198.

22. On the miracles of Pythagoras, see Burkert, *Lore and Science*, 141 ff.

23. The first extensive modern studies of the *symbola* are those by C. Hoelk, *De acusmatis sive symbolis Pythagoricis* (Diss. Kiel, 1894) and by F. Boehm, *De symbolis Pythagoreis* (Diss. Berlin, 1905). The most accessible and recent studies are those of J. A. Philip, *Pythagoras and Early Pythagoreanism* (Toronto, 1966) 134-150, and Burkert, *Lore and Science*, 166-192.

24. See I. Lévy, *Recherches sur les sources*, who gives a good survey of fourth century sources, 10 ff. Aristotle is discussed on pp. 10-18. See also Burkert, *Lore and Science*, 28-52, mainly on the Pythagoreans according to Aristotle.

25. Andron's reports are discussed by Lévy, *Recherches sur les sources*, 19-20.

26. Lévy, *Recherches sur les sources*, 20-22.

27. The phrase is that of R. Leo, *Die griechisch-römische Biographie* (Leipzig, 1901) who remarks that Aristoxenus "erscheint als der Begründer der literarischen Biographie," 102.

natural. He did not forbid eating beans, or most kinds of meat. It was Pythagoras who first introduced weights and measures into Greece, and who treated numbers theoretically, apart from their use in mercantile transactions. He refused to live under Polycrates' tyranny, and at the age of forty, migrated from Samos to Italy where his teaching attracted followers from all around: Lucanians, Messapians, Peucetians, and Romans. He later refused to accept Cylon into his community because of Cylon's violent and tyrannical character. In brief, Lévy seems correct in considering Aristoxenus' *Life* as a panegyric to the glory of one "qui unit le culte de la speculation au souci des applications pratiques, du moraliste auquel remontait l'institution de la société des sages vertueux. . . ."[29] The *Pythagorean Sayings* dealt with Pythagoras' teachings on the need for restraining the emotions. Since human beings are naturally subject to untamed emotions, education and upbringing by parents and society are necessary. Aristoxenus' *On the Pythagorean Way of Life* was also concerned with the importance of discipline, a discipline maintained by dietary regulations and life in a community which fostered friendship. Given Aristoxenus' importance for the history of ancient biography, and his interest in the Pythagoras legend, it is not surprising that he became an authority for later accounts of Pythagoras, and is often cited by Porphyry, Diogenes, and Iamblichus.

Dicaearchus, a friend of Aristoxenus, wrote *Lives* of Plato and other philosophers, and *The Greek Way of Life*, a universal history of culture until the fourth century B.C.[30] In these works, he portrayed Pythagoras as a master of the practical life ($\beta\iota\omega\varsigma$ $\pi\rho\alpha\kappa\tau\iota\kappa\acute{o}\varsigma$) and believed that Plato borrowed his doctrines from Pythagoras and Socrates. Although Dicaearchus himself denied the soul's immortality, he reported and caricatured the legend of Pythagoras' previous incarnations: first he was Euphorbus, and then Pyrandus, Aethalides, and finally Alco, a courtesan. Dicaearchus also narrated Pythagoras' success in attracting the elders, young men, and women of Croton to his teachings.[31] Later, during the revolt against the Pythagoreans, Pythagoras escaped to Metapontium where he died of starvation.

In his long *History* (thirty-eight books) concerned mainly with Sicily, Italy, and Libya, Timaeus of Tauromenium gave attention to Pythagoras and his followers.[32] According to Timaeus, for example, Pythagoras' daughter led the chorus of vir-

---

28. See Wehrli, *Aristoxenos*, 10-20, and Lévy, *Recherches sur les sources*, 44-49 who summarizes Aristoxenus' reports on Pythagoras.

29. Lévy, *Recherches sur les sources*, 45. We are indebted to Lévy's work as well as to Wehrli's *Aristoxenos* for understanding Aristoxenus' *Life*.

30. On Dicaearchus, see Lévy, *Recherches sur les sources*, 49-52, and F. Wehrli, ed. *Die Schule des Aristoteles*, vol. I: *Dikaiarchos* (Basel, 1944). As Wehrli noted "unter Bioi . . . kann ein Peripatetiker ebenso Lebensformen wie Biographien verstehen. . . ." 50.

31. Dicaearchus' report on Pythagoras' speeches at Croton has been much discussed. See, for example, Burkert, *Lore and Science*, 122.

32. On Timaeus, see, for example, Lévy, *Recherches sur les sources*, 53-59.

gins in Croton, and after her marriage, the chorus of women.[33] Timaeus also reported Pythagoras' dealings with young people who came to him: only after careful examination (δοκιμασία), were they allowed to see him face to face. Because of their great regard for Pythagoras, the citizens of Metapontium converted his house into a temple. Such details, however, do not provide an overall impression of Timaeus' treatment of Pythagoras, and he remains perhaps "the greatest unknown" among the ancient authors who dealt with the legend of Pythagoras.[34]

After Aristoxenus, Dicaearchus, and Timaeus, several authors played a role in the transmission and transformation of traditional stories about Pythagoras. Among the more important of these writers was Neanthes who gave details on Pythagoras' family and education.[35] According to Neanthes, Pythagoras' father Mnesarchus (not Mnemarchus as in Iamblichus' VP)[36] was a wealthy merchant, and Tyrian (not Samian) by birth.[37] Hence, he sent his son to Tyre where his teachers were Chaldeans. Neanthes was perhaps the first to connect Pythagoras with Phoenicia, and he also gave an account of Cylon's revolt against the Pythagoreans which differs from other sources: according to Neanthes, Pythagoras died with his companions (except Lysis and Archippus who escaped) when the house in which they gathered was set on fire.

Neanthes' identity is uncertain, but he is probably the third century B.C. historian from Cyzicus.[38] Two other third century writers, both Peripatetic biographers, are Satyrus and Hermippus.[39] Satyrus is cited by Diogenes Laertius (8.40) who relies on Heraclides Lembus' *Epitome of the Lives of Satyrus*. According to this account, Pythagoras buried his teacher Pherecydes on Delos, and then returned to Italy for a banquet at Milo's house. If this brief report be compared with Porphyry's chap. 57 (introduced by "others say"), Satyrus may also have told the story of how Pythagoras' disciples saved him when Milo's house was torched by their enemies: Pythagoras escaped the fire, and died later of starvation in Metapontium, a detail that may show Satyrus' reliance on Dicaearchus.

Hermippus is perhaps best known for his satire on Pythagoras. According to Diogenes Laertius (8.41), Pythagoras made a subterranean dwelling after his arrival in Italy, and asked his mother to inform him of all that happened while he was below. He later came up, looking like a skeleton, and told the assembly that he had been in Hades. Pythagoras thus gained credence for his belief in the soul's

---

33. Porph. *VP* 4.

34. See Burkert, *Lore and Science*, 103-105.

35. On Neanthes, see Lévy, *Recherches sur les sources*, 60-64.

36. In Iamblichus the name is consistently "Mnemarchus," not "Mnesarchus." See Burkert, *Lore and Science*, 111, n. 13, and N. Demand, "Pythagoras, son of Mnesarchos," *Phronesis* 18 (1973) 91-96.

37. On Neanthes' report, Burkert, *Lore and Science* 111, n. 12.

38. *Ibid.*, 102.

39. For brief accounts of these biographers, see Lévy, *Recherches sur les sources*, 64-66.

immortality, Hermippus' reasons for telling the story were probably satirical, and an attempt to entertain his audience.[40] In general, the satire of Hermippus, and the reports of Neanthes and of Satyrus discussed previously, seem sufficient to show "quel chaos" prevailed in third century accounts of Pythagoras.[41]

Two other names worth mention in regard to the Pythagoras legend, are Androcydes and Alexander Polyhistor. Androcydes' *On the Pythagorean Symbols*, was probably a principal source for later tradition on the *acusmata* or *symbola* of Pythagoras. But exactly who Androcydes was remains uncertain. Possibly he was a fourth century B.C. physician, but all that can be safely surmised is that his work circulated about the first century B.C.[42] It is from Alexander Polyhistor that Diogenes Laertius derived his summary of Pythagorean doctrine in 8.24-33. Alexander's *Successions of Philosophers*, or his so-called *Commentaries* (Ὑπομνήματα), probably date about the second century B.C., but these *Commentaries*, like Androcydes' work on the Pythagorean symbols, do not directly concern Pythagoras' life.[43] They perpetuated the belief that Pythagoras was a philosopher of some sophistication who used a symbolic way of teaching.

Beginning in the first century A.D., there seems to be an upsurge of interest in Pythagoras and his followers. Seneca, for example, became a vegetarian because Sotion argued for it on Pythagorean principles.[44] Plutarch of Chaeronea was interested in Pythagoras, and had a good knowledge of Pythagoreanism.[45] Two shadowy figures, important for attempts to understand how the Pythagoras legend continued, are Antonius Diogenes and Apollonius.[46] Antonius wrote a twenty-four book account of adventures and travels, *Wonders beyond Thule*, and in it he reported, for example, Mnesarchus' discovery of a miraculous child (Pythagoras?) under a lovely white poplar which nourished him with dew (Porph. *VP* 10f.). Another report from Diogenes (Porph. *VP* 32f.), gives Pythagoras' advice about shunning honors, praise, and public discussion.

Scholars have generally regarded Apollonius as very important for understanding the Pythagoras legend. He is cited once by Porphyry (chap. 2), and by Iamblichus at *VP* 254 ff. for an account of the plot against the Pythagoreans.[47] Quite

---

40. See Gottschalk, *Heraclides*, 118.

41. Lévy, *Recherches sur les sources*, 65.

42. On Androcydes see Burkert, *Lore and Science*, 167, and Lévy, *Recherches sur les sources*, 66-70.

43. The fullest discussion is that of A. J. Festugière, "Les mémoires pythagoriques cités par Alexandre Polyhistor," *REG* 58 (1945) 1-65. See also Burkert, *Lore and Science*, 53 ff. For an excellent survey of pseudo-Pythagorean writings, see H. Thesleff, *An Introduction to the Pythagorean Writings of the Hellenistic Period*, in *Acta Academiae Aboensis, Humaniora* 24.3 (Åbo, 1961) 5-140.

44. On Sotion, see E. Zeller, *Die Philosophie der Griechen*, 5th ed. III. 2 (Leipzig, 1923) 113.

45. See G. Méautis, *Recherches sur le pythagorisme* (Neuchâtel, 1922), and J. Hershbell, "Plutarch's Pythagorean Friends," *CB* 60 (1984) 73-78.

46. See Lévy, *Recherches sur les sources*, 93-95 and 104-110. See also W. Fauth, "Astraios und Zalmoxis. Über Spuren pythagoreischer Aretalogie im Thule-Roman des Antonius Diogenes," *Hermes* 106 (1978) 220-241.

likely this Apollonius is the wonder-worker of Tyana, an enthusiastic Pythagorean.[48] Although little survives of his writings, scholars have attributed other chapters of Iamblichus' *VP* to Apollonius. For example, since Porphyry used Apollonius' *On Pythagoras* for chap. 2 of his own work on Pythagoras' early years, and this chapter has similarities to Iamb. *VP* 4-5 and 11, Lévy concluded that Apollonius was Iamblichus' source for these sections of *VP*.[49] Earlier than Lévy, E. Rohde argued that sections 3-25 of Iamblichus' *VP* were taken from Apollonius.[50] Without pursuing further the intricacies of *Quellenforschung*, it seems sufficient to present Lévy's summary of the section of Iamblichus' *VP* which may go back ("semblent donc revenir") to Apollonius:

1) an account of Pythagoras' life from his birth until his last departure from Samos (3-25 and 28);

2) events in Italy, especially Pythagoras' encounter with fishermen (36), and his teaching at Croton (37-57);

3) a story of Pythagoras' encounter with Abaris and Phalaris of Agrigentum (215);

4) an account of the decline of Pythagoras' popularity, and the uprising against him and his followers (254-64).[51]

In contrast to Apollonius, "le romancier sans scrupules," Nicomachus of Gerasa (ca. 50-150 A.D.), a near contemporary of Apollonius, was considered, by E. Rohde and others, as the honest compiler who used Aristoxenus' works for his reports on Pythagoras.[52] Nicomachus is specifically cited by Porphyry in sections 20 and 59, and Iamblichus mentions him once at *VP* 252 f. as being in general agreement with Aristoxenus. Such explicit references to Nicomachus do not, however, prove that he was a principal source for Porphyry and Iamblichus, and so J.A. Philip argued that there is no evidence that Nicomachus wrote a life of Pythagoras.[53] Philip also challenged Rohde's assumption that Iamblichus did not use Porphyry's biography: according to Rohde, passages common to both authors are explained by their reliance on Nicomachus. But, according to Philip, Iamblichus' and Porphyry's works have a common pattern, a pattern explicable by Iamblichus' use of Porphyry (denied by Rohde), and the fact that both Iamblichus and

47. Burkert, *Lore and Science*, 100-101 has a brief, but good treatment of Apollonius.

48. Méautis, *Recherches sur le pythagorisme*, 91, doubted Apollonius' identity with the wonder-worker.

49. Lévy, *Recherches sur les sources*, 105-106.

50. E. Rohde, "Die Quellen des Iamblichus in seiner Biographie des Pythagoras," *RhM* 27 (1872) 23 f.

51. The summary is based on Lévy's discussion, *Recherches sur les sources*, 110.

52. *Ibid.*, 98.

53. J. A. Philip, "The Biographical Tradition - Pythagoras," *TAPA* 90 (1959) 185-194, esp. 187-88.

Porphyry had "protreptic" purposes in composing their works.[54] There is also persuasiveness to Philip's contention that anti-Christian motives were operative in both Porphyry and Iamblichus, and that they were defending Greek thought or *Hellenism* against the "revealed religions of 'barbarian audacity.'"[55]

Whether Philip's views on Nicomachus as a source for Porphyry and Iamblichus are correct or not, the fact is that from the fifth century B.C. until the third century A.D., information on Pythagoras is fragmentary, and often inconsistent. The first extant and complete works on Pythagoras are those of Diogenes Laertius, Porphyry, and Iamblichus, all three living in the third century A.D., and using earlier sources. Lack of chronological data hinders ascertaining whose work was first: there is no evidence that Iamblichus and Porphyry knew Diogenes' work. Diogenes' identity and dates remain conjectural,[56] but his life of Pythagoras is closer in spirit to Porphyry's than to Iamblichus'. If he himself wrote the preface to *Lives and Opinions of Eminent Philosophers*,[57] he believed that philosophy had a twofold origin: Anaximander on the one hand, and Pythagoras on the other, and it was with Pythagoras that the "Italian school" began (I. 13). In Bk. VIII Diogenes starts his examination of Italian philosophy with Pythagoras, and divides philosophers into two "successions," an Ionian or Eastern (I. 22-VII), and an Italian or Western (VIII); he concludes with the "sporadics," philosophers who did not establish successions (IX-X). Thus Diogenes' biography of Pythagoras is followed by accounts of various thinkers, e.g. Empedocles, Epicharmus, Eudoxus, whom he regarded as Pythagoras' successors.

Although Diogenes' reasons for writing the *Lives* are unknown, there are passages which suggest that his interests were mainly in the lives or persons of early thinkers, not in their philosophies. As J. Mejer observed, many biographies have no doxography, and the biographical sections, together with anecdotes and apophthegms, occupy more space than the doxographical. Moreover, when Diogenes mentions a philosopher's works, it is often because they are thought to reveal his character, e.g. 2.56 and 63, 6.14 and 7.180.[58] A. Delatte, who studied Diogenes' *Lives* for his commentary on the life of Pythagoras, noticed the following divisions in many biographies: 1) an account of the philosopher's origins; 2) his education, philosophical training, and journeys or voyages; 3) his foundation of a "school"; 4) his character, mannerisms, temperament, habits, often illustrated by anecdotes

---

54. *Ibid.*, 190-91. Burkert, *Lore and Science*, 98, n. 5 is not convinced by Philip's arguments about Iamblichus' use of Porphyry. In any case, Philip's remark on the "protreptic" nature of both works is correct.

55. Philip, *TAPA* 90 (1959) 192.

56. Though somewhat dated, A. Delatte's 1922 study, *La vie de Pythagore de Diogène Laërce* (New York, reprint 1979) is still useful. See also J. Mejer, *Diogenes Laertius and his Hellenistic Background*, *Hermes Einzelschriften* 40 (Wiesbaden, 1978) for a good bibliography of works until 1976.

57. See Delatte, *La vie*, 50-51.

58. See Mejer, *Diogenes Laertius*, 3-4 and 91-92.

and apophthegms; 5) important events of his life; 6) an anecdotal description of his death and epigrams on this subject; 7) his *floruit* and chronological details; 8) works; 9) doctrines; 10) documents, e.g. last will and testament, letters, etc.; 11) homonyms; 12) additional notes.[59] Two aspects of Delatte's "rubrics of a biography" perhaps deserve special notice. First, Diogenes' connection of philosophers with politics was an important concept from Hellenistic times on,[60] and second, Diogenes gave considerable attention to the philosophers' personalities: their dress, physical appearance, "amours," diet, and other habits.[61] Mejer also noted that Diogenes included anecdotes and apothegms about a philosopher in order to describe his character ($\mathring{\eta}\theta os$), not his thinking or intellectual achievements.

In his *Lives*, Diogenes often refers to his sources, and in his biography of Pythagoras, he cites, for example, Aristoxenus, Dicaearchus, Heraclides Ponticus, Heraclides Lembus, Hermippus, and Favorinus. These are in the biographical portions of his *Life of Pythagoras*. When Diogenes turns to doxographical matters in 17-35, he does not first cite his source(s) for the Pythagorean *symbola* (17-18). At 19 f., however, in discussing precepts for the Pythagorean way of life, Aristotle and Aristoxenus are mentioned as Diogenes' authorities. No sources are given for Pythagoras' teaching in 22-24, but from 25-33, Diogenes copies a long passage from Alexander Polyhistor's *Successions of Philosophers*, and at 34-35, a short passage perhaps from Aristotle's *On the Pythagoreans*. Whether this latter report was from Aristotle, Alexander, or still another source, cannot be adequately determined.[62] In any case, sections 24-33 contain Alexander's second cent. B.C. comprehensive and systematic account of Pythagoreanism. Diogenes probably included this long excerpt from Alexander (and Aristotle?) because of his interest "in old and untypical sources,"[63] for he reports that Alexander found his material in some Pythagorean $\dot{v}\pi o\mu\nu\acute{\eta}\mu\alpha\tau a$ (see 25 and 36). Moreover, Diogenes believed that Pythagoras himself wrote books, and cites poems or works of Pythagoras recorded by Heraclides Lembus in his *Epitome of Sotion*.[64]

On the whole, Diogenes' *Life of Pythagoras* illustrates Delatte's "rubrics of a biography." For example, Diogenes reports on Pythagoras' family, education, and travels (1-3); his involvement in the politics of southern Italy (3, 39-40) his writings (6-11); homonyms (46-48). Throughout the biography, there are references to Pythagoras' character, and to his way of life; for example, he was most dignified, perfected geometrical study (11-12), and practiced abstinence and moderation

59. Delatte, *La vie*, 54-63.
60. *Ibid.* 56.
61. Delatte, *La vie*, 57.
62. See Mejer, *Diogenes Laertius*, 4, n. 11; for Alexander Polyhistor in Diogenes Laertius, *ibid.*, 66-68.
63. *Ibid.* 5.
64. For an assessment of Diogenes' beliefs about Pythagoras' books, see Delatte, *La vie*, 159 ff.

(18-19). Diogenes was especially interested in Pythagoras' dietary regulations, and his beliefs about reincarnation, as Diogenes' own "jesting verses" (44-45) suggest. In sum, although Diogenes' *Lives*, including that of Pythagoras, were often governed by various rubrics, and drew on many acknowledged sources, they are not much more than a collection of second-hand information on various Greek thinkers arranged in teacher-pupil "successions." The chief value of his "Pythagoras" resides in preserving reports by much earlier authors.

Porphyry's *Life of Pythagoras* is similar to Diogenes'. It was part of the first book of his *History of Philosophy*, composed perhaps before he became Plotinus' student.[65] The *History* consisted of four books, and gave a survey of Greek thought from the Milesians to Plato. From the remarks in the Suda, it is clear that the *History* had an authority like the works of Sotion and of Aetius. Porphyry used many sources: thirty-one authors are mentioned in his *Life of Pythagoras*, e.g. Apollonius (of Tyana), Aristoxenus, Dicaearchus, Neanthes (of Cyzicus), and Timaeus of Tauromenium. Like Diogenes, he often quotes his sources, and some are quoted several times. Like Diogenes again, Porphyry's treatment of his sources sometimes seems uncritical, and does not show much effort at reconciling or evaluating their different opinions, e.g. 56-57 where Porphyry initially mentions "Dicaearchus and the more accurate authorities" for the revolt against the Pythagoreans. But later he reports what "others say" without any attempt to reconcile the different versions. Diogenes, it was seen, copies a long passage on Pythagorean teaching from Alexander Polyhistor. Porphyry similarly cites Moderatus of Gades' collection in ten books of Pythagorean doctrines (48), and the long section (48-53) on Pythagorean number theory, may well be from Moderatus. On the whole, Porphyry and Diogenes seem typical of third century A.D. scholars trying to present a portrait of Pythagoras, using sources for which no critical methods had yet been developed.

Porphyry's arrangement of material is also similar to that of Diogenes: he begins with accounts of Pythagoras' origins, his family (1-5); attention is then given to his education, e.g. learning mathematics from the Egyptians, Chaldeans, and Phoenicians, and his training by the Magi (6-17); the great sensation Pythagoras made on his arrival in Italy, and his attraction of faithful followers (18-20); then a preliminary discussion of his legal and moral teaching (21-22), followed by a collection of miracle stories (23-31); an account of his daily regimen and diet (32-35); following this, an exposition of his teachings with a careful distinction between what he taught publicly, and what he taught secretly to his closest disciples (37-53); the remaining sections deal with the revolt against the Pythagoreans, and the importance of friendship among the descendants of the Pythagoreans.

---

65. See the collection of ancient testimonia in *Porphyrii Philosophi Platonici, Opuscula selecta*, ed. A. Nauck (New York, reprint, 1977) 4-16.

Although Porphyry's *Life* shows no obvious biases, he does connect Pythagoras'
teachings with the wisdom of the Orient, a tendency found in his sources, e.g.
Neanthes and Antonius Diogenes. There is, moreover, something holy and mysterious about Pythagoras, and so Antonius Diogenes is cited (10) for a story of the
miraculous child feeding on "dew dripping down" from a poplar, a child probably
meant to be Pythagoras. Great attention is given to the miracles of Pythagoras,
and Porphyry remarks: "ten thousand other things yet more marvelous and more
divine are told about the man. . . . to put it bluntly, about no one else have greater
and more extraordinary things been believed" (28-29). On the whole, Porphyry
seems engaged in composing a hagiography, which is not surprising since Pythagoras was, in the Platonic-Plotinian tradition, the archetype of the Sage. In following this tradition, Porphyry differs notably from Diogenes Laertius whose own
philosophical allegiance remains unknown. Moreover, in view of Porphyry's anti-
Christian sentiments, it is not amiss to regard Pythagoras as a competitor of Jesus
of Nazareth, and to see parallels with the Gospels, e.g. Pythagoras' miracles, his
public and private teaching which corresponds, for example, to the distinctions
in Luke (9:18 ff.) and Mark (8:27 ff.) Like the Gospels, Porphyry's *Life* ends with
the death of Pythagoras, and the survival of his teaching through his disciples.[66]
What, of course, Porphyry's intentions were in composing the *Life*, ultimately remain, like those of Diogenes Laertius, matters for speculation.

IV. Pythagorean Communities

Persistence of ancient interest in Pythagoras has suggested to some scholars the
existence of Pythagorean communities from the fifth century B.C. on. Certainly
comic poets of the fourth century B.C. lampooned "Pythagorists" for their ascetic
and sometimes slovenly habits,[67] and Iamblichus, relying on earlier authorities
such as Timaeus of Tauromenium, gives evidence for Pythagorean communities
in the fifth century B.C. But the reliability of his sources has been questioned, and
the existence of Pythagorean communities in late antiquity remains uncertain.
For example, H. Thesleff's belief that Pythagorean schools existed in southern Italy after Pythagoras' death has not won widespread acceptance. No doubt many
"Pythagorean" writings were composed in the Hellenistic age, but these do not
confirm Thesleff's thesis about Pythagorean schools in southern Italy. On the au-

---

66. See Hadas and Smith, *Heroes and Gods*, 107. See also J. Schattenmann, "Jesus and Pythagoras," *Kairos* 21 (1979) 215-20; W. Fauth, "Jesus von Nazareth und der Helios-Apollon des
Julianus Apostata. Zu einigen Eigentümlichkeiten der spätantiken Pythagoras-Aretalogie im Ver-
gleich mit der thaumasiologischen Tradition der Evangelien," *ZNW* 78 (1987) 26-48.
67. Thesleff "An Introduction to the Pythagorean Writings," 48 ff. The evidence of comic poets is collected In Diels-Kranz, *Die Fragmente der Vorsokratiker,* I 478-480. See also R. M. Grant, "Dietary Laws among Pythagoreans, Jews, and Christians," *HTR* 73 (1980) 299-310; reprinted in his
Christian Beginnings. Apocalypse to History (London, 1983) no. 7.

thority of Aristoxenus, Diogenes Laertius mentions five thinkers as the last (τελευταῖοι) of the Pythagoreans (8.46). Iamblichus cites these names at *VP* 251, and so Aristoxenus' report was apparently accepted in later antiquity. Moreover, the "last" Pythagoreans, whom Aristoxenus knew, lived in central and northern Greece.[68]

In the nineteenth century, E. Zeller connected Pythagoreanism with Jewish thought,[69] and Lévy also later argued that Pythagorean ideas had great influence on Alexandrian Judaism. Lévy claimed, in brief, that the Essenes were influenced by Pythagoreanism, and formed a community organized on Pythagorean principles, e.g. with a novitiate, oath of initiation, and possessions in common.[70] Indeed, the only philosophical or religious group that seems to have corresponded to the Essene community in antiquity was the Pythagorean. Josephus (or his source, Nicolaus of Damascus) at *AJ* 15 , 371 described the Essenes as dependent on the Pythagorean way of life (δίαιτῃ), and it is possible that the Essenes knew Pythagorean doctrines. Direct dependence, however, seems unlikely, and despite the interesting comparisons of Lévy and others, the extent and nature of Pythagorean influence on the Essenes remains a subject for continuing conjecture. As M. Hengel noted, the important thing is not the supposed "Pythagorean" influences, but the fact that Hellenistic observers like Josephus could present the Essenes as Jewish "Pythagoreans."[71]

Whether Pythagoreanism itself was revived in the first century B.C. is also subject to debate. The alleged revival of Pythagoreanism, and possibly of Pythagorean communities, involves consideration of Roman Pythagoreanism.[72] No less an authority than Cicero claimed that his contemporary Nigidius Figulus first revived Pythagoreanism after its extinction (*Tim.* 1). In making his remarks, Cicero may have thought of a Pythagorean society gathered about its master, studying astronomy, mathematics, and observing a way of life. Moderatus of Gades in the first century A.D. tried to promote what he believed was Pythagoras' true teaching, and attracted students.[73]

---

68. For a brief, but cogent criticism of Thesleff, see C. de Vogel, *Pythagoras and Early Pythagoreanism: An Interpretation of Neglected Evidence on the Philosopher Pythagoras* (Assen, 1966) 28.

69. A brief survey of nineteenth and twentieth century views on Neopythagoreanism is in Thesleff, "An Introduction to the Pythagorean Writings," 50 ff. For Zeller's views see *Philosophie der Griechen*, III. 2, 89-93.

70. See I. Lévy, *La légende de Pythagore de Grèce en Palestine* (Paris, 1927) esp. 264-293. For a brief criticism, see W. Burkert, "Hellenistische Pseudopythagorica," *Philol.* 105 (1961) 233-34.

71. M. Hengel, *Judaism and Hellenism*, trans. J. Bowden, I (Philadelphia, 1974) 247. For Hengel's complete discussion, see pps. 243-247. See also P. Gorman, "Pythagoras Palaestinus," *Philol.* 127 (1983) 30-42. Philo's *De vita contemplativa* is a long discussion of the Therapeutae, a counterpart to the Essenes. The Therapeutae seem to have been much influenced by Pythagoreanism, and the notion of Jewish Pythagorean communities was much alive in the Graeco-Roman world.

72. For bibliography until about 1960 see Burkert, *Philol.* 105, 226 ff. L. Ferrero, *Storia del pitagorismo nel mondo Romano* (Turin, 1955) deals with the subject at great length.

Finally, A. J. Festugière claimed that Iamblichus in his *VP* projected back into Pythagoras' time the practices of philosophical schools of the third century A.D., and that section 104 of *VP*, for example, describes teaching methods used in Iamblichus' own time.[74] His views have been accepted by J. A. Philip who noted that the establishment of ascetic communities among Syrian Christians was familiar to Iamblichus, himself a Syrian.[75]

Tempting as it is to connect the Pythagoras legend with Pythagorean communities, there is no indisputable evidence for such communities in antiquity. Certainly there were political and other associations (ἑταιρεῖαι) in the fifth-fourth centuries B.C. Moreover, Moderatus of Gades in the first century A.D. had students who were attracted to Pythagoreanism. But whether the Pythagorean communities portrayed by Iamblichus or his sources ever existed, remains a subject for further examination.[76] Certainly there were individuals such as Heraclides, Aristoxenus, or Iamblichus who kept Pythagoras' memory alive, but they themselves were not members of Pythagorean communities

In conclusion, the existence of Pythagorean communities may never be proved to everyone's satisfaction, and yet the vividness and detail with which Iamblichus or his sources portray the Pythagorean way of life suggests that it once flourished among a chosen few. It is hard to believe that such communities were wholly the product of ancient imagination. What is certain is that quite early on, Pythagoras became a legendary figure, like Moses or Jesus of Nazareth, and the problems which make dispassionate investigation of these figures sometimes difficult are similar to those involving Pythagoras.

---

73. On Moderatus' student, Lucius (*Quaest. conviu* 727 B), see J. Hershbell, *CB* 60 (1984) 74 f., and J. Dillon, *The Middle Platonists*, 344-351.

74. A. J. Festugière, *Le Révélation d'Hermès Trismégiste*, II (Paris, 1949) 33-47, and more particularly, "Sur le *De Vita Pythagorica* de Iamblique," *REG* 50 (1937), 476-89 (repr. in *Etudes de Philosophie grecque*, Paris, 1971). He also makes interesting comparisons with the practices of the Essenes (as described by Josephus, *BJ* II, viii, 2-13, 119-61), and of contemporary Christian monastic communities.

75. J. A. Philip, *Pythagoras and Early Pythagoreanism*, 139 ff.

76. *Ibid.*, esp. 140-147. Philip, who doubts, for example, the reliability of Timaeus as a witness for Pythagorean communities, concludes that "though there may have been Pythagorean political associations in the 5th century, there is no early evidence for the existence of an order or brotherhood ... the notion of a Pythagorean order or brotherhood is to be ascribed to late Hellenistic times when such ascetic communities became common."

V. Iamblichus: Life and Works[77]

Of Iamblichus' life, despite the biographical sketch of the late fourth century sophist Eunapius of Sardis, in his *Lives of the Philosophers and Sophists*,[78] little of substance is known. Reading between the lines of Eunapius, and helped by pieces of information from elsewhere, reasonable conjecture can produce probable data.

Eunapius reports (*VS* 457) that Iamblichus was born in Chalcis "in Coele (Syria)". After Septimius Severus' division of the Syrian command in 194 A.D., this refers, not to southern, but to northern Syria, and so the Chalcis in question must be Chalcis ad Belum, modern Qinnesrin, a strategically important town to the east of the Orontes valley, on the road from Beroea (Aleppo) to Apamea, and from Antioch to the East.[79] The date of his birth is uncertain, but the tendency in recent scholarship has been to put it much earlier than the traditional date of c.265 A.D. A. Cameron, in "The Date of Iamblichus' Birth",[80] bases his conclusions on the assumption that the Iamblichus whose son Ariston is mentioned by Porphyry (*Plot.* 9) as having married a lady disciple of Plotinus, Amphicleia, is our Iamblichus. This assumption seems reasonable, since Porphyry expects his readers to know who this Iamblichus is, and there is no other Iamblichus in this period and milieu. Porphyry's language is ambiguous, but to gain a credible chronology, one assumes that Ariston married Amphicleia some time after Plotinus' death, and probably not long before 301 A.D., when Porphyry composed the *Life*. Even so, and accepting that Ariston was much younger than Amphicleia, one cannot postulate a date for Iamblichus' birth later than 240 A.D. Iamblichus was not, then, much younger than Porphyry himself (born in 232), which perhaps explains the rather uneasy pupil-teacher relationship they appear to have enjoyed.

According to Eunapius, Iamblichus was "of illustrious birth, and belonged to the well-to-do and fortunate classes" (*VS* 457). It is remarkable that this Semitic name[81] was preserved by a distinguished family in this region, when so many of

---

77. For a fuller version of the account given here, see J. Dillon "Iamblichus of Chalcis," in *ANRW*, pt. II, Vol. 36:2, 1987, 863-909, itself a revised version of the introduction to his edition of the fragments of Iamblichus' commentaries on the Platonic dialogues, *Iamblichi Chalcidensis in Platonis Dialogos Commentariorum Fragmenta*, Leiden, 1973.

78. Editions: W. C. Wright, Loeb Classical Library (with Philostratus, *Lives of the Sophists*), Cambridge, 1921, and G. Giangrande, *Eunapii Vitae Sophistarum*, Rome, 1956. (Page numbering from Boissonade's edition, Paris, 1822.)

79. In a recent article, "Themistios and the Origin of Iamblichos," *Hermes* 116 (1988), 125-3, J. Vanderspoel has presented an interesting argument in favor of the Chalcis in Lebanon (mod. "Anjar"). He may well be right, but the question is not, perhaps, of prime importance.

80. *Hermes* 96 (1969), 374-6.

81. The original form of Iamblichus' name is Syriac or Aramaic: *ya-mliku*, a third person singular indicative or jussive of the root MLK, with El understood, meaning "he (sc. El) is king," or "May he rule."

the well-to-do had long since taken on Greek and Roman names. But there were, in fact, ancestors of whom the family could be proud, if the philosopher Damascius may be believed. At the beginning of his *Life of Isidore*,[82] he reports that Iamblichus was descended from the royal line of the priest-kings of Emesa. Sampsigeramus, the first of these potentates to appear in history, won independence from the Seleucids in the 60's B.C., and was in the entourage of Antony at the Battle of Actium. He left a son Iamblichus to carry on the line, and the names "Sampsigeramus" and "Iamblichus" alternate in the dynasty until the end of the first century A.D., when they were dispossessed by Domitian. Inscriptional evidence, however, shows the family still dominant well into the second century.[83]

How or why a branch of the family got to Chalcis by the third century is not clear, but it may have been the result of a dynastic marriage, since Iamblichus' other distinguished ancestor mentioned by Damascius is Monimus (Arabic *Mun'eim*). This is not an uncommon name in the area, but the identity of the Monimus in question may be concealed in an entry by Stephanus of Byzantium (s.v. *Chalcis*), which reads: "*Chalcis*: fourth, a city in Syria, founded by Monicus the Arab." Monicus is a name not found elsewhere, and may well be a slip (either by Stephanus himself or a later scribe) for "Monimus." This would give Iamblichus an ancestor of suitable distinction, none other than the founder of his city.[84] What may have happened is that a daughter of the former royal house of Emesa married into the leading family of Chalcis, and one of her sons was called after his maternal grandfather.

There is no doubt, at any rate, that Iamblichus was of good family. Such an ancestry may have influenced his intellectual formation. His tendency as a philosopher, manifested in various ways, is always to connect Platonic doctrine with more ancient wisdom (preferably, but not necessarily, of a Chaldaean variety), and within Platonism itself it is he who, more than any other, is the author of the ramified hierarchy of levels of being (many identified with traditional gods and minor divinities) which is a feature of the later Athenian Platonism of Syrianus and Proclus. With Iamblichus and his advocacy of theurgy as a necessary complement to theology, Platonism also becomes more explicitly a religion. Before his time, the mystery imagery so popular with Platonist philosophers (going back to Plato himself) was, so far as can be seen, just that — imagery. With Iamblichus, there is an earnest emphasis on ritual, enabling the Emperor Julian to found his church on this rather shaky rock.

---

82. Ed. C. Zintzen, Hildesheim, 1967, 2.

83. *Inscriptions grecques et latines de la Syrie* V, 2212-2217. Cf also John Malalas, *Chron.* 296.

84. Unless, in fact, the reference is to the *god* Monimus, attested by Iamblichus himself (*ap.* Julian, *Hymn to King Helios*, 150 CD) worshipped as at Emesa in association with the sun god. The royal family may conceivably have traced their ancestry to this deity, identified with the Planet Mercury.

The mid-third century was a profoundly disturbed time to be growing up in Syria. In 256 A.D., in Iamblichus' early youth, the Persian King Shapur broke through the Roman defences around Chalcis (the so-called *limes* of Chalcis), and pillaged the whole north of Syria, including Antioch (Malalas, *Chron.* 295-6). It is not known how Iamblichus' family weathered the onslaught. Being prominent figures, especially if they were pro-Roman, they may well have withdrawn before it and sought refuge temporarily on the coast.

At this point, the problem arises of who Iamblichus' teachers in philosophy were. Eunapius simply writes of a certain Anatolius, μετὰ Πορφύριον τά δεύτερα φερόμενος (*VS* 457). This phrase in earlier times simply means "take second place to,"[85] but a parallel in Photius[86] suggests that for Eunapius the phrase meant "was successor to." If this is so, it poses a problem. It has been suggested[87] that Iamblichus' teacher is identical with the Anatolius who was a teacher of Peripatetic philosophy in Alexandria in the 260's and later (in 274) consecrated bishop of Laodicea in Syria. This suggestion seems untenable: chronology requires that Iamblichus was a student no later than the 270's, so that it must be concluded that Anatolius (who is the dedicatee of Porphyry's *Homeric Questions* (Ὁμηρικὰ ζητή-ματα), and so probably a student of his) represented in some way Porphyry during his absence (perhaps still in Sicily?). This, however, presupposes a situation for which there is no evidence, namely that Porphyry established a school in Rome between his visits to Sicily , or that Plotinus had founded a school of which Porphyry was the titular head even in his absence in Sicily. Another possibility, of course, is that Eunapius was profoundly confused, but that conclusion seems to be a counsel of despair.

When Porphyry returned from Sicily to Rome is not clear. Eusebius, writing some time after his death (c. 305 A.D.), describes him (*HE* VI 19,2) as "he who was in our time established in Sicily" (ὁ καθ'ἡμᾶς ἐν Σικελίᾳ καταστάς) which suggests a considerable stay. J. Bidez,[88] however, takes this as referring only to the publication of Porphyry's work *Against the Christians*. Porphyry refers to himself as having returned to Rome at *Plot.* 2, but when that happened he does not indicate. That he returned by the early 280's, however, is a proposition with which few would disagree, and if Iamblichus studied with him, it would have occurred in this period. The only direct evidence of their association is the dedication to Iamblichus of Porphyry's work *On the maxim 'Know Thyself*.[89]

What the relationship between the two may have been cannot be determined. In later life Iamblichus was repeatedly, and often sharply, critical of his master's

---

85. E.g. in Herodotus VIII. 104.
86. *Bibl.* 181, Dam. *Isid.*, 319, 14 Zintzen.
87. Dillon, *ANRW* 36.2 (1987) 866-7.
88. *Vie de Porphyre*, 103, n. 1.

philosophical positions. This can be seen in his *Timaeus Commentary*,[90] where, of thirty-two fragments in which Porphyry is mentioned, twenty-five are critical, only seven signifying agreement. The same position is evident also in the commentary on Aristotle's *Categories*, as preserved by Simplicius, but there Simplicius reports that Iamblichus based his own commentary on that of Porphyry[91] (something also likely for his *Timaeus Commentary*), so that such statistics given previously are misleading. However, Iamblichus' *De Mysteriis Aegyptiorum* is a point-by-point refutation of Porphyry's *Letter to Anebo* (which, in turn, was an attack on theurgy probably aimed at Iamblichus), and Iamblichus' references to Porphyry in his *De Anima* are often less than reverent. No doubt, also, Iamblichus' lost work *On Statues* had much to say in refutation of Porphyry's work of the same name.

There is no need, however, to conclude that Iamblichus learned nothing from Porphyry, or that they parted on bad terms. The refutation of one's predecessors was a necessary part of staying afloat in the scholarly world, then as now, and Iamblichus was enough of an original mind to have many modifications and elaborations to introduce into Porphyry's relatively simple metaphysical scheme. Also, contact with Plotinus was a personal experience for Porphyry, which it was not for Iamblichus. This has some bearing, along with the considerations of ancestry mentioned earlier, on Iamblichus' enthusiasm for theurgy, an enthusiasm of Porphyry himself in his youth, which was something direct contact with Plotinus tended to suppress. When Porphyry wrote his *Letter to Anebo*, he was actually providing a recantation of his earlier beliefs, as expressed in the *Philosophy from Oracles*.

Even as it is not known when or where[92] Iamblichus studied with Porphyry, so it is not known when he left him, returned to Syria and founded his own school. From the fact that he returned to Syria, rather than staying on as successor to Porphyry (he was, after all, his most distinguished pupil), one might conclude that there was tension between them. But Iamblichus by the 290's would already be, if our chronology is correct, a man of middle age, and it is natural enough that he should want to set up on his own. Porphyry, after all, did not die until after 305 at the earliest, and probably Iamblichus departed long before that.

For Iamblichus' activity on his return to Syria one is dependent on Eunapius' account, which, with all its fantastic anecdotes, is claimed by its author to rest on an oral tradition descending to him from Iamblichus' senior pupil Aedesius, *via*

---

89. Unless account is taken of Iamblichus' assertion in *De Anima* (*ap*. Stob. 1.375, 24.2) that he has 'heard' Porphyry propound a certain doctrine. The verb ἀκούω with the genitive came to be used in peculiar ways in later Greek, denoting acquaintance at various removes, so that one cannot put much trust in this testimony. There is no real reason, however, to doubt that Iamblichus and Porphyry were personally acquainted.

90. Collected in Dillon's edition, cf. n. 76 above.

91. *Categ*. 2,9 ff. Kalbfleisch.

92. It is conceivable that he went to study with him in Lilybaeum.

his own revered master Chrysanthius. Unfortunately, Eunapius is vague on details of prime importance. Where, for example, did Iamblichus establish his school? The evidence seems to be in favour of Apamea,[93] rather than his native Chalcis. This is not surprising: Apamea had been a distinguished center of philosophy for well over a century (at least), and was the home town, and probably base, of the distinguished second century Neopythagorean Numenius. It was also the place to which Plotinus' senior pupil Amelius retired in the 260's, no doubt because of admiration for Numenius. Amelius was dead by the time Porphyry wrote his *Commentary on the Timaeus* (probably in the 290's), but he left his library and possessions to his adopted son Hostilianus Hesychius,[94] who presumably continued to reside in Apamea.

Once established in Apamea, Iamblichus seems to have acquired support from a prominent local citizen, Sopater, and in Eunapius' account (*VS* 458-9), he seems in possession of a number of suburban villas (προάστεια) and a considerable group of followers. There are glimpses of him in the midst of his disciples, discoursing and fielding questions, disputing with rival philosophers, and leading school excursions to the hot springs at Gadara. Iamblichus had strong Pythagorean sympathies, inherited from Numenius and Nicomachus of Gerasa, and one would like to know how far *On the Pythagorean Way of Life* reflects life in his own school. Probably not very closely, in such matters as community of property or long periods of silence, or we would have heard about it from Eunapius. More likely the school of Iamblichus was like any contemporary philosophic school in the Platonist tradition, a group of students living in or round their teacher, meeting with him daily, and probably dining with him, pursuing a set course of reading and study in the works of Aristotle and Plato, and holding disputations on set topics.

Possibly Iamblichus' ten volumes on Pythagoreanism, entitled collectively *A Compendium of Pythagorean Doctrine* of which Περὶ τοῦ Πυθαγορείου βίου is the first, constituted an introductory course for his school. It is plain that there was study of at least some Aristotle, the logical works (Iamblichus wrote a copious commentary on the *Categories*, heavily dependent on that of Porphyry, but with transcendental interpretations of his own), the *De Anima*, and perhaps parts of the *Metaphysics*, followed by the study of Plato. For Plato, Iamblichus, building on ear-

---

93. There is some conflicting evidence, from Malalas (*Chron.* XII, 312, 11-12), indicating that Iamblichus was established with a school at Daphne, near Antioch, in the reigns of Maxentius and Galerius (305-312 A.D.), and Malalas says that he continued teaching there until his death. Malalas, despite his limitations, is not entirely unreliable on matters affecting his home area, so it is possible that Iamblichus spent some time in Daphne; there is no doubt that Apamea was his main base.

94. Porph. *Plot.* 3. Nothing more is known about this person, but excavations in Apamea may turn up some trace of him, as of other characters in this story.

lier, Middle Platonic systems of instruction (such as described in Albinus' Εἰσ-
αγωγή), prescribed a definite number and order of dialogues to be studied. In the
Anonymous Prolegomena to Platonic Philosophy[95] ch. 26, there is a course of ten dialogues attributed originally to Iamblichus, starting with the *Alcibiades* I, and continuing with *Gorgias, Phaedo, Cratylus, Theaetetus, Sophist, Statesman, Phaedrus,
Symposium* and *Philebus*, leading to the two main dialogues of Platonic philosophy,
the *Timaeus* and the *Parmenides*, the former "physical," the latter "theological." Of
these, there are fragments of evidence of commentaries by Iamblichus on the *Alcibiades, Phaedo, Sophist, Phaedrus, Philebus, Timaeus* and *Parmenides*, the most extensive (preserved in Proclus' commentary on the same dialogue) being those on the
Timaeus. It is surprising not to find any mention in this sequence of either the *Republic* or the *Laws*. They were probably regarded as too long, and in the main too
political, to be suitable for study as wholes, but there is an indication that sections
such as *Republic* VI, VII and X, and *Laws* X, received due attention.

Formal exegesis then, played a significant part in the curriculum of the school,
but notice must also be taken of the reputation which Iamblichus acquired in later times (mainly because of the excesses of such *epigoni* as Maximus of Ephesus,
the teacher of Julian in the 350's) for magical practices. He probably used the
Chaldaean Oracles in lectures, since he composed a vast commentary (in at least 28
books) on the *Oracles*. There is only one story related by Eunapius in which Iamblichus is said to have performed a magical act, and that was during the above-
mentioned visit of the school to the hot springs at Gadara. Iamblichus, in response to insistent requests, conjured up two spirits in the form of boys, identified
as Eros and Anteros, from two adjacent springs (*VS* 459). On another occasion,
however (*VS*. 458), he is recorded as dismissing with a laugh rumors that during
prayer he was accustomed to rise ten cubits into the air, and that his body and
clothing took on a golden hue. Nevertheless, his championing of theurgy (which
is really only magic with a philosophical underpinning), presented at length in
the *De Mysteriis*, introduced a new element into Platonism, which was to continue
even up to the Renaissance. Partly this was a response to a Christian emphasis on
the miracle-working holy man. It might have happened without Iamblichus, but
certain elements in his background perhaps disposed him to making Platonism
into more of a religion than had hitherto been the case.

The details of Iamblichus' philosophical system are not relevant to the present
work, since they do not obtrude on his account of Pythagoreanism.[96] The whole
sequence of Pythagorean works, being very largely compilations from previous

---

95. Ed. L. G. Westerink, Amsterdam, 1962. This sequence of dialogues was linked to a progression through the three higher levels of virtue, political, cathartic and theoretic (in the
scheme of levels of virtue propounded by Porphyry, and amplified by Iamblichus). Cf. Westerink's Introduction, xxxix-xl.

96. For a full discussion, see Dillon, *ANRW* 36.2 (1987), 878-907.

works (as is the case with the present one), has no place for the technicalities of later Neoplatonism. As in Iamblichus' *Letters*, numerous passages of which have been preserved by Stobaeus, what is found are non-technical commonplaces of Platonism, presented in a form palatable for beginners.

Iamblichus seems to have lived in Apamea until the early 320s. A terminus is found in Sopater's departure for Constantinople to try his luck with Imperial politics in 326/7, by which time his revered master was certainly dead. A most interesting testimony to Iamblichus' status in the 320's is provided by the letters included among the works of the Emperor Julian.[97] These were composed by an admirer of Iamblichus between the years 315 and 320, who was then attached to the staff of the Emperor Licinius. This person cannot be identified, but Eunapius (*VS* 458) gives the names of various disciples, Aedesius and Eustathius (who was Iamblichus' successor) from Cappadocia, and Theodorus (presumably Theodorus of Asine) and Euphrasius from mainland Greece. Besides these it is possible to identify Dexippus, author of a surviving commentary on Aristotle's *Categories*, and Hierius, master of the theurgist Maximus of Ephesus. To some of these there is a record of letters on philosophical subjects by Iamblichus (Sopater, Dexippus and Eustathius, at least). One is even tempted to wonder whether the recipient of a letter *On Ruling*, a certain Dyscolius (perhaps identical with a governor of Syria around 323)[98] may not be the mysterious correspondent. But even if that were known, we would not really be much wiser.

Iamblichus' works, apart from those already mentioned, included many commentaries on Plato and Aristotle, a treatise *On the Soul*, of which extensive fragments are preserved by Stobaeus in his *Anthologium*,[99] and much of the substance also in the *De Anima* traditionally attributed to Simplicius, but now persuasively identified by Carlos Steel[100] as the work of his contemporary Priscian of Lydia. *On the Gods*, was much used by Julian, and probably served as a chief source for the surviving work of Sallustius *On the Gods and the World*. As for the rest of the Συναγωγή of which *On the Pythagorean Way of Life* was the first volume: it consisted of a sequence of ten works, of which only the first four survive (and possibly the substance of a fifth in a curious compilation, *The Theology of Arithmetic*, which, as it has been transmitted, is largely a cento of passages from a lost work of Nicomachus of

---

97. *Eps.* 181, 183-187 Bidez-Cumont (= 76-78, 75, 74, 79 Wright, *LCL*). How they fell into the hands of Julian, or came to be included among his works, is uncertain, but he was an avid collector of Iamblichiana, and they would have been among Iamblichus' papers. On this person, see T. D. Barnes, "A Correspondent of Iamblichus," *GRBS* 19 (1978), 99-106, who sorts out the problems connected with him most lucidly.

98. See Jones, *Prosopography of the Later Roman Empire*, I, 275.

99. Vol. I, 365-458. There is a useful translation with notes by A. J. Festugière, in Vol. III of *La Révélation d'Hermès Trismégiste*, (Paris, 1953) pp. 177 ff.

100. in *The Changing Self: a Study in The Soul in later Neoplatonism: Iamblichus, Damascius and Priscianus* (Brussels, 1978).

Gerasa (by the same title) and one of Anatolius, presumably Iamblichus' teacher, *On the Decade and the Numbers within It*). The remaining volumes are the *Protrepticus*, or *Exhortation to Philosophy,* a work based on Aristotle's lost *Protrepticus*, but with large sections of Platonic dialogues, various *Pythagorica*, and an extract from the work of an unknown fifth century B.C. sophist, now known as the *Anonymus Iamblichi*; the work *On the General Principles of Mathematics* (*De Communi Mathematica Scientia*) is again a cento of previous works, borrowed without acknowledgement, like *On the Pythagorean Way of Life*, and a commentary on the *Introduction to Arithmetic* of Nicomachus of Gerasa, somewhat more original, if only by virtue of its rather different nature. D. J. O'Meara[101] has recently identified in later Byzantine sources some extracts from later volumes (such as Iamblichus planned) on Physics, Ethics, Music, Geometry and Astronomy, but it is plain that if they existed, all would probably be compilations of previous doctrines. Even that, however, would be of value, as it doubtless was to Iamblichus' students, who were the primary intended audience of these works, even as they were of the *VP.*

Respect for Iamblichus as a philosopher has increased in recent years, as his distinctive contribution to the doctrine of the later Athenian school of Neoplatonism becomes clearer. He is an influence of prime importance on Syrianus, and hence on Proclus, as both of them freely acknowledge. In this way he inaugurated a scholastic tradition of Platonism which, becoming more ramified in the works of such men as Damascius and "Dionysius the Areopagite," descended to later Byzantine writers like Michael Psellus, and, through the translations of William of Moerbeke and, later, of Marsilio Ficino, to the West. Iamblichus' commentaries seem not to have long survived the closing of the Academy in 529 A.D. Damascius, Olympiodorus and Simplicius can all quote from them, as can Priscian and John of Stobi from his *De Anima* (and John from his *Letters*), but Psellus and the Byzantine scholars after him were dependent for their references to his technical works on Proclus. Only his 'exoteric' works, the Pythagorean Sequence and the *De Mysteriis*, survived into later Byzantine times, as they still do, to give a distorted and inadequate view of his achievement.

VI. Form and Structure of On the Pythagorean Way of Life

The first thing to be noticed about Iamblichus' work is that it is not a biography of Pythagoras. Those who so considered it have tended to excoriate it irrelevantly as a verbose, disorganised, and derivative example of the genre.[102] But

---

101. "New Fragments from Iamblichus' *Collection of Pythagorean Doctrines*", *AJP* 102 (1981), 26-40. See now his book, *Pythagoras Revived* (Oxford, 1989).

102. For example, E. Rohde, in his otherwise useful article, "Die Quellen des Iamblichos," and G. Mau, in his Pauly-Wissowa article "Iamblichos" [*RE* IX (1914): 648 ff.] W. Burkert, by contrast, recognizes its true nature (*Lore and Science*, p. 97).

Iamblichus, in contrast to Porphyry, who calls his work Περὶ τοῦ Πυθαγόρου βίου, or *Life of Pythagoras*, is careful to entitle his Περὶ τοῦ Πυθαγορείου βίου, *On the Pythagorean Way of Life*.[103]

The title, then, indicates that this is not a biography like the *Lives* of Porphyry or of Diogenes Laertius. But if it is not a biography of Pythagoras that Iamblichus composes, what is it? It certainly has characteristics of a biography: it concerns one particular person, and observes a loosely chronological framework, including the deeds and sayings of the Master, and his followers; beginning in chs. 2-6 with his birth and early years, education, travels and arrival in South Italy, and ending, in ch. 35, with an account of his persecution and death. But much of the central part of the work seems hardly excusable in a biography: it concerns not Pythagoras himself, but the Pythagoreans in general, and chronological sequence is largely abandoned. The work is, in fact, a dramatised study of a way of life, with a strong protreptic purpose. If it is permissible (that is, if it be correct to recognise it as a genre transcending the strictly Christian milieu), it seems best to classify *VP* as a gospel.

Having asserted that, what is thereby claimed? How conscious was Iamblichus of a genre such as an εὐαγγέλιον? Is there any kind of writing in the purely Hellenic tradition by which he could have been influenced? To answer the second question first, there is a likely influence from enterprises of the Peripatetic School in the generation after Aristotle.[104] Apart from their concern with biography, the Peripatetics showed an interest in "ways of life," not least that of the Pythagoreans. One example is Aristoxenus' Πυθαγορικαὶ Ἀποφάσεις (*Pythagorean Sayings*), which Iamblichus knew and often quotes. Despite its rather restrictive title, it seems to have presented the Pythagorean life in many of its aspects. Again, Dicaearchus' work, *The Greek Way of Life*, recounted the habits and customs of the Greeks, enriched, perhaps, by illustrative anecdotes from Pythagorean lore. There seems, however, to be no precedent in works such as these for either narrating miraculous deeds or presenting long discourses, both of which are a feature of Iamblichus' work. The "miracles," of course, form an integral part of the Pythagoras legend, recounted in any biography of the man, but what of the discourses?

Some ancestry for these discourses can be found in the works of Heraclides Ponticus, who wrote imaginative dialogues involving figures of former times, including Pythagoras.[105] It is also profitable to look in another direction: the con-

---

103. Βίος in Greek means "way of life;" or "life-style," as well as simply "life." For an analogous title to that of Iamblichus, one might cite the Peripatetic Dicaearchus' (unfortunately lost) *Bios Hellados*, "The Greek Way of Life."

104. See the useful discussion of B.D. Larsen, in *Iamblique de Chalcis*, 80-4.

105. In particular, one passage, in ch. 32, (sects. 217-222), is argued by P. Boyancé (see n. *ad loc.*) to have been derived from Heraclides' lost dialogue, *Abaris*, but this is disputed.

text of the first set of discourses, those to the people of Croton, from chap. 8 to chap. 11. After an introductory chapter (7), which announces the beginning of Pythagoras' "ministry" to the Greeks in Italy, Iamblichus begins in chap. 8 with a promise to record in detail what Pythagoras "did and said." Interestingly enough, his first recorded "deed" on arrival in Italy, on his journey from Sybaris to Croton, involves fishermen, pulling in a catch of fish on the shore (sect. 36). This might remind readers familiar with the New Testament of the circumstances in which Jesus began his public ministry in the synoptic gospels (Matthew 1:16-20; Mark 4:18-22; Luke 5:1-11).[106] Is this simply a coincidence (the story itself is not original to Iamblichus), or is there some degree of one-up-manship going on? Porphyry, after all, who also relates the story (*VP* 25), does not place it at the start of Pythagoras' Italian ministry, or gives it any clear chronological niche. It was plainly a free-floating anecdote. There seems to be evidence here of deliberate structuring on Iamblichus' part, and it is tempting to conclude that he has the synoptics in mind.

Apart from this detail, though, the gospel which *VP* closely resembles is John, a resemblance not surprising since John is the most "philosophical" of the gospels: Plotinus' senior pupil, Amelius, read it in his seminar, and commented on it with respect.[107] Whether Amelius did this during his Apamean period or earlier is not clear, but there is no difficulty in assuming that Christian texts were available to Platonic philosophers in this period. Gnostic treatises were also known to Plotinus' circle, and Porphyry was well acquainted with the Gospels, which he used to embarrassing effect in his work *Against the Christians*.[108] Iamblichus is, admittedly, not known to have concerned himself with the Christians or their writings, but, as a pupil of Porphyry, and teaching in Syria at the end of the 3rd century A.D., it would be strange if he were unfamiliar with them.[109]

Analysis of the structure of *VP*, does not depend, however, on these speculations as to its genre. An examination of its chief sections is in order.[110]

After the proem (ch. 1) in which Iamblichus invokes the blessing of God on the enterprise, and emphasises both the usefulness and the difficulty of his proposed task, there are the following divisions:

---

106. Pythagoras' encounter with fishermen is quite different from that of Jesus but the overall effect is the same: the manifestation of power, and the gaining of disciples (though the actual fishermen do not drop everything and follow Pythagoras).

107. Eusebius, *Praeparatio Evangelica* XI 18-19.

108. Porph., *Plot.* ch. 16.

109. Porph., *Plot.* ch. 16. On the reaction of philosophers against Christianity see J.-C. Fredouille, "Heiden," *RAC* 13 (1986) 1113-1149, esp. 1135-41, with reference to A. Meredith, "Porphyry and Julian against the Christians," *ANRW*, part II, Vol. 23:2, 1980, 1119-1149.

110. It seems legitimate to use the existing chapter divisions as natural divisions of the work, since they go back at least to Byzantine times, and possibly to Iamblichus himself.

1) *Early Life* (ch. 2-5): ancestry, upbringing, travels (to Phoenicia, Egypt, Babylon), life as a teacher on Samos, initial recognition by his peers as a sage. Here the motifs worth noting are: heralded by an oracle (ch. 2 - divine birth is actually rejected by Iamblichus, in favour of Pythagoras being a favoured soul in the "chain" of Apollo, a sort of *boddhisattva*); precocity in learning (2, ss.9-12); initial rejection as a teacher (5, 20-21), overcome in this case by an amusing ruse (ss. 22-25).

2) *Beginning of Public Mission* (chs. 6-8 s. 36): departure from home; arrival at his chosen destination (Italy). Chapter 6 is a general introduction to his public life, including a summary of his organisational system and doctrines. Note the motifs of people guessing as to his identity (s. 30): "Who do men say that I am?", and the introductory miracle, mentioned earlier, the miraculous draught of fishes.

3) *A Sequence of Discourses* (ch. 8, (s.37) - 11): (a) a speech to the young men (ss. 37-44); (b) speech to the Thousand (ch. 9); (c) speech to the children (ch. 10); (d) speech to the women (ch. 11). This sequence serves as a good compendium of his teaching, directed successively at different sections of the community.

4) *A Survey of Pythagorean Philosophy and Way of Life* (chs. 12-27): this great central portion of the work reviews every aspect of Pythagoras' teaching and practice, drawing on a variety of sources which have been discussed in Part III above. There is some evidence of structuring here at the beginning and the end, but not much in the middle chapters. There is no longer any question of chronological development, and Iamblichus has no compunction about switching from Pythagoras to "the Pythagoreans" (according to whether or not his ultimate source is Aristoxenus).

A logical beginning (ch. 12) is the account of Pythagoras' own definition of philosophy (the comparison of life to a public festival), and his coining of the term *philosophia.* There follows a discussion of Pythagoras' influence over living beings, with an account of his power over animals (ch. 13); this leads to a description of his doctrine of metempsychosis and his power to recall previous lives, underpinnings for the doctrine that all levels of life are connected (ch. 14). There is, then, a description of the role of sense-perception in Pythagorean introductory training (ch. 15), and after that, a description of his methods of purifying the lower, passionate part of the soul through various practices, including music. This is followed by two chapters (17-18) on Pythagoras' procedures for examining new postulants, and into what groups he divided them. (This latter chapter is palpably anachronis-

tic, since the distinctions between *Pythagoreioi* and *Pythagoristai* and *acus-matici* and *mathematici* are introduced).

After this section, it is hard to discern much of a logical order in the topics covered, though perhaps such an order is not required. At the beginning of ch. 19, Iamblichus states that Pythagoras discovered "many roads to education" (πολλὰς ὁδοὺς παιδείας), each catering to the individual character of the candidate, and in the chapters that follow there is a survey of these "roads,"[111] prefaced by the edifying story of the visit of Abaris, and ending, in ch. 27, with a description of Pythagoras' contributions to political philosophy and to legislation, which seems a proper culmination to the whole subject.

5) *The Pythagorean Virtues* (chs. 28-33): with chapter 28 there begins a new section of the work, in which Pythagorean teaching is arranged under the various virtues: Wisdom (29), Justice (30), Self-Control (31), Courage (32), Friendship (33), with a long introductory chapter (28) on Pythagorean piety, and the divine character of Pythagoras and his teaching. The chapter begins as follows, signalling a clear break: "after this, then, let us present an ordered account of his virtuous deeds no longer in general (κοινῶς) as we have been doing, but according to the individual virtues, ." This procedure involves much verbatim repetition (which is signalled in the notes), and it is not entirely clear why Iamblichus thought it to be necessary. It may, however, serve a pedagogical purpose, as indeed the whole book does. The *VP*, after all, as we have said, is the first volume of a ten-volume educational sequence, probably designed to contribute to the initial training of pupils in Iamblichus' own school. For this purpose the reproducing of the same edifying story, or passage from a previous authority, under separate headings would not be inappropriate, as it would be in a purely literary production. E. Rohde's indignation at Iamblichus' procedure may thus be seen as misguided.

6) *Conclusion* (ch. 34-36): after a survey of the virtues, there is first, a chapter on "Odds and Ends," in which Iamblichus presents a kind of ragbag ending to the previous section ("Thus far we have treated of Pythagoras and the Pythagoreans in orderly fashion, according to topics (κατὰ γένη τεταγμέν-ως). After this, let us take into evidence the miscellaneous (σποράδην) reports which are customarily related, as many as do not fall under the

---

111. E.g. in ch. 21 there is information on the daily routine laid down by Pythagoras for his disciples; in 22 about Pythagorean doctrine on friendship, in 23 about the use of *symbola*, in 24 about diet, and in 25 about the use of music as therapy (which leads on in 26 to an account of Pythagoras' discovery of the laws of harmony). This is all coherent and comprehensive, but there seems no reason why the topics should be in precisely this order.

previously stated arrangement.") This may refer back only to chs. 28-33, or to the whole book in general, in which latter case Iamblichus himself probably saw a definite *taxis* in his presentation from chapter 12 on.

It is not clear, though, what the justification for this chapter is. There is first an encomium of the Doric dialect, its purity and antiquity, as an explanation of why Pythagoras adopted it, then a passage on diet, repeated from ch. 29, and then a condemnation of those who teach for pay, especially those who were prepared to peddle Pythagorean secret doctrines to the outside world. There is a certain concluding quality at least about the first and last of these topics, but they could have been better presented as such.

Following this, there is a return to chronological sequence, with an account of the overthrow and death of Pythagoras (ch. 35), and the fate of the Pythagoreans after the dispersal of the school - an account in which, as is noted *ad loc.*, the chronology is confused and telescoped. The work ends (ch. 36) with an account of the succession to Pythagoras, and a roll-call of eminent Pythagoreans.

What might be a contemporary judgement on such a work? It was suggested earlier, à propos the section on the virtues, that it is best judged as an instrument of pedagogy rather than as a purely literary work. In that connexion, the analogy with the gospels is relevant, whatever the possible generic connexions. Iamblichus is not aspiring to originality. He is not trying to fool anyone by failing to acknowledge the authorities that he strings together here (as he does in the *Protrepticus* and the *De Communi Mathematica Scientia*); he doubtless saw himself, not as plagiarising, but as providing a service by assembling these authorities, often difficult of access, in easily assimilable form. Periodic repetitions are probably not due to absent-mindedness or literary incompetence, but rather serve to reinforce important points, or present them in different contexts. If this be accepted as a description of the document that is before us, then a more dispassionate judgment of its value becomes possible. Looked at positively, *On the Pythagorean Way of Life* can be seen as a kind of protreptic summation of the whole ethical tradition of Greek philosophy, a tradition in which all the major schools agreed, that philosophy was not simply a set of doctrines, but a whole way of life. Of this great tradition Pythagoras is presented as the true founder and begetter.

ΙΑΜΒΛΙΧΟΥ
ΧΑΛΚΙΔΕΩΣ ΤΗΣ ΚΟΙΛΗΣ ΣΥΡΙΑΣ
ΠΕΡΙ ΤΟΥ ΠΥΘΑΓΟΡΕΙΟΥ ΒΙΟΥ

[1] Ἐπὶ πάσης μὲν φιλοσοφίας ὁρμῇ θεὸν δήπου παρακαλεῖν ἔθος ἅπασι τοῖς γε σώφροσιν, ἐπὶ δὲ τῇ τοῦ θείου Πυθαγόρου δικαίως ἐπωνύμῳ νομιζομένη πολὺ δήπου μᾶλλον ἁρμόττει τοῦτο ποιεῖν· ἐκ θεῶν γὰρ αὐτῆς παραδοθείσης τὸ κατ' ἀρχὰς οὐκ ἔνεστιν ἄλλως ἢ διὰ τῶν θεῶν ἀντιλαμβάνεσθαι. πρὸς γὰρ τούτῳ καὶ τὸ κάλλος αὐτῆς καὶ τὸ μέγεθος ὑπεραίρει τὴν ἀνθρωπίνην δύναμιν ὥστε ἐξαίφνης αὐτὴν κατιδεῖν, ἀλλὰ μόνως ἄν τίς του τῶν θεῶν εὐμενοῦς ἐξηγουμένου κατὰ βραχὺ προσιὼν ἠρέμα ἂν αὐτῆς παρα-
[2] σπάσασθαί τι δυνηθείη. διὰ πάντα δὴ οὖν ταῦτα παρακαλέσαντες τοὺς θεοὺς ἡγεμόνας καὶ ἐπιτρέψαντες αὐτοῖς ἑαυτοὺς καὶ τὸν λόγον ἑπώμεθα ᾗ ἂν ἄγωσιν, οὐδὲν ὑπολογιζόμενοι τὸ πολὺν ἤδη χρόνον ἠμελῆσθαι τὴν αἵρεσιν ταύτην καὶ τὸ μαθήμασιν ἀπεξενωμένοις καὶ τισιν ἀπορρήτοις συμβόλοις ἐπικεκρύφθαι ψευδέσι τε καὶ νόθοις πολλοῖς συγγράμμασιν ἐπισκιάζεσθαι ἄλλαις τε πολλαῖς τοιαύταις δυσκολίαις παραποδίζεσθαι. ἐξαρκεῖ γὰρ ἡμῖν ἡ τῶν θεῶν βούλησις, μεθ' ἧς καὶ τὰ τούτων ἔτι ἀπορώτερα δυνατὸν ὑπομένειν. μετὰ δὲ θεοὺς ἡγεμόνα ἑαυτῶν προστησόμεθα τὸν ἀρχηγὸν καὶ πατέρα τῆς θείας φιλοσοφίας, μικρόν γε ἄνωθεν προλαβόντες περὶ τοῦ γένους αὐτοῦ καὶ τῆς πατρίδος.

30

CHAPTER ONE

Preface to the philosophy of Pythagoras, in which invocation
of the gods takes precedence, and the excellence and
difficulty of the subject are indicated at the same time.

[1] At the start of every philosophical investigation, it is after all the custom, at least for all who are sound-minded, to invoke God.[1] But at the outset of that philosophy rightly believed to be named after the divine Pythagoras, it is surely all the more fitting to do this; for since this philosophy was at first handed down by the gods, it cannot be comprehended without the gods' aid. Moreover, its nobility and greatness exceed human ability to understand it immediately: only when the goodwill of the gods leads the way, can someone with gradual approach slowly ap-
[2] propriate something from it. For all these reasons, then, invoking the gods as leaders, and entrusting ourselves and our discourse to them, let us follow wherever they lead, in no way discouraged by the long time this philosophical school has been neglected, concealed by outlandish teachings and secret codes (*symbola*)[2] obscured by numerous false and spurious treatises,[3] and entangled in many other similar difficulties. For us the will of the gods is sufficient, with which we can endure even more difficult circumstances than these. And after the gods, we shall choose as our leader the founder and father of this divine philosophy. But let us first, by way of preliminaries, say something about his family and country.

---

1. Cf. Plato, *Timaeus* 27c: "all who have even a small share of good sense call upon God always at the outset of every undertaking, be it small or great." Contrary to E. Rohde's uncertainty as to whether the preface belongs to Iamblichus himself, or to Apollonius of Tyana (*RhM* 27 (1872) 23), the preface to *VP* reflects Iamblichus' own beliefs about human imperfection, and the need for divine aid. See von Albrecht, *Antike und Abendland* 12 (1966) 58-60.

2. The Pythagorean *symbola* or *acusmata* (the terms seem equivalent) have received much attention. See, for example, W.K.C. Guthrie, *A History of Greek Philosophy*, I (Cambridge, 1962) 183 ff., W. Burkert, *Lore and Science in Ancient Pythagoreanism*, tr. E. L. Minar, Jr. (Cambridge, Mass. 1972) 166 ff., and the dissertations of C. Hoelk, *De acusmatis sive symbolis Pythagoricis* (Kiel, 1894), and of F. Boehm, *De symbolis Pythagoreis* (Berlin, 1905). See also *VP* 82-86, and Iamblichus' *Protrepticus*, chap. 21. Iamblichus' main source for the *symbola* was probably Aristotle. See J. A. Philip, "Aristotle's Monograph *On the Pythagoreans*," *TAPA* 94 (1963) 185-198.

3. On pseudo-Pythagorean literature, see W. Burkert, "Hellenistische Pseudopythagorica," *Philologus* 105 (1961) 16-43, 226-246, and H. Thesleff, *An Introduction to the Pythagorean Writings of the Hellenistic Period* in *Acta Academiae Aboensis, Humaniora* 24.3 (Åbo, 1961), and *The Pythagorean Texts of the Hellenistic Period* = *Acta Academiae Aboensis, Humaniora* 30.1 (Åbo, 1965).

[3] Λέγεται δὴ οὖν Ἀγκαῖον τὸν κατοικήσαντα Σάμην τὴν ἐν τῇ Κεφαληνίᾳ γεγενῆσθαι μὲν ἀπὸ Διός, εἴτε δι᾽ ἀρετὴν εἴτε διὰ ψυχῆς τι μέγεθος ταύτην τὴν φήμην αὐτοῦ ἀπενεγκαμένου, φρονήσει δὲ καὶ δόξῃ τῶν ἄλλων Κεφαλήνων διαφέρειν. τούτῳ δὲ γενέσθαι χρησμὸν παρὰ τῆς Πυθίας συναγαγεῖν ἀποικίαν ἐκ τῆς Κεφαληνίας καὶ ἐκ τῆς Ἀρκαδίας καὶ ἐκ τῆς Θετταλίας, καὶ προσλαβεῖν ἐποίκους παρά τε τῶν Ἀθηναίων καὶ παρὰ τῶν Ἐπιδαυρίων καὶ παρὰ τῶν Χαλκιδέων, καὶ τούτων ἁπάντων ἡγούμενον οἰκίσαι νῆσον τὴν δι᾽ ἀρετὴν τοῦ ἐδάφους καὶ τῆς γῆς Μελάμφυλλον [4] καλουμένην, προσαγορεῦσαί τε τὴν πόλιν Σάμον ἀντὶ τῆς Σάμης τῆς ἐν Κεφαληνίᾳ. τὸν μὲν οὖν χρησμὸν συνέβη γενέσθαι τοιοῦτον·

Ἀγκαῖ᾽, εἰναλίαν νῆσον Σάμον ἀντὶ Σάμης σε
οἰκίζειν κέλομαι· Φυλλὶς δ᾽ ὀνομάζεται αὕτη.

τοῦ δὲ τὰς ἀποικίας ἐκ τῶν τόπων τῶν προειρημένων συνελθεῖν σημεῖόν ἐστιν οὐ μόνον αἱ τῶν θεῶν τιμαὶ καὶ θυσίαι, διότι μετηγμέναι τυγχάνουσιν ἐκ τῶν τόπων ὅθεν τὰ πλήθη τῶν ἀνδρῶν συνῆλθεν, ἀλλὰ καὶ ⟨τὰ⟩ τῶν συγγενειῶν καὶ τῶν μετ᾽ ἀλλήλων συνόδων, ἃς ποιούμενοι οἱ Σάμιοι τυγχάνουσι. φασὶ τοίνυν Μνήμαρχον καὶ Πυθαΐδα τοὺς Πυθαγόραν γεννήσαντας ἐκ ταύτης εἶναι τῆς οἰκίας καὶ τῆς συγγενείας τῆς ἀπ᾽ Ἀγκαίου γεγενημένης τοῦ τὴν

CHAPTER TWO

About Pythagoras: his birth and native land, his upbringing
and education, his visits abroad, and journey to his home,
and from there his departure for Italy; in short,
about his whole course of life.

[3]
The story goes, then, that Ancaeus who dwelt in Same in Cephallenia was sired by Zeus. But whether he gained this reputation by moral excellence or by greatness of soul, he surpassed the other Cephallenians in judgment and renown. [1] He received an oracle from the Pythia to assemble a colony from Cephallenia, Arcadia, and Thessaly, and to take additional settlers from Athens, Epidaurus, and Chalcis. In charge of all these, he was to colonize an island, which because of its excellent soil and land, was called "Melamphyllus," i.e. "dark-leaved"; and to name the community "Samos" after Same which is on Cephallenia.

[4]
The oracle, went as follows:

> Ancaeus, the sea-island Samos instead of Samê,
> I command you to settle, and this (island) is named "Phyllis."

Evidence that groups of colonists came together from the aforementioned places is provided not only by the honors and sacrifices given to the gods (these being transferred from the places from which the main groups of colonists came), but is also provided by the family connections and guilds which the Samians came to form.[2] The tradition is that Mnemarchus and Pythais, Pythagoras' parents, were from the household and family started by Ancaeus who founded the colony.[3]

---

1. According to Rohde, sections 3-25 of *VP* are from Apollonius: Iamblichus' borrowing ends with mention of the athlete Pythagoras in section 25 (see *RhM* 27 [1872] 24). Rohde's assignment of portions of Iamblichus' work to Apollonius was accepted by I. Lévy, *Recherches sur les sources de la légende de Pythagore* (Paris, 1926) 104 ff. who also assigned sections 28, 36-57, 215-21, and 254-64 to Apollonius. Apollonius' *On Pythagoras* is lost, but references to it in the works of Iamblichus, Porphyry, and Philostratus (his *Life of Apollonius of Tyana*) give some notion of its contents. See Lévy, *Recherches*, 130-137, for details. Iamblichus' report on Pythais, Pythagoras' mother, is in Porph. *VP* 2, where the Samian poet's verses are also quoted. Porphyry gives Apollonius' *On Pythagoras* as his source.

   Ancaeus was son either of Poseidon or of Zeus, and took part in the voyage of the Argonauts. He was also King of the Leleges on Samos. See J. Toepffer, "Ankaios" in *RE* I, cols 2218-2219. For a brief history of Samos with bibliography, see *OCD* s.v. "Samos." See also G. Shipley, *A History of Samos, 800-188 B.C.* (Oxford, 1987).

   2. See F. Poland, *Geschichte der griechischen Vereinswesens* (Leipzig, 1909) 158 ff.

[5] ἀποικίαν στείλαντος. ταύτης δὲ τῆς εὐγενείας λεγομένης παρὰ τοῖς πολίταις ποιητής τις τῶν παρὰ τοῖς Σαμίοις γεγενημένων Ἀπόλλωνος αὐτὸν εἶναί φησι λέγων οὕτως·

Πυθαγόραν θ', ὃν τίκτε Διὶ φίλῳ Ἀπόλλωνι
Πυθαΐς, ἣ κάλλος πλεῖστον ἔχεν Σαμίων.

ὁπόθεν δὲ ὁ λόγος οὗτος ἐπεκράτησεν, ἄξιον διελθεῖν. Μνημάρχῳ τούτῳ τῷ Σαμίῳ κατ' ἐμπορίαν ἐν Δελφοῖς γενομένῳ μετὰ τῆς γυναικὸς ἀδήλως ἔτι κυούσης προεῖπεν ἡ Πυθία χρωμένῳ περὶ τοῦ εἰς Συρίαν πλοῦ, τὸν μὲν θυμηρέστατον ἔσεσθαι καὶ ἐπικερδῆ, τὴν δὲ γυναῖκα κύειν τε ἤδη καὶ τέξεσθαι παῖδα τῶν πώποτε κάλλει καὶ σοφίᾳ διοίσοντα καὶ τῷ ἀνθρωπίνῳ γένει μέγιστον ὄφελος εἰς [6] σύμπαντα τὸν βίον ἐσόμενον. ὁ δὲ Μνήμαρχος συλλογισά- μενος ὅτι οὐκ ἂν μὴ πυθομένῳ αὐτῷ ἔχρησέ τι περὶ τέκνου ὁ θεός, εἰ μὴ ἐξαίρετον προτέρημα ἔμελλε περὶ αὐτὸν καὶ θεοδώρητον ὡς ἀληθῶς ἔσεσθαι, τότε μὲν εὐθὺς ἀντὶ Παρθενίδος τὴν γυναῖκα Πυθαΐδα μετωνόμασεν ἀπὸ τοῦ [7] γόνου καὶ τῆς προφήτιδος, ἐν δὲ Σιδόνι τῆς Φοινίκης ἀποτεκούσης αὐτῆς τὸν γενόμενον υἱὸν Πυθαγόραν προσηγόρευσεν, ὅτι ἄρα ὑπὸ τοῦ Πυθίου προηγορεύθη αὐτῷ. παραιτητέοι γὰρ ἐνταῦθα Ἐπιμενίδης καὶ Εὔδοξος καὶ Ξενοκράτης, ὑπονοοῦντες τῇ Παρθενίδι τότε μιγῆναι τὸν Ἀπόλλωνα καὶ κύουσαν αὐτὴν ἐκ μὴ οὕτως ἐχούσης καταστῆσαί τε καὶ προαγγεῖλαι διὰ τῆς προφήτιδος. τοῦτο μὲν οὖν οὐδαμῶς δεῖ προσίεσθαι. τὸ μέντοι τὴν Πυθαγόρου [8] ψυχὴν ἀπὸ τῆς Ἀπόλλωνος ἡγεμονίας, εἴτε συνοπαδὸν οὖσαν εἴτε καὶ ἄλλως οἰκειότερον ἔτι πρὸς τὸν θεὸν τοῦτον συντεταγμένην, καταπεπέμφθαι εἰς ἀνθρώπους οὐδεὶς ἂν ἀμφισβητήσειε τεκμαιρόμενος αὐτῇ τε τῇ γενέσει ταύτῃ καὶ τῇ σοφίᾳ τῆς ψυχῆς αὐτοῦ τῇ παντοδαπῇ. καὶ περὶ μὲν τῆς γενέσεως τοσαῦτα.

[5]   Although this noble origin is told by the citizens, a Samian poet says that Pythag-
      oras was son of Apollo. He spoke thus:

      Pythagoras, whom Pythais bore for Apollo, dear to Zeus,
      she who was loveliest of the Samians.

      It is worthwhile to relate how this story prevailed. When Mnemarchus the Samian
      was in Delphi for trade purposes with his wife pregnant, but not yet obviously so,
      the Pythia prophesied to him when he consulted the oracle about his (impend-
      ing) voyage to Syria,[4] that it would be most pleasant and profitable; and that his
      wife, now pregnant, would bear a child surpassing in beauty and wisdom those
      who had ever yet existed, and he would be of enormous help to the human race
      in its whole manner of living. Mnemarchus concluded that since he had not in-
[6]   quired about a child, the god would not have given such an oracle unless the child
      were to have some special superiority and be truly god-given. So he immediately
      gave his wife a new name, "Pythais," instead of "Parthenis," a name derived from
[7]   her offspring and from the prophetess. And when she gave birth in Sidon of Phoe-
      nicia, he called the son born "Pythagoras," because he was prophesied to him by
      Pythian Apollo.[5] We must reject here the view of Epimenides, Eudoxus, and Xe-
      nocrates, who assumed that Apollo had intercourse with Parthenis at that time,
      and when she was not pregnant, made her so, and announced it through his
[8]   prophetess. This view deserves no acceptance. Nevertheless, no one would dis-
      pute, judging from his very birth and the all around wisdom of his life, that
      Pythagoras' soul was sent down to humans under Apollo's leadership, either as a
      follower in his train, or united with this god in a still more intimate way. So much
      then, about his birth.

---

3. Diogenes Laertius and Porphyry call Pythagoras' father "Mnesarchus" and identify him as
a gem-engraver (δακτυλιογλύφος) on which see N. Demand, "Pythagoras, Son of Mnesarchos."
Phronesis 18 (1973) 91-96. This form of the name is given by Heraclitus (D.-K., B 129) and Herodotus (IV.95). Why Iamblichus (or a scribe) consistently writes "Mnemarchus" is unclear. In the
genealogy of D.L. 8.1, it is given as "Marmacus" (cf. K. von Fritz, *RE* XXIV, col. 172); Mamercus
is a son of Pythagoras in Plut. *Aem.* 1.
    4. Porph. VP 1) reports that Neanthes claimed Pythagoras' father was a Syrian from Tyre, and
introduced him to the Chaldeans. Aristoxenus, however, makes him a Tyrrhenian, and Plutarch
considers him an Etrurian. For conflicting ancient reports on Pythagoras' origins, see Burkert,
Lore and Science, III n. 12, and J. A. Philip, *Pythagoras and Early Pythagoreanism* (Toronto, 1966)
186-87.
    5. "Pythagoras" is here derived from "prophesied by the Pythian" (ὑπὸ τοῦ Πυθίου προ-
ηγορεύθη). The story of Apollo's paternity may be modelled after that of Plato's birth (see P.
Lang, *De Speusippi Academici Scriptis* (Bonn, 1911) fr. 27 = D.L. 3.2). Iamblichus' criticism of it
here may be aimed at Christian claims about Jesus. For the etymology of "Jesus," see Matt. 1:21-
24; Luke 1:30-33.

[9] ἐπεὶ δὲ ἀνεκομίσθη εἰς τὴν Σάμον ἀπὸ τῆς Συρίας ὁ
Μνήμαρχος μετὰ παμπόλλου κέρδους καὶ βαθείας περιουσίας, ἱερὸν ἐδείματο τῷ Ἀπόλλωνι, Πυθίου ἐπιγράψας, τόν
τε παῖδα ποικίλοις παιδεύμασι καὶ ἀξιολογωτάτοις ἐνέτρεφε,
νῦν μὲν Κρεοφύλῳ, νῦν δὲ Φερεκύδῃ τῷ Συρίῳ, νῦν δὲ
σχεδὸν ἅπασι τοῖς τῶν ἱερῶν προϊσταμένοις παραβάλλων
αὐτὸν καὶ ἐγχειρίζων, ὡς ἂν καὶ τὰ θεῖα κατὰ δύναμιν
αὐτάρκως ἐκδιδαχθείη. ὃ δὲ ἀνετρέφετο εὐμορφότατός τε τῶν
πώποτε ἱστορηθέντων καὶ θεοπρεπέστατος εὐτυχηθείς,
[10] ἀποθανόντος τε τοῦ πατρὸς σεμνότατος σωφρονέστατός τε
ηὐξάνετο, κομιδῇ τε νέος ἔτι ὑπάρχων ἐντροπῆς πάσης καὶ
αἰδοῦς ἠξιοῦτο ἤδη καὶ ὑπὸ τῶν πρεσβυτάτων, ὀφθείς τε καὶ
φθεγξάμενος ἐπέστρεφε πάντας, καὶ ᾧτινι οὖν προσβλέψας
θαυμαστὸς ἐφαίνετο, ὥστε ὑπὸ τῶν πολλῶν εἰκότως
βεβαιοῦσθαι τὸ θεοῦ παῖδα αὐτὸν εἶναι. ὃ δὲ ἐπιρρωννύμενος
καὶ ὑπὸ τῶν τοιούτων δοξῶν καὶ ὑπὸ τῆς ἐκ βρέφους
παιδείας καὶ ὑπὸ τῆς φυσικῆς θεοειδείας ἔτι μᾶλλον ἑαυτὸν
κατέτεινεν ἄξιον τῶν παρόντων προτερημάτων ἀποφαίνων,
καὶ διεκόσμει θρησκείαις τε καὶ μαθήμασι καὶ διαίταις
ἐξαιρέτοις, εὐσταθείᾳ τε ψυχῆς καὶ καταστολῇ σώματος, ὧν
τε ἐλάλει ἢ ἔπραττεν εὐδίᾳ καὶ ἀμιμήτῳ τινὶ γαλήνῃ, μήτε
ὀργῇ ποτε μήτε γέλωτι μήτε ζήλῳ μήτε φιλονεικίᾳ μήτε
[11] ἄλλῃ ταραχῇ ἢ προπετείᾳ ἁλισκόμενος, ὡς δὲ δαίμων τις
ἀγαθὸς ἐπιδημῶν τῇ Σάμῳ. διόπερ ἔτι ἐφήβου αὐτοῦ ὄντος
πολλὴ δόξα εἴς τε Μίλητον πρὸς Θαλῆν καὶ εἰς Πριήνην
πρὸς Βίαντα διεκομίσθη τοὺς σοφοὺς καὶ ⟨εἰς⟩ τὰς
ἀστυγείτονας πόλεις ἐξεφοίτησε, καὶ τὸν ἐν Σάμῳ κομήτην
ἤδη ἐν παροιμίᾳ πολλοὶ πολλαχοῦ τὸν νεανίαν
ἐπευφημοῦντες ἐξεθείαζον καὶ διεθρύλλουν. ὑποφυομένης δὲ
ἄρτι τῆς Πολυκράτους τυραννίδος περὶ ὀκτωκαιδέκατον
μάλιστα ἔτος γεγονὼς προορώμενός τε οἷ χωρήσει καὶ ὡς
ἐμπόδιος ἔσται τῇ αὐτοῦ προθέσει καὶ τῇ ἀντὶ πάντων αὐτῷ
σπουδαζομένῃ φιλομαθείᾳ, νύκτωρ λαθὼν πάντας μετὰ τοῦ
Ἑρμοδάμαντος μὲν τὸ ὄνομα, Κρεοφυλείου δὲ ἐπικαλου-
μένου, ὃς ἐλέγετο Κρεοφύλου ἀπόγονος εἶναι, Ὁμήρου
ξένου τοῦ ποιητοῦ ⟨, οὗ δὴ δοκεῖ⟩ γενέσθαι φίλος καὶ
διδάσκαλος τῶν ἁπάντων, μετὰ τούτου πρὸς τὸν Φερεκύδην
διεπόρθμευε καὶ πρὸς Ἀναξίμανδρον τὸν φυσικὸν καὶ πρὸς

[9]   When Mnemarchus returned to Samos from Syria with very great gain and abundant profit, he built Apollo a shrine, dedicated it to the Pythian god, and brought up his son with various and quite remarkable subjects of instruction. At one time he left and entrusted him to Creophylus; at another time to Pherecydes of Syros;[6] and at still other times to almost all who were experts in divine matters, that he might be taught thoroughly and sufficiently about divine matters as much as is humanly possible. He was thus educated, and having had this good fortune,

[10]   he became the most handsome and godlike of those ever recorded in history. After his father's death, he grew up to be most dignified and sound-minded, and while still quite young he was already thought worthy of all respect and reverence even by the oldest. Both on sight and at first hearing, he attracted everyone's attention; and on whomever he gazed, he appeared marvelous, so that by the multitude he was naturally confirmed to be a god's child.

Strengthened by such opinions, by his upbringing from infancy, and by a natural godlikeness, he strove earnestly to show himself even more worthy of his present privileges, and disciplined himself with religious observances, scientific studies, and extraordinary regimens. Having achieved stability of soul and mastery of body, his every word and action were accomplished with tranquillity and inimitable calmness. Never overcome by anger, laughter, envy, contentiousness, or any other mental disturbance or rashness, he lived on Samos like some beneficent guardian spirit (*daimon*).[7]

[11]   Hence, while still a youth, his great reputation spread abroad to the sages: Thales at Miletus and Bias at Priene, and to their neighboring cities. Many everywhere glorified the youth, now the proverbial "long-haired Samian,"[8] and lauded him to the skies with continued gossip. And when Polycrates' tyranny was just starting to grow,[9] Pythagoras, now about eighteen years old, foreseeing where it would lead,

---

6. According to Delatte, *La vie de Pythagore de Diogène Laërce*, 150, the sources linking Pythagoras to Pherecydes are so numerous and ancient that they may derive from early Pythagoreans. See also J. Philip, *Pythagoras*, 188. Pythagoras later cared for his sick teacher, and finally buried him, see *VP* 184 and 252. The chronology of Pythagoras' relationship with Pherecydes was much disputed in antiquity. See Delatte, *La vie de Pythagore*, 150-151.

7. Δαίμων is not easily translatable. For discussions of the word in connection with Pythagoreanism, see M. Detienne, *La notion de Daïmon dans le pythagorisme ancien* (Paris, 1963), and Burkert, *Lore and Science*, 73 ff. and 185 ff.

8. A pun is possibly here intended with another meaning of κομήτης "comet."

9. Since this must be dated to ca. 532 B.C., it conflicts seriously with the chronology presented later in section 17. On this chronology, Pythagoras would have been born ca. 550 B.C. Exact dates are of small concern to Iamblichus. F. Jacoby in his discussion of the chronology of Pythagoras (*Apollodors Chronik*, Berlin, 1902, 221-227) distinguished three schemes of establishing Pythagoras' dates based on Apollodorus, Eratosthenes, and an Italian tradition, none easily reconcilable with one another. See more recently, Burkert, *Lore and Science*, 110 ff., and J. Philip, *Pythagoras*, 185-199, who gives a succinct discussion of the likely dates of Pythagoras' life. It may be that the close connexion of Pythagoras' departure from Samos with the growth of Polycrates' tyranny is a later pious fabrication, designed to show Pythagoras' disapproval of tyranny.

[12] Θαλῆν εἰς Μίλητον, καὶ παραγενόμενος πρὸς ἕκαστον αὐτῶν ἀνὰ μέρος οὕτως ὡμίλησεν, ὥστε πάντας αὐτὸν ἀγαπᾶν καὶ τὴν φύσιν αὐτοῦ θαυμάζειν καὶ ποιεῖσθαι τῶν λόγων κοινωνόν. καὶ δὴ καὶ ὁ Θαλῆς ἄσμενος αὐτὸν προσήκατο, καὶ θαυμάσας τὴν πρὸς τοὺς ἄλλους νέους παραλλαγήν, ὅτι μείζων τε καὶ ὑπερβεβηκυῖα ἦν τὴν προφοιτήσασαν ἤδη δόξαν, μεταδούς τε ὅσων ἠδύνατο μαθημάτων, τὸ γῆράς τε τὸ ἑαυτοῦ αἰτιασάμενος καὶ τὴν ἑαυτοῦ ἀσθένειαν προετρέψατο εἰς Αἴγυπτον διαπλεῦσαι καὶ τοῖς ἐν Μέμφει καὶ Διος⟨πόλει⟩ μάλιστα συμβαλεῖν ἱερεῦσι· παρὰ γὰρ ἐκείνων καὶ ἑαυτὸν ἐφωδιάσθαι ταῦτα, δι' ἃ σοφὸς παρὰ τοῖς πολλοῖς νομίζεται. οὐ μὴν τοσούτων γε προτερημάτων οὔτε φυσικῶς οὔτε ὑπ' ἀσκήσεως ἐπιτετευχέναι ἑαυτὸν ἔλεγεν, ὅσων τὸν Πυθαγόραν καθορᾶν· ὥστε ἐκ παντὸς εὐηγγελίζετο, εἰ τοῖς δηλουμένοις ἱερεῦσι συγγένοιτο, θειότατον αὐτὸν καὶ σοφώτατον ὑπὲρ ἅπαντας ἔσεσθαι ἀνθρώπους.

and that it would be a hindrance to his goal and to his love of learning, which he valued above all, escaped by night without anyone noticing. He fled together with Hermodamas (surnamed Creophyleius, since he was said to be a descendant of Creophylus, host of the poet Homer,[10] whose friend and teacher in all things he seems to have been). With (Hermodamas), then, he journeyed over the sea to Pherecydes and to Anaximander, the natural philosopher, and to Thales at Mile-[12] tus.[11] And as he visited each in turn, the result of association with him was such that all cherished him and admired his character, and made him a partner in their discourses. And what is more, Thales gladly accepted him as a student, and admired his difference from other youths. Because it was greater and exceeded the reputation that already preceded him, (Thales) gave whatever lessons he could. But then, giving as an excuse his own old age and weakness, (Thales) urged him to sail to Egypt, and especially to meet with the priests in Memphis and Diospolis. For it was by these, he said, that he himself had been provided with the very things in virtue of which the multitude believed he was wise.[12] Indeed, Thales said that he himself had gained neither by nature nor by training so many privileges as he saw in Pythagoras. Hence, he could proclaim nothing but good news:[13] if Pythagoras associated with the priests, he would be most divine, and wisest beyond all humans.

---

10. Hermodamas is assigned, together with Pherecydes, as one of Pythagoras' main teachers. Creophylus is the Samian who hospitably received Homer. A purpose of the report is to suggest a Homeric association with Pythagoreanism. See M. Detienne, *Homère, Hésiode et Pythagore. Poésie et philosophie dans le Pythagorisme ancien* (Brussels 1962 = Coll. *Latomus* 57) 113 f. Cf. *RE* VIII, cols. 2150-51. Homer's friendship with Creophylus is often mentioned in antiquity (see, for example, Pl. *R.* 600 B) and he was a guest of Creophylus on Ios.

11. On Pythagoras' alleged connections with Thales and Anaximander, see Burkert, *Lore and Science*, 415 ff. Pythagoras' voyages were a favorite theme of the biographical tradition, and in Plato's Academy there was great interest in the Orient. See W. Jaeger, *Aristotle* (Oxford, 1948) 131-137. There is, however, no proof that Pythagoras knew Pherecydes.

12. Egypt is often mentioned in Pythagoras' travels. According to Isocrates (*Busiris* 28), Pythagoras "visited Egypt and became a disciple of the priests there. He was the first to introduce (their) philosophy to the Greeks . . . ." But in 12, 33 Isocrates almost concedes that this is an invention. Aristoxenus later had Pythagoras travel not only to Egypt, but to the East and to Zaratas (Zoroaster). See J. Bidez and F. Cumont, *Les mages hellénisés* vol. I(Paris, 1938) 28 and 38 ff., and F. Wehrli, *Aristoxenus* (Basel, 1945) 49 ff.

13. This is almost certainly an anti-Christian reference (cf. Luke 2:52 at the conclusion of Luke 2:41-52)

[13] Ὠφεληθεὶς οὖν παρὰ Θάλεω τά τε ἄλλα καὶ χρόνου
μάλιστα φείδεσθαι, καὶ χάριν τούτου οἰνοποσίᾳ τε καὶ
κρεωφαγίᾳ καὶ ἔτι πρότερον πολυφαγίᾳ ἀποταξάμενος, τῇ δὲ
τῶν λεπτῶν καὶ εὐαναδότων ἐδωδῇ συμμετρηθείς, κἀκ
τούτου ὀλιγοϋπνίαν καὶ ἐπεγρίαν καὶ ψυχῆς καθαρότητα
κτησάμενος ὑγείαν τε ἀκριβεστάτην καὶ ἀπαρέγκλιτον τοῦ
σώματος, ἐξέπλευσεν εἰς τὴν Σιδόνα, φύσει τε αὐτοῦ
πατρίδα πεπυσμένος εἶναι καὶ καλῶς οἰόμενος ἐκεῖθεν αὑτῷ
[14] ῥᾴονα τὴν εἰς Αἴγυπτον ἔσεσθαι διάβασιν. ἐνταῦθα δὴ
συμβαλὼν τοῖς τε Μώχου τοῦ φυσιολόγου προφήτου ἀπο-
γόνοις καὶ τοῖς ἄλλοις Φοινικικοῖς ἱεροφάνταις, καὶ πάσας
τελεσθεὶς θείας τελετὰς ἔν τε Βύβλῳ καὶ Τύρῳ καὶ κατὰ
πολλὰ τῆς Συρίας μέρη ἐξαιρέτως ἱερουργουμένας, καὶ οὐχὶ
δεισιδαιμονίας ἕνεκα τὸ τοιοῦτον ὑπομείνας, ὡς ἄν τις ἁπλῶς
ὑπολάβοι, πολὺ δὲ μᾶλλον ἔρωτι καὶ ὀρέξει θεωρίας καὶ
εὐλαβείᾳ τοῦ μή τι αὐτὸν τῶν ἀξιομαθήτων διαλάθῃ ἐν θεῶν
ἀπορρήτοις ἢ τελεταῖς φυλαττόμενον, προσμαθών τε ὅτι
ἄποικα τρόπον τινὰ καὶ ἀπόγονα τῶν ἐν Αἰγύπτῳ ἱερῶν τὰ
αὐτόθι ὑπάρχει, ἐκ τούτου τε ἐλπίσας καλλιόνων καὶ
θειοτέρων καὶ ἀκραιφνῶν μεθέξειν μνημάτων ἐν τῇ
Αἰγύπτῳ, ἀγασθεὶς κατὰ τὰς Θάλεω τοῦ διδασκάλου ὑποθήκας διεπορθμεύθη ἀμελλητὶ ὑπό τινων Αἰγυπτίων
πορθμέων καιριώτατα προσορμισάντων τοῖς ὑπὸ Κάρμηλον
τὸ Φοινικικὸν ὄρος αἰγιαλοῖς, ἔνθα ἐμόναζε τὰ πολλὰ ὁ Πυθαγόρας κατὰ τὸ ἱερόν· οἵπερ ἄσμενοι ἐδέξαντο αὐτόν, τήν
τε ὥραν αὐτοῦ κερδῆσαι καί, εἰ ἀποδοῖντο, τὴν πολυτιμίαν

CHAPTER THREE

His sailing to Phoenicia and his study there, and his journey
from there to Egypt, and how it took place.

[13] Helped, then, by Thales in other matters, especially in making the best use of his time, for the sake of which he renounced drinking wine and eating meat, and still earlier, excessive eating, (Pythagoras) limited himself to light and easily digestible food. Acquiring from this (regimen) the need for little sleep, alertness, purity of soul, real and unimpaired health of the body, he sailed to Sidon. He learned that it was his native land at birth, and rightly believed that from there his passage to Egypt would be easier.

[14] There he joined the descendants of Mochus,[1] the prophet and natural philosopher, and other Phoenician hierophants, and was initiated into all sacred rites of the mysteries celebrated especially in Byblos and in Tyre, and in many parts of Syria. (Pythagoras) did not experience these as a result of superstition, as someone might foolishly suppose, but much more with a desire and yearning for theoretical knowledge, and a reverent concern that nothing worthy of learning kept in the secrets or mystic rites of the gods escape his notice. Having learned besides that those which existed there (in Syria) were somehow derived and descended from the sacred rites in Egypt, he hoped thus to participate in the more noble, more divine and pure rites of Egypt. Filled with admiration for them, then, in accord with instructions from his teacher Thales, he was transported without delay by some Egyptian seamen who had most opportunely anchored at the shore under Carmel, the Phoenician mountain where Pythagoras spent a good deal of time alone in sacred pursuits.[2] They (the seamen) gladly welcomed him, looking forward to making profit from his youth, and, if they sold him into slavery, the high price he would bring.

---

1. The connection of "Mochus" with Moses is tenuous. Mochus appears to go back to Posidonius (see Strabo, XIV, 757) who presents him as a Phoenician sage from Sidon before the Trojan War, and who was the founder of Atomism (Sextus Empiricus, *M*, 363 = frs. 285-86, Edelstein-Kidd). Josephus (*AJ* 1,107) regards Mochus as an authority distinct from Moses. See F. Jacoby, *Frag. Gr. Hist.* III 784 F 2-6 where references to Mochus are given

2. Neanthes emphasized Pythagoras' connections with Syria. See Porph. *VP* 1-2. Both Porphyry and Iamblichus were of Syrian origin.

41

[15] προϊδόμενοι. ἔπειτα μέντοι κατὰ τὸν πλοῦν ἐγκρατῶς αὐτοῦ
τε καὶ σεμνῶς ἀκολούθως τε τῇ συντρόφῳ ἐπιτηδεύσει
διάγοντος ἄμεινον περὶ αὐτοῦ διατεθέντες καὶ μεῖζόν τι ἢ
κατὰ τὴν ἀνθρωπίνην φύσιν ἐνιδόντες τῇ τοῦ παιδὸς
εὐκοσμίᾳ, ἀναμνησθέντες τε ὡς προσορμίσασιν εὐθὺς αὐτοῖς
ὤφθη κατιὼν ἀπ' ἄκρου τοῦ Καρμήλου λόφου (ἱερώτατον δὲ
τῶν ἄλλων ὀρῶν ἠπίσταντο αὐτὸ καὶ πολλοῖς ἄβατον),
σχολαίως τε καὶ ἀνεπιστρεπτὶ βαίνων, οὔτε κρημνώδους
τινὸς οὔτε δυσβάτου πέτρας ἐνισταμένης, καὶ ἐπιστὰς τῷ
σκάφει μόνον τε ἐπιφθεγξάμενος "εἰς Αἴγυπτον ὁ
ἀπόπλους;" κατανευσάντων αὐτῶν ἐνέβη καὶ σιωπῇ ἐκάθι-
σεν ἔνθα μάλιστα οὐκ ἔμελλεν αὐτοῖς ἐμπόδιος ἔσεσθαι
[16] ναυτιλλομένοις, παρ' ὅλον (τε) τὸν πλοῦν ἐφ' ἑνός τε καὶ
τοῦ αὐτοῦ σχήματος διέμεινε δύο νύκτας καὶ τρεῖς ἡμέρας
μήτε τροφῆς μήτε ποτοῦ μετασχὼν μήτε ὕπνου, ὅτι εἰ μὴ
λαθὼν ἅπαντας ὡς εἶχεν ἐν τῇ ἑδραίᾳ καὶ ἀσαλεύτῳ ἐπιμονῇ
κατέδαρθε βραχύ, καὶ ταῦτα διηνεκοῦς καὶ σεσυρμένου παρὰ
προσδοκίαν εὐθυτενοῦς τε συμβάντος αὐτοῖς τοῦ πλοῦ ὡς ἄν
τινος παρουσίᾳ θεοῦ· πάντα συντιθέντες τὰ τοιάδε καὶ
ἐπισυλλογιζόμενοι δαίμονα θεῖον ὡς ἀληθῶς ἐπείσθησαν σὺν
αὐτοῖς ἀπὸ Συρίας εἰς Αἴγυπτον μετιέναι, καὶ τόν τε
πρόσλοιπον εὐφημότατα πλοῦν διεξήνυσαν καὶ σεμνοτέροις
ἤπερ εἰώθεσαν ὀνόμασί τε καὶ πράγμασιν ἐχρήσαντο πρός τε
ἀλλήλους καὶ πρὸς αὐτὸν μέχρι τῆς εὐτυχεστάτης συμβάσης
[17] αὐτοῖς καὶ ἀκυμάντου παρ' ὅλον εἰς τὴν Αἰγυπτίαν ἠόνα τοῦ
σκάφους προσοχῆς. ἔνθα δὴ ἐκβαίνοντα ὑπερείσαντες
σεβαστικῶς ἅπαντες καὶ διαδεξάμενοι ἐκάθισαν ἐπὶ
καθαρωτάτης ἄμμου, καὶ αὐτοσχέδιόν τινα βωμὸν πρὸ αὐτοῦ
πλάσαντες ἐπινήσαντές τε ὅσων εἶχον ἀκροδρύων οἷον
ἀπαρχάς τινας κατατιθέμενοι τοῦ φόρτου μεθώρμισαν τὸ
σκάφος, ὅπουπερ καὶ προέκειτο αὐτοῖς ὁ πλοῦς. ὃ δὲ διὰ τὴν
τοσήνδε ἀσιτίαν ἀτονώτερον τὸ σῶμα ἔχων οὔτε πρὸς τὸν
ἀποβιβασμὸν καὶ τὴν τῶν ναυτῶν ὑπέρεισιν καὶ χειρα-
γωγίαν ἠναντιώθη τότε οὔτε ἀπαλλαγέντων ἀπέσχετο ἐπὶ
πολὺ τῶν παρακειμένων ἀκροδρύων, ἀλλὰ ἐφαψάμενος
χρησίμως αὐτῶν καὶ ὑποθρέψας τὴν δύναμιν εἰς τὰς ἐγγὺς
διέσωσε συνοικίας, τὸ αὐτὸ ἦθος ἐν παντὶ ἀτάραχον καὶ
ἐπιεικὲς διαφυλάττων.

[15] On the voyage, however, since he passed the time with self-control and nobly, in accord with his habitual way of life, they became better disposed to him, and saw in the youth's good behavior something greater than human nature. And they remembered how, when they first anchored, he was seen coming from the topmost crest of Carmel[3] (for they believed it the holiest of mountains, and not accessible to the common multitude). He walked leisurely and unconcernedly, no [16] precipice or impassible rock barring his way. They also remembered how on reaching the boat, he had said only "is your voyage to Egypt?", and when they nodded "yes," he boarded and sat in silence where he would not be the slightest hindrance to those navigating. They also recalled that throughout the whole voyage, he kept the same posture for two nights and three days, without food, drink, or sleep (unless no one noticed that while in that sedentary and tranquil inactivity, he had fallen asleep for a short time) and that their voyage was uninterrupted, swift, and, contrary to expectation, went straight to its destination as if some god were present.

After reflecting on all such incidents, and drawing a reasonable conclusion, they were persuaded that truly a divine guardian spirit *(daimon)* had crossed with them from Syria to Egypt. They completed the rest of the voyage most auspiciously with a favorable wind, and spoke and acted more respectfully than usual to one another and to him, until their boat docked without mishap or rough weather at the Egyptian shore.

[17] There, on disembarking, all supported him and helped him ashore in turn, and seated him on the cleanest sand. After fashioning an impromptu altar before him, heaping up whatever fruits they had in their cargo and laying these down before him like some sacrificial offerings, they raised anchor and sailed off to their intended destination. But he, rather weak in body because of much lack of food, neither opposed the support and guidance of the sailors at his disembarking, nor, when they departed, did he abstain for long from the fruits provided. After eating them, and restoring his strength, he arrived safely at the settlements nearby, maintaining his same disposition, undisturbed and reasonable in every respect.

---

3. Carmel, a prominent mountain on the coast of Palestine, had significant associations with Elijah and Elisha; its special religious significance is indicated in I Kings, 18:19-40, and II Kings, 2:25 and 4:25. Its sanctuaries were prominent throughout antiquity. There was, for example, a shrine of Baal and later of Zeus. See G. W. Van Beek, *IDB*, s.v. Carmel, Mount; M. C. Astour, *IDB.S*, s.v. Carmel, Mount; E. Schürer, *The History of the Jewish People in the Age of Jesus Christ*, rev. and ed. by G. Vermes, F. Millar, and M. Black, II (Edinburgh, 1979) 35 n. 32; M. J. Mulder, *Theologisches Wörterbuch zum Alten Testament*, IV (Stuttgart, 1982) 340-51 (with bibliography).

[18] Ἐκεῖθέν τε εἰς πάντα ἐφοίτησεν ἱερὰ μετὰ πλείστης σπουδῆς καὶ ἀκριβοῦς ἐξετάσεως, θαυμαζόμενός τε καὶ στεργόμενος ὑπὸ τῶν συγγινομένων ἱερέων καὶ προφητῶν καὶ ἐκδιδασκόμενος ἐπιμελέστατα περὶ ἑκάστου, οὐ παραλείπων οὔτε ἄκουσμα τῶν καθ' ἑαυτὸν ἐπαινουμένων οὔτε ἄνδρα τῶν ἐπὶ συνέσει γνωριζομένων οὔτε τελετὴν τῶν ὅπου δήποτε τιμωμένων οὔτε τόπον ἀθεώρητον, εἰς ὃν ἀφικόμενος ᾠήθη τι περιττότερον εὑρήσειν. ὅθεν πρὸς ἅπαντας τοὺς ἱερέας ἀπεδήμησεν, ὠφελούμενος παρ' ἑκάστῳ ὅσα ἦν σοφὸς ἕκαστος. δύο δὴ καὶ εἴκοσιν ἔτη κατὰ τὴν Αἴγυπτον ἐν τοῖς
[19] ἀδύτοις διετέλεσεν ἀστρονομῶν τε καὶ γεωμετρῶν καὶ μυούμενος, οὐκ ἐξ ἐπιδρομῆς οὐδ' ὡς ἔτυχε, πάσας θεῶν τελετάς, ἕως ὑπὸ τῶν σὺν Καμβύσῃ αἰχμαλωτισθεὶς εἰς Βαβυλῶνα ἀνήχθη· κἀκεῖ τοῖς μάγοις ἀσμένοις ἄσμενος συνδιατρίψας καὶ ἐκπαιδευθεὶς τὰ παρ' αὐτοῖς σεμνὰ καὶ θεῶν θρησκείαν ἐντελεστάτην ἐκμαθών, ἀριθμῶν τε καὶ μουσικῆς καὶ τῶν ἄλλων μαθημάτων ἐπ' ἄκρον ἐλθὼν παρ' αὐτοῖς, ἄλλα τε δώδεκα προσδιατρίψας ἔτη, εἰς Σάμον ὑπέστρεψε περὶ ἕκτον που καὶ πεντηκοστὸν ἔτος ἤδη γεγονώς.

CHAPTER FOUR

His study in Egypt, and how he traveled from there to
Babylonia. How he kept company with the magi,
and how he returned again to Samos.

[18] From there he visited every holy place, full of great zeal, and with a desire for careful inspection. He was both admired and cherished by the priests and prophets with whom he associated. He learned everything most attentively, and neglected neither any oral instruction commended in his own time, nor anyone known for sagacity, nor any rite anywhere and at anytime honored. He also left no place unvisited where he thought he would find something exceptional. Hence, he visited all the priests, and benefited from the special wisdom of each.

[19] So he spent twenty-two years in the sanctuaries of Egypt,[1] studying astronomy and geometry and being initiated in all the mystic rites of the gods, not superficially nor haphazardly, until, taken prisoner by Cambyses' soldiers, he was brought to Babylon.[2] There he spent a mutually gratifying time with the magi. Educated thoroughly in their solemn rites, he learned perfect worship of the gods with them, and reached the highest point in knowledge of numbers, music, and other mathematical sciences. After spending another twelve years there, he returned to Samos, now about fifty-six years of age.

---

1. See note 12 of Chap. 2. Pythagoras' connection with Egypt is as early as Herodotus (II. 81), but even that evidence cannot be considered reliable.

2. This report must be dated to 525 B. C., and involves a serious chronological contradiction with Aristoxenus' testimony (Wehrli, fr. 16) that Pythagoras left Samos to escape Polycrates' tyranny in 532/1 B.C. Given Pythagoras' twenty-two years in Egypt, twelve years in Babylon, a return to Samos, and a trip to Magna Graecia, it can only be concluded that Iamblichus presents an impossible chronology, or spins a very tall tale.

[20] Ἀναγνωρισθεὶς δὲ ὑπό τινων πρεσβυτέρων καὶ οὐκ ἔλαττον ἢ πρόσθεν θαυμασθείς (καλλίων τε γὰρ καὶ σοφώτερος καὶ θεοπρεπέστερος αὐτοῖς ἐφάνη), παρακαλούσης αὐτὸν δημοσίᾳ τῆς πατρίδος ὠφελεῖν ἅπαντας καὶ μεταδιδόναι τῶν ἐνθυμίων, οὐκ ἀντιτείνων τὸν τῆς διδασκαλίας τρόπον συμβολικὸν ποιεῖν ἐπεχείρει καὶ πάντῃ ὅμοιον τοῖς ἐν Αἰγύπτῳ διδάγμασι, καθ᾽ ἃ ἐπαιδεύθη, εἰ καὶ μὴ σφόδρα προσίεντο τὸν τοιοῦτον τρόπον οἱ Σάμιοι μηδὲ ἁρμονίως καὶ
[21] ὡς ἐχρῆν προσεφύησαν αὐτῷ. μηδενὸς οὖν αὐτῷ προστρέχοντος μηδὲ γνησίως ὀρεγομένου τῶν μαθημάτων, ἃ τοῖς Ἕλλησιν ἐνοικίζειν παντὶ τρόπῳ ἐπειρᾶτο, μὴ περιφρονῶν μηδὲ ὀλιγωρῶν τῆς Σάμου διὰ τὸ πατρίδα εἶναι, γεῦσαί τε πάντως βουλόμενος τῆς τῶν μαθημάτων καλλονῆς τοὺς πατριώτας, εἰ καὶ μὴ ἑκόντας, ἀλλ᾽ οὖν ἐπινοίᾳ καὶ μεθόδῳ, παρατηρήσας εὐφυῶς τινα καὶ εὐκινήτως ἐν τῷ γυμνασίῳ σφαιρίζοντα τῶν φιλογυμναστούντων μὲν καὶ σωμασκούντων, πενήτων δ᾽ ἄλλως καὶ ἀπορωτέρων, λογισάμενος ὅτι εὐπειθῆ ἕξει, εἰ τὰ ἐπιτήδεια ἔκπλεά τις αὐτῷ ἀμεριμνοῦντι παρέχοι, προσκαλεσάμενος μετὰ τὸ λουτρὸν τὸν νεανίαν ἐπηγγείλατο αὐτάρκη αὐτῷ ἐφόδια εἰς τὴν τῆς σωμασκίας ὑποτροφὴν καὶ ἐπιμέλειαν διηνεκῶς παρέξειν, εἰ διαδέξαιτο αὐτοῦ κατὰ βραχύ τε καὶ ἀπόνως ἐνδελεχῶς τε, ὥστε μὴ ἀθρόως φορτισθῆναι, μαθήματά τινα, ἃ παρὰ βαρβάρων μὲν ἐξέμαθεν αὐτὸς νέος ὤν, ἀπολείπει δ᾽ αὐτὸν ταῦτα ἤδη διὰ τὸ γῆρας καὶ τὴν τούτου ἀμνημοσύνην. ὑποσχομένου δὲ τοῦ νεανίου καὶ τῇ τῶν ἐπιτηδείων ἐλπίδι ὑπομείναντος τὴν δι᾽ ἀριθμῶν μάθησιν καὶ γεωμετρίας ἐνάγειν αὐτῷ ἐπειρᾶτο, ἐπ᾽ ἄβακος τὰς ἑκάστου ἀποδείξεις
[22] ποιούμενος, καὶ διδάσκων παντὸς σχήματος, ὅ ἐστι διαγράμματος, μισθὸν καὶ ἀντίπονον παρεῖχε τῷ νεανίᾳ τριώβολον. καὶ τοῦτο μέχρι πολλοῦ χρόνου διετέλεσε ποιῶν, φιλοτιμότατα μὲν καὶ σπουδαίως τάξει τε βελτίστῃ ἐμβιβάζων εἰς τὴν θεωρίαν, καθ᾽ ἑκάστου δὲ σχήματος παρά-

CHAPTER FIVE

*What he studied during his stay in Samos, and how he
educated his namesake with amazing skill; his journeys
to the Hellenes and ascetical mode of life in Samos.*

[20] Recognized by some of the older inhabitants, he was no less admired than before
(for he appeared to them more handsome, wiser, and more god-like). When his
country summoned him by public consent to benefit all and to share his reflec-
tions, he did not refuse but tried to present his symbolic manner of instruction,
entirely like the teachings which he learned in Egypt. The Samians did not greatly
take to such a method of teaching, nor were they attached to him in harmonious
fashion, as was required.

[21] Although no one rushed up to him or was truly devoted to his teachings, he
tried to introduce these in every way among the Hellenes. Since he neither despised nor thought little of Samos, because it was his native land, he hoped by all
means to give his fellow countrymen a taste of the fineness of his teachings, even
if they were unwilling. Therefore, with purpose and a plan, he closely watched
someone who skillfully and agilely played ball in the gymnasium. The player was
one of those who loves sports and body training, but who was otherwise poor and
needy. Pythagoras calculated that if one were to provide this youth with abundant
provisions, and hence free him from daily cares, he would have a compliant student. So he summoned him after his bath, and told him that he would furnish
sufficient provisions for him, and help him with his sustenance and concern for
bodily exercise. The youth was to receive from him, gradually and easily, so as not
to be suddenly burdened, some instructions which as a youth he himself (Pythag-
[22] oras) had learned as a young man from the barbarians. Because of his old age
and forgetfulness these (instructions) were now leaving him. When the youth ac-
quiesced and took on this task in the hope of provisions, Pythagoras encouraged
him in learning numbers and geometry, and made each of his demonstrations on
a reckoning-board.[1] And after teaching each figure of a geometrical proposition,
he provided the youth with a three obol piece as a wage and reward for labor. And
this he continued to do for a long time while he guided the very enthusiastic and
earnest youth in the best way possible to theoretical thinking, and gave him a
three obol piece for learning each geometrical figure.[2]

---

1. Probably covered with dust or sand.
2. Παράληψις is literally "receiving from another," and suggests a continuing tradition.

[23] ληψιν τριώβολον ἐπιδιδούς. ἐπεὶ δὲ ὁ νεανίας ὁδῷ τινι
ἐμμελεῖ ἀγόμενος τῆς ἐκπρεπείας ἤδη ἀντελαμβάνετο καὶ τῆς
ἡδονῆς καὶ ἀκολουθίας τῆς ἐν τοῖς μαθήμασι, συνιδὼν τὸ
γινόμενον ὁ σοφὸς καὶ ὅτι οὐκ ἂν ἑκὼν ἔτι ἀποσταίη οὐδὲ
ἀπόσχοιτο τῆς μαθήσεως, οὐδ' εἰ πάντα πάθοι, πενίαν
ὑπετιμήσατο καὶ ἀπορίαν τῶν τριωβόλων. ἐκείνου δὲ εἰπόν-
[24] τος "ἀλλὰ καὶ χωρὶς τούτων οἷός τέ εἰμι μανθάνειν καὶ
διαδέχεσθαί σου τὰ μαθήματα", ἐπήνεγκεν "ἀλλ' οὐδ' αὐτὸς
τὰ πρὸς τροφὴν ἐπιτήδεια ἔχω ἔτι οὐδ' εἰς ἐμαυτόν· δέον οὖν
σχολάζειν εἰς πορισμὸν τῶν καθ' ἡμέραν ἀναγκαίων καὶ τῆς
ἐφημέρου τροφῆς οὐ καλῶς ἔχει ἄβακι καὶ ἀνονήτοις
ματαιοπονήμασιν ἑαυτὸν ἀντιπερισπᾶν". ὥστε τὸν νεανίαν
δυσαποσπάστως τοῦ συνείρειν τὴν θεωρίαν ἔχοντα "καὶ
ταῦτ'" εἰπεῖν "ἐγώ σοι λοιπὸν ποριῶ καὶ ἀντιπελαργήσω
τρόπον τινά· κατὰ γὰρ ἕκαστον σχῆμα τριώβολον καὐτός σοι
ἀντιπαρέξω". καὶ τὸ ἀπὸ τοῦδε οὕτως ἑάλω ὑπὸ τῶν
μαθημάτων, ὥστε μόνος Σαμίων συναπῆρε Πυθαγόρᾳ,
[25] ὁμώνυμος μὲν ὢν αὐτῷ, Ἐρατοκλέους δὲ υἱός. τούτου δὴ καὶ
τὰ ἀλειπτικὰ συγγράμματα φέρεται καὶ ἡ ἀντὶ ἰσχάδων τοῖς
τότε ἀθληταῖς κρεώδους τροφῆς διάταξις, οὐ καλῶς εἰς
Πυθαγόραν τὸν Μνημάρχου τούτων ἀναφερομένων.

λέγεται δὲ περὶ τὸν αὐτὸν χρόνον θαυμασθῆναι αὐτὸν περὶ
τὴν Δῆλον, προσελθόντα αὐτὸν πρὸς τὸν ἀναίμακτον
λεγόμενον καὶ τοῦ Γενέτορος Ἀπόλλωνος βωμὸν καὶ τοῦτον
θεραπεύσαντα. ὅθεν εἰς ἅπαντα τὰ μαντεῖα παρέβαλε. καὶ ἐν
Κρήτῃ δὲ καὶ ἐν Σπάρτῃ τῶν νόμων ἔνεκα διέτριψε. καὶ
τούτων ἁπάντων ἀκροατής τε καὶ μαθητὴς γενόμενος, εἰς
[26] οἶκον ἐπανελθὼν ὥρμησεν ἐπὶ τὴν τῶν παραλελειμμένων
ζήτησιν. καὶ πρῶτον μὲν διατριβὴν ἐν τῇ πόλει κατεσκεύασε
τὸ Πυθαγόρου καλούμενον ἔτι καὶ νῦν ἡμικύκλιον, ἐν ᾧ νῦν
Σάμιοι περὶ τῶν κοινῶν βουλεύονται, νομίζοντες δεῖν περὶ
τῶν καλῶν καὶ τῶν δικαίων καὶ τῶν συμφερόντων ἐν τούτῳ
τῷ τόπῳ ποιεῖσθαι τὴν ζήτησιν, ὃν κατεσκεύασεν ὁ πάντων
[27] τούτων ποιησάμενος τὴν ἐπιμέλειαν. ἔξω τε τῆς πόλεως
οἰκεῖον τῆς αὐτοῦ φιλοσοφίας ἄντρον ποιησάμενος, ἐν τούτῳ
τὰ πολλὰ τῆς νυκτὸς καὶ τῆς ἡμέρας διέτριβε καὶ τὴν
ζήτησιν ἐποιεῖτο τῶν ἐν τοῖς μαθήμασι χρησίμων, τὸν αὐτὸν
τρόπον Μίνῳ τῷ τοῦ Διὸς υἱῷ διανοηθείς. καὶ τοσοῦτον
διήνεγκε τῶν ὕστερον τοῖς ἐκείνου μαθήμασι χρησαμένων,

[23] When the youth, led on a proper path of excellence, now understood both the pleasure and consistency of his lessons, the sage, seeing what was happening, and that the youth would still not willingly shun or separate himself from learning under any circumstances, pleaded poverty as an excuse for lack of three obol pieces.

[24] And when the youth said, "Yet even without these, I am ready to learn and to receive your teachings," Pythagoras replied: "But I myself no longer have provisions for nourishment, not even for myself. Since it is necessary to spend time on getting daily necessities and nourishment, it is not good to divert oneself with the reckoning-board and foolish vain tasks." And so the youth, unwilling to discontinue his theoretical studies, said: "these things I will provide for you in the future, and, so to speak, cherish you in turn:[3] for every geometrical figure I myself will furnish a three obol piece for you!"

[25] From then on, the youth was so taken by his studies, that he alone of the Samians sailed away with Pythagoras. He had the same name, but was son of Eratocles.[4] Treatises on the art of athletic training are ascribed to this one, including the decree that athletes have a meat diet instead of dried figs. These treatises are not correctly attributed to Pythagoras, son of Mnemarchus.

It is reported that, about the same time, Pythagoras was an object of wonder at Delos, after he visited the altar called "unstained with blood" of Father Apollo, and worshipped this.[5] From there he went to all the centers of oracles, and spent time in Crete and in Sparta for the sake of their laws. And after becoming a pupil and learner of all these, he returned home, and undertook the investigation of subjects which he had previously neglected.

[26] First, he established in the city a school called even now the "semi-circle of Pythagoras," in which the Samians still deliberate about public affairs.[6] They believed it necessary to make inquiry about things noble, just, and advantageous in [27] this place, which he who had made a practice of all these things, established. Outside the city, after preparing a cave suitable for his own philosophical pursuit,

---

3. The image of the stork feeding its young (ἀντιπελαργεῖν) suggests Christian imagery: the stork feeds its young from the blood of its breast, and so the Christ nourishes the faithful with his own blood.

4. Cf. Porph. VP 15, who reports that the athlete Eurymenes "on Pythagoras' advice was the first to strengthen his body by eating a fixed daily portion of meat." Eratosthenes identified the philosopher Pythagoras with Pythagoras of Samos, an Olympic victor in 588 B.C. On homonyms, see Burkert, Lore and Science, 110, note 5, 111 note 12, 118 f., and 181, note 111.

5. Diogenes Laertius (8. 13) describes this as "the altar of Apollo Genetor, behind the altar of Horns at Delos" on which offerings of grain, but not of animals were placed. He gives Aristotle's Constitution of Delos as his source. According to Rohde, RhM 27 (1872) 24 f., Iamblichus' "it is reported," marks the end of his borrowing from Apollonius. He thinks Nicomachus is Iamblichus' source for section 25 and sections 30 and 33-34.

6. Sections 26-27 (clearly not a reference to Iamblichus' own time) are believed by Rohde (ibid. 25 f.) to be from Antiphon's On the Life of Those Who Excelled in Virtue quoted by Porphyry in a parallel passage of his VP 9.

ὥστε ἐκεῖνοι μὲν ἐπὶ σμικροῖς θεωρήμασι μέγιστον ἐφρόνησαν, Πυθαγόρας δὲ συνετέλεσε τὴν περὶ τῶν οὐρανίων ἐπιστήμην καὶ ταῖς ἀποδείξεσιν αὐτὴν ὅλαις ταῖς ἀριθμητικαῖς καὶ ταῖς γεωμετρικαῖς διέλαβεν.

Pythagoras spent much of both day and night in it. He investigated things useful to the sciences, of like mind with Minos, Zeus' son.[7] And he greatly surpassed those who later made use of his teachings. Whereas they took greatest pride in minor speculations, Pythagoras acquired complete knowledge about celestial matters, and grasped it with a full range of arithmetical and geometrical proofs.

---

7. Iamblichus (or his source) may well be thinking of Minos' employment of Daedalus, the great inventor and craftsman of antiquity.

[28] Οὐ μὴν ἀλλὰ καὶ διὰ τῶν ὕστερον ὑπ' αὐτοῦ πραχθέντων ἔτι μᾶλλον αὐτὸν θαυμαστέον. ἤδη γὰρ μεγάλην ἐπίδοσιν τῆς φιλοσοφίας ἐχούσης καὶ τῆς Ἑλλάδος ἁπάσης θαυμάζειν αὐτὸν προαιρουμένης καὶ τῶν ἀρίστων καὶ τῶν φιλοσοφωτάτων εἰς τὴν Σάμον δι' ἐκεῖνον παραγεγονότων καὶ βουλομένων κοινωνεῖν τῆς παρ' ἐκείνου παιδείας, ὑπὸ τῶν αὐτοῦ πολιτῶν εἰς τὰς πρεσβείας πάσας ἑλκόμενος καὶ μετέχειν ἀναγκαζόμενος τῶν αὐτῶν λειτουργιῶν, καὶ συνιδὼν ὅτι τοῖς τῆς πατρίδος νόμοις πειθόμενον χαλεπὸν αὐτοῦ μένοντα φιλοσοφεῖν, καὶ διότι πάντες οἱ πρότερον φιλοσοφήσαντες ἐπὶ ξένης τὸν βίον διετέλεσαν, ταῦτα πάντα παρ' αὐτῷ διανοηθεὶς καὶ φεύγων τὰς πολιτικὰς ἀσχολίας, ὡς δ' ἔνιοι λέγουσι, τὴν περὶ παιδείαν ὀλιγωρίαν τῶν τότε τὴν Σάμον οἰκούντων παραιτούμενος, ἀπῆρεν εἰς τὴν Ἰταλίαν, πατρίδα ἡγησάμενος τὴν πλειόνων εὖ ἐχόντων πρὸς τὸ μανθάνειν οἰστικῶς ἔχουσαν χώραν. καὶ ἐν πρώτῃ [29] Κρότωνι ἐπισημοτάτῃ πόλει προτρεψάμενος πολλοὺς ἔσχε ζηλωτάς, ὥστε [ἱστορεῖται ἑξακοσίους αὐτὸν ἀνθρώπους ἐσχηκέναι, οὐ μόνον ὑπ' αὐτοῦ κεκινημένους εἰς τὴν φιλο-σοφίαν, ἧς μετεδίδου, ἀλλὰ καὶ τὸ λεγόμενον κοινοβίους, καθὼς προσέταξε, γενομένους· καὶ οὗτοι μὲν ἦσαν οἱ φιλο-
[30] σοφοῦντες, οἱ δὲ πολλοὶ ἀκροαταί, οὓς ἀκουσματικοὺς καλοῦσιν] ἐν μιᾷ μόνον ἀκροάσει, ὥς φασιν, ἣν πρωτίστην καὶ πάνδημον μόνος ἐπιβὰς τῆς Ἰταλίας ὁ ἄνθρωπος ἐποιή-σατο, πλέονες ἢ δισχίλιοι τοῖς λόγοις ἐνεσχέθησαν,

CHAPTER SIX

*His reasons for journeying to Italy and about his life in this
land; also the nature of the general division made by Pythagoras,
and about his philosophy.*

[28] He is, however, to be even more admired because of his later deeds. For his philosophy had now made great progress, and all Hellas chose to admire him. Both the best and wisest came to Samos because of him, and desired to share in his teaching and training.[1] Drawn into all their embassies by his fellow citizens,[2] and compelled to take part in their public services, he saw that it was difficult to obey the laws of his country while continuing to philosophize, and that all who had formerly philosophized had spent their lives on foreign soil. After reflecting on all these things by himself, shunning political occupations, and, as some say,[3] deprecating the light esteem those who then lived on Samos had for his teaching and training, he sailed to Italy. He considered his fatherland whatever country was productive of a greater number well disposed to learning.

[29] He first established himself in the famous city of Croton,[4] where he discovered that he had many devotees, so that [it is recounted that he had six hundred followers; they were drawn to him not only by the philosophy which he imparted, but
[30] also, to use the technical term, by the "cenobitic" life,[5] just as he ordered it. These were the "philosophers," but the majority were the disciples who are called "acus-

---

1. According to Rohde, *RhM* 27 (1872) 25, Iamblichus returns to Apollonius' account in section 28: a passage from Nicomachus begins at section 30.

2. An anachronism in Pythagoras' own lifetime, but suitable to later ages. The great sophists and rhetors of the fifth century B.C. such as Gorgias of Leontini and Hippias of Elis, were the first intellectuals sent on embassies.

3. This is at variance with what was just stated. Porphyry follows Aristoxenus' version, according to which Pythagoras avoided Polycrates' tyranny.

4. Pythagoras' connections with Croton have been much discussed, and even the coinage of Croton (and other ancient places) has been associated with Pythagoreanism. See Guthrie, *History* I, 174 ff., Burkert, *Lore and Science*, 113 ff., and C. de Vogel, *Pythagoras and Pythagoreanism* (Assen 1966) 36 ff. for discussions of "Pythagorean" coinage. Famous for athletes, physicians, a cult of Heracles, and a Pythagorean community, Croton attained prominence after destroying Sybaris ca. 510 B.C. Its subsequent defeat by Locri and Rhegium marked the beginnings of its decline.

5. κοινόβιος is first found in Ptolemy's *Tetrabiblos*, 119. Later it is used of the monastic life: see *LSJ, s.v.* This may, as Deubner believed, be a scholion inserted into the text: the syntax flows smoothly without it. It could also be an insertion by Iamblichus into the text of Nicomachus whom he apparently used at this point (see Porph. *VP* 20). See also Lampe, *Patristic Greek Lexicon*, s.v.

αἱρεθέντες αὐτοὶ κατὰ κράτος οὕτως, ὥστε οὐκέτι οἴκαδε ἀπέστησαν, ἀλλὰ ὁμοῦ παισὶ καὶ γυναιξὶν ὁμακοεῖόν τι
παμμέγεθες ἱδρυσάμενοι καὶ πολίσαντες αὐτοὶ τὴν πρὸς
πάντων ἐπικληθεῖσαν Μεγάλην Ἑλλάδα, νόμους τε παρ'
αὐτοῦ δεξάμενοι καὶ προστάγματα ὡσανεὶ θείας ὑποθήκας,
ὧν ἐκτὸς οὐδὲν ἔπραττον, παρέμειναν ὁμονοοῦντες ὅλῳ τῷ
τῶν ὁμιλητῶν ἀθροίσματι, εὐφημούμενοι καὶ παρὰ τῶν
πέριξ μακαριζόμενοι, τάς τε οὐσίας κοινὰς ἔθεντο, ὡς
προελέχθη, καὶ μετὰ τῶν θεῶν τὸν Πυθαγόραν λοιπὸν
κατηρίθμουν ὡς ἀγαθόν τινα δαίμονα καὶ φιλανθρωπότατον,
οἳ μὲν τὸν Πύθιον, οἳ δὲ τὸν ἐξ Ὑπερβορέων Ἀπόλλωνα, οἳ
δὲ τὸν Παιᾶνα, οἳ δὲ τῶν τὴν σελήνην κατοικούντων
δαιμόνων ἕνα, ἄλλοι δὲ ἄλλον τῶν Ὀλυμπίων θεῶν
φημίζοντες εἰς ὠφέλειαν καὶ ἐπανόρθωσιν τοῦ θνητοῦ βίου
[λέγοντες] ἐν ἀνθρωπίνῃ μορφῇ φανῆναι τοῖς τότε, ἵνα τὸ
τῆς εὐδαιμονίας τε καὶ φιλοσοφίας σωτήριον ἔναυσμα
χαρίσηται τῇ θνητῇ φύσει, οὗ μεῖζον ἀγαθὸν οὔτε ἦλθεν
οὔτε ἥξει ποτὲ δωρηθὲν ἐκ θεῶν [διὰ τούτου τοῦ
Πυθαγόρου]. διόπερ ἔτι καὶ νῦν ἡ παροιμία τὸν ἐκ Σάμου
[31] κομήτην ἐπὶ τῷ σεμνοτάτῳ διακηρύττει. ἱστορεῖ δὲ καὶ
Ἀριστοτέλης ἐν τοῖς περὶ τῆς Πυθαγορικῆς φιλοσοφίας
διαίρεσίν τινα τοιάνδε ὑπὸ τῶν ἀνδρῶν ἐν τοῖς πάνυ
ἀπορρήτοις διαφυλάττεσθαι· τοῦ λογικοῦ ζῴου τὸ μέν ἐστι
θεός, τὸ δὲ ἄνθρωπος, τὸ δὲ οἷον Πυθαγόρας. καὶ πάνυ
εὐλόγως τοιοῦτον αὐτὸν ὑπελάμβανον, δι' ὃν περὶ θεῶν μὲν
καὶ ἡρώων καὶ δαιμόνων καὶ κόσμου, σφαιρῶν τε καὶ
ἀστέρων κινήσεως παντοίας, ἐπιπροσθήσεών τε καὶ
ὑπολείψεων καὶ ἀνωμαλιῶν, ἐκκεντροτήτων τε καὶ
ἐπικύκλων, καὶ τῶν ἐν κόσμῳ πάντων, οὐρανοῦ καὶ γῆς καὶ
τῶν μεταξὺ φύσεων ἐκδήλων τε καὶ ἀποκρύφων, ὀρθή τις καὶ
ἐοικυῖα τοῖς οὖσι παρεισῆλθεν ἔννοια, μηδενὶ τῶν
φαινομένων ἢ δι' ἐπινοίας λαμβανομένων μηδαμῶς

matici"][6] in only one lecture, so they say, which he made on his first arrival in Italy, to the general public, more than two thousand were captivated by his words, so powerfully that they no longer returned home, but together with children and women, they established a very great school, and built a community in that which is called by all "Magna Graecia." After receiving from him laws and ordinances, as if they were divine precepts, without which they did nothing, they remained of like mind with the entire gathering of disciples. Praised and deemed blessed by those all around them, they held their possessions in common, as stated before,[7] and reckoned Pythagoras henceforth among the gods, as a beneficent guardian spirit (*daimon*) and most benevolent to humanity. Some spread a report that he was the Pythian Apollo, others that he was Apollo from the Hyperboreans,[8] others that he was Paean, others that he was one of the spirits (*daimones*) dwelling in the moon. Still others reported that he was one of the Olympian gods, claiming that he appeared in human form to those then alive for the benefit and improvement of the mortal way of life, in order that he might give mortal nature a saving spark of well-being and philosophy. A greater good than this never came, nor will it ever come, as a gift from the gods than [through this Pythagoras].[9] Hence even now [31] the proverb celebrates "the long haired Samian"[10] with greatest respect. And Aristotle records, in his writings on the Pythagorean philosophy,[11] that the following division was preserved by these men in their very secret doctrines: that of rational, living beings one kind is divine, another human, and another such as Pythagoras. And it was quite understandable that they should consider him to be of this kind, since he proposed a correct theory, appropriate to reality, and in no way contradicting either natural phenomena or rational conceptions of gods, heroes, daemons, and the cosmos. He also had a correct theory about every kind of motion of the spheres and stars, of eclipses and occultations and irregular motions, of eccentricities and epicycles, and of all things in the cosmos, both heaven and earth,

---

6. L. Deubner, "Bemerkungen zum Text der *Vita Pythagorae* des Iamblichos," *Sitzungsberichte der preussischen Akademie der Wissenschaften* (1935) 663, believed that the entire section in brackets was inserted into the text. Much has been written on the *acusmatici*. See, for example, K. von Fritz, "Mathematiker und Akusmatiker bei den alten Pythagoreern," *Sitzungsberichte der bayerischen Akademie der Wissenschaften*, Philos.-hist. Kl. 11 (1960); Guthrie, *History*, I 191 ff. See also Iamblichus, *VP* 81-82, and *De Comm. Math. Sc.* 76, 16 ff. In *VP* 81-82, Iamblichus makes a distinction between *acusmatici* and *mathematici*.

7. Where is this stated in Iamblichus' text? It seems to refer to κοινόβιος above, which is an argument for considering this as a passage from Nicomachus into which the bracketed passage has been interpolated.

8. Aristotle said that Pythagoras himself was believed to be the "Hyperborean Apollo," according to his Περὶ τῶν Πυθαγορείων (fr. 191 Rose; or fr. 1 Ross). See Burkert, *Lore and Science*, 141 ff. *ibid.*, 149 n. 154 on the Hyperboreans.

9. Excised by Cobet, probably correctly, though von Albrecht would defend it.

10. Cf. section 11 above.

11. Fr. 192 Rose; fr. 2 Ross.

ἀντιπαίουσα, μαθήματα δὲ καὶ θεωρία καὶ τὰ ἐπιστημονικὰ πάντα, ὅσαπερ ὀμματοποιὰ τῆς ψυχῆς ὡς ἀληθῶς καὶ καθαρτικὰ τῆς ὑπὸ τῶν ἄλλων ἐπιτηδευμάτων τοῦ νοῦ τυφλώσεως, πρὸς τὸ κατιδεῖν δυνηθῆναι τὰς ὄντως τῶν ὅλων ἀρχὰς καὶ αἰτίας ἐνῳκίσθη τοῖς Ἕλλησι. πολιτεία δὲ ἡ [32] βελτίστη καὶ ὁμοδημία καὶ "κοινὰ τὰ φίλων" καὶ θρησκεία θεῶν καὶ ὁσιότης πρὸς κατοιχομένους, νομοθεσία τε καὶ παιδεία καὶ ἐχεμυθία καὶ φειδὼ τῶν ἄλλων ζῴων καὶ ἐγκράτεια καὶ σωφροσύνη καὶ ἀγχίνοια καὶ θειότης καὶ τὰ ἄλλα ἀγαθά, ὡς ἑνὶ ὀνόματι περιλαβεῖν, ταῦτα πάντα τοῖς φιλομαθοῦσιν ἀξιέραστα καὶ περισπούδαστα δι' αὐτὸν ἐφάνη. εἰκότως δὴ οὖν διὰ πάντα ταῦτα, ὃ δὴ νῦν ἔλεγον, οὕτως ὑπερφυῶς ἐθαύμαζον τὸν Πυθαγόραν.

and of the visible and invisible substances between them.[12] And the mathematical sciences, metaphysics, and all scientific matters which cause the soul to "see" truly[13] and which purify the blindness imposed on the mind by other pursuits, were introduced by him to the Hellenes, and enabled them to behold the actual principles and causes of all things. Again, the best civil polity, living with others, "friends have things in common," worship of the gods, reverence for the dead, legislation and education, silence and forbearance for other living beings, self-control and sound-mindedness, sagacity and piety, and other good things: to summarize in a word, all these appeared, thanks to him, worthy of desire and much sought after by those eager for learning. Naturally then, on account of all these things, which I have just now mentioned, they admired Pythagoras so exceedingly.

[32]

12. Pythagoras is credited here with all the discoveries of later astronomy. See D. R. Dicks, *Early Greek Astronomy* (London and Ithaca, 1970) 62-91, and Burkert, *Lore and Science*, 322-337.

13. A reference to Plato, *R.* 533d, thus by implication claiming the Platonic curriculum of *Republic VII* for Pythagoras.

[33] Δεῖ τοίνυν μετὰ τοῦτο εἰπεῖν, πῶς ἐπεδήμησε καὶ τίσι
πρώτοις, τίνας τε λόγους ἐποιήσατο καὶ περὶ τίνων καὶ πρὸς
τίνας· οὕτω γὰρ ἂν γένοιτο εὔληπτα ἡμῖν τὰ τῆς διατριβῆς
αὐτοῦ τίνα ἦν καὶ ὁποῖα ἐν τῷ τότε βίῳ. λέγεται τοίνυν ὡς
ἐπιδημήσας Ἰταλίᾳ καὶ Σικελίᾳ, ἃς κατέλαβε πόλεις
δεδουλωμένας ὑπ' ἀλλήλων, τὰς μὲν πολλῶν ἐτῶν, τὰς δὲ
νεωστί, ταύτας φρονήματος ἐλευθερίου ὑποπλήσας διὰ τῶν
ἐφ' ἑκάστης ἀκουστῶν αὐτοῦ ἀνερρύσατο καὶ ἐλευθέρας
ἐποίησε, Κρότωνα καὶ Σύβαριν καὶ Κατάνην καὶ Ῥήγιον καὶ
Ἱμέραν καὶ Ἀκράγαντα καὶ Ταυρομένιον καὶ ἄλλας τινάς,
αἷς καὶ νόμους ἔθετο διὰ Χαρώνδα τε τοῦ Καταναίου καὶ
Ζαλεύκου τοῦ Λοκροῦ, δι' ὧν εὐνομώταται καὶ ἀξιοζήλωτοι
ταῖς περιοίκοις μέχρι πολλοῦ διετέλεσαν. ἀνεῖλε δὲ ἄρδην
[34] στάσιν καὶ διχοφωνίαν καὶ ἁπλῶς ἑτεροφροσύνην οὐ μόνον
ἀπὸ τῶν γνωρίμων καὶ τῶν ἀπογόνων δὲ αὐτῶν μέχρι
πολλῶν, ὡς ἱστορεῖται, γενεῶν, ἀλλὰ καὶ καθόλου ἀπὸ τῶν
ἐν Ἰταλίᾳ καὶ Σικελίᾳ πόλεων πασῶν κατά τε ἑαυτὰς καὶ
πρὸς ἀλλήλας. πυκνὸν γὰρ ἦν αὐτῷ πρὸς ἅπαντας πανταχῇ
πολλοὺς καὶ ὀλίγους (τὸ τοιοῦτον) ἀπόφθεγμα, χρησμῷ θεοῦ
συμβουλευτικῷ ὅμοιον, ἐπιτομή τις ὡσπερεὶ καὶ
ἀνακεφαλαίωσίς τις τῶν αὐτῷ δοκούντων [τὸ τοιοῦτον
ἀπόφθεγμα]· "φυγαδευτέον πάσῃ μηχανῇ καὶ περικοπτέον
πυρὶ καὶ σιδήρῳ καὶ μηχαναῖς παντοίαις ἀπὸ μὲν σώματος
νόσον, ἀπὸ δὲ ψυχῆς ἀμαθίαν, κοιλίας δὲ πολυτέλειαν,
πόλεως δὲ στάσιν, οἴκου δὲ διχοφροσύνην, ὁμοῦ δὲ πάντων
ἀμετρίαν", δι' ὧν φιλοστοργότατα ἀνεμίμνησκεν ἕκαστον
[35] τῶν ἀρίστων δογμάτων. ὁ μὲν οὖν κοινὸς τύπος αὐτοῦ τῆς
ζωῆς ἔν τε τοῖς λόγοις καὶ ταῖς πράξεσι τοιοῦτος ἦν ἐν τῷ
τότε χρόνῳ.

CHAPTER SEVEN

*General sketches, as it were, of his deeds in Italy, and the
kinds of sayings given for public use to human beings.*

[33]   After this, it is further necessary to state how he lived, whom he first visited, what speeches he made, on what subjects and to whom. Thus we will most easily understand his manner of study, and all aspects of his way of life at that time. Well then,[1] it is said that when he came to stay in Italy and Sicily, he found, on arrival, which cities were enslaved by one another, some for many years, others recently. Having filled these cities with a spirit of freedom by placing his disciples in each, he rescued and liberated them: Croton, Sybaris, Catania, Rhegium, Himera, Acragas, Tauromenium, and some others. For these (cities) he established laws through Charondas the Catanian and Zaleucus the Locrian;[2] with their laws the cities were very well governed for a long time, and much envied by their neigh-

[34]   bors. He wholly abolished sedition, discord, and, in a word, difference of opinion, not only among his own students and their descendants for many generations, as is recorded, but generally in all cities of Italy and Sicily, both within themselves and with one another.

For he often delivered the following pronouncement to all audiences everywhere, both large and small, and it was like a god's hortatory oracle, an abridgment, as it were, and summation of his opinions: "There must be banished with every means, cut away with fire and iron and with all sorts of devices, from the body, disease; from the soul, ignorance; from the belly, extravagance; from the city, sedition; from the family, discord, and from everything in general, lack of measure." Through this pronouncement he reminded everyone of the best of his doctrines.[3] Such, then, was the general pattern of his life in sayings and deeds at that time.

---

1. With this remark Iamblichus seems to return to Nicomachus (see Porph. *VP* 21-22).
2. Cf. D.L. 8.16 and Delatte, *La vie de Pythagore*, 185.
3. Cf. sections 68 and 147 below.

59

Εἰ δὲ δεῖ καὶ τὰ καθ' ἕκαστον ἀπομνημονεῦσαι ὧν ἔπραξε
καὶ εἶπε, ῥητέον ὡς παρεγένετο μὲν εἰς Ἰταλίαν κατὰ τὴν
ὀλυμπιάδα τὴν δευτέραν ἐπὶ ταῖς ἑξήκοντα, καθ' ἣν Ἐρυξίας
ὁ Χαλκιδεὺς στάδιον ἐνίκησεν, εὐθὺς δὲ περίβλεπτος καὶ
περίστατος ἐγένετο, καθάπερ καὶ πρότερον, ὅτε εἰς Δῆλον
κατέπλευσεν· ἐκεῖ τε γὰρ πρὸς μόνον τὸν βωμὸν τὸν τοῦ
Γενέτορος Ἀπόλλωνος προσευξάμενος, ὃς μόνος ἀναίμακτός
ἐστιν, ἐθαυμάσθη παρὰ τοῖς ἐν τῇ νήσῳ, καὶ κατ' ἐκεῖνον τὸν
[36] καιρὸν πορευόμενος ἐκ Συβάριδος εἰς Κρότωνα παρὰ τὸν
αἰγιαλὸν δικτυουλκοῖς ἐπέστη, ἔτι τῆς σαγήνης κατὰ βυθοῦ
ἐμφόρτου ἐπισυρομένης, ὅσον τε πλῆθος ἐπισπῶνται εἶπεν,
ἰχθύων ὁρίσας ἀριθμόν. καὶ τῶν ἀνδρῶν ὑπομεινάντων ὅ τι
ἂν κελεύσῃ πράξειν, εἰ τοῦθ' οὕτως ἀποβαίη, ζῶντας
ἀφεῖναι πάλιν κελεῦσαι τοὺς ἰχθῦς, πρότερόν γε ἀκριβῶς
διαριθμήσαντας. καὶ τὸ θαυμασιώτερον, οὐδεὶς ἐν τοσούτῳ
τῆς ἀριθμήσεως τῷ χρόνῳ τῶν ἰχθύων ἐκτὸς ὕδατος
μεινάντων ἀπέπνευσεν, ἐφεστῶτός γε αὐτοῦ. δοὺς δὲ καὶ τὴν
τῶν ἰχθύων τιμὴν τοῖς ἁλιεῦσιν ἀπῄει εἰς Κρότωνα. οἳ δὲ τὸ
πεπραγμένον διήγγειλαν καὶ τοὔνομα μαθόντες παρὰ τῶν
παίδων εἰς ἅπαντας ἐξήνεγκαν. οἳ δὲ ἀκούσαντες ἐπεθύμουν
ἰδεῖν τὸν ξένον, ὅπερ ἐν ἑτοίμῳ κατέστη· τήν τε γὰρ ὄψιν ἦν
οἷον ἐξεπλάγη τις ἂν ἰδὼν καὶ καθυπενόει εἶναι τοιοῦτον οἷος
ὡς ἀληθῶς ἦν.

CHAPTER EIGHT

*When and how he traveled to Croton, what he did on
his first appearance, and what words he spoke to the youth.*

But if one must record in detail both his actions and his sayings, it need be stated that he arrived in Italy in the sixty-second Olympiad,[1] at which time Eryxias, of Chalcis, won the stadion. Immediately he was admired and surrounded by a crowd, just as before when he sailed to Delos. For there, after worshipping only at the altar of Father Apollo, which is unique in being unstained with blood,[2] he became an object of admiration to those on the island. And so, at that time,[3] journeying from Sybaris to Croton, he stopped on the shore near some fishermen, and while their large drag-net, still in deep water, was being drawn up laden with fish, he determined the number of fish, and announced how many they were drawing in. When the men undertook to do whatever he ordered (if the count turned out to be accurate) he decreed that the fish, once they had been exactly counted, should be released again alive. And still more marvelous, while he himself stood near, not one fish died, even though they were out of the water for some time during the count. After paying the fishermen for their catch, he departed for Croton. The fishermen proclaimed what happened, and on learning his name from their servants, declared it to all. And those who heard desired to see the stranger, which was readily accomplished; for he was of such an appearance that anyone seeing him would be impressed, and would perceive what sort of person he truly was.

[36]

---

1. 532 B.C. This date seems acceptable, but is at variance with other chronological data Iamblichus has been giving. Clement of Alexandria (*Strom.* I 65) also gives this date.

2. Cf. section 25 above.

3. See Porph. *VP* 25, presumably from Nicomachus. The story has a resemblance to the marvelous draft of fishes which begins Jesus' ministry in Luke 5:1-11, but it would be rash to assert any direct influence (cf. Intro. p. 26); cf. John 21:1-11 where the number of fish is mentioned. See R. Bultmann, *The Gospel of John* (Oxford, 1971) 709, n.2. Plutarch (*Mor.* 91C and 729E) and Apuleius (*Apol.* 31) also knew this story, though apparently without the detail of guessing the number of fish.

[37] καὶ μετ᾽ ὀλίγας ἡμέρας εἰσῆλθεν εἰς τὸ γυμνάσιον.
περιχυθέντων δὲ τῶν νεανίσκων παραδέδοται λόγους τινὰς
διαλεχθῆναι πρὸς αὐτούς, ἐξ ὧν εἰς τὴν σπουδὴν παρεκάλει
τὴν περὶ τοὺς πρεσβυτέρους, ἀποφαίνων ἔν τε τῷ κόσμῳ καὶ
τῷ βίῳ καὶ ταῖς πόλεσι καὶ τῇ φύσει μᾶλλον τιμώμενον τὸ
προηγούμενον ἢ τὸ τῷ χρόνῳ ἑπόμενον, οἷον τὴν ἀνατολὴν
τῆς δύσεως, τὴν ἕω τῆς ἑσπέρας, τὴν ἀρχὴν τῆς τελευτῆς,
τὴν γένεσιν τῆς φθορᾶς, παραπλησίως δὲ καὶ τοὺς
αὐτόχθονας τῶν ἐπηλύδων, ὁμοίως δὲ αὖ τῶν ἐν ταῖς
ἀποικίαις τοὺς ἡγεμόνας καὶ τοὺς οἰκιστὰς τῶν πόλεων, καὶ
καθόλου τοὺς μὲν θεοὺς τῶν δαιμόνων, ἐκείνους δὲ τῶν
ἡμιθέων, τοὺς ἥρωας δὲ τῶν ἀνθρώπων, ἐκ τούτων δὲ τοὺς
[38] αἰτίους τῆς γενέσεως τῶν νεωτέρων. ἐπαγωγῆς δὲ ἕνεκα
ταῦτα ἔλεγε πρὸς τὸ περὶ πλείονος ποιεῖσθαι τοὺς γονεῖς
ἑαυτῶν, οἷς ἔφη τηλικαύτην ὀφείλειν αὐτοὺς χάριν, ἡλίκην
ἂν ὁ τετελευτηκὼς ἀποδοίη τῷ δυνηθέντι πάλιν αὐτὸν εἰς τὸ
φῶς ἀγαγεῖν. ἔπειτα δίκαιον μὲν εἶναι τοὺς πρώτους καὶ τοὺς
τὰ μέγιστα εὐηργετηκότας ὑπὲρ ἅπαντας ἀγαπᾶν καὶ
μηδέποτε λυπεῖν· μόνους δὲ τοὺς γονεῖς προτερεῖν τῆς
γενέσεως ταῖς εὐεργεσίαις, καὶ πάντων τῶν κατορθουμένων
ὑπὸ τῶν ἐγγόνων αἰτίους εἶναι τοὺς προγόνους, οὓς οὐδενὸς
ἔλαττον ἑαυτοὺς εὐεργετεῖν ἀποδεικνύντας εἰς θεοὺς οὐχ οἷόν
τέ ἐστιν ἐξαμαρτάνειν. καὶ γὰρ τοὺς θεοὺς εἰκός ἐστι
συγγνώμην ἂν ἔχειν τοῖς μηδενὸς ἧττον τιμῶσι τοὺς
[39] πατέρας· καὶ γὰρ τὸ θεῖον παρ᾽ αὐτῶν μεμαθήκαμεν τιμᾶν.
ὅθεν καὶ τὸν Ὅμηρον τῇ αὐτῇ προσηγορίᾳ τὸν βασιλέα τῶν
θεῶν αὔξειν, ὀνομάζοντα πατέρα τῶν θεῶν καὶ τῶν θνητῶν,
πολλοὺς δὲ καὶ τῶν ἄλλων μυθοποιῶν παραδεδωκέναι τοὺς
βασιλεύοντας τῶν θεῶν τὴν μεριζομένην φιλοστοργίαν παρὰ
τῶν τέκνων πρὸς τὴν ὑπάρχουσαν συζυγίαν τῶν γονέων καθ᾽
αὐτοὺς περιποιήσασθαι πεφιλοτετιμημένους, καὶ διὰ ταύτην
τὴν αἰτίαν ἅμα τὴν τοῦ πατρὸς καὶ τῆς μητρὸς ὑπόθεσιν
λαβόντας, τὸν μὲν τὴν Ἀθηνᾶν, τὴν δὲ τὸν Ἥφαιστον
ἐναντίαν γεννῆσαι φύσιν ἔχοντας τῆς ἰδίας ἕνεκα τοῦ καὶ τῆς
πλεῖον ἀφεστώσης φιλίας μετασχεῖν. ἁπάντων δὲ τῶν
παρόντων τὴν τῶν ἀθανάτων κρίσιν ἰσχυροτάτην εἶναι
[40] συγχωρησάντων, ἀποδεῖξαι τοῖς Κροτωνιάταις διὰ τὸ τὸν
Ἡρακλέα τοῖς κατῳκισμένοις οἰκεῖον ὑπάρχειν, διότι δεῖ τὸ
προσταττόμενον ἑκουσίως τοῖς γονεῦσιν ὑπακούειν,

[37] A few days later, he entered the gymnasium. When the youths crowded about him, it is related that he gave them talks in which he encouraged them to have esteem for their elders.[4] He demonstrated that in the cosmos and life, cities and nature, what precedes in time is more honorable than what follows: for example, the sun's rising is more honorable than its setting, the dawn more than the evening, the beginning more than the end, birth more than death. Similarly, natives are more to be honored than foreigners, and in like manner, founders of cities and leaders of colonies. And universally, the gods are more honorable than daemons, and the latter more than demigods, and heroes more than humans. And among the latter, those responsible for birth are more honorable than their [38] offspring. He said these things to encourage the youths to value their parents more than themselves: He said that they owed as much thanks to their parents as one deceased would owe to someone able to lead them back again to daylight. Further, it is right to cherish above all and never to pain those who have done one the first and greatest services. For only parents precede birth itself with their good deeds, and forebears are responsible for everything accomplished successfully by their descendants, so that if we recognize that they are second to none in benefitting us, we cannot sin against the gods. And it is likely the gods would judge kindly [39] those who honor their fathers second to none, for from our fathers we have learned to honor the divine. Hence Homer also glorified the ruler of the gods with this very appellation, naming him "father of gods and mortals." Many other myth-makers have also handed down by tradition that the rulers of the gods vied to keep for themselves the affection that children normally divide between their parents. And for this reason, the gods took the role of both father and mother: one (Zeus) bore Athena, another (Hera) bore Hephaestus, each having a nature opposite to their own. They did so for the sake of sharing in the affection of their [40] offspring which would be more removed from themselves.[5] And when all those present agreed that the immortals' judgment was most compelling, he showed the Crotoniates by citing the example of Heracles, who was the patron hero of the colonists, why it is necessary to obey willingly that which is ordered by parents. For they had the tradition that he, being himself a god, yet obedient to someone older

---

4. Cf. D.L. 8. 22-23, which is verbally quite close, as if the same document were available to them both. In Iamblichus' *VP*, these discourses of the Crotoniates fulfill a function similar to those of Jesus which John works into his Gospel. They serve to set out Pythagoras' program.

5. The train of thought is awkward, and no clear moral lesson is given. But if Iamblichus had one, it is that the youth of Croton, looking up to the rulers of the gods who acted simultaneously as father and mother, should love parents with an equal love, without preferring one to the other. Homer refers to Athena's birth from Zeus' head at *Il.* 5.875 ff. See also *H. Hom.* 28, 4-5, and Hesiod's *Theogony*, 924 ff. In 927, Hesiod recited that Hera "without union with Zeus, for she was very angry and quarreled with her mate, bore famous Hephaestus." Just as Zeus took on the role of a mother in bringing forth Athena, so Hera in begetting Hephaestus played the role of father as well.

παρειληφότας αὐτὸν τὸν θεὸν ἑτέρῳ πρεσβυτέρῳ πειθόμενον
διαθλῆσαι τοὺς πόνους καὶ τῷ πατρὶ θεῖναι τῶν
κατειργασμένων ἐπινίκιον τὸν ἀγῶνα τὸν Ὀλύμπιον.
ἀπεφαίνετο δὲ καὶ ταῖς πρὸς ἀλλήλους ὁμιλίαις οὕτως ἂν
χρωμένους ἐπιτυγχάνειν, ὡς μέλλουσι τοῖς μὲν φίλοις
μηδέποτε ἐχθροὶ καταστῆναι, τοῖς δὲ ἐχθροῖς ὡς τάχιστα
φίλοι γίνεσθαι, καὶ μελετᾶν ἐν μὲν τῇ πρὸς τοὺς
πρεσβυτέρους εὐκοσμίᾳ τὴν πρὸς τοὺς πατέρας εὔνοιαν, ἐν
δὲ τῇ πρὸς ἄλλους φιλανθρωπίᾳ τὴν πρὸς τοὺς ἀδελφοὺς
[41] κοινωνίαν. ἐφεξῆς δὲ ἔλεγε περὶ σωφροσύνης, φάσκων τὴν
τῶν νεανίσκων ἡλικίαν πεῖραν τῆς φύσεως λαμβάνειν, καθ᾽
ὃν καιρὸν ἀκμαζούσας ἔχουσι τὰς ἐπιθυμίας. εἶτα
προετρέπετο θεωρεῖν [ἄξιον], ὅτι μόνης τῶν ἀρετῶν ταύτης
καὶ παιδὶ καὶ παρθένῳ καὶ γυναικὶ καὶ τῇ τῶν πρεσβυτέρων
τάξει ἀντιποιεῖσθαι προσήκει, καὶ μάλιστα τοῖς νεωτέροις.
ἔτι δὲ μόνην αὐτὴν ἀποφαίνειν περιειληφέναι καὶ τὰ τοῦ
σώματος ἀγαθὰ καὶ τὰ τῆς ψυχῆς, διατηροῦσαν τὴν ὑγείαν
καὶ τὴν τῶν βελτίστων ἐπιτηδευμάτων ἐπιθυμίαν. φανερὸν
[42] δὲ εἶναι καὶ διὰ τῆς ἀντικειμένης ἀντιθέσεως· τῶν γὰρ
βαρβάρων καὶ τῶν Ἑλλήνων περὶ τὴν Τροίαν ἀντιτα-
ξαμένων ἑκατέρους δι᾽ ἑνὸς ἀκρασίαν ταῖς δεινοτάταις
περιπεσεῖν συμφοραῖς, τοὺς μὲν ἐν τῷ πολέμῳ, τοὺς δὲ κατὰ
τὸν ἀνάπλουν, καὶ μόνης ⟨ταύτης⟩ τῆς ἀδικίας τὸν θεὸν
δεκετῆ καὶ χιλιετῆ τάξαι τὴν τιμωρίαν, χρησμῳδήσαντα τήν
τε τῆς Τροίας ἅλωσιν καὶ τὴν τῶν παρθένων ἀποστολὴν
παρὰ τῶν Λοκρῶν εἰς τὸ τῆς Ἀθηνᾶς τῆς Ἰλιάδος ἱερόν.
παρεκάλει δὲ τοὺς νεανίσκους καὶ πρὸς τὴν παιδείαν,
ἐνθυμεῖσθαι κελεύων ὡς ἄτοπον ἂν εἴη πάντων μὲν
σπουδαιότατον κρίνειν τὴν διάνοιαν καὶ ταύτῃ βουλεύεσθαι
περὶ τῶν ἄλλων, εἰς δὲ τὴν ἄσκησιν τὴν ταύτης μηδένα
χρόνον μηδὲ πόνον ἀνηλωκέναι, καὶ ταῦτα τῆς μὲν τῶν
σωμάτων ἐπιμελείας τοῖς φαύλοις τῶν φίλων ὁμοιουμένης
καὶ ταχέως ἀπολειπούσης, τῆς δὲ παιδείας καθάπερ οἱ καλοὶ
κἀγαθοὶ τῶν ἀνδρῶν μέχρι θανάτου παραμενούσης, ἐνίοις δὲ
[43] καὶ μετὰ τὴν τελευτὴν ἀθάνατον δόξαν περιποιούσης. καὶ
τοιαῦθ᾽ ἕτερα, τὰ μὲν ἐξ ἱστοριῶν, τὰ δὲ καὶ ἀπὸ δογμάτων,
κατεσκεύασε, τὴν παιδείαν ἐπιδεικνύων κοινὴν οὖσαν
εὐφυΐαν τῶν ἐν ἑκάστῳ τῷ γένει πεπρωτευκότων· τὰ γὰρ
ἐκείνων εὑρήματα ταῦτα τοῖς ἄλλοις γεγονέναι παιδείαν.

than himself, struggled through his labors and established for his father (Zeus) the triumphal contest at Olympia in commemoration of his achievements. He also directed them to be so disposed in their associations with one another, that they never become enemies to their friends, but become, as quickly as possible, friends to their enemies.[6] Also they should practice, on the one hand, in decency toward those older, the good will due their fathers, and, on the other hand, in benevolence[7] toward others, the fellowship due their brothers.

[41]   Next he spoke about temperance,[8] saying that the age of youths puts their nature to the test, at the time when they have desires in full bloom. Then he urged them to consider that of the virtues, this alone was fitting for youths, maidens, women, and those older to seek after, but especially for those younger. He declared, moreover, that this virtue alone embraced goods of the body and those of [42] the soul, since it maintained health and a desire for the best pursuits. This is also made clear by setting out the opposite situation: for when the barbarians and Hellenes were arrayed against each other at Troy because of the incontinence of a single person, they encountered terrible misfortunes, some in the war, others in sailing home. And for this single injustice, the god decreed punishment for ten years and for a thousand years, and prophesied both Troy's capture, and the dispatching of maidens by the Locrians to the temple of Trojan Athena.[9] He encouraged the young men also in regard to mental culture,[10] urging them to consider that it would be absurd to judge the intellect the most important of all things, and with this to deliberate about other matters, but to have spent no time or effort on its training. Indeed, care bestowed on bodies is like bad friends and quickly departs, whereas mental culture, like good and noble persons, lasts until death, and [43] for some it even attains immortal fame after death. And he provided other examples, some from history, some from philosophical teachings, demonstrating that mental culture is the sum total of the natural excellence of those who are out-

---

6. Cf. D.L. 8. 23: "so as to behave to one another as not to make friends into enemies, but to turn enemies into friends." This is an edifying adaptation of the saying attributed to Bias of Priene, one of the Seven Sages: "love your friends as if you would one day hate them, and hate your enemies as if you would one day love them."

7. Or "loving-kindness" φιλανθρωπία. The word appears often from the fourth century B.C. on; e.g. in Xenophon, Cyrus appears as the model of φιλανθρωπία See S. Tromp de Ruiter, "De vocis quae est φιλανθρωπία significatione atque usu," Mnemosyne 59 (1931), 271-306.

8. Or "self-control" or "sound-mindedness" (σωφροσύνη). .

9. See C. Robert, Griechische Heldensage (Berlin 1920-26) 1269 ff. and F. Schwenn, Die Menschenopfer bei den Griechern und Römern, Religionsgeschichtliche Versuche und Vorarbeiten XV, 3 (Giessen, 1915). See also de Vogel, Pythagoras, 84-89, for a discussion of the ancient sources, e.g. Strabo XIII, 1.40 or Polybius XII, 5.

10. Παιδεία. De Vogel, Pythagoras, 93 ff. notes that the style and substance of this passage on mental culture or education seems reminiscent of Isocrates in the fourth century B.C. Yet there are differences between the views of Isocrates, and those expressed here. Παιδεία is, in any case, a difficult word to translate. See W. Jaeger's justly famous work, Paideia: the Ideals of Greek Culture, trans. G. Highet, I-III (Oxford, 1939).

οὕτω δ᾽ ἐστὶ τῇ φύσει σπουδαῖον τοῦτο, ὥστε τῶν μὲν
ἄλλων τῶν ἐπαινουμένων τὰ μὲν οὐχ οἷόν τε εἶναι παρ᾽
ἑτέρου μεταλαβεῖν, οἷον τὴν ῥώμην, τὸ κάλλος, τὴν ὑγείαν,
τὴν ἀνδρείαν, τὰ δὲ τὸν προέμενον οὐκ ἔχειν αὐτόν, οἷον τὸν
πλοῦτον, τὰς ἀρχάς, ἕτερα πολλὰ τῶν παραλειπομένων, τὴν
δὲ δυνατὸν εἶναι καὶ παρ᾽ ἑτέρου μεταλαβεῖν καὶ τὸν δόντα
[44] μηδὲν ἧττον αὐτὸν ἔχειν. παραπλησίως δὲ τὰ μὲν οὐκ ἐπὶ
τοῖς ἀνθρώποις εἶναι κτήσασθαι, παιδευθῆναι δὲ ἐνδέχεσθαι
κατὰ τὴν ἰδίαν προαίρεσιν, εἶθ᾽ οὕτως προσιόντα φανῆναι
πρὸς τὰς τῆς πατρίδος πράξεις, οὐκ ἐξ ἀναιδείας, ἀλλ᾽ ἐκ
παιδείας. σχεδὸν γὰρ ταῖς ἀγωγαῖς διαφέρειν τοὺς μὲν
ἀνθρώπους τῶν θηρίων, τοὺς δὲ ῞Ελληνας τῶν βαρβάρων,
τοὺς δὲ ἐλευθέρους τῶν οἰκετῶν, τοὺς δὲ φιλοσόφους τῶν
τυχόντων, ὅλως δὲ τηλικαύτην ἔχοντας ὑπεροχήν, ὥστε
τοὺς μὲν θᾶττον τρέχοντας τῶν ἄλλων ἐκ μιᾶς πόλεως τῆς
ἐκείνων ἑπτὰ κατὰ τὴν Ὀλυμπίαν εὑρεθῆναι, τοὺς δὲ τῇ
σοφίᾳ προέχοντας ἐξ ἁπάσης τῆς οἰκουμένης ἑπτὰ
συναριθμηθῆναι. ἐν δὲ τοῖς ἑξῆς χρόνοις, ἐν οἷς ἦν αὐτός,
ἕνα φιλοσοφίᾳ προέχειν τῶν πάντων· καὶ γὰρ τοῦτο τὸ
ὄνομα ἀντὶ τοῦ σοφοῦ ἑαυτὸν ἐπωνόμασε. ταῦτα μὲν ἐν τῷ
γυμνασίῳ τοῖς νέοις διελέχθη.

standing in each generation. For the discoveries of these have become mental culture for others.

An index of its value is this: some praiseworthy things such as strength, beauty, health, or courage, cannot be shared with someone else; other praiseworthy things such as wealth, political power, and many others one could mention, are no longer possessed when given away. But it is possible both to share in someone [44] else's mental culture, and for the one who has given it to be in no way diminished. Similarly, some things are not in the power of human beings to acquire, but it is possible to be educated according to one's own deliberate choice, and so to appear attending to the affairs of one's country, not out of impudence, but out of experience.[11] For generally speaking, it is because of education that human beings differ from beasts, Hellenes from barbarians, free persons from slaves, philosophers from ordinary people. In short, there is such a degree of superiority to be discerned here that while those found running faster than others at Olympia were seven from one city,[12] those superior in wisdom from the whole inhabited world were reckoned as seven in number.[13] And in later times, in which he himself lived, one man alone surpassed all others in philosophy. For he called himself by this name, i.e. "philosopher," instead of "wise."[14] These things he said to the youths in the gymnasium.

---

11. There is a deliberate antithesis here between ἐξ ἀναιδείας and ἐκ παιδείας which we have tried to reproduce.

12. Croton, in fact; cf. Strabo VI, 262.

13. Sc. the Seven Sages.

14. Cf. below, section 58. On the much disputed question of the origin of "philosopher' and "philosophy," see de Vogel, *Pythagoras*, 96 ff. who reviews and summarizes recent discussions of the origin of the terms.

[45] Ἀπαγγελθέντων δ' οὖν ὑπὸ τῶν νεανίσκων πρὸς τοὺς πατέρας τῶν εἰρημένων ἐκάλεσαν οἱ χίλιοι τὸν Πυθαγόραν εἰς τὸ συνέδριον, καὶ προεπαινέσαντες ἐπὶ τοῖς πρὸς τοὺς υἱοὺς ῥηθεῖσιν ἐκέλευσαν, εἴ τι συμφέρον ἔχει λέγειν τοῖς Κροτωνιάταις, ἀποφήνασθαι τοῦτο πρὸς τοὺς τῆς πολιτείας προκαθημένους. ὃ δὲ πρῶτον μὲν αὐτοῖς συνεβούλευεν ἱδρύσασθαι Μουσῶν ἱερόν, ἵνα τηρῶσι τὴν ὑπάρχουσαν ὁμόνοιαν· ταύτας γὰρ τὰς θεὰς καὶ τὴν προσηγορίαν τὴν αὐτὴν ἁπάσας ἔχειν καὶ μετ' ἀλλήλων παραδεδόσθαι καὶ ταῖς κοιναῖς τιμαῖς μάλιστα χαίρειν, καὶ τὸ σύνολον ἕνα καὶ τὸν αὐτὸν ἀεὶ χορὸν εἶναι τῶν Μουσῶν, ἔτι δὲ συμφωνίαν, ἁρμονίαν, ῥυθμόν, ἅπαντα περιειληφέναι τὰ παρασκευάζοντα τὴν ὁμόνοιαν. ἐπεδείκνυε δὲ αὐτῶν τὴν δύναμιν

[46] οὐ περὶ τὰ κάλλιστα θεωρήματα μόνον ἀνήκειν, ἀλλὰ καὶ περὶ τὴν συμφωνίαν καὶ ἁρμονίαν τῶν ὄντων. ἔπειτα ὑπολαμβάνειν αὐτοὺς ἔφη δεῖν κοινῇ παρακαταθήκην ἔχειν τὴν πατρίδα παρὰ τοῦ πλήθους τῶν πολιτῶν. δεῖν οὖν ταύτην διοικεῖν οὕτως, ὡς μέλλουσι τὴν πίστιν παραδόσιμον τοῖς ἐξ αὐτῶν ποιεῖν. ἔσεσθαι δὲ τοῦτο βεβαίως, ἐὰν ἅπασιν ἴσοι τοῖς πολίταις ὦσι καὶ μηδενὶ μᾶλλον ἢ τῷ δικαίῳ προσέχωσι. τοὺς γὰρ ἀνθρώπους εἰδότας, ὅτι τόπος ἅπας προσδεῖται δικαιοσύνης, μυθοποιεῖν τὴν αὐτὴν τάξιν ἔχειν παρά τε τῷ Διὶ τὴν Θέμιν καὶ παρὰ τῷ Πλούτωνι τὴν Δίκην

[47] καὶ κατὰ τὰς πόλεις τὸν νόμον, ἵν' ὁ μὴ δικαίως ἐφ' ἃ τέτακται ποιῶν ἅμα φαίνηται πάντα τὸν κόσμον συναδικῶν.

CHAPTER NINE

What words he spoke to the Thousand who were leaders
of the whole body of citizens concerning the best
ways of speaking and living.

[45] When the things said were reported by the youths to their fathers, the Thousand called Pythagoras to the council. After first praising him for the things said to their sons, they urged that if he had anything advantageous to say to the Crotoniates, to declare this to those presiding over the community. He first advised them to dedicate a temple to the Muses in order that they might preserve their existing civic concord;[1] for these goddesses all have the same title (that of "Muse"), and they have been handed down in a common tradition with one another and especially delight in common honors. In general, the dance of the Muses is always one and the same, encompassing unison of sound, harmony, rhythm, and all things which provide for concord. He showed that their power extended not only to the finest arts and sciences, but even to the concordance and harmony of existing things.[2]

[46] Then he said it was necessary for them to understand that they held their country as a common deposit entrusted to their care by the majority of citizens. It was thus necessary to govern this so that they were likely to make their trusteeship hereditary for their descendants. This would certainly happen if they were equal with all the citizens and surpassed them in nothing more than justice. For knowing that every place needs justice, human beings created the myth that the same place is occupied by Themis at the side of Zeus, and Dike at the side of Pluto, as is occupied by law in cities.[3] Thus he who does not act justly toward what has been ordained may appear simultaneously to wrong the whole cosmos.[4]

---

1. According to the tradition followed by Porphyry and Diogenes Laertius, Pythagoras fled to the temple of the Muses after Cylon's attack (D.L. 8. 40, and Porph., *VP* 57, both drawing on Dicaearchus). According to Iamblichus, the street where Pythagoras lived in Metapontum was called the "Mouseion" (*VP*, 170).

2. With this passage we may compare Iamblichus' praise of ὁμόνοια in his *Letter to Macedonius* on the subject, ap. Stob. II 257, 5 ff. Wachsmuth.

3. This triadic scheme has parallels in "Theages," *On Virtue*, ap. Stob. III 79, 5 ff. (= p. 191, 5 ff. Thesleff, *Pythagorean Texts*): "it (sc. Justice) is called *themis* among the heavenly gods, *dika* among the chthonic gods, and *nomos* among men."

4. The entire passage raises many problems on which see de Vogel, *Pythagoras*, 108-109.

προσήκειν δὲ τοῖς συνεδρίοις μηδενὶ καταχρήσασθαι τῶν
θεῶν εἰς ὅρκον, ἀλλὰ τοιούτους προχειρίζεσθαι λόγους, ὥστε
καὶ χωρὶς ὅρκων εἶναι πιστούς, καὶ τὴν ἰδίαν οἰκίαν οὕτως
οἰκονομεῖν, ὥστε τὴν ἀναφορὰν ἐξεῖναι τῆς προαιρέσεως εἰς
ἐκείνην ἀνενεγκεῖν. πρός τε τοὺς ἐξ αὐτῶν γενομένους
διακεῖσθαι γνησίως, ὡς καὶ τῶν ἄλλων ζῴων μόνης ταύτης
τῆς ἐννοίας αἴσθησιν εἰληφότων, καὶ πρὸς τὴν γυναῖκα τὴν
τοῦ βίου μετέχουσαν ὁμιλοῦντας ὡς τῶν μὲν πρὸς τοὺς
ἄλλους συνθηκῶν τιθεμένων ἐν γραμματειδίοις καὶ στήλαις,
τῶν δὲ πρὸς τὰς γυναῖκας ἐν τοῖς τέκνοις. καὶ πειρᾶσθαι
παρὰ τοῖς ἐξ αὐτῶν ἀγαπᾶσθαι μὴ διὰ τὴν φύσιν, ἧς οὐκ
αἴτιοι γεγόνασιν, ἀλλὰ διὰ τὴν προαίρεσιν· ταύτην γὰρ εἶναι
[48]   τὴν εὐεργεσίαν ἑκούσιον. σπουδάζειν δὲ καὶ τοῦτο, ὅπως
αὐτοί τε μόνας ἐκείνας εἰδήσωσιν, αἵ τε γυναῖκες μὴ
νοθεύωσι τὸ γένος ὀλιγωρίᾳ καὶ κακίᾳ τῶν συνοικούντων·
ἔτι δὲ τὴν γυναῖκα νομίζειν ἀπὸ τῆς ἑστίας εἰληφότα μετὰ
σπονδῶν καθάπερ ἱκέτιν ἐναντίον τῶν θεῶν εἰσῆχθαι πρὸς
αὐτόν. καὶ τῇ τάξει καὶ τῇ σωφροσύνῃ παράδειγμα γενέσθαι
τοῖς τε κατὰ τὴν οἰκίαν, ἣν οἰκεῖ, καὶ τοῖς κατὰ τὴν πόλιν,
καὶ προνοεῖν τοῦ μηδένα μηδ' ὁτιοῦν ἐξαμαρτάνειν, ὅπως μὴ
φοβούμενοι τὴν ἐκ τῶν νόμων ζημίαν ἀδικοῦντες
λανθάνωσιν, ἀλλ' αἰσχυνόμενοι τὴν τοῦ τρόπου καλοκαγαθίαν εἰς τὴν δικαιοσύνην ὁρμῶσι. διεκελεύετο δὲ κατὰ τὰς

[47]   The council members should not misuse the gods' (names) in an oath,[5] but indulge only in such statements as would be trustworthy even without oaths. They
were to manage their own households so that it would be possible to refer to this
management as the standard for their policy.[6] They were to be genuinely well-disposed to their own offspring, since this is the only attitude taken up by all other
animals as well.[7] They should also let their relationship with wives who share their
lives be guided by the thought that, while compacts with others are placed on tab-
lets and steles, those with wives are placed in children. They should also try to be
loved by their offspring, not because of their kinship, for which they were not responsible, but because of their character;[8] for this kindness is voluntary.[9] They
[48]   should also pay serious attention to this: that they know only their wives, and that
their wives not produce bastard offspring because of the neglect and meanness of
their spouses.[10] Moreover, they should believe that they took their wives like suppliants from the hearth in the presence of the gods, and have led them to their
homes.[11] By their discipline and sound-mindedness, they should become examples both to those in the households where they live, and to those in the whole
community. Moreover, they were to take care that none of them did anything
wrong, so that the people be motivated, not by fear of the penalty of the laws
which might induce them to do wrong if they could get away with it, but rather by
shame before their noble way of life, which would induce them to strive after justice.

---

5. Cf. section 144 below, and D.L. 8. 22: μηδ' ὀμνύναι θεούς, and Philo, Decal. 84.

6. Cf. section 169 below.

7. Von Albrecht's emendation is misguided. It seems wrong to allege that *no* other animals are
well-disposed to their offspring.

8. This meaning of προαίρεσις is attested first in Epictetus, and becomes widespread in later
Platonism. See J. M. Rist, "Prohairesis: Proclus, Plotinus, et alia," in *De Jamblique à Proclus: Entretiens Classique de la Fondation Hardt* XXI, ed H. Dörrie et al. (Geneva, Fondation Hardt, 1975)
103-122.

9. Rohde, *RhM.* 26 (1879) 261, notes that ταύτην γὰρ εἶναι τὴν εὐργεσίαν ἑκούσιον cannot be
correct since no εὐεργεσία has been mentioned before. He suggests the reading ταύτης, sc. τῆς
προαιρέσεως, the benefit or good conduct (εὐεργεσία) contained in what is voluntary.

10. The Crotoniates seem to have been much attached to concubines and other non-mono-
gamous unions. Cf. Hermippus of Rhodes, according to D.L. 8. 21.

11. Cf. section 85 below.

[49] πράξεις ἀποδοκιμάζειν τὴν ἀργίαν· εἶναι γὰρ οὐχ ἕτερόν τι
ἀγαθὸν ἢ τὸν ἐν ἑκάστῃ τῇ πράξει καιρόν. ὡρίζετο δὲ
μέγιστον εἶναι τῶν ἀδικημάτων παῖδας καὶ γονεῖς ἀπ'
ἀλλήλων διασπᾶν. νομίζειν δὲ κράτιστον μὲν εἶναι τὸν καθ'
αὑτὸν δυνάμενον προϊδεῖν τὸ συμφέρον, δεύτερον δὲ τὸν ἐκ
τῶν τοῖς ἄλλοις συμβεβηκότων κατανοοῦντα τὸ λυσιτελοῦν,
χείριστον δὲ τὸν ἀναμένοντα διὰ τοῦ κακῶς παθεῖν αἰσθέσθαι
τὸ βέλτιον ἔφη δὲ καὶ τοὺς φιλοτιμεῖσθαι βουλομένους οὐκ
ἂν διαμαρτάνειν μιμουμένους τοὺς ἐν τοῖς δρόμοις στεφανου-
μένους· καὶ γὰρ ἐκείνους οὐ τοὺς ἀνταγωνιστὰς κακῶς
ποιεῖν, ἀλλ' αὑτοὺς τῆς νίκης ἐπιθυμεῖν τυχεῖν. καὶ τοῖς
πολιτευομένοις ἁρμόττειν οὐ τοῖς ἀντιλέγουσι δυσαρεστεῖν,
ἀλλὰ τοὺς ἀκούοντας ὠφελεῖν. παρεκάλει δὲ τῆς ἀληθινῆς
ἀντεχόμενον εὐδοξίας ἕκαστον εἶναι τοιοῦτον οἷος ἂν βούλοιτο φαίνεσθαι τοῖς ἄλλοις· οὐ γὰρ οὕτως ὑπάρχειν τὴν
συμβουλὴν ἱερὸν ὡς τὸν ἔπαινον, ἐπειδὴ τῆς μὲν ἡ χρεία
πρὸς μόνους ἐστὶ τοὺς ἀνθρώπους, τοῦ δὲ πολὺ μᾶλλον πρὸς
τοὺς θεούς. εἶθ' οὕτως ἐπὶ πᾶσιν εἶπεν ὅτι τὴν πόλιν αὐτῶν
[50] ᾠκίσθαι συμβέβηκεν, ὡς λέγουσιν, Ἡρακλέους, ὅτε τὰς
βοῦς διὰ τῆς Ἰταλίας ἤλαυνεν, ὑπὸ Λακινίου μὲν
ἀδικηθέντος, Κρότωνα δὲ βοηθοῦντα τῆς νυκτὸς παρὰ τὴν
ἄγνοιαν ὡς ὄντα τῶν πολεμίων διαφθείραντος, καὶ μετὰ
ταῦτα ἐπαγγειλαμένου περὶ τὸ μνῆμα συνώνυμον ἐκείνῳ
κατοικισθήσεσθαι πόλιν, ἄν περ αὐτὸς μετάσχῃ τῆς ἀθανασίας, ὥστε τὴν χάριν τῆς ἀποδοθείσης εὐεργεσίας
προσήκειν αὐτοὺς ἔφη δικαίως οἰκονομεῖν. οἳ δὲ ἀκούσαντες
τό τε Μουσεῖον ἱδρύσαντο καὶ τὰς παλλακίδας, ἃς ἔχειν ἐπι-
χώριον ἦν αὐτοῖς, ἀφῆκαν καὶ διαλεχθῆναι χωρὶς αὐτὸν ἐν
μὲν τῷ Πυθαίῳ πρὸς τοὺς παῖδας, ἐν δὲ τῷ τῆς Ἥρας ἱερῷ
πρὸς τὰς γυναῖκας ἠξίωσαν.

[49]   He also admonished them to reject laziness in their activities as unworthy; for in every action there is nothing better than the right time.[12] And the greatest of wrongs he defined as separation of parents and children from one another. He believed the most powerful is the one able to foresee what is advantageous for himself; second best is he who understands the advantageous from what happens to others; but worst is he who waits until he perceives the better course through having himself suffered misfortune.[13] He also said that those who are ambitious would not go far wrong by imitating those crowned in the race-courses, for they do not desire to harm their competitors, but rather to win victory for themselves. Those taking part in public life should not be annoyed with those speaking in opposition, but should benefit those listening. He also encouraged everyone laying claim to genuine good repute to *be* such as he wished to *appear* to others. For counsel is not so sacred a thing as praise: need for the former pertains only to human beings, but praise much more to the gods.

[50]   Then, in addition to all these things, he said that their city was founded, so they report, by Heracles[14] when he drove the oxen through Italy, after having been wronged by Lacinius. In ignorance he (Heracles) slew Croton at night, believing him an enemy even though he was helping. As a result, Heracles promised that a city with the same name as Croton should be established about his tomb when he himself partook of immortality. So he (Pythagoras) said it was fitting for them to administer justly the favor of the kindness rendered to them.

Upon hearing this, they built a temple to the Muses and dismissed the concubines whom they were accustomed to keep; and they requested him (Pythagoras) to discourse separately to the boys in the temple of Pythian Apollo, and to the women in the temple of Hera.

---

12. Pythagorean respect for καιρός is well attested, cf. sections 180-3 below, and Procl. *In Alc.* 121-2 West. The Pythagoreans were even said to have called the first principle καιρός. It is an old concept in Greek thought, and is found, for example, in the wisdom of the Seven Sages, e.g. Solon's "seal your words with silence, and your silence with timeliness." On section 49 as a whole, and its possible connections with Gorgias who also stressed the concept of καιρός see de Vogel, *Pythagoras*, 113-123.

13. A rephrasing of Hesiod, *Works and Days*, 293-97. The concept of καιρός is in Hesiod, *ibid.* 692.

14. Cf. Diodorus Siculus, IV. 24.7.

[51] Τὸν δὲ πεισθέντα λέγουσιν εἰσηγήσασθαι τοῖς παισὶ τοιάδε ὥστε μήτε ἄρχειν λοιδορίαν μηδὲ ἀμύνεσθαι τοὺς λοιδορουμένους, καὶ περὶ τὴν παιδείαν τὴν ἐπώνυμον τῆς ἐκείνων ἡλικίας κελεῦσαι σπουδάζειν. ἔτι δὲ ὑποθέσθαι τῷ μὲν ἐπιεικεῖ παιδὶ ῥᾴδιον πεφυκέναι πάντα τὸν βίον τηρῆσαι τὴν καλοκαγαθίαν, τῷ δὲ μὴ εὖ πεφυκότι κατὰ τοῦτον τὸν καιρὸν χαλεπὸν καθεστάναι, μᾶλλον δὲ ἀδύνατον, ἐκ φαύλης ἀφορμῆς ἐπὶ τὸ τέλος εὖ δραμεῖν. πρὸς δὲ τούτοις θεοφιλεστάτους αὐτοὺς ὄντας ἀποφῆναι, καὶ διὰ τοῦτο φῆσαι κατὰ τοὺς αὐχμοὺς ὑπὸ τῶν πόλεων ἀποστέλλεσθαι παρὰ τῶν θεῶν ὕδωρ αἰτησομένους, ὡς μάλιστα ἐκείνοις ὑπακούσαντος τοῦ δαιμονίου καὶ μόνοις διὰ τέλους ἁγνεύου-

[52] σιν ἐξουσίας ὑπαρχούσης ἐν τοῖς ἱεροῖς διατρίβειν. διὰ ταύτην δὲ τὴν αἰτίαν καὶ τοὺς φιλανθρωποτάτους τῶν θεῶν, τὸν Ἀπόλλωνα καὶ τὸν Ἔρωτα, πάντας ζωγραφεῖν καὶ ποιεῖν τὴν τῶν παίδων ἔχοντας ἡλικίαν. συγκεχωρῆσθαι δὲ καὶ τῶν στεφανιτῶν ἀγώνων ⟨τινὰς⟩ τεθῆναι διὰ παῖδας, τὸν μὲν Πυθικὸν κρατηθέντος τοῦ Πύθωνος ὑπὸ παιδός, ἐπὶ παιδὶ δὲ τὸν ἐν Νεμέᾳ καὶ τὸν ἐν Ἰσθμῷ, τελευτήσαντος Ἀρχεμόρου καὶ Μελικέρτου. χωρὶς δὲ τῶν εἰρημένων ἐν τῷ κατοικισθῆναι τὴν πόλιν τῶν Κροτωνιατῶν ἐπαγγείλασθαι τὸν Ἀπόλλωνα τῷ ἡγεμόνι τοῦ οἰκισμοῦ δώσειν γενεάν,

[53] ἐὰν ἀγάγῃ τὴν εἰς Ἰταλίαν ἀποικίαν. ἐξ ὧν ὑπολαβόντας δεῖν τῆς μὲν γενέσεως αὐτῶν πρόνοιαν πεποιῆσθαι τὸν Ἀπόλλωνα, τῆς δ' ἡλικίας ἅπαντας τοὺς θεούς, ἀξίους εἶναι τῆς ἐκείνων φιλίας καὶ μελετᾶν ἀκούειν, ἵνα δύνωνται

CHAPTER TEN

What advice he gave to the boys of Croton in the
temple of Apollo during his first visit.

[51]   They say he was persuaded and advised the boys as follows: neither to begin a quarrel nor to defend themselves against those doing so. He also urged them to be eager about that "learning" which takes its name from their time of life.[1] Then, he instructed them that, for a good boy, it is easy to preserve moral excellence throughout one's whole life. But for one who does not behave well at this critical time, it is difficult, if not impossible, to finish a course well after a bad start. Moreover, he declared that boys are most dear to the gods. Because of this, he said that in times of drought, they are sent by cities to request rain from the gods, since the divinity especially listens to them.[2] Since they alone are completely pure, they have authority to spend time in temples. For this reason, all paint and represent

[52]   the most benevolent of gods, Apollo and Eros, as boys in age.[3] And it is agreed that even some contests in which a wreath was a prize, were instituted because of boys: the Pythian since the Python was conquered by a boy, and for boys the Nemean and Isthmian games were founded when Archemorus and Melicertes died.[4]

[53]   Moreover, when the city of the Crotoniates was founded, Apollo promised to give offspring to the leader of its colonization if he led the settlement to Italy.[5] Hence assuming that Apollo took thought for their origin, and all the gods for their

---

1. Originally παιδεία referred to childhood, and not to "learning." In any case, παιδεία is derived from παῖς, a child.

2. "Rain-making" was practiced in Graeco-Roman antiquity (see M. P. Nilsson, *Geschichte der griechischen Religion* I, 3rd. ed. (Munich, 1967) 395, 400f). Children are not mentioned, but because drought was considered a divine punishment, persons free of (sexual) impurity would be favored. The precept that after sexual intercourse one must not enter a temple until ritual purification is well known. See E. Fehrle, *Die kultische Keuschheit im Altertum*, 155 ff.

3. The representation of Eros as a boy is common in antiquity. It seems less likely that Apollo was so depicted by "all." See de Vogel, *Pythagoras*, 128-130, for a discussion of the problems posed by Iamblichus' remark.

4. Both Archemorus and Melicertes perished as babies. The Isthmian games were instituted in honor of the latter who is also called "Palaemon" (see Pausanias II 2, 3; Hypoth. Pind. *I.*). Melicertes' mother, Ino (Leucothea) jumped into the sea at Megara, holding him in her arms (see also Ovid, *Metam.* IV, 512 ff; Hyg. *Fab.* 2). Archemorus (nicknamed "Opheltes") came from Nemea, and was buried there. According to the legend, the Argive army of the "Seven against Thebes" came to Nemea, and, being thirsty, was guided to a pool by Opheltes' nurse. The child who was left behind, was strangled by a snake. See Pausanias VIII 48. 2, Hyg. *Fab.* 74, 273.

5. This story is told in more detail by Diodorus Siculus (VIII, 17, 1). The founder of Croton was Myskellus of Achaea, and he consulted the god at Delphi because he was childless.

λέγειν, ἔτι δέ, ἣν μέλλουσιν εἰς τὸ γῆρας βαδίζειν, ταύτην εὐθὺς ἐξορμῶντας τοῖς ἐληλυθόσιν ἐπακολουθεῖν καὶ τοῖς πρεσβυτέροις μηδὲν ἀντιλέγειν· οὕτω γὰρ εἰκότως ὕστερον ἀξιώσειν μηδὲ αὐτοῖς τοὺς νεωτέρους ἀντιδικεῖν. διὰ δὲ τὰς παραινέσεις ὁμολογεῖται παρασκευάσαι μηδένα τὴν ἐκείνου προσηγορίαν ὀνομάζειν, ἀλλὰ πάντας θεῖον αὐτὸν καλεῖν.

growing to manhood, they should see that they were worthy of the gods' friendship. Also they should practice listening in order to be able to speak. Moreover, whatever path they intended to take to old age, this they should set out on at once, following those who had gone before. And they should not contradict their elders, for thus later they will reasonably expect those younger not to contradict them.

Because of these exhortations, it is agreed that no one used his personal name, but that all called him "divine."[6]

---

6. The people give Pythagoras the epithet common for the θεῖος ἀνήρ; see H.D. Betz, "Gottmensch II (Griechisch-römische Antike und Urchristentum)." *RAC* XII (1983) 234-312, especially 235-38. By comparison with section 255 below, it seems that Pythagoras' followers referred to him as "the divine one" or something similar during his lifetime, and "that man" after his death. Iamblichus' source may be Apollonius of Tyana, but the tradition is obviously old. See D.L. 8. 41, who mentions Hermippus as his source. There was also the Pythagorean custom of referring to Pythagoras simply as "himself" (αὐτός).

[54] Ταῖς δὲ γυναιξὶν ὑπὲρ μὲν τῶν θυσιῶν ἀποφήνασθαι
λέγεται πρῶτον μέν, καθάπερ ἑτέρου μέλλοντος ὑπὲρ αὐτῶν
ποιεῖσθαι τὰς εὐχὰς βούλοιντ' ἂν ἐκεῖνον εἶναι καλὸν κἀγα-
θόν, ὡς τῶν θεῶν τούτοις προσεχόντων, οὕτως αὐτὰς περὶ
πλείστου ποιεῖσθαι τὴν ἐπιείκειαν, ἵν' ἑτοίμους ἔχωσι τοὺς
ταῖς εὐχαῖς ὑπακουσομένους· ἔπειτα τοῖς θεοῖς προσφέρειν ἃ
μέλλουσι, ταῖς χερσὶν αὐτὰς ποιεῖν καὶ χωρὶς οἰκετῶν πρὸς
τοὺς βωμοὺς προσενεγκεῖν, οἷον πόπανα καὶ ψαιστὰ καὶ
κηρία καὶ λιβανωτόν, φόνῳ δὲ καὶ θανάτῳ τὸ δαιμόνιον μὴ
τιμᾶν, μηδ' ὡς οὐδέποτε πάλιν προσιούσας ἑνὶ καιρῷ πολλὰ
δαπανᾶν. περὶ δὲ τῆς πρὸς τοὺς ἄνδρας ὁμιλίας κελεῦσαι
κατανοεῖν, ὅτι συμβαίνει καὶ τοὺς πατέρας ἐπὶ τῆς θηλείας
φύσεως παρακεχωρηκέναι μᾶλλον ἀγαπᾶσθαι τοὺς
γεγαμηκότας ἢ τοὺς τεκνώσαντας αὐτάς. διὸ καλῶς ἔχειν ἢ
μηδὲ ἐναντιοῦσθαι πρὸς τοὺς ἄνδρας, ἢ τότε νομίζειν νικᾶν,
[55] ὅταν ἐκείνων ἡττηθῶσι. ἔτι δὲ τὸ περιβόητον γενόμενον
ἀποφθέγξασθαι κατὰ τὴν σύνοδον, ὡς ἀπὸ μὲν τοῦ
συνοικοῦντος ἀνδρὸς ὅσιόν ἐστιν αὐθημερὸν προσιέναι τοῖς
ἱεροῖς, ἀπὸ δὲ τοῦ μὴ προσήκοντος οὐδέποτε. παραγγεῖλαι δὲ
καὶ κατὰ πάντα τὸν βίον αὐτάς τε εὐφημεῖν καὶ τοὺς ἄλλους
ὁρᾶν ὁπόσα ὑπὲρ αὐτῶν εὐφημήσουσι, καὶ τὴν δόξαν τὴν
διαδεδομένην μὴ καταλύσωσι μηδὲ τοὺς μυθογράφους
ἐξελέγξωσιν, οἳ θεωροῦντες τὴν τῶν γυναικῶν δικαιοσύνην
ἐκ τοῦ προΐεσθαι μὲν ἀμάρτυρον τὸν ἱματισμὸν καὶ τὸν
κόσμον, ὅταν τινὶ ἄλλῳ δέῃ χρῆσαι, μὴ γίγνεσθαι δὲ ἐκ τῆς
πίστεως δίκας μηδ' ἀντιλογίας, ἐμυθοποίησαν τρεῖς γυναῖκας
ἑνὶ κοινῷ πάσας ὀφθαλμῷ χρωμένας διὰ τὴν εὐχερῆ
κοινωνίαν· ὅπερ ἐπὶ τοὺς ἄρρενας μετατεθέν, ὡς ὁ προλαβὼν
ἀπέδωκεν εὐκόλως, ἑτοίμως καὶ τῶν ἑαυτοῦ μεταδιδούς,

CHAPTER ELEVEN

His discourse to the women of Croton in the
temple of Hera during his first visit.

To the women he is said to have talked first about sacrifices: just as they would wish someone else about to make prayers on their behalf to be good and noble, (since the gods pay attention to these) so they themselves should pay most attention to goodness, in order that they have the gods ready to hear their prayers. Then they were to make what they intended to offer to the gods with their own hands, and to offer them at the altars without slaves; for example, round cakes, cakes of ground barley, honeycombs and incense. But they were not to honor the divine with slaughter and death, nor to indulge in great expenditure at one time as if they were never to approach (the altars) again.[1] He urged them to reflect about relations with their husbands: even their fathers allowed the female sex to love those who married them more than those who bore them. Hence, it is well neither to oppose their husbands, nor to believe they were victorious when yielding to them.

Moreover, in this assembly Pythagoras stated that opinion of his which has become very famous: that after sleeping with her lawful husband, it is holy to enter temples on the same day, but after (sleeping) with someone not married to her, never.[2] He also encouraged them to speak auspiciously throughout their entire lives, and to see that others speak auspiciously in matters concerning themselves. He also urged that they neither ruin their traditional popular reputation nor contradict those myth-makers who recognized women's sense of justice in giving away, without witness, their apparel and adornment, whenever someone else needed to use them. Since neither law-suits nor quarrels arose from this good faith, a story was told about three women who together used one common eye for the sake of open-handed[3] fellowship. Such a story if transposed to males (that one who re-

---

1. The moral restrictions on sacrifice and prayer, especially the need for simplicity and avoidance of killing, may go back to Pythagoras himself (cf. Diodorus X. 7, and, 9,6, and Porph. *VP* 36).

2. This remark is attributed to Theano, and to Deino, wife of Brontinus. Cf. section 132 below. Moreover, προσιέναι τοῖς ἱεροῖς suggests not only entering temples, but also attending sacrifices (which took place outside the temple).

3. Presumably a reference to the Graiae, on which see, for example, the entry in *OCD* s.v. "Graiae." On women giving precious things to one another without witnesses, cf. Aristophanes *Ec.* 446-451.

[56] οὐδένα ἂν προσδέξασθαι λεγόμενον, ὡς μὴ οἰκεῖον αὐτῶν τῇ φύσει. ἔτι δὲ τὸν σοφώτατον τῶν ἁπάντων λεγόμενον καὶ συντάξαντα τὴν φωνὴν τῶν ἀνθρώπων καὶ τὸ σύνολον εὑρετὴν καταστάντα τῶν ὀνομάτων, εἴτε θεὸν εἴτε δαίμονα εἴτε θεῖόν τινα ἄνθρωπον, συνιδόντα διότι τῆς εὐσεβείας οἰκειότατόν ἐστι τὸ γένος τῶν γυναικῶν ἑκάστην τὴν ἡλικίαν αὐτῶν συνώνυμον ποιήσασθαι θεῷ, καὶ καλέσαι τὴν μὲν ἄγαμον κόρην, τὴν δὲ πρὸς ἄνδρα δεδομένην νύμφην, τὴν δὲ τέκνα γεννησαμένην μητέρα, τὴν δὲ παῖδας ἐκ παίδων ἐπιδοῦσαν κατὰ τὴν Δωρικὴν διάλεκτον μαῖαν· ᾧ σύμφωνον εἶναι τὸ καὶ τοὺς χρησμοὺς ἐν Δωδώνῃ καὶ Δελφοῖς δηλοῦσθαι διὰ γυναικός. διὰ δὲ τῶν εἰς τὴν εὐσέβειαν ἐπαίνων πρὸς τὴν εὐτέλειαν τὴν κατὰ τὸν ἱματισμὸν τηλικαύτην παραδέδοται κατασκευάσαι τὴν μεταβολήν, ὥστε τὰ πολυτελῆ τῶν ἱματίων μηδεμίαν ἐνδύεσθαι τολμᾶν, ἀλλὰ θεῖναι πάσας εἰς τὸ τῆς Ἥρας ἱερὸν πολλὰς μυριάδας

[57] ἱματίων. λέγεται δὲ καὶ τοιοῦτόν τι διελθεῖν, ὅτι περὶ τὴν χώραν τῶν Κροτωνιατῶν ἀνδρὸς μὲν ἀρετὴ πρὸς γυναῖκα διαβεβόηται, Ὀδυσσέως οὐ δεξαμένου παρὰ τῆς Καλυψοῦς ἀθανασίαν ἐπὶ τῷ τὴν Πηνελόπην καταλιπεῖν, ὑπολείποιτο δὲ ταῖς γυναιξὶν εἰς τοὺς ἄνδρας ἀποδείξασθαι τὴν καλοκαγαθίαν, ὅπως εἰς ἴσον καταστήσωσι τὴν εὐλογίαν. ἁπλῶς δὲ μνημονεύεται διὰ τὰς εἰρημένας ἐντεύξεις περὶ Πυθαγόραν οὐ μετρίαν τιμὴν καὶ σπουδὴν καὶ κατὰ τὴν πόλιν τῶν Κροτωνιατῶν γενέσθαι καὶ διὰ τὴν πόλιν περὶ τὴν Ἰταλίαν.

ceived an advance was happy to give it back, readily sharing his own things) would be accepted by no one since it doesn't belong to a male's nature.

[56] Moreover, he who is said to be wisest of all, having structured human speech and generally having become the discoverer of names, whether god, daemon, or some divine man, on realizing that the feminine gender is most suitable for piety, gave each of their ages the same name as a deity. He called the unmarried one "Korê"; the one given to a man (a bride) "Nymphê"; the woman who bore children "Mêter";[4] the one who produces a child by means of children (a grandmother), "Maia" according to the Doric dialect. Consonant with this, the oracles at Dodona and Delphi are revealed by a woman. And by praising their piety, it is recorded that he brought about such a great change towards thrift in regard to apparel, that no one dared to wear expensive clothes, but all placed countless

[57] articles of clothing in the temple of Hera. He is also said to have remarked as follows: in the land of the Crotoniates a man's fidelity to his wife received wide publicity when Odysseus would not accept immortality from Calypso on condition that he abandon Penelope;[5] and it remained now for the women to show nobility to their husbands in order that they establish a good reputation on an equal basis.

In brief, it is recorded that by means of the mentioned discourses great honor and enthusiasm arose for Pythagoras within the city of Croton, and through the agency of this city, all round Italy.

---

4. This remark is reported by Timaeus of Tauromenium in Bk. X of his *History* (*ap.* D.L. 8.11).
5. Is this to place Calypso's island in the vicinity of Croton?

[58]   Λέγεται δὲ Πυθαγόρας πρῶτος φιλόσοφον ἑαυτὸν προσ-
αγορεῦσαι, οὐ καινοῦ μόνον ὀνόματος ὑπάρξας, ἀλλὰ καὶ
πρᾶγμα οἰκεῖον προεκδιδάσκων χρησίμως. ἐοικέναι γὰρ ἔφη
τὴν εἰς τὸν βίον τῶν ἀνθρώπων πάροδον τῷ ἐπὶ τὰς
πανηγύρεις ἀπαντῶντι ὁμίλῳ. ὡς γὰρ ἐκεῖσε παντοδαποὶ
φοιτῶντες ἄνθρωποι ἄλλος κατ' ἄλλου χρείαν ἀφικνεῖται (ὃ
μὲν χρηματισμοῦ τε καὶ κέρδους χάριν ἀπεμπολῆσαι τὸν
φόρτον ἐπειγόμενος, ὃ δὲ δόξης ἕνεκα ἐπιδειξόμενος ἥκει τὴν
ῥώμην τοῦ σώματος· ἔστι δὲ καὶ τρίτον εἶδος καὶ τό γε
ἐλευθεριώτατον, συναλιζόμενον τόπων θέας ἕνεκα καὶ
δημιουργημάτων καλῶν καὶ ἀρετῆς ἔργων καὶ λόγων, ὧν αἱ
ἐπιδείξεις εἰώθεσαν ἐν ταῖς πανηγύρεσι γίνεσθαι), οὕτως δὴ
κἀν τῷ βίῳ παντοδαποὺς ἀνθρώπους ταῖς σπουδαῖς εἰς ταὐτὸ
ἀθροίζεσθαι· τοὺς μὲν γὰρ χρημάτων καὶ τρυφῆς αἱρεῖ πόθος,
τοὺς δὲ ἀρχῆς καὶ ἡγεμονίας ἵμερος φιλονεικίαι τε
δοξομανεῖς κατέχουσιν. εἰλικρινέστατον δὲ εἶναι τοῦτον
ἀνθρώπου τρόπον, τὸν ἀποδεξάμενον τὴν τῶν καλλίστων
[59] θεωρίαν, ὃν καὶ προσονομάζειν φιλόσοφον. καλὴν μὲν οὖν
εἶναι τὴν τοῦ σύμπαντος οὐρανοῦ θέαν καὶ τῶν ἐν αὐτῷ
φορουμένων ἀστέρων εἴ τις καθορῴη τὴν τάξιν· κατὰ
μετουσίαν μέντοι τοῦ πρώτου καὶ τοῦ νοητοῦ εἶναι αὐτὸ
τοιοῦτον. τὸ δὲ πρῶτον ἦν ἐκεῖνο, ἡ τῶν ἀριθμῶν τε καὶ
λόγων φύσις διὰ πάντων διαθέουσα, καθ' οὓς τὰ πάντα
ταῦτα συντέτακταί τε ἐμμελῶς καὶ κεκόσμηται πρεπόντως,
καὶ σοφία μὲν ἡ τῷ ὄντι ἐπιστήμη τις ἡ περὶ τὰ καλὰ τὰ
πρῶτα καὶ θεῖα καὶ ἀκήρατα καὶ ἀεὶ κατὰ τὰ αὐτὰ καὶ
ὡσαύτως ἔχοντα ἀσχολουμένη, ὧν μετοχῇ καὶ τὰ ἄλλα ἂν
εἴποι τις καλά· φιλοσοφία δὲ ἡ ζήλωσις τῆς τοιαύτης
θεωρίας. καλὴ μὲν οὖν καὶ αὕτη παιδείας ἦν ἐπιμέλεια ἡ
συντείνουσα αὐτῷ πρὸς τὴν τῶν ἀνθρώπων ἐπανόρθωσιν.

CHAPTER TWELVE

His discourse about philosophy:
the fact that he was the first to call himself a
philosopher and the reason for that.

[58]   It is also said that Pythagoras was the first to call himself a philosopher. He introduced not only a new word, but taught beforehand the reality corresponding to it in a useful manner.[1] For he said that the entrance of human beings into life is like a crowd meeting at festal assemblies. For as there, while all sorts of humans gather, each arrives with a different need: one hurries to sell wares for the sake of money and gain; another comes to display bodily strength for fame's sake, and there is a third group, the most free, which comes to take in the sights, the fine creations of craftsmen, and the deeds and speeches of excellence, the displays of which usually occur at festivals. So also in life all sorts of men gather together in the same place to pursue their several interests: longing for money and luxuriousness seize some, desire for public office, leadership, eagerness for rivalry, and mad desires for fame, possess others. But the purest way of life for a human being [59] is that which embraces the contemplation of the noblest objects, which is what one may term "philosophical." Noble, for a start, is the sight of the whole heaven and the stars revolving in it, if one observes their order; for after all, it is such by participation in that which is primary and intelligible. And that which is primary is the nature of numbers and ratios running through all things, according to which all these things are harmoniously arranged and suitably ordered. And wisdom is truly a knowledge concerned with first things, noble, divine, undefiled, and always the same and in the same state, by participation in which all other things may be termed noble.[2] And philosophy is zealous pursuit of such contemplation. Noble also is this care bestowed on education which is directed to improvement of human beings.

---

1. Cf. section 44, and the reference there to de Vogel who believes, contrary to other scholars, that Pythagoras might have first coined the term "philosopher."
2. A thoroughly Platonic formulation.

[60]   Εἰ δὲ καὶ πιστευτέον τοσούτοις ἱστορήσασι περὶ αὐτοῦ
παλαιοῖς τε ἅμα οὖσι καὶ ἀξιολόγοις, μέχρι τῶν ἀλόγων ζώ-
ων ἀναλυτικόν τι καὶ νουθετητικὸν ἐκέκτητο Πυθαγόρας ἐν
τῷ λόγῳ, διὰ τούτου συμβιβάζων, ὡς διδασκαλίᾳ πάντα
περιγίνεται τοῖς νοῦν ἔχουσιν, ὅπου καὶ τοῖς ἀνημέροις τε
καὶ ἀμοιρεῖν λόγου νομιζομένοις. τὴν μὲν γὰρ Δαυνίαν
ἄρκτον, χαλεπώτατα λυμαινομένην τοὺς ἐνοίκους, κατα-
σχών, ὥς φασι, καὶ ἐπαφησάμενος χρόνον συχνόν, ψωμίσας
τε μάζῃ καὶ ἀκροδρύοις, ὁρκώσας μηκέτι ἐμψύχου
καθάπτεσθαι ἀπέλυσεν· ἢ δὲ εὐθὺς εἰς τὰ ὄρη καὶ τοὺς
δρυμοὺς ἀπαλλαγεῖσα οὐκέτ᾽ ἔκτοτε ὤφθη τὸ παράπαν
ἐπιοῦσα οὐδὲ ἀλόγῳ ζώῳ. βοῦν δὲ ἐν Τάραντι ἰδὼν ἐν
[61]   παμμιγεῖ νομῇ καὶ κυάμων χλωρῶν παραπτόμενον, τῷ
βουκόλῳ παραστὰς συνεβούλευσεν εἰπεῖν τῷ βοῒ τῶν
κυάμων ἀπέχεσθαι. προσπαίξαντος δὲ αὐτῷ τοῦ βουκόλου
περὶ τοῦ εἰπεῖν καὶ οὐ φήσαντος εἰδέναι βοϊστὶ εἰπεῖν, εἰ δὲ
αὐτὸς οἶδε, καὶ περισσῶς συμβουλεύειν, δέον τῷ βοῒ
παραινεῖν, προσελθὼν αὐτὸς καὶ εἰς τὸ οὖς πολλὴν ὥραν
προσψιθυρίσας τῷ ταύρῳ, οὐ μόνον τότε αὐτὸν ἀμελλητὶ
ἑκόντα ἀπέστησε τοῦ κυαμῶνος, ἀλλὰ καὶ εἰσαῦθις λέγουσι
μηκέτι γεγεῦσθαι κυάμων τὸ παράπαν τὸν βοῦν ἐκεῖνον,
μακροχρονιώτατον δὲ ἐν τῇ Τάραντι κατὰ τὸ τῆς Ἥρας ἱερὸν
γηρῶντα διαμεμενηκέναι, τὸν ἱερὸν ἀνακαλούμενον
Πυθαγόρου βοῦν ὑπὸ πάντων, ἀνθρωπίναις τροφαῖς
[62]   σιτούμενον, ἃς οἱ ἀπαντῶντες αὐτῷ προσώρεγον. ἀετόν τε
ὑπεριπτάμενον Ὀλυμπίασι προσομιλοῦντος αὐτοῦ τοῖς
γνωρίμοις ἀπὸ τύχης περί τε οἰωνῶν καὶ συμβόλων καὶ
διοσημειῶν, ὅτι παρὰ θεῶν εἰσὶν ἀγγελίαι τινὲς καὶ ἀετοὶ
τοῖς ὡς ἀληθῶς θεοφιλέσι τῶν ἀνθρώπων, καταγαγεῖν
λέγεται καὶ καταψήσαντα πάλιν ἀφεῖναι. διὰ τούτων δὴ καὶ
τῶν παραπλησίων τούτοις δέδεικται τὴν Ὀρφέως ἔχων ἐν
τοῖς θηρίοις ἡγεμονίαν καὶ κηλῶν αὐτὰ καὶ κατέχων τῇ ἀπὸ
τοῦ στόματος τῆς φωνῆς προϊούσῃ δυνάμει.

CHAPTER THIRTEEN

That Pythagoras possessed a power of education
through reason extending to wild beasts and irrational
animals: sundry proofs of this.

[60]   If one were to believe the many ancient and noteworthy stories about him, Pythagoras had a soothing and monitory quality to his speech which extended even to irrational beings. He taught that, with instruction, all things are overcome by those possessing intellect, whenever they deal with things untamed and with no share in reason.[1] For they report that after detaining the Daunian bear which most cruelly harmed the inhabitants (of the land), he petted it lightly for a long time. After feeding it barley-cakes and nuts, he released it on exacting an oath from it never again to attack a living thing. The bear left at once for the mountains and woods, and was no longer seen attacking anything at all, not even a wild animal.

[61]   And when he saw a bull in Tarentum in mixed pasturage, grazing on green beans, he approached the herdsman, and advised him to tell the bull to abstain from the beans. But the herdsman jested with him about how to communicate with it, and said he did not know how to speak "bull-talk". If he himself knew, then it was superfluous to urge him on, if the bull had to be admonished.[2] So he himself approached, and whispered in the bull's ear for a long time, and the bull then not only willingly, but immediately abstained from the beans. Even afterwards, they say, that bull no longer ate any beans, but lived for a very long time growing old in Tarentum in the temple of Hera. Called by all the "sacred ox of Pythago-
[62] ras," he was fed with human provisions which passersby offered to him. (Pythagoras) is also said to have drawn down an eagle which flew overhead, while he was conversing with his disciples at the Olympic Games about bird omens, secret signs, and omens from the sky: these are special messages from the gods to those human beings truly dear to them. And after stroking it, he released it again. By means of these and similar incidents, then, he was shown to have Orpheus' domination over wild beasts, both enchanting and restraining them with the power of his speech.

---

1. This and the subsequent chapter follow Porphyry's account virtually verbatim through section 63 (cf. Porph. *VP* 23-26).

2. Melampus had the ability to learn the language of animals. Hes. fr. 261 Merkelbach-West, Apollod. Bibl. 1.9.11. Oxen have a special significance in Pythagorean legend, e.g. the ox sacrificed to celebrate discovery of a geometrical theorem. See Burkert, *Lore and Science*, 180-1 and 428 f.

Ἀλλὰ μὴν τῆς γε τῶν ἀνθρώπων ἐπιμελείας ἀρχὴν
ἐποιεῖτο τὴν ἀρίστην, ἥπερ ἔδει προειληφέναι τοὺς μέλ-
λοντας καὶ περὶ τῶν ἄλλων τὰ ἀληθῆ μαθήσεσθαι.
ἐναργέστατα γὰρ καὶ σαφῶς ἀνεμίμνησκε τῶν ἐντυγχανόντων πολλοὺς τοῦ προτέρου βίου, ὃν αὐτῶν ἡ ψυχὴ πρὸ
τοῦ τῷδε τῷ σώματι ἐνδεθῆναι πάλαι ποτὲ ἐβίωσε, καὶ
ἑαυτὸν δὲ ἀναμφιλέκτοις τεκμηρίοις ἀπέφαινεν Εὔφορβον
γεγονέναι Πάνθου υἱόν, τὸν Πατρόκλου καταγωνιστήν, καὶ
τῶν Ὁμηρικῶν στίχων μάλιστα ἐκείνους ἐξύμνει καὶ μετὰ
λύρας ρικῶν στίχων μάλιστα ἐκείνους ἐξύμνει καὶ μετὰ λύρας
ἐμμελέστατα ἀνέμελπε καὶ πυκνῶς ἀνεφώνει, τοὺς ἐπιτα-
φίους ἑαυτοῦ,

> αἵματί οἱ δεύοντο κόμαι Χαρίτεσσιν ὁμοῖαι
> πλοχμοί θ', οἳ χρυσῷ τε καὶ ἀργύρῳ εὖ ἤσκηντο.
> οἷον δὲ τρέφει ἔρνος ἀνὴρ ἐριθηλὲς ἐλαίης
> χώρῳ ἐν οἰοπόλῳ, ὅθ' ἅλις ἀναβέβρυχεν ὕδωρ,
> καλὸν τηλεθάον, τὸ δέ τε πνοιαὶ δονέουσι
> παντοίων ἀνέμων, καί τε βρύει ἄνθεϊ λευκῷ,
> ἐλθὼν δ' ἐξαπίνης ἄνεμος σὺν λαίλαπι πολλῇ
> βόθρου τ' ἐξέστρεψε καὶ ἐξετάνυσσ' ἐπὶ γαίης·
> τοῖον Πάνθου υἱὸν ἐυμελίην Εὔφορβον
> Ἀτρείδης Μενέλαος, ἐπεὶ κτάνε, τεύχε' ἐσύλα.

τὰ γὰρ ἱστορούμενα περὶ τῆς ἐν Μυκήναις ⟨ἀνακειμένης⟩
σὺν Τρωϊκοῖς λαφύροις τῇ Ἀργείᾳ Ἥρᾳ Εὐφόρβου τοῦ
Φρυγὸς τούτου ἀσπίδος παρίεμεν ὡς πάνυ δημώδη. πλὴν ὅ
γε διὰ πάντων τούτων βουλόμεθα δεικνύναι, ἐκεῖνό ἐστιν,
ὅτι αὐτός τε ἐγίγνωσκε τοὺς προτέρους ἑαυτοῦ βίους καὶ τῆς
τῶν ἄλλων ἐπιμελείας ἐντεῦθεν ἤρχετο, ὑπομιμνήσκων
αὐτοὺς ἧς εἶχον πρότερον ζωῆς.

CHAPTER FOURTEEN

That he made the starting-point of education the reminiscence
of the previous lives which souls lived through before
entering the bodies in which they happened to be living.

[63] He established as the best starting-point for the care of human beings the following, one which those who expect to learn the truth on this and other matters must first master. For he reminded many who met him most distinctly and clearly about the former mode of life their souls lived long ago before being bound to their present body, and demonstrated with convincing proofs that he himself had been Euphorbus,[1] son of Panthous, conqueror of Patroclus. And he especially liked to chant those Homeric verses, and with the lyre raised the strain most harmoniously and uttered them often, those lines which are his own funeral verses:

> "Drenched with blood are his hair and locks,
> like those of the Graces, which were well
> adorned[2] with silver and gold. And as a man
> tends the flourishing young shoot of an
> olive tree in a lonely place, where water has
> sufficiently gushed up; it is a lovely bloom
> which breezes of all sorts of winds shake
> and it swells with white flower: suddenly a
> wind came with great storm and rooted it from
> its hollow and stretched it on the earth; so
> Menelaus, son of Atreus, when he slew graceful
> Euphorbus, son of Panthous, stripped off his armor."[3]

The story told about the shield of this Euphorbus, the Phrygian, dedicated to Argive Hera among the Trojan spoils at Mycenae, we omit since it is very hackneyed. But what we wish to show by means of all these anecdotes is that he himself recognized his own former lives, and on this he based his care for others, reminding them of the life which they formerly had.

---

1. On Pythagoras as a reincarnation of Euphorbus, see Burkert, *Lore and Science*, 138-141, who accepts Kerényi's interpretation, to wit "if someone wanted to say, 'I am perhaps Apollo,' he could, in Homeric terms, call himself Euphorbus . . ."

2. Iamblichus apparently read εὖ ἤσκηντο for ἐσφήκωντο of the Homeric mss. preserved by Porphyry. Since Iamblichus hardly made this alteration himself, there is likelihood of his dependence on a common source with Porphyry (Nicomachus?). Porphyry may have emended his text to conform with Homer (on whom he was an authority).

3. *Il.* 17. 51-60.

[64] Ἡγούμενος δὲ πρώτην εἶναι τοῖς ἀνθρώποις τὴν δι᾽ αἰσθήσεως προσφερομένην ἐπιμέλειαν, εἴ τις καλὰ μὲν ὁρώη καὶ σχήματα καὶ εἴδη, καλῶν δὲ ἀκούοι ῥυθμῶν καὶ μελῶν, τὴν διὰ μουσικῆς παίδευσιν πρώτην κατεστήσατο διά τε μελῶν τινῶν καὶ ῥυθμῶν, ἀφ᾽ ὧν τρόπων τε καὶ παθῶν ἀνθρωπίνων ἰάσεις ἐγίγνοντο ἁρμονίαι τε τῶν τῆς ψυχῆς δυνάμεων, ὥσπερ εἶχον ἐξ ἀρχῆς, συνήγοντο, σωματικῶν τε καὶ ψυχικῶν νοσημάτων καταστολαὶ καὶ ἀφυγιασμοὶ ὑπ᾽ αὐτοῦ ἐπενοοῦντο. καὶ νὴ Δία τὸ ὑπὲρ πάντα ταῦτα λόγου ἄξιον, ὅτι τοῖς μὲν γνωρίμοις τὰς λεγομένας ἐξαρτύσεις τε καὶ ἐπαφὰς συνέταττε καὶ συνηρμόζετο, δαιμονίως μη- χανώμενος κεράσματά τινων μελῶν διατονικῶν τε καὶ χρωματικῶν καὶ ἐναρμονίων, δι᾽ ὧν ῥᾳδίως εἰς τὰ ἐναντία περιέτρεπε καὶ περιῆγε τὰ τῆς ψυχῆς πάθη νέον ἐν αὐτοῖς ἀλόγως συνιστάμενα καὶ ὑποφυόμενα, λύπας καὶ ὀργὰς καὶ ἐλέους καὶ ζήλους ἀτόπους καὶ φόβους, ἐπιθυμίας τε παν- τοίας καὶ θυμοὺς καὶ ὀρέξεις καὶ χαυνώσεις καὶ ὑπτιότητας καὶ σφοδρότητας, ἐπανορθούμενος πρὸς ἀρετὴν τούτων ἕκαστον διὰ τῶν προσηκόντων μελῶν ὡς διά τινων σωτη-
[65] ρίων συγκεκραμένων φαρμάκων. ἐπί τε ὕπνον ἑσπέρας τρεπομένων τῶν ὁμιλητῶν, ἀπήλλαττε μὲν αὐτοὺς τῶν ἡμερινῶν ταραχῶν καὶ ἐνηχημάτων διεκάθαιρέ τε συγκεκλυ- δασμένον τὸ νοητικόν, ἡσύχους τε καὶ εὐονείρους, ἔτι δὲ μαντικοὺς τοὺς ὕπνους αὐτοῖς ἀπειργάζετο· ἀπό τε τῆς εὐνῆς πάλιν ἀνισταμένων, τοῦ νυκτερινοῦ κάρου καὶ τῆς ἐκλύσεως καὶ τῆς νωχελίας αὐτοὺς ἀπήλλασσε διά τινων ἰδιοτρόπων ᾀσμάτων καὶ μελισμάτων, ψιλῇ τῇ κράσει, διὰ λύρας ἢ καὶ φωνῆς, συντελουμένων. ἑαυτῷ δὲ οὐκέθ᾽ ὁμοίως, δι᾽ ὀργάνων ἢ καὶ ἀρτηρίας, τὸ τοιοῦτον ὁ ἀνὴρ συνέταττε καὶ ἐπόριζεν, ἀλλὰ ἀρρήτῳ τινὶ καὶ δυσεπινοήτῳ θειότητι χρώμενος ἐνητένιζε τὰς ἀκοὰς καὶ τὸν νοῦν ἐνήρειδε ταῖς μεταρσίαις τοῦ κόσμου συμφωνίαις, ἐνακούων, ὡς ἐνέφαινε, μόνος αὐτὸς καὶ συνιεὶς τῆς καθολικῆς τῶν σφαιρῶν καὶ τῶν κατ᾽ αὐτὰς κινουμένων ἀστέρων ἁρμονίας τε καὶ συνῳδίας, πληρέστερόν τι τῶν θνητῶν καὶ κατακορέστερον μέλος φθεγγομένης διὰ τὴν ἐξ ἀνομοίων μὲν καὶ ποικίλως διαφερόντων ῥοιζημάτων ταχῶν τε καὶ μεγεθῶν καὶ ἐποχήσεων, ἐν λόγῳ δέ τινι πρὸς ἄλληλα μουσικωτάτῳ διατεταγμένων, κίνησιν καὶ περιπόλησιν εὐμελεστάτην ἅμα καὶ ποικίλως περικαλλεστάτην ἀποτελουμένην. ἀφ᾽ ἧς

CHAPTER FIFTEEN

What the primary step was in education through sense-perception
in his system, and how he used to correct the souls of his
associates through music, and how he himself
attained perfection in this area.

[64]

Since he believed that the first level of care for humans is that brought about through sense perception: for example, when someone sees lovely shapes and forms, or hears fine rhythms and tunes, he based primary education on music and certain tunes and rhythms, from which arose cures for human attitudes and emotions; and harmonisation of the soul's powers, back to their original state, was brought about, and he devised remissions and healing of bodily and spiritual diseases.[1] And, by Zeus, what is more worthy of mention than all these is this: for his disciples he arranged and adapted those things called musical arrangements and treatments,[2] after marvelously devising combinations of diatonic, chromatic, and enharmonic tunes. By means of these he easily turned around and led in the opposite direction the emotions of the soul, when these newly and irrationally arose and developed among them: pains and angers, pangs of pity, absurd jealousies and fears, all sorts of desires, outbursts of indignation, yearnings, feelings of superiority, outbreaks of laziness and violence. He corrected each of these in the direction of moral excellence by means of proper tunes, as though by means of some well-blended, health-giving drugs.

[65]

When his disciples went to sleep in the evening, he freed them from daily disturbances and reverberations in their ears, purified their confused intelligence, and made them restful, their dreams auspicious and their slumbers even prophetic. And when they arose again from their beds, he freed them from deep nocturnal sleep, feebleness and sluggishness with distinctive hymns and melodies, performed, in a simple mode, either with a lyre or with a voice.

For himself, however, he no longer prescribed and provided a procedure of this kind, (using) instruments or a wind-pipe. But employing some ineffable and abstruse divine power, he extended his hearing and fixed his intellect in the heav-

---

1. For the content of section 64, cf. 110-111 below, see Plut. *De virt. mor.* 441e, and H. John "Das musikerzieherische Wirken Pythagoras' und Damon," *Das Altertum* 8 (1962) 67-72, esp. p. 68.
2. Cf. "Hippodamos" *On the State,* p. 99, 18 ff. Thesleff, *Pythagorean Texts* (= Stob. 4. 1. 94), "Kallikratidas," *On Happiness in the Home* (esp. 103, 19ff (= Stob. 4. 26.16), and "Euryphamos," *On Life,* 86, 15 ff. Thes. (= Stob. 4.39.27). In all these passages, the distinctive terms ἐξαρτύσεις and ἐπαφαί appear.

[66] ἀρδόμενος ὥσπερ καὶ τὸν τοῦ νοῦ λόγον εὐτακτούμενος καὶ
ὡς εἰπεῖν σωμασκούμενος εἰκόνας τινὰς τούτων ἐπενόει
παρέχειν τοῖς ὁμιληταῖς ὡς δυνατὸν μάλιστα, διά τε ὀργάνων καὶ διὰ ψιλῆς τῆς ἀρτηρίας ἐκμιμούμενος. ἑαυτῷ μὲν
γὰρ μόνῳ τῶν ἐπὶ γῆς ἁπάντων συνετὰ καὶ ἐπήκοα τὰ
κοσμικὰ φθέγματα ἐνόμιζε, καὶ ἀπ' αὐτῆς τῆς φυσικῆς
πηγῆς τε καὶ ῥίζης ἄξιον ἑαυτὸν ἡγεῖτο διδάσκεσθαί τι καὶ
ἐκμανθάνειν καὶ ἐξομοιοῦσθαι κατ' ἔφεσιν καὶ ἀπομίμησιν
τοῖς οὐρανίοις, ὡς ἂν οὕτως ἐπιτυχῶς πρὸς τοῦ φύσαντος
αὐτὸν δαιμονίου μόνον διωργανωμένον. ἀγαπητὸν δὲ τοῖς
ἄλλοις ἀνθρώποις ὑπελάμβανεν εἰς αὐτὸν ἀφορῶσι καὶ τὰ
παρ' αὐτοῦ χαριστήρια δι' εἰκόνων τε καὶ ὑποδειγμάτων
ὠφελεῖσθαι καὶ διορθοῦσθαι, μὴ δυναμένοις τῶν πρώτων καὶ
εἰλικρινῶν ἀρχετύπων ὡς ἀληθῶς ἀντιλαμβάνεσθαι·
[67] καθάπερ ἀμέλει καὶ τοῖς οὐχ οἵοις τε ἀτενὲς ἐνορᾶν τῷ ἡλίῳ
διὰ τὴν τῶν ἀκτίνων ὑπερφέγγειαν ἐν βαθείᾳ συστάσει
ὕδατος ἢ καὶ διὰ τετηκυίας πίσσης ἢ κατόπτρου τινὸς
μελαναυγοῦς δεικνύειν ἐπινοοῦμεν τὰς ἐκλείψεις, φειδόμενοι
τῆς τῶν ὄψεων ἀσθενείας αὐτῶν καὶ ἀντίρροπόν τινα
κατάληψιν αὐτοῖς τὸ τοιοῦτον ἀγαπῶσιν εἰ καὶ ἀνειμενω-
τέραν μηχανώμενοι. τοῦτο φαίνεται καὶ Ἐμπεδοκλῆς περὶ
αὐτοῦ αἰνίττεσθαι καὶ τῆς ἐξαιρέτου καὶ θεοδωρήτου περὶ
αὐτὸν ὑπὲρ τοὺς ἄλλους διοργανώσεως ἐν οἷς φησί·

ἦν δέ τις ἐν κείνοισιν ἀνὴρ περιώσια εἰδώς,
ὃς δὴ μήκιστον πραπίδων ἐκτήσατο πλοῦτον
παντοίων τε μάλιστα σοφῶν ἐπιήρανος ἔργων·
ὁππότε γὰρ πάσῃσιν ὀρέξαιτο πραπίδεσσι,
ῥεῖά γε τῶν ὄντων πάντων λεύσσεσκεν ἕκαστα
καί τε δέκ' ἀνθρώπων καί τ' εἴκοσιν αἰώνεσσι.

τὸ γὰρ "περιώσια" καὶ "τῶν ὄντων πάντων λεύσσεσκεν
ἕκαστα" καὶ "πραπίδων πλοῦτον" καὶ τὰ ἐοικότα ἐμφαντικὰ
μάλιστα τῆς ἐξαιρέτου καὶ ἀκριβεστέρας παρὰ τοὺς ἄλλους
διοργανώσεως ἦν ἔν τε τῷ ὁρᾶν καὶ τῷ ἀκούειν καὶ τῷ νοεῖν.

enly harmonious sounds of the cosmos. He alone could hear and understand, so he indicated, the universal harmony and concord of the spheres,[3] and the stars moving through them, which sound a tune fuller and more intense than any mortal ones. (This harmony) is caused by a movement and most graceful revolution, very beautiful in its simultaneous variety, which arises from unlike and variously different sonic motions, speeds, magnitudes and conjunctions, arranged together in a most musical proportion.

[66]   Irrigated, as it were, by this music, and well ordered in the principle of his intellect, and exercised, so to speak, in body, he conceived the idea of furnishing certain likenesses of these (sounds) to his disciples as far as possible, imitating faithfully (these sounds) by instruments and by the voice alone. He believed that to himself alone, of all those on earth, the cosmic sounds were comprehensible and audible. From this natural source and foundation, he considered himself worthy to be taught something and to learn thoroughly, and to be assimilated, in accordance with desire and imitation, to heavenly beings, since he alone was so fortunately fashioned by the divine spirit (*daimonion*) which begot him. He believed that it would be enough for other humans to look to him, since they were not able to apprehend the truly first and pure archetypes, and be benefited and
[67] improved by his favors through images and signs. Indeed, just as for those not able to look directly at the sun because of its intense shining rays, we contrive to show eclipses either in a deep pool of water or even by means of melted pitch or a dark-gleaming mirror, sparing the weakness of their eyes and devising, if somewhat inadequately , some compensatory perception for those who must be content with this sort of thing.

     Empedocles also seems to have made an allusion to him, and his superior and god-given formation above the rest of men, when he says:

> "There was a man among them of outstanding knowledge,
> who possessed the greatest wealth of wit, especially
> master of all sorts of clever deeds. For whenever
> he reached out with all his thoughts, easily he gazed
> on each of all existing things both in the tenth and
> twentieth generations of the human race."[4]

For "outstanding" and "gazed on each of all existing things," and "wealth of wit" and the like, were especially expressive of his superior and genuine formation above others in seeing, hearing, and thinking.

---

3. Much has been written on the harmony of the spheres, on which see, for example, Burkert, *Lore and Science*, 350 ff., and J. Pépin, "Harmonie der Sphären," *RAC* 13 (1986) 593-618, especially 609-610.

4. D.-K. B129. Empedocles did not give any name, but Timaeus understood the verses as applying to Pythagoras; others, thought that they referred to Parmenides. See Burkert, *Lore and Science*, 137-38.

[68]   Αὕτη μὲν οὖν ἡ διὰ μουσικῆς ἐπετηδεύετο αὐτῷ κατάρτυσις τῶν ψυχῶν· ἄλλη δὲ κάθαρσις τῆς διανοίας ἅμα καὶ τῆς
ὅλης ψυχῆς διὰ παντοδαπῶν ἐπιτηδευμάτων οὕτως ἠσκεῖτο
παρ' αὐτῷ. τὸ γεννικὸν τῶν περὶ τὰ μαθήματα καὶ
ἐπιτηδεύματα πόνων ᾤετο δεῖν ὑπάρχειν καὶ τὰς τῆς
ἐμφύτου πᾶσιν ἀκρασίας τε καὶ πλεονεξίας βασάνους τε
ποικιλωτάτας τε κολάσεις καὶ ἀνακοπάς, πυρὶ καὶ σιδήρῳ
κατ' αὐτῆς συντελουμένας, διαθεσμοθετῆσαι τοῖς χρωμένοις,
ἃς οὔτε καρτερεῖν οὔτε ὑπομένειν δύναταί τις κακὸς ὤν. πρὸς
δὲ τούτοις ἐμψύχων ἀποχὴν πάντων καὶ ἔτι βρωμάτων
τινῶν ταῖς ἐπεγρίαις τοῦ λογισμοῦ καὶ εἰλικρινείαις
ἐμποδιζόντων κατέδειξεν [ἐν] τοῖς ἑταίροις, ἐχεμυθίαν τε καὶ
παντελῆ σιωπήν, πρὸς τὸ γλώσσης κρατεῖν συνασκοῦσαν
ἐπὶ ἔτη πολλά, σύντονόν τε καὶ ἀδιάπνευστον περὶ τὰ
δυσληπτότατα τῶν θεωρημάτων ἐξέτασίν τε καὶ ἀνάληψιν·
[69]   διὰ ταῦτὰ δὲ καὶ ἀνοινίαν καὶ ὀλιγοσιτίαν καὶ ὀλιγοϋπνίαν,
δόξης δὲ καὶ πλούτου καὶ τῶν ὁμοίων ἀνεπιτήδευτον (περι-)
φρόνησίν τε καὶ κατεξανάστασιν, καὶ αἰδῶ μὲν ἀνυπόκριτον
πρὸς τοὺς προήκοντας, πρὸς δὲ τοὺς ὁμήλικας ἄπλαστον
ὁμοιότητα καὶ φιλοφροσύνην, συνεπίτασίν τε καὶ παρόρμη-
σιν πρὸς τοὺς νεωτέρους φθόνου χωρίς, φιλίας δὲ πάντων
πρὸς ἅπαντας, εἴτε θεῶν πρὸς ἀνθρώπους δι' εὐσεβείας καὶ
ἐπιστημονικῆς θεραπείας, εἴτε δογμάτων πρὸς ἄλληλα καὶ
καθόλου ψυχῆς πρὸς σῶμα λογικοῦ τε πρὸς τὰ τοῦ ἀλόγου
διὰ φιλοσοφίας καὶ τῆς κατὰ ταύτην θεωρίας, εἴτε
ἀνθρώπων πρὸς ἀλλήλους, πολιτῶν μὲν διὰ νομιμότητος
ὑγιοῦς, ἑτεροφύλων δὲ διὰ φυσιολογίας ὀρθῆς, ἀνδρὸς δὲ
πρὸς γυναῖκα ἢ ἀδελφοὺς καὶ οἰκείους διὰ κοινωνίας ἀδιαστρόφου, εἴτε συλλήβδην πάντων πρὸς ἅπαντας καὶ
προσέτι τῶν ἀλόγων ζῴων τινὰ διὰ δικαιοσύνης καὶ φυσικῆς
ἐπιπλοκῆς καὶ κοινότητος, εἴτε καὶ σώματος καθ' ἑαυτὸ θνητοῦ τῶν ἐγκεκρυμμένων αὐτῷ ἐναντίων δυνάμεων εἰρήνευσιν
καὶ συμβιβασμὸν δι' ὑγείας καὶ τῆς εἰς ταύτην διαίτης καὶ
σωφροσύνης κατὰ μίμησιν τῆς ἐν τοῖς κοσμικοῖς στοιχείοις

CHAPTER SIXTEEN

The nature of the purificatory training he enjoined, which he also
practiced, and his more perfect theory of friendship,
itself serving as a preparation for
those suited to philosophy.

[68] So then, this training of souls was undertaken by him through music. Another purification of the intellect, and simultaneously of the whole soul, was practiced by him with a variety of pursuits,[1] and is as follows. He thought that a noble attitude towards labors concerned with studies and ascetic exercises is a prerequisite. And for all those subject to inborn incontinence and greediness, he prescribed most varied tests, punishments and restraints accomplished by fire and sword, which someone with a bad character is able neither to bear patiently nor to endure. Moreover, he taught his disciples abstinence from all animal flesh and also from certain foods, which are a hindrance to alert and pure reasoning. He also taught reserve and absolute silence which helped them to practice mastery of the tongue for many years;[2] and he taught intense and untiring close examination and repetition of theories about subjects most difficult to comprehend. For these
[69] reasons he prescribed abstinence from wine, moderation in food and sleep, an unaffected contempt for, and resistance to fame, wealth, and similar things; a sincere respect for those advanced in age; with those of the same age, a true affinity and friendliness, joint pressure on and stimulation of those younger than themselves without jealousy; and friendship of all with all:[3] either of gods with human beings by means of piety and scientific worship, or of doctrines with one another, and generally of the soul with the body; also of the rational part of the soul with all forms of the irrational, through philosophy and contemplation in accord with this; or of human beings with one another: of citizens through observance of law,

---

1. This passage, down to the beginning of section 69, is repeated almost verbatim at sections 225-26 below, and more loosely in sections 187-88.

2. The Pythagorean requirement of silence was famous and involved five years at the outset (see section 72 below, and D.L. 8. 10). This is a good shamanistic and yogic practice. Cf. G. Mensching, *Das heilige Schweigen* (Giessen, 1926). The disciples heard Pythagoras' discourses without ever seeing him since he lectured at night. Cf. Aulus Gellius, *NA*, I, 9 (an account which Aulus claims to owe to his instructor in Platonism, Calvenus Taurus).

3. Iamblichus or his sources often reflect on "friendship" (φιλία) in *VP*. See, for example, sections 230-37, especially 234-37 on Damon and Phintias. See also de Vogel, *Pythagoras*, 151 ff. In any case, this passage, until the beginning of section 70, is repeated at the start of the sections on friendship, sections 229-30 below.

[70] εὐετηρίας. πάντων τούτων [ἐν] ἑνὸς καὶ τοῦ αὐτοῦ κατὰ
σύλληψιν καὶ συγκεφαλαίωσιν ὀνόματος ⟨ὄντος⟩, τοῦ τῆς
φιλίας, εὑρετὴς καὶ νομοθέτης ὁμολογουμένως Πυθαγόρας,
καὶ διόλου τῆς ἐπιτηδειοτάτης πρὸς θεοὺς ὁμιλίας ὕπαρ τε
καὶ κατὰ τοὺς ὕπνους αἰτιώτατος τοῖς περὶ αὐτόν, ὅπερ οὔτε
ὑπὸ ὀργῆς τεθολωμένη περιγίνεταί ποτε ψυχῇ, οὔτε ὑπὸ
λύπης οὔτε ὑπὸ ἡδονῆς οὔτε τινὸς ἄλλης αἰσχρᾶς ἐπιθυμίας
παρηλλαγμένη, μὰ Δία, οὐδὲ τῆς τούτων ἁπασῶν ἀνοσιω-
τάτης τε καὶ χαλεπωτάτης ἀμαθίας. ἀπὸ δὴ τούτων ἁπάντων
δαιμονίως ἰᾶτο καὶ ἀπεκάθαιρε τὴν ψυχὴν καὶ ἀνεζωπύρει τὸ
θεῖον ἐν αὐτῇ καὶ ἀπέσῳζε καὶ περιῆγεν ἐπὶ τὸ νοητὸν τὸ
θεῖον ὄμμα, κρεῖττον ὂν σωθῆναι κατὰ τὸν Πλάτωνα μυρίων
σαρκίνων ὀμμάτων. μόνῳ γὰρ αὐτῷ διαβλέψαντι καὶ οἷς
προσῆκε βοηθήμασι τονωθέντι καὶ διαρθρωθέντι ἡ περὶ τῶν
ὄντων ἁπάντων ἀλήθεια διορᾶται. πρὸς δὴ τοῦτο ἀναφέρων
ἐποιεῖτο τὴν τῆς διανοίας κάθαρσιν, καὶ ἦν αὐτῷ τῆς
παιδεύσεως ὁ τύπος τοιοῦτος καὶ πρὸς ταῦτα ἀποβλέπων.

those of another race by correct inquiry into natural laws, or of a husband with a wife, or with brothers and kindred, through an unperverted spirit of community; in short, friendship of all with all, and furthermore with certain brute animals through justice and natural union and affability; and (friendship) of the mortal body with itself by pacification and reconciliation of the opposite powers concealed in it, accomplished through health and a way of life conducive to this and temperance conducive to this, in imitation of the efficient functioning in the cosmic elements.[4]

[70] For all these instances taken together and summed up, there is one and the same word: "friendship," of which, by common consent, Pythagoras was the discoverer and legislator. And he was especially responsible to those about him for the most suitable association with the gods both when awake and when asleep, which never occurs in a soul disturbed by anger or in one changed by pain, pleasure, or any other base desire, or even by ignorance, which, by Zeus, is most unholy and miserable of all. From all these, he marvellously healed and purified the soul, rekindled and preserved that which is divine in it, and brought the divine eye which is, according to Plato,[5] more worth saving than ten thousand fleshly eyes, round to the intelligible. For only by the clear vision of this eye (when it is braced up and thoroughly developed with appropriate aids) is the truth about all existing things perceived. With a view to this, then, he purified the intellect, and such was the model of his teaching and training, and to this he directed his attention.

---

4. It is not clear what is meant by εὐετηρία. The word has connotations of "good season," "prosperity," "plenty." See *LSJ* s.v. and R. Renehan, *Greek Lexicographical Notes*, Hyp. (Göttingen, 1975) 96. The cosmic elements were usually four: earth, air, fire, and water, and the seasons corresponded, in turn, to these elements. See Burkert, *Lore and Science*, esp. 355 f. See also section 229 below.

5. *R.*, 527 d-e.

[71] Παρεσκευασμένῳ δὲ αὐτῷ οὕτως εἰς τὴν παιδείαν τῶν
ὁμιλητῶν, προσιόντων τῶν νεωτέρων καὶ βουλομένων συν-
διατρίβειν οὐκ εὐθὺς συνεχώρει, μέχρις ἂν αὐτῶν τὴν
δοκιμασίαν καὶ τὴν κρίσιν ποιήσηται, πρῶτον μὲν πυνθανό-
μενος πῶς τοῖς γονεῦσι καὶ τοῖς οἰκείοις τοῖς λοιποῖς
πάρεισιν ὡμιληκότες, ἔπειτα θεωρῶν αὐτῶν τούς τε γέλω-
τας τοὺς ἀκαίρους καὶ τὴν σιωπὴν καὶ τὴν λαλιὰν παρὰ τὸ
δέον, ἔτι δὲ τὰς ἐπιθυμίας τίνες εἰσὶ καὶ τοὺς γνωρίμους οἷς
ἐχρῶντο καὶ τὴν πρὸς τούτους ὁμιλίαν καὶ πρὸς τίνι
μάλιστα τὴν ἡμέραν σχολάζουσι καὶ τὴν χαρὰν καὶ τὴν
λύπην ἐπὶ τίσι τυγχάνουσι ποιούμενοι. προσεθεώρει δὲ καὶ
τὸ εἶδος καὶ τὴν πορείαν καὶ τὴν ὅλην τοῦ σώματος
κίνησιν, τοῖς τε τῆς φύσεως γνωρίσμασι φυσιογνωμονῶν
αὐτοὺς σημεῖα τὰ φανερὰ ἐποιεῖτο τῶν ἀφανῶν ἠθῶν ἐν τῇ
[72] ψυχῇ. καὶ ὅντινα δοκιμάσειεν οὕτως, ἐφίει τριῶν ἐτῶν
ὑπερορᾶσθαι, δοκιμάζων πῶς ἔχει βεβαιότητος καὶ
ἀληθινῆς φιλομαθείας, καὶ εἰ πρὸς δόξαν ἱκανῶς
παρεσκεύασται ὥστε καταφρονεῖν τιμῆς. μετὰ δὲ τοῦτο τοῖς
προσιοῦσι προσέταττε σιωπὴν πενταετῆ, ἀποπειρώμενος
πῶς ἐγκρατείας ἔχουσιν, ὡς χαλεπώτερον τῶν ἄλλων
ἐγκρατευμάτων τοῦτο, τὸ γλώσσης κρατεῖν, καθὰ καὶ ὑπὸ
τῶν τὰ μυστήρια νομοθετησάντων ἐμφαίνεται ἡμῖν. ἐν δὴ
τῷ χρόνῳ τούτῳ τὰ μὲν ἑκάστου ὑπάρχοντα, τουτέστιν αἱ
οὐσίαι, ἐκοινοῦντο, διδόμενα τοῖς ἀποδεδειγμένοις εἰς τοῦτο
γνωρίμοις, οἵπερ ἐκαλοῦντο πολιτικοί, καὶ οἰκονομικοί
τινες καὶ νομοθετικοὶ ὄντες. αὐτοὶ δὲ εἰ μὲν ἄξιοι ἐφαίνοντο
τοῦ μετασχεῖν δογμάτων, ἔκ τε βίου καὶ τῆς ἄλλης
ἐπιεικείας κριθέντες, μετὰ τὴν πενταετῆ σιωπὴν ἐσωτερικοὶ
λοιπὸν ἐγίνοντο καὶ ἐντὸς σινδόνος ἐπήκουον τοῦ
Πυθαγόρου μετὰ τοῦ καὶ βλέπειν αὐτόν· πρὸ τούτου δὲ
ἐκτὸς αὐτῆς καὶ μηδέποτε αὐτῷ ἐνορῶντες μετεῖχον τῶν
λόγων διὰ ψιλῆς ἀκοῆς, ἐν πολλῷ χρόνῳ διδόντες βάσανον

CHAPTER SEVENTEEN

*How Pythagoras conducted the examination of the disciples who
first came to him, and what tests of character he imposed
on them before introducing them to philosophy.*

[71] After he thus prepared himself for his disciples' education, when young people came and wished to study with him, he did not immediately agree until he examined and tested them,[1] and first inquired how they associated with their parents and other relatives. Then he watched them for untimely laughter, and silence and chatting beyond what was proper. Also he looked at the nature of their desires, the acquaintances with whom they had dealings and their company with these. Most of all, he looked at leisure occupations in which they spent the day, and what things gave them joy and pain. He observed, moreover, their physique, manner of walking and their whole bodily movement. Studying the features by which their nature is made known,[2] he took the visible things as signs of the invisible charac-
[72] ter traits in their souls. And whomever he examined in this way, he left to be supervised for three years, to test how he was disposed to stability and true love of learning, and if he was sufficiently equipped against popular repute so as to despise honor. After this, he ordered a five year silence for those coming to him, testing how they were disposed to self-control, since more difficult than other forms of self-control is mastery of the tongue, as is revealed to us by those who instituted the mysteries.

At this time, then, the things belonging to each, that is, their possessions, were held in common, given to those disciples appointed for this purpose who were called "politicians," and experienced in household management and skilled in legislation.[3] The candidates themselves, then, if they appeared worthy of sharing

---

1. This first sentence is taken almost verbatim from Timaeus of Tauromenium, Bk. V of his *History* (as reported in *Schol.* to Plato *Phdr.* 279c). Timaeus goes on to talk of friends building things in common, which Iamblichus gets to in the next section. It is possible that the contents of 71-74 as a whole go back to Timaeus. See Burkert, *Lore and Science*, 192, n. 1.

2. For Pythagoras' practice of physiognomics, cf. below, section 74, Porph. *VP* 13, and Aulus Gellius, *NA* I, 9, 2.

3. On these πολιτικοί see below section 150, where they are ranked with the ἀκουσματικοί lower than the philosophers. But Varro (*ap.* Aug. *Ord.* 2, 20) represents the πολιτικοί as the highest group. There need be no great contradiction here, since they are presumably the ruling element politically in a Pythagorean state (cf. sections 108 and 129 below). For an attempt to deal with the ranks and "degrees" of Pythagorean wisdom, see Burkert, *Lore and Science*, 192 ff. who is mainly concerned with the distinction between the *acusmatici* and *mathematici*.

[73] τῶν οἰκείων ἠθῶν. εἰ δ' ἀποδοκιμασθείησαν, τὴν μὲν
οὐσίαν ἐλάμβανον διπλῆν, μνῆμα δὲ αὐτοῖς ὡς νεκροῖς
ἐχώννυντο ὑπὸ τῶν ὁμακόων (οὕτω γὰρ ἐκαλοῦντο πάντες οἱ
περὶ τὸν ἄνδρα), συντυγχάνοντες δὲ αὐτοῖς οὕτως
συνετύγχανον ὡς ἄλλοις τισίν, ἐκείνους δὲ ἔφασαν τεθνά-
ναι, οὓς αὐτοὶ ἀνεπλάσσοντο, καλοὺς κἀγαθοὺς
προσδοκῶντες ἔσεσθαι ἐκ τῶν μαθημάτων· ἀδιοργανώτους
τε καὶ ὡς εἰπεῖν ἀτελεῖς τε καὶ στειρώδεις ᾤοντο τοὺς
[74] δυσμαθεστέρους. εἰ γοῦν, μετὰ τὸ ἐκ μορφῆς τε καὶ
βαδίσματος καὶ τῆς ἄλλης κινήσεώς τε καὶ καταστάσεως
ὑπ' αὐτῶν φυσιογνωμονηθῆναι καὶ ἐλπίδα ἀγαθὴν περὶ
αὐτοῦ παρασχεῖν, μετὰ τὴν πενταετῆ σιωπὴν καὶ [τὴν]
μετὰ τοὺς ἐκ τῶν τοσῶνδε μαθημάτων ὀργιασμοὺς καὶ
μυήσεις ψυχῆς τε ἀπορρύψεις καὶ καθαρμοὺς τοσούτους τε
καὶ τηλικούτους καὶ ἐκ ποικίλων οὕτως θεωρημάτων
προοδεύσαντας, δι' οὓς ἀγχίνοιαί τε καὶ ψυχῆς εὐάγειαι
πᾶσιν ἐκ παντὸς ἐνεφύοντο, δυσκίνητος ἔτι τις καὶ
δυσπαρακολούθητος ηὑρίσκετο, στήλην δή τινα τῷ τοιούτῳ
καὶ μνημεῖον ἐν τῇ διατριβῇ χώσαντες (καθὰ καὶ Περίλλῳ
τῷ Θουρίῳ λέγεται καὶ Κύλωνι τῷ Συβαριτῶν ἐξάρχῳ,
ἀπογνωσθεῖσιν ὑπ' αὐτῶν) ἐξήλαυνον ἂν τοῦ ὁμακοείου,
φορτίσαντες χρυσοῦ τε καὶ ἀργύρου πλῆθος (κοινὰ γὰρ
αὐτοῖς καὶ ταῦτα ἀπέκειτο, ὑπό τινων εἰς τοῦτο ἐπιτηδείων
κοινῇ διοικονομούμενα, οὓς προσηγόρευον οἰκονομικοὺς ἀπὸ
τοῦ τέλους)· καὶ εἴ ποτε συντύχοιεν ἄλλως αὐτῷ, πάντα
ὁντινοῦν μᾶλλον ἢ ἐκεῖνον ἡγοῦντο εἶναι, τὸν κατ' αὐτοὺς
τεθνηκότα.

[75]　　διόπερ καὶ Λῦσις Ἱππάρχῳ τινὶ ἐπιπλήττων, μεταδιδόντι
τῶν λόγων τοῖς ἀνεισάκτοις καὶ ἄνευ μαθημάτων καὶ θεωρίας
ἐπιφυομένοις, φησί· "φαντὶ δέ σε καὶ δαμοσίᾳ φιλοσοφὲν
τοῖς ἐντυγχάνουσι, τόπερ ἀπαξίωσε Πυθαγόρας, ὡς ἔμαθες
μέν, Ἵππαρχε, μετὰ σπουδᾶς, οὐκ ἐφύλαξας δέ,
γευσάμενος, ὦ γενναῖε, Σικελικᾶς πολυτελείας, ἃς οὐκ
ἐχρῆν τοι γενέσθαι δεύτερον. εἰ μὲν ὦν μεταβάλοιο, χαρη-
σοῦμαι· εἰ δὲ μή γε, τέθνακας. διαμεμνᾶσθαι γάρ, φησίν,
ὅσιον εἴη κα τῶν τήνου θείων τε καὶ ἀνθρωπείων παραγ-
γελμάτων, μηδὲ κοινὰ ποιεῖσθαι τὰ σοφίας ἀγαθὰ τοῖς οὐδ'
ὄναρ τὰν ψυχὰν κεκαθαρμένοις. οὐ γὰρ θέμις ὀρέγεν τοῖς
ἀπαντῶσι τὰ μετὰ τοσούτων ἀγώνων σπουδᾷ πορριχθέντα,

in his teachings, having been judged by their way of life and other virtuousness, after the five year silence, became "esoterics" and heard Pythagoras within the curtain,[4] and also saw him. Before this, they shared his discourses through mere hearing, being outside the curtain and never seeing him, while submitting over a

[73] long period to a test of their characters. If they were rejected, they received double their property, and a tomb was raised by their "fellow-hearers" (for so all those about the man were called) as if they were dead. And on meeting them, they met them as if they were somebody else; for they said those whom they themselves had been moulding were dead, since they expected them to be good and noble as a

[74] result of their lessons. They thought those slower at learning both disorganized and, so to speak, imperfect and barren. If, at any rate, after his features were studied by them, and from his physique, walk, and other movement and condition, the candidate provided good expectation about himself, after the five year silence, and after ritual celebrations and initiations in so many sciences, and after many and great cleansings and purifications of the soul, emanating from so many complex theories (through which ready wit and alertness of the soul are fully implanted in all) if he were found still clumsy and hard of understanding, after raising for such a one a stele and memorial in the school (just as is said to have been done for Perillus the Thurian, and Cylon, leader of the Sybarites, who were rejected by them) they would expel him from the school of the Pythagoreans. They would load him with much gold and silver (for these things were stored in common for them, and were administered in common by those suitable for this purpose, whom they called "managers" because of their post). And if they ever met him by chance, they considered him someone wholly other than he who, according to them, had died.

[75] Hence also Lysis, in rebuking Hipparchus for having shared doctrines with uninitiated persons who had attached themselves to him without training in the sciences and theory, says:[5] "They say you philosophize in public with ordinary people, the very thing Pythagoras deemed unworthy, as you learned, Hipparchus, with zeal, but you did not maintain, having tasted, good fellow, Sicilian extravagance, which ought not to happen to you a second time. If you repent of your decision, I will be pleased, but if not, you are dead." "For," he says, "it is pious to remember the divine and human precepts of the famous one, not to share the

---

4. Or "veil" (σινδών). According to Ath. 4. 145 b-c, the king of Persia eats behind a curtain.

5. The full text is in Hercher, *Epistolographi Graeci*, 601 (Thesleff, *Pythagorean Texts*, 111-114). The letter is in bogus Doric which we do not attempt to reproduce. Iamblichus first quotes from the end of the letter, then goes back to the beginning. Lysis was one of the two survivors of the disaster which befell the Pythagorean ruling group in Croton (perhaps around 450 B.C.), who then emigrated to Thebes where he later became the teacher of the Theban leader, Epaminondas, cf. below, sections 244-50 and D.L., 8. 7 and 39. The letter is treated in great detail by Burkert, *Philol.* 105 (1961) 17-28.

οὐδὲ μὰν βεβάλοις τὰ ταῖν Ἐλευσινίαιν θεαῖν μυστήρια
διαγέεσθαι· κατ᾽ ἰσότατα δὲ ἄδικοι καὶ ἀσεβέες οἱ ταῦτα
πράξαντες. διαλογίζεσθαι δὲ καλόν, ὅσον χρόνου μᾶκος
[76] ἐκμεμετρήκαμεν ἀπορρυπτόμενοι ⟨σπίλως⟩ τὼς ἐν τοῖς
στάθεσσιν ἁμῶν ἐγκεκολαμμένως, ἕως ποκὰ διελθόντων
ἐτέων ἐγενόμεθα δεκτικοὶ τῶν τήνου λόγων. καθάπερ γὰρ οἱ
βαφεῖς προεκκαθάραντες ἔστυψαν τὰ βάψιμα τῶν ἱματίων,
ὅπως ἀνέκπλυτον τὰν βαφὰν ἀναπίωντι καὶ μηδέποτε
γενησουμέναν ἐξίταλον, τὸν αὐτὸν τρόπον καὶ ὁ δαιμόνιος
ἀνὴρ προπαρεσκεύαζε τὰς ψυχὰς τῶν φιλοσοφίας
ἐρασθέντων, ὅπως μὴ διαψευσθῇ περί τινα τῶν ἐλπισθέντων
ἐσεῖσθαι καλῶν τε κἀγαθῶν. οὐ γὰρ κιβδήλως ἐνεπορεύετο
λόγως οὐδὲ πάγας, ταῖς τοὶ πολλοὶ τῶν σοφιστᾶν τὼς νέως
ἐμπλέκοντι, ποτ᾽ οὐδὲν κράγυον σχολάζοντες, ἀλλὰ θείων
καὶ ἀνθρωπίνων πραγμάτων ἦς ἐπιστάμων. τοὶ δὲ πρόσχημα
ποιησάμενοι τὰν τήνω διδασκαλίαν πολλὰ καὶ δεινὰ δρῶντι,
σαγηνεύοντες οὐ κατὰ κόσμον οὐδ᾽ ὡς ἔτυχε τὼς νέως.
[77] τοιγαροῦν χαλεπῶς τε καὶ προαλεῖς ἀπεργάζονται τὼς
ἀκουστάς. ἐγκίρναντι γὰρ ἤθεσι τεταραγμένοις τε καὶ
θολεροῖς θεωρήματα καὶ λόγως θείως, καθάπερ εἴ τις εἰς
φρέαρ βαθὺ βορβόρω πλῆρες ἐγχέοι καθαρὸν καὶ διειδὲς
ὕδωρ· τόν τε γὰρ βόρβορον ἀνετάραξε καὶ τὸ ὕδωρ
ἐπαφάνιξεν. ὁ αὐτὸς δὴ τρόπος τῶν οὕτω δὴ διδασκόντων τε
καὶ διδασκομένων· πυκιναὶ γὰρ καὶ λάσιαι λόχμαι περὶ τὰς
φρένας καὶ τὰν καρδίαν πεφύκαντι τῶν μὴ καθαρῶς τοῖς
μαθήμασιν ὀργιασθέντων, πᾶν τὸ ἄμερον καὶ πρᾷον καὶ
λογιστικὸν τᾶς ψυχᾶς ἐπισκιάζουσαι καὶ κωλύουσαι
προφανῶς αὐξηθῆμεν καὶ προκύψαι τὸ νοατικόν. ὀνομάξαιμι
δέ κα πρῶτον ἐπελθὼν αὐτῶν τὰς ματέρας, ἀκρασίαν τε καὶ
[78] πλεονεξίαν· ἄμφω δὲ πολύγονοι πεφύκαντι. τᾶς μέν νυν
ἀκρασίας ἐκβεβλαστάκαντι ἄθεσμοι γάμοι καὶ φθοραὶ καὶ
μέθαι καὶ παρὰ φύσιν ἀδοναὶ καὶ σφοδραί τινες ἐπιθυμίαι,
μέχρι βαράθρων καὶ κρημνῶν διώκουσαι· ἤδη γάρ τινας
ἀνάγκαξαν ἐπιθυμίαι μήτε ματέρων μήτε θυγατέρων
ἀποσχέσθαι, καὶ δὴ παρεωσάμεναι πόλιν καὶ νόμον καθάπερ
τύραννος, ἐκπεριαγαγοῦσαι τὼς ἀγκῶνας ὥσπερ αἰχμάλωτον
ἐπὶ τὸν ἔσχατον ὄλεθρον μετὰ βίας ἄγουσαι κατέστασαν.
τᾶς δὲ πλεονεξίας ἐκπέφυκαν ἁρπαγαί, λᾳστεῖαι,
πατροκτονίαι, ἱεροσυλίαι, φαρμακεῖαι, καὶ ὅσα τούτων

good things of wisdom with those who have their souls in no way purified. For it is not lawful to give to any random person things acquired with diligence after so many struggles, or to divulge to the profane the mysteries of the Eleusinian goddesses.[6] For those who have done these things are equally unjust and impious. It

[76] is well to reckon how great a span of time we measured out when cleansing (the stain) so settled in our hearts until at some time after years passed, we became capable of receiving the doctrines of that (famous) one. For just as dyers, while cleaning garments, treat what is to be dyed with a mordant, in order that the dye be indelible in that which absorbs it, and never fade, so the divine man prepared the souls of those in love with philosophy in order that he not be mistaken about anyone whom he hoped to be among those noble and good.[7] For he did not traffic in fraudulent doctrines or snares with which many sophists, who never devote themselves to anything good, entrap young men, and he had a knowledge of things divine and human. But these (sophists), having made this one's teaching a pretext for doing many dreadful things, catch the youth as in a net neither in orderly fashion nor by chance. Accordingly, they make their hearers undisciplined

[77] and heedless. For they pour theories and divine discourses all mixed up into characters agitated and disturbed, just as if someone were to pour clean and clear water into a deep well full of mud; for such a one both stirs up the mud, and also spoils the water. The same, then, is the method of those teaching, and being taught in this way. For dense and bushy thickets grow about the wits and heart of those not purely initiated in the sciences, overshadowing all that is civilized, gentle, and rational in the soul, and hindering the intellectual part from clearly increasing and emerging. At the outset, I would first name the mothers of these thickets incontinence and greediness; and both are by nature prolific. From in-

[78] continence blossom forth unlawful marriages, corruptions, drunkenness, pleasures and vehement desires contrary to nature which pursue (their possessors) even to pits and cliffs (of ruin). For already desires have forced some to abstain neither from ravaging mothers nor daughters, and to reject city and law just like a tyrant. Led with arms tied like a captive of war, led by force, they are appointed for final destruction. From greediness spring forth rapes, robberies, parricide, sacrilege, sorcery, and whatever are sisters of these. One must first, then, clear the woods in which these passions dwell, both with fire and sword and all the devices of science, and after having cleared the rational part of so many evils, provide something good to plant in it."

---

6. Demeter and Persephone.
7. Cf. Pl. *R.* 429 d ff., where a similar dye analogy is developed at some length; Cic. *Hortens.* fr. 23, p. 315, 6 ff. Mueller.

ἀδελφά. δεῖ ὧν πρᾶτον μὲν τὰς ὕλας, αἷς ἐνδιαιτῆται ταῦτα τὰ πάθη, πυρὶ καὶ σιδήρῳ καὶ πάσαις μαθημάτων μηχαναῖς ἐκκαθαίροντας καὶ ῥυομένως τὸν λογισμὸν ἐλεύθερον τῶν τοσούτων κακῶν, τὸ τανικάδε ἐμφυτεύεν τι χρήσιμον αὐτῷ καὶ παραδιδόμεν."

[79]   τοσαύτην ἐπιμέλειαν καὶ οὕτως ἀναγκαιοτάτην ᾤετο δεῖν μαθημάτων πρὸ φιλοσοφίας ποιεῖσθαι Πυθαγόρας, τιμήν τε ἐξαίρετον ἐτίθετο καὶ ἐξέτασιν ἀκριβεστάτην περὶ τὴν διδασκαλίαν καὶ μετάδοσιν τῶν αὐτῷ δεδογμένων, βασανίζων τε καὶ διακρίνων τὰς τῶν ἐντυγχανόντων ἐννοίας διδάγμασί τε ποικίλοις καὶ θεωρίας ἐπιστημονικῆς μυρίοις εἴδεσι.

[79]   Such indispensable attention as this Pythagoras believed must be given to studies prior to philosophy, and he ordered that both exceptional value and most exact investigation be given to the teaching and communication of his doctrines.
And he examined and judged the conceptions of candidates with every sort of
teaching, and a vast array of scientific theory.

[80] Μετὰ δὴ τοῦτο λέγωμεν ὅπως τοὺς ἐγκριθέντας ὑφ' ἑαυτοῦ διήρηκε χωρὶς κατὰ τὴν ἀξίαν ἑκάστους. οὔτε γὰρ τῶν αὐτῶν μετέχειν ἐπ' ἴσης πάντας ἦν ἄξιον, μὴ τῆς ὁμοίας ὄντας φύσεως, οὔτε ἄξιον ἦν τοὺς μὲν πάντων τῶν τιμιωτάτων ἀκροαμάτων μετέχειν, τοὺς δὲ μηδενὸς [ἢ] μηδόλως μετέχειν· καὶ γὰρ τοῦτο ἦν ἀκοινώνητον καὶ ἄνισον. τῷ μέντοι μεταδοῦναι τῶν ἐπιβαλλόντων λόγων ἑκάστοις τὴν προσήκουσαν μοῖραν τήν τε ὠφέλειαν ἀπένεμεν ἅπασι κατὰ τὸ δυνατὸν καὶ τὸν τῆς δικαιοσύνης λόγον ἐφύλαττεν, ὅτι μάλιστα τὴν ἀξίαν ἑκάστοις ἀποδιδοὺς ἀκρόασιν. κατὰ δὴ τοῦτον τὸν λόγον τοὺς μὲν Πυθαγορείους καλέσας, τοὺς δὲ Πυθαγοριστάς, ὥσπερ Ἀττικούς τινας ὀνομάζομεν, ἑτέρους δὲ Ἀττικιστάς, διελὼν οὕτως πρεπόντως τὰ ὀνόματα τοὺς μὲν γνησίους εἶναι ἐνεστήσατο, [81] τοὺς δὲ ζηλωτὰς τούτων δηλοῦσθαι ἐνομοθέτησε. τῶν μὲν οὖν Πυθαγορείων κοινὴν εἶναι τὴν οὐσίαν διέταξε καὶ τὴν συμβίωσιν ἅμα διὰ παντὸς τοῦ χρόνου διατελεῖν, τοὺς δὲ ἑτέρους ἰδίας μὲν κτήσεις ἔχειν ἐκέλευσε, συνιόντας δὲ εἰς ταὐτὸ συσχολάζειν ἀλλήλοις.

καὶ οὕτω τὴν διαδοχὴν ταύτην ἀπὸ Πυθαγόρου κατ' ἀμφοτέρους τοὺς τρόπους συστῆναι. κατ' ἄλλον δὲ αὖ τρόπον δύο ἦν εἴδη τῆς φιλοσοφίας· δύο γὰρ ἦν γένη καὶ τῶν μεταχειριζομένων αὐτήν, οἱ μὲν ἀκουσματικοί, οἱ δὲ μαθηματικοί. τουτωνὶ δὲ οἱ μὲν μαθηματικοὶ ὡμολογοῦντο Πυθαγόρειοι εἶναι ὑπὸ τῶν ἑτέρων, τοὺς δὲ ἀκουσματικοὺς οὗτοι οὐχ ὡμολόγουν, οὔτε τὴν πραγματείαν αὐτῶν εἶναι Πυθαγόρου, ἀλλ' Ἱππάσου· τὸν δὲ Ἵππασον οἱ μὲν Κροτωνιάτην φασίν, οἱ δὲ Μεταποντῖνον. ἔστι δὲ ἡ μὲν τῶν

CHAPTER EIGHTEEN

*Into how many groups and on what principles Pythagoras
divided his disciples, and for what reasons he
separated them in this way.*

[80]   After this, then, let us discuss how he divided into separate groups those whom
he accepted, each according to worth. For it was not right that all should partake
equally of the same things, since they were not alike by nature. Nor was it right
that some should share in all the most prized lectures, and others should have no
share in them whatever: for this would have been most unsocial and unfair. By giving each, however, the fitting portion of the appropriate teachings, he gave assistance to all as much as possible, and preserved the rule of justice, especially
because he gave to each an appropriate kind of lecture. According to this rule,
then, he called some "Pythagoreans," other "Pythagorists" (just as we name some
"Attics," but others "Atticists") and after suitably distinguishing the names, he
identified the former as his true followers, and decreed that the latter show them-
[81]   selves emulators of these.[1] Then he ordered that the property of the Pythagoreans
be held in common, and that their common life should be permanent. The others he ordered to retain their own possessions, but to meet together to study with
one another.

And so this tradition was established from Pythagoras' time in both these
modes. But taking it from another point of view, there were two kinds of philosophy, for there were two kinds of those pursuing it: some were *acusmatici* (proba-
tioners) and others were *mathematici* (advanced students). Of these, the
mathematici are agreed to be Pythagoreans by the others, but the *mathematici* do
not agree that the *acusmatici* are Pythagoreans, or that their mode of study derived
from Pythagoras, but from Hippasus. Some say Hippasus was a Crotoniate, others
that he was a Metapontine.[2]

---

1. On the previous lines cf. Procl. in *Plat. Tim.* I, 22, 7 ff. Diehl. For the distinction between
"Attics" and "Atticists," cf. Hipp. *Ref.* 1, 2, 4, and *Schol. Theaet.* 14.5. It may go back to classical
times, but the comparison with "Atticists" can hardly antedate the first century B.C. The contrast
between *acusmatici* and *mathematici* (just below) goes back at least to Timaeus of Tauromenium.
See Burkert, *Lore and Science*, 192-208, and K. von Fritz, "Mathematiker und Akusmatiker bei den
alten Pythagoreern," *Sitzungsberichte der bayerischen Akademie der Wissenschaften*, Phil.-hist. Kl. 11
(1960).

[82] ἀκουσματικῶν φιλοσοφία ἀκούσματα ἀναπόδεικτα καὶ ἄνευ
λόγου, ὅτι οὕτως πρακτέον, καὶ τἆλλα, ὅσα παρ' ἐκείνου
ἐρρέθη, ταῦτα πειρῶνται διαφυλάττειν ὡς θεῖα δόγματα,
αὐτοὶ δὲ παρ' αὑτῶν οὔτε λέγειν προσποιοῦνται οὔτε λεκ-
τέον εἶναι, ἀλλὰ καὶ αὐτῶν ὑπολαμβάνουσι τούτους ἔχειν
βέλτιστα πρὸς φρόνησιν, οἵτινες πλεῖστα ἀκούσματα ἔσχον.
πάντα δὲ τὰ οὕτως ⟨καλούμενα⟩ ἀκούσματα διῄρηται εἰς τρία
εἴδη· τὰ μὲν γὰρ αὐτῶν τί ἐστι σημαίνει, τὰ δὲ τί μάλιστα,
τὰ δὲ τί δεῖ πράττειν ἢ μὴ πράττειν. τὰ μὲν οὖν τί ἐστι
τοιαῦτα, οἷον τί ἐστιν αἱ μακάρων νῆσοι; ἥλιος καὶ σελήνη.
τί ἐστι τὸ ἐν Δελφοῖς μαντεῖον; τετρακτύς· ὅπερ ἐστὶν ἡ
ἁρμονία, ἐν ᾗ αἱ Σειρῆνες. τὰ δὲ τί μάλιστα, οἷον τί τὸ
δικαιότατον; θύειν. τί τὸ σοφώτατον; ἀριθμός· δεύτερον δὲ
τὸ τοῖς πράγμασι τὰ ὀνόματα τιθέμενον. τί σοφώτατον τῶν
παρ' ἡμῖν; ἰατρική. τί κάλλιστον; ἁρμονία. τί κράτιστον;
γνώμη. τί ἄριστον; εὐδαιμονία. τί δὲ ἀληθέστατον λέγεται;
ὅτι πονηροὶ οἱ ἄνθρωποι. διὸ καὶ ποιητὴν Ἱπποδάμαντά
φασιν ἐπαινέσαι αὐτὸν τὸν Σαλαμίνιον, ὃς ἐποίησεν·

ὦ θεοί, πόθεν ἐστέ, πόθεν τοιοίδ' ἐγένεσθε;
ἄνθρωποι, πόθεν ἐστέ, πόθεν κακοὶ ὧδ' ἐγένεσθε;

[83] ταῦτα καὶ τοιαῦτά ἐστι τὰ τούτου τοῦ γένους ἀκούσματα·
ἕκαστον γὰρ τῶν τοιούτων μάλιστά τί ἐστιν. ἔστι δ' αὕτη ἡ
αὐτὴ τῇ τῶν ἑπτὰ σοφιστῶν λεγομένῃ σοφίᾳ. καὶ γὰρ
ἐκεῖνοι ἐζήτουν, οὐ τί ἐστι τἀγαθόν, ἀλλὰ τί μάλιστα· οὐδὲ
τί τὸ χαλεπόν, ἀλλὰ τί τὸ χαλεπώτατον (ὅτι τὸ αὑτὸν
γνῶναί ἐστιν)· οὐδὲ τί τὸ ῥᾴδιον, ἀλλὰ τί τὸ ῥᾷστον (ὅτι τὸ
ἔθει χρῆσθαι). τῇ τοιαύτῃ γὰρ σοφίᾳ μετηκολουθηκέναι ἔοικε
τὰ τοιαῦτα ἀκούσματα· πρότεροι γὰρ οὗτοι Πυθαγόρου
ἐγένοντο. τὰ δὲ τί πρακτέον ἢ οὐ πρακτέον τῶν ἀκουσμάτων
τοιαῦτά ἐστιν, οἷον ὅτι δεῖ τεκνοποιεῖσθαι (δεῖ γὰρ
ἀντικαταλιπεῖν τοὺς θεραπεύοντας τὸν θεόν), ἢ ὅτι δεῖ τὸν
δεξιὸν ὑποδεῖσθαι πρότερον, ἢ ὅτι οὐ δεῖ τὰς λεωφόρους
βαδίζειν ὁδοὺς οὐδὲ εἰς περιρραντήριον ἐμβάπτειν οὐδὲ ἐν

[82]   The philosophy of the *acusmatici* consists of oral instructions without demonstration and without argument: e.g. "in this way one must act". And the other things said by that one (Pythagoras), these they try to preserve as divine teachings.[3] They do not claim to speak for themselves; nor must one so speak, but even among themselves they suppose those have made best progress towards practical wisdom who have absorbed the fullest oral instructions. All these so-called oral instructions are divided into three kinds: for some indicate what a thing is; others, what is the best in any category; and others, what it is necessary to do or not to do.[4] Those, then, on what a thing is, are as follows: for example, what are the islands of the blessed? Sun and moon. What is the oracle at Delphi? The tetraktys, which is the harmony in which the Sirens are. Those on what is best, are, for example: what is the most just thing? To sacrifice. What is the wisest? Number; and in the second place is that which gives names to things.[5] What is the wisest of things among us? Medicine. What is the loveliest? Harmony. What is the most powerful? Intelligence. What is the best? Well-being. What is most truly said? Human beings are bad. Hence they say he (Pythagoras) praised the Salaminian poet Hippodamas who composed the following:

> O gods, whence are you?
> Whence did you become such?
> Mortals, whence are you,
> Whence did you become so wicked?

[83]   These and similar things are oral instructions of this kind; for each of these concerns what is the top of a given category. And this method is the same as that called the wisdom of the Seven Sages. For these sought not what is good, but what is the best; not what is difficult, but what is most difficult (that is, to know oneself); not what is easy, but what is easiest (that is, to indulge in a habit). For such oral instructions seem to follow the pattern of this sort of wisdom; for these sages lived before Pythagoras. The oral instructions about what must be done or what must not be done were of this sort: for example, that one must beget children (for it is necessary to leave in one's stead someone to serve God), or that one must put the right shoe on first, or that one must not walk on roads traveled by the public, or dip (the hand) in a vessel for lustral water (at sacrifices), or wash oneself in a bath-

---

2. From a parallel passage in *Comm. math. sc.* p. 76, 19-78, 8, one can see that Iamblichus has here altered the information of his sources: (a) it was the *mathematici* who were accused by the *acusmatici* of deriving from Hippasus, and (b) sections 82-86 are an insertion into a continuous passage which picks up again in 87. See von Fritz's article cited in the preceding note, and Delatte, *Études*, 272.

3. This passage through section 86 is derived originally from Aristotle's lost work *On the Pythagoreans* (cf. D.L. 8. 34); see Burkert's discussion, *Lore and Science*, 166-192.

4. On this triple division, see Burkert, *Lore and Science*, 167-9.

5. Here in the neuter, but generally in the masculine; cf. section 56 above, and Ael. *NA* 17.

[84] βαλανείῳ λούεσθαι· ἄδηλον γὰρ ἐν πᾶσι τούτοις εἰ
καθαρεύουσιν οἱ κοινωνοῦντες. καὶ ἄλλα τάδε· φορτίον μὴ
συγκαθαιρεῖν (οὐ γὰρ δεῖ αἴτιον γίνεσθαι τοῦ μὴ πονεῖν),
συνανατιθέναι δέ. χρυσὸν ἐχούσῃ μὴ πλησιάζειν ἐπὶ
τεκνοποιίᾳ. μὴ λέγειν ἄνευ φωτός. σπένδειν τοῖς θεοῖς κατὰ
τὸ οὖς τῆς κύλικος οἰωνοῦ ἕνεκεν, καὶ ὅπως μὴ ἀπὸ τοῦ
αὐτοῦ πίνηται. ἐν δακτυλίῳ μὴ φέρειν σημεῖον θεοῦ εἰκόνα,
ὅπως μὴ μιαίνηται· ἄγαλμα γάρ, ὅπερ δεῖ φυτεῦσαι ἐν τῷ
οἴκῳ. γυναῖκα οὐ δεῖ διώκειν τὴν αὐτοῦ, ἱκέτις γάρ· διὸ καὶ
ἀφ' ἑστίας ἀγόμεθα, καὶ ἡ λῆψις διὰ δεξιᾶς. μηδὲ
ἀλεκτρυόνα λευκὸν ⟨θύειν⟩· ἱκέτης γάρ, ἱερὸς τοῦ Μηνός, διὸ
[85] καὶ σημαίνουσιν ὥραν. καὶ συμβουλεύειν μηδὲν παρὰ τὸ
βέλτιστον τῷ συμβουλευομένῳ· ἱερὸν γὰρ συμβουλή.
ἀγαθὸν οἱ πόνοι, αἱ δὲ ἡδοναὶ ἐκ παντὸς τρόπου κακόν· ἐπὶ
κολάσει γὰρ ἐλθόντας δεῖ κολασθῆναι. θύειν χρὴ ἀνυπόδητον
καὶ πρὸς τὰ ἱερὰ προσιέναι. εἰς ἱερὸν οὐ δεῖ ἐκτρέπεσθαι· οὐ
γὰρ πάρεργον δεῖ ποιεῖσθαι τὸν θεόν. ὑπομένοντα καὶ ἔχοντα
τραύματα ἐν τῷ ἔμπροσθεν τελευτῆσαι ἀγαθόν, ἐναντίως δὲ
ἐναντίον. εἰς μόνα τῶν ζῴων οὐκ εἰσέρχεται ἀνθρώπου
ψυχή, οἷς θέμις ἐστὶ τυθῆναι· διὰ τοῦτο τῶν θυσίμων χρὴ
ἐσθίειν μόνον, οἷς ἂν τὸ ἐσθίειν καθήκῃ, ἄλλου δὲ μηδενὸς
ζῴου. τὰ μὲν οὖν τοιαῦτα τῶν ἀκουσμάτων ἐστί, τὰ δὲ
πλεῖστον ἔχοντα μῆκος περί τε θυσίας καθ' ἑκάστους τοὺς
καιροὺς πῶς χρὴ ποιεῖσθαι τάς τε ἄλλας ⟨θεῶν τιμὰς⟩ καὶ
περὶ μετοικήσεως τῆς ἐντεῦθεν καὶ περὶ τὰς ταφάς, πῶς δεῖ
καταθάπτεσθαι. ἐπ' ἐνίων μὲν οὖν ἐπιλέγεται τί δεῖ, οἷον ὅτι
[86] δεῖ τεκνοποιεῖσθαι ἕνεκα τοῦ καταλιπεῖν ἕτερον ἀνθ' ἑαυτοῦ
θεῶν θεραπευτήν, τοῖς δὲ οὐδεὶς λόγος πρόσεστι. καὶ ἔνια
μὲν τῶν ἐπιλεγομένων δόξει προσπεφυκέναι ἀπ' ἀρχῆς, ἔνια
δὲ πόρρω· οἷον περὶ τοῦ τὸν ἄρτον μὴ καταγνύναι, ὅτι πρὸς
τὴν ἐν ᾅδου κρίσιν οὐ συμφέρει. αἱ δὲ προστιθέμεναι
εἰκοτολογίαι περὶ τῶν τοιούτων οὐκ εἰσὶ Πυθαγορικαί, ἀλλ'
ἐνίων ἔξωθεν ἐπισοφιζομένων καὶ πειρωμένων προσάπτειν
εἰκότα λόγον, οἷον καὶ περὶ τοῦ νῦν λεχθέντος, διὰ τί οὐ δεῖ
καταγνύναι τὸν ἄρτον· οἳ μὲν γάρ φασιν ὅτι οὐ δεῖ τὸν
συνάγοντα διαλύειν (τὸ δὲ ἀρχαῖον βαρβαρικῶς πάντες ἐπὶ
ἕνα ἄρτον συνῇσαν οἱ φίλοι), οἳ δ' ὅτι οὐ δεῖ οἰωνὸν
ποιεῖσθαι τοιοῦτον ἀρχόμενον καταγνύντα καὶ συντρίβοντα.

ἅπαντα μέντοι, ὅσα περὶ τοῦ πράττειν ἢ μὴ πράττειν
διορίζουσιν, ἐστόχασται πρὸς τὸ θεῖον, καὶ ἀρχὴ αὕτη ἐστί,

ing house; for it is unclear if those sharing in all these things are clean. And others are the following: do not join in putting a burden down (for one should not be-
[84] come a cause of someone's not working), but join in taking it up. Don't have intercourse with a woman who wears gold with a view to begetting children. Do not speak without light. Pour libations to the gods from a drinking cup's handle for the sake of the omen, and so that you not drink from the same part (from which you poured out). Do not wear a god's image as signet on a ring, so that it may not be polluted; for it is an image which ought to be set up in the house. One ought not drive out one's own wife, for she is a suppliant; hence, we also lead her from the hearth, and take her by the right hand. Not to sacrifice a white cock, for he is a suppliant and sacred to the Moon ((*Mên*), which is why they indicate the time of day. And to advise nothing short of the best for one asking advice; for counsel
[85] is sacred. Labors are good, but pleasures are bad in every way; for having come for punishment, one must be punished. One should sacrifice and enter temples without shoes. One ought not turn aside into a temple; for the god must not be made secondary. It is right to die standing one's ground and having wounds in the front, but to have them on the opposite side is wrong. Only into those animals which it is lawful to sacrifice does there not enter a human soul; for this reason one may eat only sacrificial animals, such as are suitable for eating, but no other living being.[6]

Such, then, were some of his oral instructions, but those of greatest length concerned sacrifices: how one should perform them on each particular occasion, and (observe) the other prerogatives of the gods; also about transmigration of souls
[86] from the present life and about burials, and how one should be buried. In the case of some, a reason why is added; for example, one must bear children in order to leave behind another in the place of oneself for worship of the gods. But for other (instructions), no reason is added. And some of the reasons given seem to have been attached from the beginning and others later; for example, not to break bread, because it is not advantageous for judgment in Hades. The probable reasons given about such matters are not Pythagorean, but were devised by some outside the school trying to give a likely reason, as, for example, that now mentioned: why one ought not break bread; (for in the past, all who were friends came together in foreign fashion for one loaf of bread), but others say that such an omen ought not be made at the beginning meal by breaking and crushing.

All such injunctions, however, which define what is to be done or what is not to be done, are directed toward the divine, and this is a first principle, and their

---

6. This is interesting testimony contrary to reports on an absolute prohibition in Pythagoreanism against meat-eating. Cf. Burkert, *Lore and Science*, 180-2. Other authorities reconciled the contradiction by explaining that absolute abstention from living things was only required for the highest grade of Pythagoreans (the doctrine of chapter 24 is based on that assumption).

καὶ ὁ βίος ἄπας συντέτακται πρὸς τὸ ἀκολουθεῖν τῷ θεῷ, καὶ
[87] ὁ λόγος αὐτὸς ταύτης ἐστὶ τῆς φιλοσοφίας. γελοῖον γὰρ
ποιοῦσιν ἄνθρωποι ἄλλοθέν ποθεν ζητοῦντες τὸ εὖ ἢ παρὰ
τῶν θεῶν, καὶ ὅμοιον ὥσπερ ἂν εἴ τις ἐν βασιλευομένῃ χώρᾳ
τῶν πολιτῶν τινὰ ὕπαρχον θεραπεύοι, ἀμελήσας αὐτοῦ τοῦ
πάντων ἄρχοντος· τοιοῦτον γὰρ οἴονται ποιεῖν καὶ τοὺς
ἀνθρώπους. ἐπεὶ γὰρ ἔστι τε θεὸς καὶ οὗτος πάντων κύριος,
δεῖν ὁμολογεῖται παρὰ τοῦ κυρίου τὸ ἀγαθὸν αἰτεῖν· πάντες
γάρ, οὓς μὲν ἂν φιλῶσι καὶ οἷς ἂν χαίρωσι, τούτοις διδόασι
τἀγαθά, πρὸς οὓς δὲ ἐναντίως ἔχουσι, τὰ ἐναντία.

τούτων μὲν αὕτη καὶ τοιαύτη σοφία. ἦν δέ τις Ἱππομέδων ['Αργεῖος] 'Ασινεὺς Πυθαγόρειος τῶν ἀκουσματικῶν,
ὃς ἔλεγεν ὅτι πάντων τούτων ἐκεῖνος λόγους καὶ ἀποδείξεις
εἶπεν, ἀλλὰ διὰ τὸ παραδεδόσθαι διὰ πολλῶν καὶ ἀεὶ
ἀργοτέρων τὸν μὲν λόγον περιῃρῆσθαι, λελεῖφθαι δὲ αὐτὰ τὰ
προβλήματα. οἱ δὲ περὶ τὰ μαθήματα τῶν Πυθαγορείων
τούτους τε ὁμολογοῦσιν εἶναι Πυθαγορείους, καὶ αὐτοί
φασιν ἔτι μᾶλλον, καὶ ἃ λέγουσιν αὐτοί, ἀληθῆ εἶναι. τὴν δὲ
αἰτίαν τῆς ἀνομοιότητος τοιαύτην γενέσθαι φασίν.
ἀφικέσθαι τὸν Πυθαγόραν ἐξ 'Ιωνίας καὶ Σάμου κατὰ τὴν
[88] Πολυκράτους τυραννίδα, ἀκμαζούσης 'Ιταλίας, καὶ γενέσθαι
συνήθεις αὐτῷ τοὺς πρώτους ἐν ταῖς πόλεσι. τούτων δὲ τοῖς
μὲν πρεσβυτέροις καὶ ἀσχόλοις διὰ τὸ ἐν πολιτικοῖς
πράγμασι κατέχεσθαι, ὡς χαλεπὸν ὂν διὰ τῶν μαθημάτων
καὶ ἀποδείξεων ἐντυγχάνειν, ψιλῶς διαλεχθῆναι, ἡγούμενον
οὐδὲν ἧττον ὠφελεῖσθαι καὶ ἄνευ τῆς αἰτίας εἰδότας τί δεῖ
πράττειν, ὥσπερ καὶ οἱ ἰατρευόμενοι, οὐ προσακούοντες διὰ
τί αὐτοῖς ἕκαστα πρακτέον, οὐδὲν ἧττον τυγχάνουσι τῆς
ὑγείας· ὅσοις δὲ νεωτέροις ἐνετύγχανε καὶ δυναμένοις πονεῖν
καὶ μανθάνειν, τοῖς τοιούτοις δι' ἀποδείξεως καὶ τῶν
μαθημάτων ἐνετύγχανεν. αὐτοὶ μὲν οὖν εἶναι ἀπὸ τούτων,
ἐκείνους δὲ ἀπὸ τῶν ἑτέρων. περὶ δ' 'Ιππάσου μάλιστα, ὡς
ἦν μὲν τῶν Πυθαγορείων, διὰ δὲ τὸ ἐξενεγκεῖν καὶ
γράψασθαι πρώτως σφαῖραν τὴν ἐκ τῶν δώδεκα πενταγώνων
ἀπώλετο κατὰ θάλατταν ὡς ἀσεβήσας, δόξαν δὲ λάβοι ὡς
εὑρών, εἶναι δὲ πάντα ἐκείνου τοῦ ἀνδρός· προσαγορεύουσι

[87] whole way of life is arranged for following the deity, and this is the rationale of their philosophy. For human beings act ridiculously in seeking the good anywhere else than from the gods, just like someone who pays court to a subordinate governor of the citizens in a country ruled by a king, neglecting him who is the ruler of all; for just so do they think humans behave.[7] For since there is a god, and he is lord of all, it is agreed one ought to ask for the good from the lord. For all give good things to those whom they cherish and with whom they are pleased, but to those toward whom they are oppositely disposed, they give the opposite.[8]

Such, indeed, is the very wisdom of these men (the *acusmatici*). There was a certain Hippomedon, an Argive from Asine,[9] a Pythagorean of the *acusmatici*, who said that that one (Pythagoras) declared the reasons for and gave demonstrations of all these precepts, but because they were handed down through many intermediaries, who became progressively lazier, the reason was omitted, while the bare precepts remained. And they who are concerned with the mathematical doctrines of the Pythagoreans (the *mathematici*), agree that these (the *acusmatici*) are Pythagoreans,[10] but they claim even more strongly, that what they themselves say is true.

[88] They say that the following was the cause of the dissimilarity (between the groups). When Pythagoras arrived from Ionia and Samos during Polycrates' tyranny, while Italy was flourishing, the foremost men in the cities became well acquainted with him. To the older amongst these, who were busy with civic affairs, he spoke simply, since it was difficult to get an audience for scientific lessons and demonstrations; he considered it no less beneficial for them to do what was necessary without knowing the cause, just as those medically treated, even when not learning the reason why each thing must be done to them, no less attain health. But all he met who were younger and able to work hard and to learn, to such he spoke with demonstration and scientific lessons. They themselves (the *mathematici*), then, descend from these, but those (the *acusmatici*) descend from the others.

On the matter of Hippasus in particular: he was a Pythagorean, but because of having disclosed and given a diagram for the first time of the sphere from the twelve pentagons,[11] he perished in the sea since he committed impiety.[12] He acquired fame as having made the discovery, but all the discoveries were of that

---

7. This image is also used by Philo, *Decal.* 61 with specific reference to the Great King and his satraps, indicating, presumably, a common source (perhaps Aristotle himself).

8. This paragraph is repeated virtually verbatim in section 137 below.

9. The mss. have here Ἀργεῖος Ἀσινεύς. Deubner brackets Ἀργεῖος; Nauck suggests Ἀργεῖος ἢ Ἀσινεύς. The Ἀργεῖος may have been inserted to agree with the list of Pythagoreans at the end of *VP* where Hippomedon is listed as an Argive.

10. This seems to refer back directly to section 81, indicating that all between is an insertion (or insertions). All that follows down to the beginning of section 89, is repeated in *Comm. math. sc.* chap. 25, p. 76, 24 ff. Festa.

11. The parallel passage in *Comm. math. sc.* has "hexagons" (p. 77, 20) which is incorrect. Neither passage seems to be copied from the other, but both are probably from the same work (Nicomachus?)

[89] γὰρ οὕτω τὸν Πυθαγόραν καὶ οὐ καλοῦσιν ὀνόματι. λέγουσι δὲ οἱ Πυθαγόρειοι ἐξενηνέχθαι γεωμετρίαν οὕτως. ἀποβαλεῖν τινα τὴν οὐσίαν τῶν Πυθαγορείων· ὡς δὲ τοῦτο ἠτύχησε, δοθῆναι αὐτῷ χρηματίσασθαι ἀπὸ γεωμετρίας. ἐκαλεῖτο δὲ ἡ γεωμετρία πρὸς Πυθαγόρου ἱστορία. περὶ μὲν οὖν τῆς διαφορᾶς ἑκατέρας τῆς πραγματείας καὶ ἑκατέρων τῶν ἀνδρῶν τῶν ἀκροωμένων Πυθαγόρου ταῦτα παρειλήφαμεν· τοὺς γὰρ εἴσω σινδόνος καὶ ἔξω ἀκροωμένους τοῦ Πυθαγόρου καὶ τοὺς μετὰ τοῦ ὁρᾶν ἀκούοντας ἢ ἄνευ τοῦ ὁρᾶν καὶ τοὺς εἴσω καὶ ἔξω διωρισμένους οὐκ ἄλλους ἢ τοὺς εἰρημένους ὑπολαμβάνειν προσήκει, καὶ τοὺς πολιτικοὺς δὲ καὶ οἰκονομικοὺς καὶ νομοθετικοὺς ἐν τοῖς αὐτοῖς ὑποτίθεσθαι χρή.

[89] man, for so they refer to Pythagoras, and do not call him by his name. The Pythagoreans say that geometry was revealed in this manner: some Pythagorean lost his property and, since this happened, he was allowed to make a profit from geometry. Geometry was called by Pythagoras "inquiry" (*historia*).[13]

About the difference, then, between each of the two types of philosophical study, and between each of the groups of followers of Pythagoras, we have ascertained these things: those who heard Pythagoras either within or without the curtain, those who heard him accompanied with seeing, or without seeing him, and who are divided into the "in" (esoteric) and "out" (exoteric) groups are properly not to be considered other than those already mentioned; and the political, economic, and legislative divisions are to be ranked as subdivisions of the same groups.

---

12. On Hippasus, see Burkert, *Lore and Science*, 206-8. The story of his drowning is not attested elsewhere, but seems to be known to Plutarch (*Num.* 22,4).

13. On Pythagorean geometry, see Burkert, *Lore and Science*, 447-465.

[90] Καθόλου δὲ εἰδέναι ἄξιον, ὡς πολλὰς ὁδοὺς Πυθαγόρας παιδείας ἀνεῦρε καὶ κατὰ τὴν οἰκείαν φύσιν ἑκάστου καὶ δύναμιν παρεδίδου τῆς σοφίας τὴν ἐπιβάλλουσαν μοῖραν. τεκμήριον δὲ μέγιστον· ὅτε γὰρ Ἄβαρις ὁ Σκύθης ἐξ Ὑπερβορέων, ἄπειρος τῆς Ἑλληνικῆς παιδείας ὢν καὶ ἀμύητος καὶ τῇ ἡλικίᾳ προβεβηκώς, ἦλθε, τότε οὐ διὰ ποικίλων αὐτὸν εἰσήγαγε θεωρημάτων, ἀλλ' ἀντὶ τῆς πενταετοῦς σιωπῆς καὶ τῆς ἐν τῷ τοσούτῳ χρόνῳ ἀκροάσεως καὶ τῶν ἄλλων βασάνων ἀθρόως αὐτὸν ἐπιτήδειον ἀπειργάσατο πρὸς τὴν ἀκρόασιν τῶν αὐτῷ δογματιζομένων, καὶ τὸ περὶ φύσεως σύγγραμμα καὶ ἄλλο τὸ περὶ θεῶν ὡς ἐν βραχυτάτοις αὐτὸν [91] ἀνεδίδαξεν. ἦλθε μὲν γὰρ Ἄβαρις ἀπὸ Ὑπερβορέων, ἱερεὺς τοῦ ἐκεῖ Ἀπόλλωνος, πρεσβύτης καθ' ἡλικίαν καὶ τὰ ἱερατικὰ σοφώτατος, ἀπὸ τῆς Ἑλλάδος ὑποστρέφων εἰς τὰ ἴδια, ἵνα τὸν ἀγερθέντα χρυσὸν τῷ θεῷ ἀποθῆται εἰς τὸ ἐν Ὑπερβορέοις ἱερόν. γενόμενος δὲ ἐν παρόδῳ κατὰ τὴν Ἰταλίαν καὶ τὸν Πυθαγόραν ἰδὼν καὶ μάλιστα εἰκάσας τῷ θεῷ, οὗπερ ἦν ἱερεύς, καὶ πιστεύσας μὴ ἄλλον εἶναι, μηδὲ ἄνθρωπον ὅμοιον ἐκείνῳ, ἀλλ' αὐτὸν ὄντως τὸν Ἀπόλλωνα, ἔκ τε ὧν ἑώρα περὶ αὐτὸν σεμνωμάτων καὶ ἐξ ὧν προεγίνωσκεν ὁ ἱερεὺς γνωρισμάτων, Πυθαγόρᾳ ἀπέδωκεν ὀιστόν, ὃν ἔχων ἀπὸ τοῦ ἱεροῦ ἐξῆλθε, χρήσιμον αὐτῷ ἐσόμενον πρὸς τὰ συμπίπτοντα δυσμήχανα κατὰ τὴν τοσαύτην ἄλην. ἐποχούμενος γὰρ αὐτῷ καὶ τὰ ἄβατα διέβαινεν, οἷον ποταμοὺς καὶ λίμνας καὶ τέλματα καὶ ὄρη καὶ τὰ τοιαῦτα, καὶ προσλαλῶν, ὡς λόγος, καθαρμούς τε ἐπετέλει καὶ λοιμοὺς ἀπεδίωκε καὶ ἀνέμους ἀπὸ τῶν εἰς τοῦτο ἀξιουσῶν πόλεων βοηθὸν αὐτὸν γενέσθαι. [92] Λακεδαίμονα γοῦν παρειλήφαμεν μετὰ τὸν ὑπ' ἐκείνου γενόμενον αὐτῇ καθαρμὸν μηκέτι λοιμῶξαι, πολλάκις πρότερον τούτῳ τῷ παθήματι περιπεσοῦσαν διὰ τὴν δυστραπελίαν τοῦ τόπου, καθ' ὃν ᾤκισται, τῶν Ταϋγέτων ὀρῶν πνῖγος ἀξιόλογον αὐτῇ παρεχόντων διὰ τὸ ὑπερκεῖσθαι, καὶ Κρήτης Κνωσσόν. καὶ ἄλλα τοιαῦτα τεκμήρια ἱστορεῖται τῆς τοῦ Ἀβάριδος δυνάμεως. δεξάμενος δὲ Πυθαγόρας τὸν ὀιστὸν καὶ μὴ ξενισθεὶς πρὸς τοῦτο, μηδὲ τὴν αἰτίαν ἐπερωτήσας δι' ἣν ἐπέδωκεν, ἀλλ' ὡς ἂν ὄντως ὁ θεὸς αὐτὸς ὤν, ἰδίᾳ καὶ αὐτὸς ἀποσπάσας τὸν Ἄβαριν τόν τε μηρὸν τὸν ἑαυτοῦ ἐπέδειξε χρύσεον, γνώρισμα παρέχων

CHAPTER NINETEEN

Pythagoras discovered many ways of instruction useful to human beings
In this connection we hear of the visit of Abaris to him,
and how he led him to the summit of wisdom
through different modes of education.

[90]   In general it is worth knowing that Pythagoras discovered many ways of teaching and training, and transmitted the appropriate portion of wisdom according to each one's own nature and ability. And the greatest evidence is this: when Abaris the Scythian came from the Hyperboreans,[1] inexperienced and uninitiated in Hellenic learning, and advanced in age, he (Pythagoras) did not instruct him at that time by means of complex theories. Instead of the five year silence, a lengthy course of instruction and the other tests, he made him immediately fit for learning his doctrines, and taught him in the shortest way possible his treatises *On Nature* and *On the Gods*. For Abaris came from the Hyperboreans, a priest of Apollo
[91] there, an old man and most wise in sacred matters. He was returning from Hellas to his own people, in order to deposit the gold that had been gathered for the god in the temple of the Hyperboreans. Passing through Italy and seeing Pythagoras, he recognized in him a particular likeness to the god whose priest he was. Indeed he believed him to be truly none other than Apollo himself, and not just a mortal resembling that god. In consequence of the greatness which he saw in Pythagoras and the tokens of recognition which in his priestly capacity[2] he recognized beforehand, he gave to Pythagoras an arrow which he had when he left his temple,[3] and which would be useful to him in the many difficulties encountered on a very long journey. For riding on it he crossed impassible places; for example, rivers, lakes, swamps, mountains and the like. And talking to the arrow, so goes the story, he performed purifications and drove off plagues and winds from the cities which
[92] asked for his assistance. At any rate, we have ascertained that Lacedaemon after being purified by him never suffered from plague again; formerly it was often afflicted by this misfortune because of the unhealthiness of the area in which it was situated (since the Taygetus range, towering over the city, provides a notable de-

---

1. On Abaris, see sections 140-41 and 215-18, and Porph. *VP,* 28-9. The legend of Abaris goes back to Herodotus IV, 36, though he makes no connection with Pythagoreans: that perhaps derives from either Heraclides of Pontus, or Hermippus.

2. Reading ὡς for ὁ with Wilamowitz.

3. In section 140 below, it is stated that Pythagoras *took* the arrow from Abaris. There may be a conflict of sources here.

τοῦ μὴ διεψεῦσθαι, καὶ τὰ καθ᾽ ἕκαστα τῶν ἐν τῷ ἱερῷ κειμένων ἐξαριθμησάμενος αὐτῷ καὶ πίστιν ἱκανὴν παρασχών, ὡς οὐκ εἴη κακῶς εἰκάσας, προσθείς τε ὅτι ἐπὶ θεραπείᾳ καὶ εὐεργεσίᾳ τῶν ἀνθρώπων ἥκοι, καὶ διὰ τοῦτο ἀνθρωπόμορφος, ἵνα μὴ ξενιζόμενοι πρὸς τὸ ὑπερέχον ταράσσωνται καὶ τὴν παρ᾽ αὐτῷ μάθησιν ἀποφεύγωσιν· ἐκέλευσέ τε μένειν αὐτοῦ καὶ συνδιορθοῦν τοὺς ἐντυγχάνοντας, τὸν δὲ χρυσόν, ὃν συνήγειρε, κοινῶσαι τοῖς ἐπιτηδείοις, ὅσοιπερ ἐτύγχανον οὕτως ὑπὸ τοῦ λόγου ἠγμένοι, ὥστε βεβαιοῦν τὸ δόγμα τὸ λέγον "κοινὰ τὰ [93] φίλων" δι᾽ ἔργου. οὕτω δὴ καταμείναντι αὐτῷ, ὃ νῦν δὴ ἐλέγομεν, φυσιολογίαν τε καὶ θεολογίαν ἐπιτετμημένην παρέδωκε, καὶ ἀντὶ τῆς διὰ τῶν θυσιῶν ἱεροσκοπίας τὴν διὰ τῶν ἀριθμῶν πρόγνωσιν παρέδωκεν, ἡγούμενος ταύτην καθαρωτέραν εἶναι καὶ θειοτέραν καὶ τοῖς οὐρανίοις τῶν θεῶν ἀριθμοῖς οἰκειοτέραν, ἄλλα τε τὰ ἁρμόζοντα τῷ Ἀβάριδι παρέδωκεν ἐπιτηδεύματα. ἀλλ᾽ οὗ δὴ ἕνεκα ὁ παρὼν λόγος, ἐπ᾽ ἐκεῖνο πάλιν ἐπανέλθωμεν, ὡς ἄρα ἄλλους ἄλλως, ὡς ἔχει ἕκαστος φύσεως καὶ δυνάμεως, ἐπανορθοῦν ἐπειρᾶτο. πάντα μὲν οὖν τὰ τοιαῦτα οὔτε παρεδόθη εἰς τοὺς ἀνθρώπους, οὔτε τὰ μνημονευόμενα ῥᾴδιον διελθεῖν· ὀλίγα [94] δὲ καὶ τὰ γνωριμώτατα διέλθωμεν δείγματα τῆς Πυθαγορικῆς ἀγωγῆς καὶ ὑπομνήματα τῶν ὑπαρχόντων τοῖς ἀνδράσιν ἐκείνοις ἐπιτηδευμάτων.

gree of stifling heat); and also he purified Knossos in Crete. And other such signs of Abaris' power are on record.

When Pythagoras received the arrow, he was neither astonished nor asked the reason why he gave it, but as if he were truly the god himself, he took Abaris aside in private, and showed him his golden thigh,[4] giving a sign that he (Abaris) had not been mistaken. After enumerating for him each of the things deposited in the temple, and providing sufficient guarantee that he had not made a wrong comparison, he added that he came for the care and benefit of human beings, and that it was for this reason that he had taken on human form, lest, being astonished at his superiority, they be disturbed and avoid his teaching. He bade Abaris remain there with him and join in the improvement of those who came their way, and share the gold which he collected with those suitable, those who were so guided by reason that they made good by deeds his doctrine which is: "common are

[93] the things of friends." So then, when Abaris agreed to remain with him, as we have just now said, he taught him his doctrine of nature and theology in abridged form. Instead of divination by the entrails of sacrificed animals, he taught him fore-knowledge through numbers, believing this to be purer, more divine, and more suitable to the heavenly number of the gods; and he also taught other studies suitable to Abaris' interests. But to return to the topic for which the present account was entered upon: he attempted to improve others in various ways, each according to their natural constitution and ability. Details of all this have not been

[94] handed down to later human beings, nor is it easy to recount what has been recorded; but let us recount a few, the best known examples of the Pythagorean training, together with some accounts of the pursuits of those men.

---

4. The legend of the golden thigh appears to derive from Aristotle (Apollon. *Mir.* 6), but is elaborated by Hermippus (D.L. 8. 11). It may be a confused recollection of initiation rituals; see Burkert, *Lore and Science* 159-60.

Πρῶτον μὲν οὖν ἐν τῷ λαμβάνειν τὴν διάπειραν ἐσκόπει
εἰ δύνανται ἐχεμυθεῖν (τούτῳ γὰρ δὴ καὶ ἐχρῆτο τῷ ὀνόματι)
καὶ καθεώρα εἰ μανθάνοντες ὅσα ἂν ἀκούσωσιν οἷοί τέ εἰσι
σιωπᾶν καὶ διαφυλάττειν, ἔπειτα εἴ εἰσιν αἰδήμονες·
ἐποιεῖτό τε πλείονα σπουδὴν τοῦ σιωπᾶν ἤπερ τοῦ λαλεῖν.
ἐσκόπει δὲ καὶ τὰ ἄλλα πάντα, μὴ ἄρα πρὸς πάθος ἢ
ἐπιθυμίαν ἀκρατήτως ἐπτόηνται, οὐ παρέργως τὰ τοιαῦτα
ἀεὶ ἐπιβλέπων, οἷον πῶς πρὸς ὀργὴν ἔχουσιν ἢ πῶς πρὸς
ἐπιθυμίαν, ἢ εἰ φιλόνικοί εἰσιν ἢ φιλότιμοι, ἢ πῶς πρὸς
φιλονεικίαν ἔχουσιν ἢ πῶς πρὸς φιλίαν. εἰ δὲ πάντα
ἀκριβῶς αὐτῷ ἐπιβλέποντι ἐξηρτυμένοι ἐφαίνοντο τοῖς
ἀγαθοῖς ἤθεσι, τότε περὶ εὐμαθείας καὶ μνήμης ἐσκόπει·
πρῶτον μὲν εἰ δύνανται ταχέως καὶ σαφῶς παρακολουθεῖν
τοῖς λεγομένοις, ἔπειτα εἰ παρέπεταί τις αὐτοῖς ἀγάπησις
καὶ σωφροσύνη πρὸς τὰ διδασκόμενα. ἐπεσκόπει γὰρ πῶς
[95] ἔχουσι φύσεως πρὸς ἡμέρωσιν, ἐκάλει δὲ τοῦτο κατάρτυσιν.
πολέμιον δὲ ἡγεῖτο τὴν ἀγριότητα πρὸς τοιαύτην διαγωγήν·
ἀκολουθεῖν γὰρ ἀγριότητι ἀναίδειαν, ἀναισχυντίαν,
ἀκολασίαν, ἀκαιρίαν, δυσμάθειαν, ἀναρχίαν, ἀτιμίαν καὶ τὰ
ἀκόλουθα, πραότητι δὲ καὶ ἡμερότητι τὰ ἐναντία. ἐν μὲν οὖν
τῇ διαπείρᾳ τοιαῦτα ἐπεσκόπει καὶ πρὸς ταῦτα ἤσκει τοὺς
μανθάνοντας, τούς τε ἁρμόζοντας τοῖς ἀγαθοῖς τῆς παρ'
ἑαυτῷ σοφίας ἐνέκρινε καὶ οὕτως ἐπὶ τὰς ἐπιστήμας ἀνάγειν
ἐπειρᾶτο· εἰ δὲ ἀνάρμοστον κατίδοι τινά, ὥσπερ ἀλλόφυλόν
τινα καὶ ὀθνεῖον ἀπήλαυνε.

CHAPTER TWENTY

*What the particular practices of Pythagorean philosophy were, and
how Pythagoras imparted them, and how he trained those who
from time to time partook of his philosophy.*

First, then, in testing (those who came to him) he considered whether they
were able to "hold their talk"[1] for this was the term he used). And he observed
whether they were able to keep silence and to preserve carefully whatever they
heard while learning. Next (he observed) if they were modest; for he made much
more ado about silence than talking. He also considered all other aspects of their
personality: that they not be excited immoderately by feeling or desire, and he always examined thoroughly how, for example, they were disposed to anger or desire, or if they were fond of victory or honor, or how, they were disposed to rivalry,
or to friendship. And if, while he observed carefully all these things, they appeared furnished with good characters, he then examined their readiness in
learning and memory: first, if they were able to follow his instructions quickly and
[95] clearly; next, if they showed enthusiasm and good sense in regard to what was
taught. For he observed closely how they were disposed by nature to civilizing influence, and he called this "training."[2] But he believed boorishness resistant to
such a course of instruction: for shamelessness, impudence, intemperance, tact-
lessness, slowness in learning, lawlessness, dishonor, and things consistent with
these, accompany boorishness, but things opposite accompany mildness and gentleness. In the first period, then, he watched closely for such indications, and exercised his pupils in these traits. And those adapted to the benefits of his own
wisdom he accepted, and so tried to lead them up to the sciences. But if he saw
someone not fitting in, he drove him off like some alien or stranger.

---

1. Pythagorean ἐχεμυθία is referred to by Plutarch, *Num.* 8, *Quaest. conu.* 728 e, Lucian, *Gall.*
2, and Ath. 7.308 d. See also Burkert, *Lore and Science.* 178-79.

2. Κατάρτυσις ("training") is used by Hippodamos, *On the State* (p. 100, 22 Thesleff), but otherwise attested only in Plu. *Them.* 2.

119

Περὶ δὲ τῶν ἐπιτηδευμάτων, ἃ παρέδωκε δι' ὅλης ἡμέρας τοῖς ἑταίροις, μετὰ τοῦτο φράσω· κατὰ γὰρ τὴν ὑφήγησιν [96] αὐτοῦ ὧδε ἔπρασσον οἱ ὑπ' αὐτοῦ ὁδηγούμενοι. τοὺς μὲν ἑωθινοὺς περιπάτους ἐποιοῦντο οἱ ἄνδρες οὗτοι κατὰ μόνας τε καὶ εἰς τοιούτους τόπους, ἐν οἷς συνέβαινεν ἠρεμίαν τε καὶ ἡσυχίαν εἶναι σύμμετρον, ὅπου τε ἱερὰ καὶ ἄλση καὶ ἄλλη τις θυμηδία. ᾤοντο γὰρ δεῖν μὴ πρότερόν τινι συντυγχάνειν, πρὶν ἢ τὴν ἰδίαν ψυχὴν καταστήσουσι καὶ συναρμόσονται τὴν διάνοιαν· ἁρμόδιον δὲ εἶναι τῇ καταστάσει τῆς διανοίας τὴν τοιαύτην ἡσυχίαν. τὸ γὰρ εὐθὺς ἀναστάντας εἰς τοὺς ὄχλους ὠθεῖσθαι θορυβῶδες ὑπειλήφεισαν. διὸ δὴ πάντες οἱ Πυθαγόρειοι τοὺς ἱεροπρεπεστάτους τόπους ἀεὶ ἐξελέγοντο. μετὰ δὲ τὸν ἑωθινὸν περίπατον τότε πρὸς ἀλλήλους ἐνετύγχανον, μάλιστα μὲν ἐν ἱεροῖς, εἰ δὲ μή γε, ἐν ὁμοίοις τόποις. ἐχρῶντο δὲ τῷ καιρῷ τούτῳ πρός τε διδασκαλίας καὶ μαθήσεις καὶ πρὸς τὴν τῶν ἠθῶν ἐπανόρθωσιν. μετὰ δὲ τὴν τοιαύτην διατριβὴν ἐπὶ τὴν [97] τῶν σωμάτων ἐτρέποντο θεραπείαν. ἐχρῶντο δὲ ἀλείμμασί τε καὶ δρόμοις οἱ πλεῖστοι, ἐλάττονες καὶ πάλαις ἔν τε κήποις καὶ ἐν ἄλσεσιν, οἳ δὲ καὶ ἁλτηροβολίᾳ ἢ χειρονομίᾳ, πρὸς τὰς τῶν σωμάτων ἰσχῦς τὰ εὔθετα ἐπιτηδεύοντες ἐκλέγεσθαι γυμνάσια. ἀρίστῳ δὲ ἐχρῶντο ἄρτῳ καὶ μέλιτι ἢ κηρίῳ, οἴνου δὲ μεθ' ἡμέραν οὐ μετεῖχον. τὸν δὲ μετὰ τὸ ἄριστον χρόνον περὶ τὰς πολιτικὰς οἰκονομίας κατεγίνοντο, περί τε τὰς ἐξωτικὰς καὶ τὰς ξενικάς, διὰ τὴν τῶν νόμων πρόσταξιν· πάντα γὰρ ἐν ταῖς μετ' ἄριστον ὥραις ἐβούλοντο διοικεῖν. δείλης δὲ γινομένης εἰς τοὺς περιπάτους πάλιν ὁρμᾶν, οὐχ ὁμοίως κατ' ἰδίαν, ὥσπερ ἐν τῷ ἑωθινῷ περιπάτῳ, ἀλλὰ σύνδυο καὶ σύντρεις ποιεῖσθαι τὸν περίπατον, ἀναμιμνησκομένους τὰ μαθήματα καὶ ἐγγυμνα-

CHAPTER TWENTY-ONE

Concerning the procedures which Pythagoras established and
taught his disciples to perform assiduously throughout
the whole day, and certain exhortations
which accord with those procedures.

After this, I will speak about the procedures which he taught his disciples to be observed throughout the whole day. For those under his guidance, according to his instruction, acted as follows:[1] they made their morning walks alone and in

[96]

such places where there was suitable calmness and stillness, and where there were temples and sacred groves and anything else that gladdened the heart. For they thought it necessary not to meet anyone until they set their own soul in order and were composed in their intellect; and such quietness is agreeable to the composure of the intellect. For to be shoved together in crowds immediately on arising they considered disturbing. Thus all Pythagoreans always selected places most becoming the sacred. And after the morning walk, they associated with one another, especially in temples; but if not, at least in similar places. They used this time for instruction and lessons, and for the improvement of their characters.

[97]

After such study, they turned to the care of their bodies. Most used oil-rubs and took part in foot-races; a lesser number wrestled in gardens and groves: some engaged in long-jumping[2] or in shadow boxing, taking care to choose exercises well-adapted to their bodily strength. For lunch they ate bread and honey or honeycomb, but during the day they did not drink wine. After lunch they engaged in civic transactions, those concerned with foreigners and guests, because of the laws' command; for they wished to manage everything in the time after lunch. But when it was late afternoon, they were again eager for walks, not privately like the morning walk, but two or three walked together, recalling their lessons, and training themselves in noble pursuits.

---

1. This chapter, with its emphasis on "the Pythagoreans" rather than Pythagoras himself, is possibly borrowed, as Rohde suggested, *RhM* 27 (1872) 35-36, from Aristoxenus' *Pythagorean Sayings* (referred to below in section 101).

2. Ἀλτηροβολία is a *hapax legomenon*; from the practice of using ἀλτῆρες, weights held in the hands to give impetus in jumping. This is an emendation of Arcerius for ἀρτηροβολία (in the mss.) which has no obvious meaning.

[98] ζομένους τοῖς καλοῖς ἐπιτηδεύμασι. μετὰ δὲ τὸν περίπατον
λουτρῷ χρῆσθαι, λουσαμένους τε ἐπὶ τὰ συσσίτια ἀπαντᾶν·
ταῦτα δ' εἶναι μὴ πλεῖον ἢ δέκα ἀνθρώπους συνευωχεῖσθαι.
ἀθροισθέντων δὲ τῶν συσσιτούντων γίνεσθαι σπονδάς τε καὶ
θυσίας θυημάτων τε καὶ λιβανωτοῦ. ἔπειτα ἐπὶ τὸ δεῖπνον
χωρεῖν, ὡς πρὸ ἡλίου δύσεως ἀποδεδειπνηκέναι. χρῆσθαι δὲ
καὶ οἴνῳ καὶ μάζῃ καὶ ἄρτῳ καὶ ὄψῳ καὶ λαχάνοις ἑφθοῖς τε
καὶ ὠμοῖς. παρατίθεσθαι δὲ κρέα ζῴων θυσίμων [ἱερείων],
τῶν δὲ θαλασσίων ὄψων σπανίως [χρῆσθαι]· εἶναι γάρ τινα
αὐτῶν δι' αἰτίας τινὰς οὐ χρήσιμα πρὸς τὸ χρῆσθαι. μετὰ δὲ
[99] τόδε τὸ δεῖπνον ἐγίνοντο σπονδαί, ἔπειτα ἀνάγνωσις
ἐγίνετο. ἔθος δ' ἦν τὸν μὲν νεώτατον ἀναγινώσκειν, τὸν δὲ
πρεσβύτατον ἐπιστατεῖν ὃ δεῖ ἀναγινώσκειν καὶ ὡς δεῖ. ἐπεὶ
δὲ μέλλοιεν ἀπιέναι, σπονδὴν αὐτοῖς ἐνέχει ὁ οἰνοχόος,
σπεισάντων δὲ ὁ πρεσβύτατος παρήγγελλε τάδε· ἥμερον
φυτὸν καὶ ἔγκαρπον μήτε βλάπτειν μήτε φθείρειν, ὡσαύτως
δὲ καὶ ζῷον, ὃ μὴ πέφυκε βλαβερὸν τῷ ἀνθρωπίνῳ γένει,
μήτε βλάπτειν μήτε φθείρειν. ἔτι πρὸς τούτοις περί τε τοῦ
[100] θείου καὶ περὶ τοῦ δαιμονίου καὶ περὶ τοῦ ἡρωικοῦ γένους
εὔφημόν τε καὶ ἀγαθὴν ἔχειν διάνοιαν, ὡσαύτως δὲ καὶ περὶ
γονέων τε καὶ εὐεργετῶν διανοεῖσθαι, νόμῳ τε βοηθεῖν καὶ
ἀνομίᾳ πολεμεῖν. τούτων δὲ ῥηθέντων ἀπιέναι ἕκαστον εἰς
οἶκον. ἐσθῆτι δὲ χρῆσθαι λευκῇ καὶ καθαρᾷ, ὡσαύτως δὲ καὶ
στρώμασι λευκοῖς τε καὶ καθαροῖς. εἶναι δὲ τὰ στρώματα
ἱμάτια λινᾶ· κωδίοις γὰρ οὐ χρῆσθαι. περὶ δὲ θήραν οὐ
δοκιμάζειν καταγίνεσθαι, οὐδὲ χρῆσθαι τοιούτῳ γυμνασίῳ.
τὰ μὲν οὖν ἐφ' ἡμέρᾳ ἑκάστῃ τῷ πλήθει τῶν ἀνδρῶν
παραδιδόμενα εἴς τε τροφὴν καὶ τὴν τοῦ βίου ἀναγωγὴν
τοιαῦτα ἦν.

[98] After the walk, they would take a bath, and having washed themselves, they met in common meals; in these no more than ten men dined together. When the diners came together, there were libations and offerings of aromatic herbs and incense. Then they went to dinner, so as to finish dining before the sun's setting. And they consumed wine, barley-cake, bread, relishes, boiled and raw vegetables. Meat of sacrificial animals was set before them, but they rarely ate fish:[3] for certain reasons, some of these were not proper for consumption. After dinner, libations [99] were again made. Then there was a public reading; it was a custom for the youngest to read aloud, and the oldest was in charge of what was to be read, and how it was to be read. And when they were about to leave, the cup-bearer poured out a libation for them, and when the libations were made, the oldest proclaimed these things: not to harm or destroy a cultivated and fruitful plant, and in like manner, not to harm or destroy a living being harmless by nature to the human race. In [100] addition to these proclamations, (they were ordered) to have a reverent and good attitude to the divine, daemonic, and heroic orders of being, and to think in like manner about parents and benefactors; to assist the law, and to war with lawlessness. After this exhortation, each departed to his house. They also wore white and clean clothing, and, in like manner, they used white and clean bed coverings. Clothes and bed coverings were of linen; for they did not use sheepskin.[4] They did not approve of hunting, nor did they indulge in such activity. Such, then were the things transmitted each day to the association of the men for their nurture, and for the elevation[5] of their way of life.

---

3. Abstinence from certain fish (including τρίγλη [red mullet], ἀκαλήφη [sea anemone], μελάνουρος [blacktail]) is among the Pythagorean *acusmata*. Cf. D.L. 8. 19 f. for a discussion of Pythagorean diet. Aristoxenus is probably Iamblichus' source. See Delatte, *La vie de Pythagore*, 188 ff.

4. Herodotus (II. 81) mentions the prohibition of burying the dead in woolen garments. See also Burkert, *Lore and Science*, 127.

5. Or, reading διαγωγή for ἀναγωγή with Cobet: "conduct."

[101] Παραδίδοται δὲ καὶ ἄλλος τρόπος παιδεύσεως διὰ τῶν Πυθαγορικῶν ἀποφάσεων καὶ τῶν εἰς τὸν βίον καὶ τὰς ἀνθρωπίνας ὑπολήψεις διατεινουσῶν, ἀφ' ὧν ὀλίγας ἐκ πολλῶν παραθήσομαι. παρήγγελλον γὰρ ἐκ φιλίας ἀληθινῆς ἐξαιρεῖν ἀγῶνά τε καὶ φιλονεικίαν, μάλιστα μὲν ἐκ πάσης, εἰ δυνατόν, εἰ δὲ μή, ἔκ γε τῆς πατρικῆς καὶ καθόλου ἐκ τῆς πρὸς τοὺς πρεσβυτέρους· ὡσαύτως δὲ καὶ ἐκ τῆς πρὸς τοὺς εὐεργέτας. τὸ γὰρ διαγωνίζεσθαι ἢ διαφιλονεικεῖν πρὸς τοὺς τοιούτους ἐμπεσούσης ὀργῆς ἢ ἄλλου τινὸς τοιούτου πάθους οὐ σωτήριον τῆς ὑπαρχούσης φιλίας. ἔφασαν δὲ δεῖν ὡς ἐλαχίστας ἀμυχάς τε καὶ ἑλκώσεις ἐν ταῖς φιλίαις ἐγγίνεσθαι· τοῦτο δὲ γίνεσθαι, ἂν ἐπίστωνται εἴκειν καὶ κρατεῖν ὀργῆς ἀμφότεροι μέν, μᾶλλον μέντοι ὁ νεώτερός τε καὶ τῶν εἰρημένων τάξεων ἔχων ἡνδήποτε. τὰς ἐπανορθώσεις τε καὶ νουθετήσεις, ἃς δὴ πεδαρτάσεις ἐκάλουν ἐκεῖνοι, μετὰ πολλῆς εὐφημίας τε καὶ εὐλαβείας ᾤοντο δεῖν γίνεσθαι παρὰ τῶν πρεσβυτέρων τοῖς νεωτέροις, καὶ πολὺ ἐμφαίνεσθαι ἐν τοῖς νουθετοῦσι τὸ κηδεμονικόν τε καὶ οἰκεῖον· οὕτω γὰρ εὐσχήμονά τε γίνεσθαι καὶ ὠφέλιμον τὴν [102] νουθέτησιν. ἐκ φιλίας μηδέποτε ἐξαιρεῖν πίστιν μήτε παίζοντας μήτε σπουδάζοντας· οὐ γὰρ ἔτι ῥᾴδιον εἶναι διυγιᾶναι τὴν ὑπάρχουσαν φιλίαν, ὅταν ἅπαξ παρεμπέσῃ τὸ ψεῦδος εἰς τὰ τῶν φασκόντων φίλων εἶναι ἤθη. φιλίαν μὴ ἀπογινώσκειν ἀτυχίας ἕνεκα ἢ ἄλλης τινὸς ἀδυναμίας τῶν εἰς τὸν βίον ἐμπιπτουσῶν, ἀλλὰ μόνην εἶναι δόκιμον ἀπόγνωσιν φίλου τε καὶ φιλίας τὴν γινομένην διὰ κακίαν μεγάλην τε καὶ ἀνεπανόρθωτον. τοιοῦτος μὲν οὖν ὁ τύπος ἦν τῆς διὰ τῶν ἀποφάσεων παρ' αὐτοῖς γινομένης ἐπανορθώσεως, εἴς τε πάσας τὰς ἀρετὰς καὶ ὅλον τὸν βίον διατείνων.

CHAPTER TWENTY-TWO

What the mode was of education in the Pythagorean
precepts referring to the conduct of everyday life and
the beliefs of ordinary men.

[101]   Another mode of education has also been handed down through the
"Pythagorean Sayings,"[6] both those which relate to the conduct of life and to the
beliefs of ordinary men. From these I will give a few of many examples. They advised removal of competition and rivalry especially from true friendship and from
all friendship if possible. But if this was not possible, at least from friendship with
one's father, and generally, from friendship with one's elders, and also similarly
from friendship with benefactors. For persistence in contention or disputation
with such, when anger or a similar emotion occurs, do not tend to preserve the
existence of friendship. They said that as few wounds and ulcerations as possible
should occur in friendships. And this happens if both know how to draw back
from and master anger, especially the younger of the two and one in any of the
aforementioned relationships.[7] Corrections and admonitions, which they called
"right tunings,"[8] they thought ought to be delivered with much caution and respect by elders to those younger, and that much solicitude and fellowship should
be shown in the admonitions; for thus the admonition is both kind and beneficial.
[102] Trust should never be removed from friendship, neither in jest nor in earnest.

For it is no longer easy for a friendship to remain healthy when falsehood once
creeps into the characters of those who claim to be friends.[9] Friendship is not to
be rejected on account of misfortune or any other disability in life, and the only
acceptable reason for rejection of a friend and friendship is that which arises from
great and incorrigible vice. Such then, was the form of the "improvement" arising
among them as a result of their precepts, and it extended to all types of virtue and
to their whole way of life.

---

6. Presumably a reference to Aristoxenus' work with that title.
7. Cf. 230 below.
8. Πεδαρτάσεις, a Doric word, meaning "setting to rights" or "re-tuning." The musical over-
tone is probably dominant. Cf. section 197 below, and D.L. 8.20.
9. Cf. 232 below.

[103] Ἀναγκαιότατος δὲ παρ' αὐτῷ τρόπος διδασκαλίας ὑπῆρχε
καὶ ὁ διὰ τῶν συμβόλων. ὁ γὰρ χαρακτὴρ οὗτος καὶ παρ'
Ἕλλησι μὲν σχεδὸν ἅπασιν ἅτε παλαιότροπος ὢν ἐσπου-
δάζετο, ἐξαιρέτως δὲ παρ' Αἰγυπτίοις ποικιλώτατα
ἐπρεσβεύετο. κατὰ τὰ αὐτὰ δὲ καὶ παρὰ Πυθαγόρᾳ μεγάλης
σπουδῆς ἐτύγχανεν, εἴ τις διαρθρώσειε σαφῶς τὰς τῶν
Πυθαγορικῶν συμβόλων ἐμφάσεις καὶ ἀπορρήτους ἐννοίας,
ὅσης ὀρθότητος καὶ ἀληθείας μετέχουσιν ἀποκαλυφθεῖσαι
καὶ τοῦ αἰνιγματώδους ἐλευθερωθεῖσαι τύπου, προσοικειω-
θεῖσαι δὲ κατὰ ἁπλῆν καὶ ἀποίκιλον παράδοσιν ταῖς τῶν
φιλοσόφων τούτων μεγαλοφυΐαις καὶ ὑπὲρ ἀνθρωπίνην
[104] ἐπίνοιαν θεωθεῖσι. καὶ γὰρ οἱ ἐκ τοῦ διδασκαλείου τούτου,
μάλιστα δὲ οἱ παλαιότατοι καὶ αὐτῷ συγχρονίσαντες καὶ
μαθητεύσαντες τῷ Πυθαγόρᾳ πρεσβύτῃ νέοι, Φιλόλαός τε
καὶ Εὔρυτος καὶ Χαρώνδας καὶ Ζάλευκος καὶ Βρύσων,
Ἀρχύτας τε ὁ πρεσβύτερος καὶ Ἀρισταῖος καὶ Λῦσις καὶ
Ἐμπεδοκλῆς καὶ Ζάμολξις καὶ Ἐπιμενίδης καὶ Μίλων, Λεύ-
κιππός τε καὶ Ἀλκμαίων καὶ Ἵππασος καὶ Θυμαρίδας καὶ οἱ
κατ' αὐτοὺς ἅπαντες, πλῆθος ἐλλογίμων καὶ ὑπερφυῶν
ἀνδρῶν, τάς τε διαλέξεις καὶ τὰς πρὸς ἀλλήλους ὁμιλίας καὶ
τοὺς ὑπομνηματισμούς τε καὶ ὑποσημειώσεις καὶ αὐτὰ ἤδη
τὰ συγγράμματα καὶ ἐκδόσεις πάσας, ὧν τὰ πλείονα μέχρι
καὶ τῶν ἡμετέρων χρόνων διασῴζεται, οὐ τῇ κοινῇ καὶ
δημώδει καὶ δὴ καὶ τοῖς ἄλλοις ἅπασιν εἰωθυίᾳ λέξει συνετὰ
ἐποιοῦντο ἐξ ἐπιδρομῆς τοῖς ἀκούουσι, πειρώμενοι
εὐπαρακολούθητα τὰ φραζόμενα ὑπ' αὐτῶν τίθεσθαι, ἀλλὰ
κατὰ τὴν νενομοθετημένην αὐτοῖς ὑπὸ Πυθαγόρου ἐχεμυθίαν
θείων μυστηρίων καὶ πρὸς τοὺς ἀτελέστους ἀπορρήτων
τρόπων ἥπτοντο καὶ διὰ συμβόλων ἐπέσκεπον τὰς πρὸς

CHAPTER TWENTY-THREE

What his mode was of exhortation to philosophy through symbols,
and the secret and hidden meaning of his teachings, which was
transmitted by Pythagoras as education only to those who
knew (the key to it), according to the accustomed procedure
of the Egyptians and the most ancient of the Hellenes.

[103]

Most indispensable for him (Pythagoras) was his manner of teaching by means of "symbols."[1] For this style of teaching was treated with respect by nearly all Hellenes inasmuch as it was of ancient origin, and especially employed by the Egyptians in very subtle ways. Likewise, Pythagoras considered it of great importance if someone carefully and clearly elucidated the meanings and secret conceptions of the Pythagorean symbols, (and discerned) how much rightness and truth they contained when revealed and freed from their enigmatic form, and when adapted with simple and unadorned teaching for the lofty geniuses of these philosophers, deified beyond human thought.

[104]

For they who were from this school, especially the oldest generation, contemporary with him, and who were young pupils when Pythagoras was old (are): Philolaus, Eurytus, Charondas, Zaleucus, Bryson, Archytas the elder, Aristaeus, Lysis, Empedocles, Zamolxis, Epimenides, Milo, Leucippus, Alcmaeon, Hippasus, Thymaridas, and all those associated with them, a throng of eloquent and extraordinary men.[2] And their dialogues and talks with one another, their memoranda and notes (of conversations), and further their treatises and all their publications, of which the greater number are preserved until our own times, they did not make readily intelligible to their audience, in a common or popular manner, or in a style customary for all others who (try) to make the things said by them easy to follow. But in accord with the "silence" legislated for them by Pythagoras, they engaged in divine mysteries and methods of instruction forbidden to the uninitiated,[3] and through symbols, they protected their talks with one another and their

---

1. With this chapter we seem to be back to Iamblichus himself.
2. Compare these names with the catalogue of Pythagoreans below in section 267. See also Burkert, *Lore and Science*, 105, n. 40.
3. Iamblichus often suggests similarities between the mysteries and the Pythagorean society, e.g. at section 75 above. The initiate at Eleusis, for example, fasted, abstained from domestic fowl, especially the cock, and avoided fish and beans (Porph. *Abst.* 4.16). Pythagoras' name was avoided (see, for example, *VP* 53, 88, 255), and the hierophant at Eleusis was not called by name. See P. Foucart, *Les mystères d'Eleusis* (Paris, 1914) 173 ff.

[105] ἀλλήλους διαλέξεις ἢ συγγραφάς. καὶ εἰ μή τις αὐτὰ τὰ σύμβολα ἐκλέξας διαπτύξειε καὶ ἀμώκῳ ἐξηγήσει ⟨περι-λάβοι⟩, γελοῖα ἂν καὶ γραώδη δόξειε τοῖς ἐντυγχάνουσι τὰ λεγόμενα, λήρου μεστὰ καὶ ἀδολεσχίας. ἐπειδὰν μέντοι κατὰ τὸν τῶν συμβόλων τούτων τρόπον διαπτυχθῇ καὶ φανὰ καὶ εὐαγῆ ἀντὶ σκοτεινῶν τοῖς πολλοῖς γένηται, θεοπροπίοις καὶ χρησμοῖς τισι τοῦ Πυθίου ἀναλογεῖ καὶ θαυμαστὴν ἐκφαίνει διάνοιαν, δαιμονίαν τε ἐπίπνοιαν ἐμποιεῖ τοῖς νενοηκόσι τῶν φιλολόγων. οὐ χεῖρον δὲ ὀλίγων μνημονεῦσαι ἕνεκα τοῦ σαφέστερον γενέσθαι τὸν τύπον τῆς διδασκαλίας. "ὁδοῦ πάρεργον οὔτε εἰσιτέον εἰς ἱερὸν οὔτε προσκυνητέον τὸ παράπαν, οὐδ' εἰ πρὸς ταῖς θύραις αὐταῖς παριὼν γένοιο. ἀνυπόδητος θύε καὶ προσκύνει. τὰς λεωφόρους ὁδοὺς ἐκκλίνων διὰ τῶν ἀτραπῶν βάδιζε. περὶ Πυθαγορείων ἄνευ φωτὸς μὴ λάλει." τοιοῦτος, ὡς ἐν τύποις εἰπεῖν, ὁ τρόπος ἦν αὐτοῦ τῆς διὰ συμβόλων διδασκαλίας.

[105] treatises. And if someone, after singling out the actual symbols, does not explicate and comprehend them with an interpretation free from mockery,[4] the things said will appear laughable and trivial to ordinary persons, full of nonsense and rambling. When, however, these utterances are explicated in accord with the manner of these symbols, they become splendid and sacred instead of obscure to the many, rather analogous to the prophecies and oracles of the Pythian god. And they reveal marvelous thought, and produce divine inspiration in those scholars who have grasped their meaning. It is well to mention a few in order that the general character of their teaching may become clearer: "as secondary purpose of a journey neither enter a temple nor worship at all, not even if you be passing before the very doors." "Sacrifice and worship unshod." "Walk on paths, avoiding roads traveled by the public." "Do not talk about Pythagorean matters without light." Such, in outline, was the manner of his teaching through symbols.

---

4. Ἄμωκος is a *hapax legomenon* formed from μῶκος, "mockery," itself a rare and late word; μωκάομαι seems more common.

[106]   Ἐπεὶ δὲ καὶ ἡ τροφὴ μεγάλα συμβάλλεται πρὸς τὴν
ἀρίστην παιδείαν, ὅταν καλῶς καὶ τεταγμένως γίγνηται,
σκεψώμεθα τίνα καὶ περὶ ταύτην ἐνομοθέτησε. τῶν δὴ
βρωμάτων καθόλου τὰ τοιαῦτα ἀπεδοκίμαζεν, ὅσα πνευμα-
τώδη καὶ ταραχῆς αἴτια, τὰ δ' ἐναντία ἐδοκίμαζέ τε καὶ
χρῆσθαι ἐκέλευεν, ὅσα τὴν τοῦ σώματος ἕξιν καθίστησί τε
καὶ συστέλλει· ὅθεν ἐνόμιζεν εἶναι καὶ τὴν κέγχρον ἐπι-
τηδείαν εἰς τροφήν. καθόλου δὲ ἀπεδοκίμαζε καὶ τὰ τοῖς θεοῖς
ἀλλότρια ὡς ἀπάγοντα ἡμᾶς τῆς πρὸς τοὺς θεοὺς οἰκειώσεως.
κατ' ἄλλον δὲ αὖ τρόπον καὶ τῶν νομιζομένων εἶναι ἱερῶν
σφόδρα ἀπέχεσθαι παρήγγελλεν ὡς τιμῆς ἀξίων ὄντων,
ἀλλ' οὐχὶ τῆς κοινῆς καὶ ἀνθρωπίνης χρήσεως, καὶ ὅσα δὲ εἰς
μαντικὴν ἐνεπόδιζεν ἢ πρὸς καθαρότητα τῆς ψυχῆς καὶ
[107] ἁγνείαν ἢ πρὸς σωφροσύνης καὶ ἀρετῆς ἕξιν, παρήνει
φυλάττεσθαι. καὶ τὰ πρὸς εὐάγειαν δὲ ἐναντίως ἔχοντα καὶ
ἐπιθολοῦντα τῆς ψυχῆς τάς τε ἄλλας καθαρότητας καὶ τὰ ἐν
τοῖς ὕπνοις φαντάσματα παρῃτεῖτο. κοινῶς μὲν οὖν ταῦτα
ἐνομοθέτησε περὶ τροφῆς, ἰδίᾳ δὲ τοῖς θεωρητικωτάτοις τῶν
φιλοσόφων καὶ ὅτι μάλιστα ἀκροτάτοις καθάπαξ περιῄρει τὰ
περιττὰ καὶ ἄδικα τῶν ἐδεσμάτων, μήτε ἔμψυχον μηδὲν
μηδέποτε ἐσθίειν εἰσηγούμενος μήτε οἶνον ὅλως πίνειν μήτε
θύειν ζῷα θεοῖς μήτε καταβλάπτειν μηδ' ὁτιοῦν αὐτά, διασ-
[108] ῴζειν δὲ καὶ τὴν πρὸς αὐτὰ δικαιοσύνην ἐπιμελέστατα. καὶ
αὐτὸς οὕτως ἔζησεν, ἀπεχόμενος τῆς ἀπὸ τῶν ζῴων τροφῆς
καὶ τοὺς ἀναιμάκτους βωμοὺς προσκυνῶν, καὶ ὅπως μηδὲ
ἄλλοι ἀναιρήσωσι τὰ ὁμοφυῆ πρὸς ἡμᾶς ζῷα προθυμούμενος,
τά τε ἄγρια ζῷα σωφρονίζων μᾶλλον καὶ παιδεύων διὰ
λόγων καὶ ἔργων, ἀλλ' οὐχὶ διὰ κολάσεως καταβλάπτων.
ἤδη δὲ καὶ τῶν πολιτικῶν τοῖς νομοθέταις προσέταξεν
ἀπέχεσθαι τῶν ἐμψύχων· ἅτε γὰρ βουλομένους ἄκρως
δικαιοπραγεῖν ἔδει δήπου μηδὲν ἀδικεῖν τῶν συγγενῶν ζῴων.
ἐπεὶ πῶς ἂν ἔπεισαν δίκαια πράττειν τοὺς ἄλλους αὐτοὶ
ἁλισκόμενοι ἐν πλεονεξίᾳ; συγγενικὴ δ' ἡ τῶν ζῴων μετοχή,

CHAPTER TWENTY-FOUR

The foods Pythagoras avoided entirely, and from which he
ordered his disciples to abstain, and how he laid down different
laws about this according to the particular way of
life followed by each group, and for what reasons.

[106]   Since diet also contributes much to the best education when it is provided in a well-ordered way, let us consider what he decreed about this. He rejected entirely, then, all such foods as cause flatulence and disturbance, and he approved and urged eating foods with an opposite effect, those which set in order and control the functions of the body. Hence, for instance, he considered millet suitable for nourishment. He entirely rejected foods which are foreign to the gods because they divert us from kinship with the gods. Again, on another basis, he emphatically commended abstention from foods believed sacred since they are worthy of honor, and not for common and human consumption. And he advised one to guard against whatever hindered prophesy, purity of soul and chastity, or a settled

[107]   condition of sound-mindedness and virtue. He also deprecated things opposed to alertness and which muddy the soul's purity in general, and visions in dreams in particular.[1]

This, then, was his general legislation about nourishment. In particular, he removed once for all from the most contemplative group of philosophers, especially those at the highest level, the use of superfluous and ill-gotten foods, by instructing them never to eat anything animate and never to drink wine; neither to sacrifice living beings to the gods nor to harm them in any way, but to maintain justice most carefully towards them.

[108]   He himself lived according to these precepts, abstaining from food provided by living beings and worshipping before altars unstained with blood, desiring eagerly that others not destroy animals kindred in nature with us; rather he chastened and educated wild animals by words and deeds, and did not harm them with punishment.[2] And he ordered law-givers of communities to abstain from living beings; for since they wished to act completely in justice, it was necessary, surely, not to injure kindred animals, since how could they persuade others to behave justly if they themselves be caught in greediness? There is a congenital partnership of

---

1. This section might be compared with D.L. 8. 24.
2. Pythagorean prohibitions on sacrifice and eating meat discussed by Burkert, *Lore and Science*, 180 ff.

ἅπερ διὰ τὴν τῆς ζωῆς καὶ τῶν στοιχείων τῶν αὐτῶν
κοινωνίαν καὶ τῆς ἀπὸ τούτων συνισταμένης συγκράσεως
[109] ὡσανεὶ ἀδελφότητι πρὸς ἡμᾶς συνέζευκται. τοῖς μέντοι
ἄλλοις ἐπέτρεπέ τινων ζῴων ἅπτεσθαι, ὅσοις ὁ βίος μὴ πάνυ
ἦν ἐκκεκαθαρμένος καὶ ἱερὸς καὶ φιλόσοφος· καὶ τούτοις
χρόνον τινὰ ὥριζε τῆς ἀποχῆς ὡρισμένον. ἐνομοθέτησε δὲ
τοῖς αὐτοῖς καρδίαν μὴ τρώγειν, ἐγκέφαλον μὴ ἐσθίειν, καὶ
τούτων εἴργεσθαι πάντας τοὺς Πυθαγορικούς· ἡγεμονίαι γάρ
εἰσι καὶ ὡσανεὶ ἐπιβάθραι καὶ ἕδραι τινὲς τοῦ φρονεῖν καὶ
τοῦ ζῆν. ἀφωσιοῦτο δὲ αὐτὰ διὰ τὴν τοῦ θείου λόγου φύσιν.
οὕτως καὶ μαλάχης εἴργεσθαι ἐκέλευεν, ὅτι πρώτη ἄγγελος
καὶ σημάντρια συμπαθείας οὐρανίων πρὸς ἐπίγεια. καὶ
μελανούρου δὲ ἀπέχεσθαι παρήγγελλε· χθονίων γάρ ἐστι
θεῶν. καὶ ἐρυθρῖνον μὴ προσλαμβάνειν δι' ἕτερα τοιαῦτα
αἴτια. καὶ "κυάμων ἀπέχου" διὰ πολλὰς ἱεράς τε καὶ φυσικὰς
καὶ εἰς τὴν ψυχὴν ἀνηκούσας αἰτίας. καὶ ἄλλα τοιαῦτα
διεθεσμοθέτησε τούτοις ὅμοια, καὶ διὰ τῆς τροφῆς ἀρχόμενος
εἰς ἀρετὴν ὁδηγεῖν τοὺς ἀνθρώπους.

living beings, since, through sharing life and the same elements and the mixture arising from these, they are yoked together with us by brotherhood, as it were.

[109]   He permitted the rest, nevertheless, to eat certain animals, those whose way of life was not entirely purified, holy, and philosophic; even for these, however, he set a definite period of abstinence. He decreed that they not "munch on the heart" nor 'eat brain,' and from these all Pythagoreans are banned; for these organs are the ruling parts and, as it were, stepping-stones and seats of practical thinking and living. And these same things he eschewed on religious grounds because of the nature of the divine reason. So also he commanded them to abstain from mallow, because it is the first messenger and indicator of an affinity of heavenly things with things earthly. And he ordered them to abstain from black-tail, for it belongs to the earth gods; and not to eat *erythrinus*[3] for similar reasons. And to "abstain from beans"[4] because of many sacred and physical reasons, and reasons pertaining to the soul. He prescribed other rules like these, and thus, beginning with food, he led human beings to moral excellence.

---

3. A sea-fish, probably Pagellus erythrinus. See *LSJ*, s.v. See also *VP* 98, n.3.

4. Pythagorean abstinence from beans is fully discussed by Burkert, *Lore and Science*, 183-185.

[110] Ὑπελάμβανε δὲ καὶ τὴν μουσικὴν μεγάλα συμβάλλεσθαι πρὸς ὑγείαν, ἄν τις αὐτῇ χρῆται κατὰ τοὺς προσήκοντας τρόπους. εἰώθει γὰρ οὐ παρέργως τῇ τοιαύτῃ χρῆσθαι καθάρσει· τοῦτο γὰρ δὴ καὶ προσηγόρευε τὴν διὰ τῆς μουσικῆς ἰατρείαν. ἥπτετο δὲ περὶ τὴν ἐαρινὴν ὥραν τῆς τοιαύτης μελῳδίας· ἐκάθιζε γὰρ ἐν μέσῳ τινὰ λύρας ἐφαπτόμενον, καὶ κύκλῳ ἐκαθέζοντο οἱ μελῳδεῖν δυνατοί, καὶ οὕτως ἐκείνου κρούοντος συνῇδον παιῶνάς τινας, δι' ὧν εὐφραίνεσθαι καὶ ἐμμελεῖς καὶ ἔνρυθμοι γίνεσθαι ἐδόκουν. χρῆσθαι δ' αὐτοὺς καὶ κατὰ τὸν ἄλλον χρόνον τῇ μουσικῇ ἐν

[111] ἰατρείας τάξει, καὶ εἶναί τινα μέλη πρὸς τὰ ψυχῆς πεποιημένα πάθη, πρός τε ἀθυμίας καὶ δηγμούς, ἃ δὴ βοηθητικώτατα ἐπινενόητο, καὶ πάλιν αὖ ἕτερα πρός τε τὰς ὀργὰς καὶ πρὸς τοὺς θυμοὺς καὶ πρὸς πᾶσαν παραλλαγὴν τῆς τοιαύτης ψυχῆς, εἶναι δὲ καὶ πρὸς τὰς ἐπιθυμίας ἄλλο γένος μελοποιίας ἐξευρημένον. χρῆσθαι δὲ καὶ ὀρχήσεσιν. ὀργάνῳ δὲ χρῆσθαι λύρᾳ· τοὺς γὰρ αὐλοὺς ὑπελάμβανεν ὑβριστικόν τε καὶ πανηγυρικὸν καὶ οὐδαμῶς ἐλευθέριον τὸν ἦχον ἔχειν. χρῆσθαι δὲ καὶ Ὁμήρου καὶ Ἡσιόδου λέξεσιν ἐξειλεγμέναις

[112] πρὸς ἐπανόρθωσιν ψυχῆς. λέγεται δὲ καὶ ἐπὶ τῶν ἔργων Πυθαγόρας μὲν σπονδειακῷ ποτὲ μέλει διὰ τοῦ αὐλητοῦ κατασβέσαι τοῦ Ταυρομενίτου μειρακίου μεθύοντος τὴν λύσσαν, νύκτωρ ἐπικωμάζοντος ἐρωμένῃ παρὰ ἀντεραστοῦ πυλῶνι, ἐμπιπράναι μέλλοντος· ἐξήπτετο γὰρ καὶ ἀνεζωπυρεῖτο ὑπὸ τοῦ Φρυγίου αὐλήματος. ὃ δὴ κατέπαυσε τάχιστα ὁ Πυθαγόρας. ἐτύγχανε δὲ αὐτὸς ἀστρονομούμενος ἀωρί· καὶ τὴν εἰς τὸν σπονδειακὸν μεταβολὴν ὑπέθετο τῷ αὐλητῇ, δι' ἧς ἀμελλητὶ κατασταλὲν κοσμίως οἴκαδε ἀπηλλάγη τὸ μειράκιον, πρὸ βραχέος μηδ' ἐφ' ὅσον οὖν ἀνασχόμενον μηδ' ἁπλῶς ὑπομεῖναν νουθεσίας ἐπιβολὴν παρ' αὐτοῦ, πρὸς δὲ καὶ ἐμπλήκτως ἀποσκοράκισαν τὴν τοῦ

CHAPTER TWENTY-FIVE

How through music and melodies he trained men at fixed times, when
they were particularly troubled by passions, and what
purifications from diseases of both soul and body he
performed through music, and how he performed them.

[110]   Pythagoras also believed that music contributed greatly to health if one used it in proper ways. For he accorded a major role to purification by this means. Indeed, he called this "medical treatment through music." In the spring season he used to employ the following choral arrangement: he seated in the middle someone holding a lyre; round about in a circle sat those able to sing, and thus while the first one played the lyre, they chanted certain paeans in unison, through which they expected to induce feelings of joy, and to become graceful and rhythmical.

[111]   At other times they used music as a medical treatment. There are[1] certain melodies created for the soul's emotions which, in fact, were designed to be most helpful against despondency and mental suffering; and again, other melodies against rages, angers, and against every mental disturbance of a soul so afflicted; there is also another kind of musical composition invented for the desires. They also made use of dances. As an instrument they used the lyre; for he believed that pipes had a wanton, showy, and wholly ignoble sound. He also used selected verses of Homer and Hesiod for the improvement of the soul.[2]

[112]   Also among Pythagoras' deeds, it is told that once with a spondaic tune played by a piper he quelled the rage of a drunken Tauromenian youth, who made a riotous assault at night on his mistress at the gate of a rival, intending to burn the house down around her. For he was inflamed and excited by the Phrygian mode of music for the pipe, which Pythagoras then stopped as quickly as possible (he himself happened to be studying astronomy at the dead of night). And (Pythagoras) suggested to the piper a change to the spondaic, by means of which the youth, immediately restrained, went home in an orderly manner, though a little before he was not in the least patient or responsive to Pythagoras' attempt at admonition, but even madly cursed Pythagoras' intervention.

---

1. This passage is repeated in section 224 virtually verbatim.
2. Cf. Porph. *VP* 32. One should also note the use of Homeric verses in the Greek magical papyri as charms and incantations. See H. D. Betz, ed. *The Greek Magical Papyri in Translation, Including the Demotic Spells* (Chicago 1985) 47,54,76, and 260.

[113] Πυθαγόρου συντυχίαν. Ἐμπεδοκλῆς δὲ σπασαμένου τὸ ξίφος ἤδη νεανίου τινὸς ἐπὶ τὸν αὐτοῦ ξενοδόχον Ἄγχιτον, ἐπεὶ δικάσας δημοσίᾳ τὸν τοῦ νεανίου πατέρα ἐθανάτωσε, καὶ ἀίξαντος, ὡς εἶχε συγχύσεως καὶ θυμοῦ, ξιφήρους παῖσαι τὸν τοῦ πατρὸς καταδικαστήν, ὡσανεὶ φονέα, Ἄγχιτον, μεθαρμοσάμενος ὡς εἶχε τὴν λύραν καὶ πεπαντικόν τι μέλος καὶ κατασταλτικὸν μεταχειρισάμενος εὐθὺς ἀνεκρούσατο τὸ

νηπενθὲς ἄχολόν τε, κακῶν ἐπίληθον ἁπάντων

κατὰ τὸν ποιητήν, καὶ τόν τε ἑαυτοῦ ξενοδόχον Ἄγχιτον [114] θανάτου ἐρρύσατο καὶ τὸν νεανίαν ἀνδροφονίας. ἱστορεῖται δ' οὗτος τῶν Ἐμπεδοκλέους γνωρίμων ὁ δοκιμώτατος ἔκτοτε γενέσθαι. ἔτι τοίνυν σύμπαν τὸ Πυθαγορικὸν διδασκαλεῖον τὴν λεγομένην ἐξάρτυσιν καὶ συναρμογὰν καὶ ἐπαφὰν ἐποιεῖτο, μέλεσί τισιν ἐπιτηδείοις εἰς τὰ ἐναντία πάθη περιάγον χρησίμως τὰς τῆς ψυχῆς διαθέσεις. ἐπί τε γὰρ εὐνὰς τρεπόμενοι τῶν μεθ' ἡμέραν ταραχῶν καὶ περιηχημάτων ἐξεκάθαιρον τὰς διανοίας ᾠδαῖς τισι καὶ μελῶν ἰδιώμασι καὶ ἡσύχους παρεσκεύαζον ἑαυτοῖς ἐκ τούτου καὶ ὀλιγονείρους τε καὶ εὐονείρους τοὺς ὕπνους, ἐξανιστάμενοί τε ἐκ τῆς κοίτης νωχελίας πάλιν καὶ κάρους δι' ἀλλοτρόπων ἀπήλλασσον ᾀσμάτων, ἔστι δὲ καὶ ὅτε ἄνευ λέξεως μελισμάτων. (ἔστι) τε ὅπου καὶ πάθη καὶ νοσήματά τινα ἀφυγίαζον, ὥς φασιν, ἐπᾴδοντες ὡς ἀληθῶς, καὶ εἰκὸς ἐντεῦθέν ποθεν τοὔνομα τοῦτο εἰς μέσον παρεληλυθέναι, τὸ τῆς ἐπῳδῆς. οὕτω μὲν οὖν πολυωφελεστάτην κατεστήσατο Πυθαγόρας τὴν διὰ τῆς μουσικῆς τῶν ἀνθρωπίνων ἠθῶν τε [115] καὶ βίων ἐπανόρθωσιν. ἐπεὶ δὲ ἐνταῦθα γεγόναμεν ἀφηγούμενοι τὴν Πυθαγόρου παιδευτικὴν σοφίαν, οὐ χεῖρον καὶ τὸ τούτῳ παρακείμενον ἐφεξῆς εἰπεῖν, ὅπως ἐξεῦρε τὴν ἁρμονικὴν ἐπιστήμην καὶ τοὺς ἁρμονικοὺς λόγους. ἀρξώμεθα δὲ μικρὸν ἄνωθεν.

[113]   Likewise Empedocles once (saved) his host Anchitus when some youth drew a sword on him. As a judge (Anchitus) had sentenced the youth's father to death. Confused and angry, the youth rushed, sword in hand, to strike him who condemned his father as if he, Anchitus, were a murderer. Since he had the lyre, Empedocles changed the mode and playing some soothing and sedating strain, immediately struck up the "freer from sorrow and allayer of anger, a forgetting of all ills," in the words of the poet[3] and he saved both his own host, Anchitus, from death, and the youth from murder. It is recorded that this youth then became the
[114] most famous of Empedocles' pupils.[4]

Moreover, the entire Pythagorean school created what is called "musical arrangement" and "musical combination" and (musical) treatment, skillfully reversing dispositions of the soul to opposite emotions with certain suitable tunes. For on going to bed they purified their intellects from the disturbances and pervasive noise of the day with certain odes and special types of tunes, and secured for themselves by this means quiet sleep with few and good dreams. And on rising again from bed, they got rid of sluggishness and drowsiness by means of a different type of chant, and sometimes even with melodies without words.[5] There are cases in which they healed emotions and certain sicknesses, as they say, truly by means of singing as an incantation and it is probable that thence this noun, "incantation" passed into common use. So Pythagoras established this most useful method of improvement of human characters and ways of life by means of music.

Since we have reached this point in our account of Pythagoras' skill in educa-
[115] tion, we may as well discuss next a topic which is closely connected with this: how he discovered the harmonic science and the harmonic ratios. But let us first fill in some background.

---

3. Hom. *Od.* 4.221.

4. Anchitus is mentioned at D.L. 8. 61. Cf. Boethius 1.1 (185, 23 ff.). It is to Anchitus' son, Pausanias, that Empedocles dedicates his poem *On Nature*.

5. Possibly the chanting of sequences of vowels, such as are frequently prescribed in the magical papyri. These practices are akin to the chanting of mantras.

Ἐν φροντίδι ποτὲ καὶ διαλογισμῷ συντεταμένῳ ὑπάρχων,
εἰ ἄρα δύναιτο τῇ ἀκοῇ βοήθειάν τινα ὀργανικὴν ἐπινοῆσαι,
παγίαν καὶ ἀπαραλόγιστον, οἵαν ἡ μὲν ὄψις διὰ τοῦ δια-
βήτου καὶ διὰ τοῦ κανόνος ἢ νὴ Δία διὰ διόπτρας ἔσχεν, ἡ
δ' ἀφὴ διὰ τοῦ ζυγοῦ ἢ διὰ τῆς τῶν μέτρων ἐπινοίας, παρά
τι χαλκοτυπεῖον περιπατῶν ἔκ τινος δαιμονίου συντυχίας
ἐπήκουσε ῥαιστήρων σίδηρον ἐπ' ἄκμονι ῥαιόντων καὶ τοὺς
ἤχους παραμὶξ πρὸς ἀλλήλους (συμφωνοτάτους) ἀπο-
διδόντων, πλὴν μιᾶς συζυγίας. ἐπεγίνωσκε δ' ἐν αὐτοῖς τήν
τε διὰ πασῶν τήν τε διὰ πέντε καὶ τὴν διὰ τεσσάρων
συνῳδίαν, τὴν δὲ μεταξύτητα τῆς τε διὰ τεσσάρων καὶ τῆς
διὰ πέντε ἀσύμφωνον μὲν ἑώρα αὐτὴν καθ' ἑαυτήν,
συμπληρωτικὴν δὲ ἄλλως τῆς ἐν αὐτοῖς μειζονότητος.
[116] ἄσμενος δὴ ὡς κατὰ θεὸν ἀννομένης αὐτῷ τῆς προθέσεως
εἰσέδραμεν εἰς τὸ χαλκεῖον, καὶ ποικίλαις πείραις παρὰ τῶν
ἐν τοῖς ῥαιστῆρσιν ὄγκων εὑρὼν τὴν διαφορὰν τοῦ ἤχου,
ἀλλ' οὐ παρὰ τὴν τῶν ῥαιόντων βίαν οὐδὲ παρὰ τὰ σχήματα
τῶν σφυρῶν οὐδὲ παρὰ τὴν τοῦ ἐλαυννομένου σιδήρου
μετάθεσιν, σηκώματα ἀκριβῶς ἐκλαβὼν καὶ ῥοπὰς ἰσαιτάτας
τῶν ῥαιστήρων πρὸς ἑαυτὸν ἀπηλλάγη, καὶ ἀπό τινος ἑνὸς
πασσάλου διὰ γωνίας ἐμπεπηγότος τοῖς τοίχοις, ἵνα μὴ κἀκ
τούτου διαφορά τις ὑποφαίνηται ἢ ὅλως ὑπονοῆται
πασσάλων ἰδιαζόντων παραλλαγή, ἀπαρτίσας τέσσαρας
χορδὰς ὁμούλους καὶ ἰσοκώλους, ἰσοπαχεῖς τε καὶ
ἰσοστρόφους, ἑκάστην ἀφ' ἑκάστης ἐξήρτησεν, ὁλκὴν
προσδήσας ἐκ τοῦ κάτωθεν μέρους, τὰ δὲ μήκη τῶν χορδῶν
[117] μηχανησάμενος ἐκ παντὸς ἰσαίτατα. εἶτα κρούων ἀνὰ δύο
ἅμα χορδὰς ἐπαλλὰξ συμφωνίας εὕρισκε τὰς προλεχθείσας,

CHAPTER TWENTY-SIX

How and by what method Pythagoras made the discovery
of harmony and the harmonic ratios, and how he
communicated to his disciples the
whole science of this.

Once, deep in thought and calculation,[1] he was pondering how he could invent some instrumental aid for hearing, steadfast and unerring, such as sight has by means of the compass, the ruler or, indeed, by the diopter, or touch has by means of the balance or by the invention of measures. He happened, by a marvelous chance, to be walking past a forge where he heard hammers beating iron on an anvil, and making mixed sounds in full harmony[2] with one another, except for one combination. He recognized in these the octave and the fifth and the fourth, and he saw the interval between the fourth and the fifth was dissonant in itself, but was capable of completing the range of greatness between them. Delighted, [116] then, that his project had the backing of divinity, he rushed into the forge, and with varied tests found that difference of the sound was produced by the weights (sizes) of the hammers, not by the force of the blows or by the shapes of the hammers or by the position of the iron being struck.[3] When he had noted accurately the weights and exact balancing of the hammers, he went home. From a single peg fixed to an angle between two walls, which he chose lest any differentiation should make itself felt on this account, or there should be any variation owing to the difference between particular pegs, he suspended four strings of the same material, of the same number of strands, of equal thickness, and of equal torsion. And from each string he hung one weight by attaching the weight at the bottom and making certain that all the strings had equal lengths. Then, striking groups [117] of two strings alternately, he found the aforementioned consonances sounded in the various combinations of strings. He found that the string stretched by the

---

1. This whole chapter is taken virtually verbatim from Nicomachus of Gerasa's *Harmonikon Encheiridion*, chaps. 6 and 7. The passage might also have appeared in his *Life of Pythagoras* (assuming that he wrote such a work). Iamblichus tells the story more briefly at *In Nic.* p. 123, 13 ff. We are grateful to Jon Solomon, University of Arizona, for his expertise in ancient music, and help in translating this very difficult and technical part of Iamblichus' *VP.*

2. Supplied from Nicomachus.

3. This is actually false (see Burkert, *Lore and Science* 375 ff.) and so the story must have been invented by someone with no knowledge of music. It is refuted already by Ptolemy, *Harm.*, p. 16, 32 ff. In reality, the pitch or frequency is proportional to the square root of the tension of the object being struck, not to its weight. The story perhaps distorts a real discovery.

ἄλλην ἐν ἄλλῃ συζυγίᾳ. τὴν μὲν γὰρ ὑπὸ τοῦ μεγίστου
ἐξαρτήματος τεινομένην πρὸς τὴν ὑπὸ τοῦ μικροτάτου διὰ
πασῶν φθεγγομένην κατελάμβανεν· ἦν δὲ ἣ μὲν δώδεκα
τινῶν ὁλκῶν, ἣ δὲ ἕξ. ἐν διπλασίῳ δὴ λόγῳ ἀπέφαινε τὴν
διὰ πασῶν, ὅπερ καὶ αὐτὰ τὰ βάρη ὑπέφαινε. τὴν δ' αὖ
μεγίστην πρὸς τὴν παρὰ τὴν μικροτάτην, οὖσαν ὀκτὼ
ὁλκῶν, διὰ πέντε συμφωνοῦσαν, ἔνθεν ταύτην ἀπέφαινεν ἐν
ἡμιολίῳ λόγῳ, ἐν ᾧπερ καὶ αἱ ὁλκαὶ ὑπῆρχον πρὸς ἀλλήλας·
πρὸς δὲ τὴν μεθ' ἑαυτὴν μὲν τῷ βάρει, τῶν δὲ λοιπῶν
μείζονα, ἐννέα σταθμῶν ὑπάρχουσαν, τὴν διὰ τεσσάρων,
ἀναλόγως τοῖς βρίθεσι. καὶ ταύτην δὴ ἐπίτριτον ἄντικρυς
κατελαμβάνετο, ἡμιολίαν τὴν αὐτὴν φύσει ὑπάρχουσαν τῆς
[118] μικροτάτης (τὰ γὰρ ἐννέα πρὸς τὰ ἕξ οὕτως ἔχει)· ὅνπερ
τρόπον ἡ παρὰ τὴν μικρὰν ἡ ὀκτὼ πρὸς μὲν τὴν τὰ ἕξ
ἔχουσαν ἐν ἐπιτρίτῳ λόγῳ ἦν, πρὸς δὲ τὴν τὰ δώδεκα ἐν
ἡμιολίῳ. τὸ ἄρα μεταξὺ τῆς διὰ πέντε καὶ τῆς διὰ τεσσάρων,
ᾧ ὑπερέχει ἡ διὰ πέντε τῆς διὰ τεσσάρων, ἐβεβαιοῦτο ἐν

ϛ   η   θ   ιβ   ἐπογδόῳ λόγῳ ὑπάρχειν, ἐν
                        ᾧπερ τὰ ἐννέα πρὸς τὰ
                        ὀκτώ, ἑκατέρως τε ἡ διὰ
                        πασῶν σύστημα ἠλέγχετο,
                        ἤτοι τῆς διὰ πέντε καὶ διὰ
                        τεσσάρων ἐν συναφῇ, ὡς ὁ
                        διπλάσιος λόγος ἡμιολίου τε
                        καὶ ἐπιτρίτου, οἷον δώδεκα,
                        ὀκτώ, ἕξ, ἢ ἀναστρόφως τῆς
                        διὰ τεσσάρων καὶ τῆς διὰ
διὰ τεσσάρων διὰ τεσσάρων πέντε, ὡς τὸ διπλάσιον ἐπι-
                        τρίτου τε καὶ ἡμιολίου, οἷον
διὰ πέντε   διὰ πέντε   δώδεκα, ἐννέα, ἕξ, ἐν τάξει
       διὰ πασῶν

τοιαύτῃ διὰ πασῶν. τυλώσας δὲ καὶ τὴν χεῖρα καὶ τὴν ἀκοὴν
πρὸς τὰ ἐξαρτήματα καὶ βεβαιώσας πρὸς αὐτὰ τὸν τῶν
σχέσεων λόγον, μετέθηκεν εὐμηχάνως τὴν μὲν τῶν χορδῶν
κοινὴν ἀπόδεσιν, τὴν (ἐκ) τοῦ διαγωνίου πασσάλου, εἰς τὸν
τοῦ ὀργάνου βατῆρα, ὃν χορδότονον ὠνόμαζε, τὴν δὲ ποσὴν
ἐπίτασιν ἀναλόγως τοῖς βάρεσιν εἰς τὴν τῶν κολλάβων
[119] ἄνωθεν σύμμετρον περιστροφήν. ἐπιβάθρᾳ τε ταύτῃ
χρώμενος καὶ οἷον ἀνεξαπατήτῳ γνώμονι εἰς ποικίλα ὄργανα
τὴν πεῖραν λοιπὸν ἐξέτεινε, λεκίδων τε κροῦσιν καὶ αὐλοὺς

greatest weight sounded together with that stretched by the smallest weight, produced an octave; the former string supported twelve weights and the latter six, so he determined that the octave was in duple proportion, as was shown, indeed, by the weights themselves. And again, he showed that the string with the greatest weight when sounded together with the string with the next to least weight, that is, the string with eight weights, produces the consonance of the fifth; in doing so, he showed this consonance to consist of a proportion of 3:2, the same proportion in which the weights themselves stand in relation to each other; while, in combination with the string second greatest in weight, that consisting of nine weights, a fourth was produced, proportionately with the weights. And he found this string
[118] (with 9 weights) to be in a proportion of 4:3 with the greatest string; yet he found this same string to be in a natural proportion of 3:2 with the smallest string, for 9 stands in such a relationship with 6. In the same way, the second smallest string, that from which 8 weights are suspended, stood in a proportion of 4:3 with that having 6 weights, but in a relationship of 2:3 with that having 12 weights. Therefore, that interval between the fifth and the fourth (that by which the fifth is greater than the fourth), was confirmed to be a proportion of 9:8, so the system of the octave proved itself to be put together in two ways: either with the fifth and fourth in conjunction as the duple proportion of the sesquialteral plus the epitritic (12:8:6), or, conversely, the fourth and fifth as the duple proportion of the epitritic and sesquialteral (12:9:6), in such an arrangement of the octave.[4]

Having accustomed both his hands and hearing to these weights, and establishing for them the proportional relationships, he skillfully transferred the common tying of the strings from the peg in the corner of the wall to the bridge of the instrument (sc. the lyre), which he named the "string-stretcher." And the amount of tightening was proportionate to the amount of weight to the corresponding turning of the pegs.
[119] Using this as a basis for proceeding, and, as it were, an infallible control,[5] he extended his experiment then to various instruments: to cymbals, *auloi*, syrinxes, monochords, *trigôna*, and the like[6]. And he found that the arithmetical relationship was unvaryingly harmonious in all of them. He named *hypatê* ("lowest")[7] the note corresponding to the number 6, *mesê* ("middle") that corresponding to 8 and epitritic to 6, *paramesê* ("next to middle"), that corresponding to 9 and higher than *mesê* by a whole tone and therefore in a 9:8 relationship to it, and *nêtê* ("highest"), that corresponding to 12. Filling out in this way the intervals of the diatonic

---

4. On this whole section, see Burkert, *Lore and Science*, 369 ff.

5. A *gnomon* is properly a carpenter's square.

6. *Auloi* are double-reeded wind instruments. *Trigôna* are musical instruments of triangular forms with strings of unequal lengths.

7. Literally, "highest" because placed highest, but lowest in pitch, even as the *nete* is the lowest in position, but highest in pitch.

καὶ σύριγγας καὶ μονόχορδα καὶ τρίγωνα καὶ τὰ παραπλήσια,
καὶ σύμφωνον εὕρισκεν ἐν ἅπασι καὶ ἀπαράλλακτον τὴν δι᾽
ἀριθμοῦ κατάληψιν. ὀνομάσας δὲ ὑπάτην μὲν τὸν τοῦ ἓξ
ἀριθμοῦ κοινωνοῦντα φθόγγον, μέσην δὲ τὸν τοῦ ὀκτώ,
ἐπίτριτον αὐτοῦ τυγχάνοντα, παραμέσην δὲ τὸν τοῦ ἐννέα,
τόνῳ τοῦ μέσου ὀξύτερον καὶ δὴ καὶ ἐπόγδοον, νήτην δὲ τὸν
τοῦ δώδεκα, καὶ τὰς μεταξύτητας κατὰ τὸ διατονικὸν γένος
συναναπληρώσας φθόγγοις ἀναλόγοις, οὕτως τὴν ὀκτάχορ-
[120] δον ἀριθμοῖς συμφώνοις ὑπέταξε, διπλασίῳ, ἡμιολίῳ,
ἐπιτρίτῳ, καὶ τῇ τούτων διαφορᾷ, ἐπογδόῳ. τὴν δὲ
πρόβασιν ἀνάγκῃ τινὶ φυσικῇ ἀπὸ τοῦ βαρυτάτου ἐπὶ τὸ
ὀξύτατον κατὰ τοῦτο τὸ διατονικὸν γένος οὕτως εὕρισκε. τὸ
γὰρ χρωματικὸν καὶ ἐναρμόνιον γένος αὖθίς ποτε ἐκ τούτου
αὐτοῦ διετράνωσεν, ὡς ἐνέσται ποτὲ δεῖξαι, ὅταν περὶ
μουσικῆς λέγωμεν. ἀλλὰ τό γε διατονικὸν γένος τοῦτο τοὺς
βαθμοὺς καὶ τὰς προόδους τοιαύτας τινὰς φυσικὰς ἔχειν
φαίνεται, ἡμιτόνιον, εἶτα τόνος, ⟨εἶτα τόνος,⟩ καὶ τοῦτ᾽ ἔστι
διὰ τεσσάρων, σύστημα δύο τόνων καὶ τοῦ λεγομένου
ἡμιτονίου. εἶτα προσληφθέντος ἄλλου τόνου, τουτέστι τοῦ
μεσεμβοληθέντος, ἡ διὰ πέντε γίνεται, σύστημα τριῶν
τόνων καὶ ἡμιτονίου ὑπάρχουσα. εἶθ᾽ ἑξῆς τούτῳ ἡμιτόνιον
καὶ τόνος καὶ τόνος, ἄλλο διὰ τεσσάρων, τουτέστιν ἄλλο
ἐπίτριτον. ὥστε ἐν μὲν τῇ ἀρχαιοτέρᾳ τῇ ἑπταχόρδῳ πάντας
ἐκ τοῦ βαρυτάτου τοὺς ἀπ᾽ ἀλλήλων τετάρτους τὴν διὰ
τεσσάρων ἀλλήλοις δι᾽ ὅλου συμφωνεῖν, τοῦ ἡμιτονίου κατὰ
μετάβασιν τήν τε πρώτην καὶ τὴν μέσην καὶ τὴν τρίτην
χώραν μεταλαμβάνοντος κατὰ τὸ τετράχορδον ἐν δὲ τῇ
[121] Πυθαγορικῇ τῇ ὀκταχόρδῳ, ἤτοι κατὰ συναφὴν συστήματι
ὑπαρχούσῃ τετραχόρδου τε καὶ πενταχόρδου, ἢ κατὰ
διάζευξιν δυεῖν τετραχόρδων τόνῳ χωριζομένων ἀπ᾽
ἀλλήλων, ἀπὸ τῆς βαρυτάτης ἡ προχώρησις ὑπάρξει, ὥστε
τοὺς ἀπ᾽ ἀλλήλων πέμπτους πάντας φθόγγους τὴν διὰ πέντε
συμφωνεῖν ἀλλήλοις, τοῦ ἡμιτονίου προβάδην εἰς τέσσαρας
χώρας μεταβαίνοντος, πρώτην, δευτέραν, τρίτην, τετάρτην.
οὕτω μὲν οὖν τὴν μουσικὴν εὑρεῖν λέγεται, καὶ
συστησάμενος αὐτὴν παρέδωκε τοῖς ὑπηκόοις ἐπὶ πάντα τὰ
κάλλιστα.

genus with proportionate notes, he arranged the octachord with numerical consonances: the duple, sesquialteral, epitritic, and, as the difference between these
latter two, the epogdoic.

[120]   Pythagoras discovered in this way the necessary natural progression from the
lowest to the highest in the diatonic genus, and beginning with the diatonic, he
proceeded to articulate the chromatic and enharmonic genera as well, as we will
show when we come to discuss music.[8] The diatonic genus, however, exhibits the
following stages and natural progressions: semitone, then whole tone, <then
whole tone>,[9] and this is the fourth, a system of two whole tones plus the so-called
"semitone." Then if another whole tone be added to this, that is to say, the inter-
calated whole tone, one gets the fifth, a system consisting of three whole tones
plus a semitone. Then, following this, there is a semitone, whole tone, and whole
tone, which produces another fourth, that is to say, another epitritic interval.
Thereby, in the more ancient heptachord, every fourth tone from the lowest
sounded throughout the system the consonance of the fourth, with the semitone,
taking in turn the first, middle, and third positions in the tetrachord. In the
[121] Pythagorean octachord, however, whether in a system consisting of a conjunction
of tetrachord and pentachord or in a system consisting of a disjunction of two tet-
rachords separated from each other by a whole tone,[10] the progression begins at
the lowest tone, so that every fifth note sounds the consonance of a fifth, with the
semitone here proceeding in turn into four places—the first, second, third, and
fourth.[11] In this way, then, he is said to have discovered music, organized it into a
system, and presented it to his followers for all noblest purposes.

---

8. This is slightly adapted from Nicomachus. Iamblichus may refer to a later work in his
Pythagorean sequence, *The Introduction to Music* (now lost) which is mentioned in the future
tense. See *In Nic.*, p. 122, 12. He may, however (as Rohde thinks, *RhM* 27 [1872] 39) be simply
copying from Nicomachus, who also makes a reference forward at this point (p. 249 of Jahn)
though not quite so specific.

9. Supplied, necessarily, from Nicomachus.

10. These alternatives describe the well-known terms συνημμένον and διεζευγμένον.

11. The order is actually "first, fourth, second, third." Here the extract from Nicomachus
ends, and the chapter is rounded off by an Iamblichean bridge-phrase.

[122]   Ἐπαινεῖται δὲ πολλὰ καὶ τῶν κατὰ τὰς πολιτείας πραχθέντων ὑπὸ τῶν ἐκείνῳ πλησιασάντων. φασὶ γάρ,
ἐμπεσούσης μέν ποτε παρὰ τοῖς Κροτωνιάταις ὁρμῆς
πολυτελεῖς ποιεῖσθαι τὰς ἐκφορὰς καὶ ταφάς, εἰπεῖν τινα
πρὸς τὸν δῆμον ἐξ αὐτῶν, ὅτι Πυθαγόρου διεξιόντος
ἀκούσειεν ὑπὲρ τῶν θεῶν, ὡς οἱ μὲν Ὀλύμπιοι ταῖς τῶν
θυόντων διαθέσεσιν, οὐ τῷ τῶν θυομένων πλήθει
προσέχουσιν, οἱ δὲ χθόνιοι τοὐναντίον, ὡς ἂν ἐλαττόνων
κληρονομοῦντες, τοῖς κομμοῖς καὶ θρήνοις, ἔτι δὲ ταῖς
συνεχέσι χοαῖς καὶ τοῖς ἐπιφορήμασι καὶ τοῖς μετὰ μεγάλης
[123]   δαπάνης ἐναγισμοῖς χαίρουσι. ὅθεν διὰ τὴν προαίρεσιν τῆς
⟨τοιαύτης⟩ ὑποδοχῆς Πλούτωνα καλεῖσθαι τὸν Ἅιδην, καὶ
τοὺς μὲν ἀφελῶς αὐτὸν τιμῶντας ἐᾶν κατὰ τὸν ἄνω κόσμον
χρονίους, ἀπὸ δὲ τῶν ἐκκεχυμένως πρὸς τὰ πένθη
διακειμένων ἀεί τινα κατάγειν ἕνεκα τοῦ τυγχάνειν τῶν
τιμῶν τῶν ἐπὶ τοῖς μνήμασι γινομένων. ἐκ δὲ τῆς
συμβουλίας ταύτης ὑπόληψιν ἐμποιῆσαι τοῖς ἀκούουσιν, ὅτι
μετριάζοντες μὲν ἐν τοῖς ἀτυχήμασι τὴν ἰδίαν σωτηρίαν
διατηροῦσιν, ὑπερβάλλοντες δὲ τοῖς ἀναλώμασιν ἅπαντες
[124]   πρὸ μοίρας καταστρέψουσιν. ἕτερον δὲ διαιτητὴν γενόμενόν
τινος ἀμαρτύρου πράγματος, χωρὶς μεθ' ἑκατέρου τῶν
ἀντιδίκων ὁδῷ προάγοντα, κατὰ μνῆμά τι στάντα φῆσαι τὸν
ἐν τούτῳ κείμενον ἐπιεικῆ καθ' ὑπερβολὴν γενέσθαι. τῶν δὲ
ἀντιδίκων τοῦ μὲν πολλὰ κἀγαθὰ κατευξαμένου τῷ
τετελευτηκότι, τοῦ δὲ εἰπόντος· "μή τι οὖν αὐτῷ πλεῖόν
ἐστι;" καταδοξάσαι, καὶ παρεσχῆσθαί τινα ῥοπὴν εἰς τὴν
πίστιν τὸν ἐγκωμιάσαντα τὴν καλοκαγαθίαν. ἄλλον δὲ
δίαιταν εἰληφότα μεγάλην, ἑκάτερον πείσαντα τῶν
ἐπιτρεψάντων, τὸν μὲν ἀποτῖσαι τέσσαρα τάλαντα, τὸν δὲ
λαβεῖν δύο, καταγνῶναι τρία, καὶ δόξαι δεδωκέναι τάλαντον

CHAPTER TWENTY-SEVEN

What public-spirited and generally useful benefits he himself
and his followers conferred on human beings through words and deeds,
both through the establishment of constitutions and the laying
down of laws, and through many other excellent regulations.

[122]   Many things done by his disciples in the area of civic affairs are also praised.[1] For they say that when desire for celebrating costly funerals and burials afflicted the Crotoniates, a Pythagorean said to the people that he once heard Pythagoras say when discoursing on the gods, that the Olympians pay attention to the attitudes of those who make sacrifice, not to the quantity of the things sacrificed. The gods of the underworld, on the contrary, since they are inheritors of lesser things, rejoice in lamentations and dirges, and moreover, in continuous libations, grave offerings, and offerings to the dead involving great expense. Hence, on account [123] of his preference for such hospitality, the god Hades is called "Pluto" ("the wealthy one"); he allows those who honor him simply to remain a long while in the upper world, but from those extravagantly disposed to mournings for the dead, he always brings someone down to the nether world for the sake of obtaining the offerings made at tombs. By this advice, Pythagoras created in his hearers the belief that by being moderate in their misfortunes, they would maintain their own well-being; but by being excessive in their expenses, they would all die before [124] their appointed time.

     Another Pythagorean became arbiter in a legal affair without witnesses; after he led separately each of the adversaries in the law-suit on a path, and stopped at a certain tomb, he said that the man lying there had been exceedingly equitable. When one of the adversaries prayed for many good things for the departed, and the other asked "Does he have any advantage from all that?" he became suspicious of this latter, and had reason for trusting him who had praised the departed's nobility.

     Another Pythagorean had taken on a great arbitration; after persuading each party referring the legal issue to him, one to repay four talents, the other to take only two, he gave judgment for three, and thus seemed to have given a talent to each.

---

1. From here to the beginning of section 129, there are a series of anecdotes loosely related to "civic affairs" (πολιτεῖαι), and which diverge increasingly from this theme until Iamblichus returns to the subject. He may, as Rohde suggests, *RhM* 27 (1872) 40-41, be following a source not all of whose anecdotes were relevant to his theme, and went on copying.

145

ἑκατέρῳ. θεμένων δέ τινων ἐπὶ κακουργίᾳ πρὸς γύναιον τῶν
ἀγοραίων ἱμάτιον καὶ διειπομένων μὴ διδόναι θατέρῳ μέχρις
ἂν ἀμφότεροι παρῶσι, μετὰ δὲ ταῦτα παραλογισαμένων, καὶ
σύνεγγυς τοῦ κοινῇ θεμένου λαβόντος θατέρου καὶ φήσαντος
συγκεχωρηκέναι τὸν ἕτερον, εἶτα συκοφαντοῦντος ἑτέρου
τοῦ μὴ προσελθόντος καὶ τὴν ἐξ ἀρχῆς ὁμολογίαν τοῖς
ἄρχουσιν ἐμφανίζοντος, ἐκδεξάμενον τῶν Πυθαγορείων τινὰ
φῆσαι τὰ συγκείμενα τὴν ἄνθρωπον ποιήσειν, ἂν ἀμφότεροι
[125] παρῶσιν. ἄλλων δέ τινων ἐν ἰσχυρᾷ μὲν φιλίᾳ πρὸς
ἀλλήλους εἶναι δοκούντων, εἰς σιωπωμένην δὲ ὑποψίαν διά
τινα τῶν κολακευόντων τὸν ἕτερον ἐμπεπτωκότων, ὃς εἴρηκε
πρὸς αὐτὸν ὡς τῆς γυναικὸς ὑπὸ θατέρου διεφθαρμένης, ἀπὸ
τύχης εἰσελθόντα τὸν Πυθαγόρειον εἰς χαλκεῖον, ἐπεὶ δείξας
ἠκονημένην μάχαιραν ὁ νομίζων ἀδικεῖσθαι τῷ τεχνίτῃ
προσέκοπτεν ὡς οὐχ ἱκανῶς ἠκονηκότι, καθυπονοήσαντα
ποιεῖσθαι τὴν παρασκευὴν αὐτὸν ἐπὶ τὸν διαβεβλημένον,
"αὕτη σοι" φῆσαι "τῶν ἄλλων ἐστὶν ἁπάντων ὀξυτέρα, πλὴν
διαβολῆς". καὶ τοῦτ' εἴπαντα ποιῆσαι τὸν ἄνθρωπον
ἐπιστῆσαι τὴν διάνοιαν καὶ μὴ προπετῶς εἰς τὸν φίλον, ὃς
[126] ἔνδον ἦν προκεκλημένος, ἐξαμαρτεῖν. ἕτερον δέ, ξένου τινὸς
ἐκβεβληκότος ἐν Ἀσκληπιείῳ ζώνην χρυσίον ἔχουσαν καὶ
τῶν μὲν νόμων τὸ πεσὸν ἐπὶ τὴν γῆν κωλυόντων
ἀναιρεῖσθαι, τοῦ δὲ ξένου σχετλιάζοντος, κελεῦσαι τὸ μὲν
χρυσίον ἐξελεῖν, ὃ μὴ πέπτωκεν ἐπὶ τὴν γῆν, τὴν δὲ ζώνην
ἐᾶν· εἶναι γὰρ ταύτην ἐπὶ τῆς γῆς. καὶ τὸ μεταφερόμενον δὲ
ὑπὸ τῶν ἀγνοούντων εἰς τόπους ἑτέρους ἐν Κρότωνι
γενέσθαι λέγουσιν, ὅτι θέας οὔσης καὶ γεράνων ὑπὲρ τοῦ
θεάτρου φερομένων, εἰπόντος τινὸς τῶν καταπεπλευκότων
πρὸς τὸν πλησίον καθήμενον· "ὁρᾷς τοὺς μάρτυρας;"
ἐπακούσας τις τῶν Πυθαγορείων ἤγαγεν αὐτοὺς ἐπὶ τὸ τῶν
χιλίων ἀρχεῖον, ὑπολαβών, ὅπερ ἐλέγχοντες τοὺς παῖδας
ἐξεῦρον, καταπεποντικέναι τινὰς τὰς ὑπὲρ τῆς νεὼς
πετομένας γεράνους μαρτυρομένους. καὶ πρὸς ἀλλήλους δέ
τινες, ὡς ἔοικε, διενεχθέντες, νεωστὶ πρὸς Πυθαγόραν
παραβαλόντες, ὡς ὁ νεώτερος προσελθὼν διελύετο, φάσκων
οὐ δεῖν ἐφ' ἕτερον ποιεῖσθαι τὴν ἀναφοράν, ἀλλ' ἐν αὐτοῖς
ἐπιλαθέσθαι τῆς ὀργῆς, τὰ μὲν ἄλλα αὐτῷ φῆσαι τὸν
ἀκούοντα διαφερόντως ἀρέσκειν, αἰσχύνεσθαι δὲ ἐπὶ τῷ
πρεσβύτερος ὢν μὴ πρότερος [ὢν] αὐτὸς προξελθεῖν.

Once two men with malicious intent left a garment with a common woman of the market-place, and agreed she not give it to either until both be present. Then they perpetrated the following fraud: quite soon after, one of them collected that which had been jointly deposited (with the woman), and said the other had agreed; then the other, who had not been present, informed against her, and showed the initial agreement to the magistrates. A Pythagorean, taking up the case, said the woman would do the things agreed on if both men were present.[2]

[125]   On another occasion, two men who seemed to have a strong friendship with one another, fell into silent mutual suspicion because a sycophantic trouble-maker told the one that his wife had been seduced by his friend. By chance, a Pythagorean entered a forge when the man who believed himself wronged was showing his sharpened sword in annoyance with the smith because he had not sharpened it enough. The Pythagorean, suspecting that it was being readied for use on the one who had been slandered, said: "For you this sword is sharper than all others, except slander." And having said this, he made the man check his intention and not hastily wrong his friend, who had been already invited to his house.

[126]   Another Pythagorean, when a visitor dropped a belt containing gold in a shrine of Asclepius, and complained indignantly because the laws prohibited taking up that which was on the ground, urged him to remove the gold, which had not fallen on the ground, and to leave the belt, for this was on the ground.

The following story too, which is shifted by the ignorant to other places, they say happened in Croton: that during a performance while cranes flew over the theater, one of the audience, who had returned from a voyage, said to his neighbour "Do you see the witnesses?" A Pythagorean, overhearing them, led them to the council house of the Thousand. He suspected, what was discovered to be the case on cross-examining their slaves, that they had thrown some persons into the sea, for whom the cranes, flying over the ship, bore witness.[3] Again, two men, so it seems, after having lately joined Pythagoras, quarreled; when the younger one approached the other and offered reconciliation, saying that it was not necessary to call in a third party as arbiter, but that it was in their own power to forget their anger, the other hearing his apology said that in every way he was greatly satisfied, but he was ashamed that being older, he had not first made the approach.

---

2. The point of this story becomes clear if it is assumed that one of the shysters involved has already decamped, and so both cannot appear. It has some elements of folktale. Cf. R. Baumgartner, "Susanna. Die Geschichte einer Legende," *ARW* 24 (1926) 259-80, esp. 270 ff.

3. This story was indeed "shifted to other places." It is best known as attached to the poet Ibycus (e.g. Plut. *De garr.* 509 F), and has been appropriated by the Pythagoreans.

[127] *** καὶ ταῦτα πρὸς ἐκεῖνον εἰπεῖν καὶ τὰ περὶ Φιντίαν καὶ Δάμωνα, περί τε Πλάτωνος καὶ Ἀρχύτου, καὶ τὰ περὶ Κλεινίαν καὶ Πρῶρον. χωρὶς τοίνυν τούτων Εὐβούλου τοῦ Μεσηνίου πλέοντος εἰς οἶκον καὶ ληφθέντος ὑπὸ Τυρρηνῶν καὶ καταχθέντος εἰς Τυρρηνίαν, Ναυσίθοος ὁ Τυρρηνός, Πυθαγόρειος ὤν, ἐπιγνοὺς αὐτὸν ὅτι τῶν Πυθαγόρου μαθητῶν ἐστιν, ἀφελόμενος τοὺς λῃστὰς μετ᾽ ἀσφαλείας [128] πολλῆς εἰς τὴν Μεσήνην αὐτὸν κατέστησε. Καρχηδονίων τε πλείους ἢ πεντακισχιλίους ἄνδρας, τοὺς παρ᾽ αὐτοῖς στρατευομένους, εἰς νῆσον ἔρημον ἀποστέλλειν μελλόντων, ἰδὼν ἐν τούτοις Μιλτιάδης ὁ Καρχηδόνιος Ποσιδῆν Ἀργεῖον, ἀμφότεροι τῶν Πυθαγορείων ὄντες, προσελθὼν αὐτῷ τὴν μὲν πρᾶξιν τὴν ἐσομένην οὐκ ἐδήλωσεν, ἠξίου δ᾽ αὐτὸν εἰς τὴν ἰδίαν ἀποτρέχειν τὴν ταχίστην, καὶ παραπλεούσης νεὼς συνέστησεν αὐτὸν ἐφόδιον προσθεὶς καὶ τὸν ἄνδρα διέσωσεν ἐκ τῶν κινδύνων. ὅλως δὲ πάσας εἴ τις λέγοι τὰς γεγενημένας ὁμιλίας τοῖς Πυθαγορείοις πρὸς ἀλλήλους, ὑπεραίροι ἂν τῷ μήκει τὸν ὄγκον καὶ τὸν καιρὸν τοῦ συγγράμματος.

[129] μέτειμι οὖν μᾶλλον ἐπ᾽ ἐκεῖνα, ὡς ἦσαν ἔνιοι τῶν Πυθαγορείων πολιτικοὶ καὶ ἀρχικοί. καὶ γὰρ νόμους ἐφύλαττον καὶ πόλεις Ἰταλικὰς διῴκησάν τινες, ἀποφαινόμενοι μὲν καὶ συμβουλεύοντες τὰ ἄριστα ὧν ὑπελάμβανον, ἀπεχόμενοι δὲ δημοσίων προσόδων. πολλῶν δὲ γιγνομένων κατ᾽ αὐτῶν διαβολῶν ὅμως ἐπεκράτει μέχρι τινὸς ἡ τῶν Πυθαγορείων καλοκαγαθία καὶ ἡ τῶν πόλεων αὐτῶν βούλησις, ὥστε ὑπ᾽ ἐκείνων οἰκονομεῖσθαι βούλεσθαι τὰ περὶ τὰς πολιτείας. ἐν τούτῳ δὲ τῷ χρόνῳ δοκοῦσιν αἱ κάλλισται τῶν πολιτειῶν ἐν [130] Ἰταλίᾳ γενέσθαι καὶ ἐν Σικελίᾳ. Χαρώνδας τε γὰρ ὁ Καταναῖος, εἷς εἶναι δοκῶν τῶν ἀρίστων νομοθετῶν, Πυθαγόρειος ἦν, Ζάλευκός τε καὶ Τιμάρης οἱ Λοκροί, ὀνομαστοὶ γεγενημένοι ἐπὶ νομοθεσίᾳ, Πυθαγόρειοι ἦσαν, οἵ τε τὰς Ῥηγινικὰς πολιτείας συστήσαντες, τήν τε γυμνασιαρχικὴν κληθεῖσαν καὶ τὴν ἐπὶ Θεοκλέους ὀνομαζομένην, Πυθαγόρειοι λέγονται εἶναι, Φύτιός τε καὶ Θεοκλῆς καὶ Ἑλικάων καὶ Ἀριστοκράτης· διήνεγκαν ⟨δὲ⟩ ἐπιτηδεύμασί τε καὶ ἔθεσιν, οἷς καὶ αἱ ἐν ἐκείνοις τοῖς τόποις πόλεις κατ᾽ ἐκείνους τοὺς χρόνους ἐχρήσαντο.

[127]   And besides these stories he says he told him[4] those about Phintias and Damon,
Plato and Archytas, and about Cleinias and Prorus. Apart from these (stories),
there is the one about Eubulus of Messene. He, when sailing homeward, was captured by Etruscans and landed in Etruria. Nausithous, the Etruscan, who was a
Pythagorean, recognized him as a pupil of Pythagoras; and, taking him away from
the pirates, brought him back to Messene in complete safety.

[128]   Again,[5] when the Carthaginians were about to send more than five thousand
soldiers serving with them to a deserted island, the Carthaginian Miltiades saw
among these the Argive Possides (both were Pythagoreans). Approaching him, he
did not reveal the action about to take place, but requested him to depart as
quickly as possible to his own land, and put him on a ship sailing near, giving him
provisions for travel, and saved the man from danger.

    In general, if someone were to relate all dealings the Pythagoreans had with
one another, he would exceed in length the size and balance of this treatise. I thus
[129] pass on instead to the following topic:[6] how excellent certain Pythagoreans were
as statesmen, and rulers. For some maintained laws and directed Italian cities pro-
claiming and counseling things they believed best, but kept their hands off public
revenues. And although many slanders were leveled at them, nevertheless the noble goodness of the Pythagoreans prevailed for some time as well as the resolve of
the cities themselves, so that they were willing to be managed by them in govern-
mental matters. It is at this time, as is generally agreed, that the best governments
[130] came into being in Italy and in Sicily. Charondas of Catana, who is considered to
be one of the best legislators, was a Pythagorean; Zaleucus and Timares the Locrians, who are famous for their legislation, were Pythagoreans; those who framed
the constitutions of Rhegium, that which is called the "gymnasiarchic," and that
which is named after Theocles, are said to have been Pythagoreans, Phytius, Theocles, Helicaon, and Aristocrates. They were distinguished in their way of life and
customs, which the cities in those places also enjoyed in those times. In short, they
say that Pythagoras was the inventor of political education in general. He asserted
that nothing of existing things is unmixed;[7] earth shares in fire, and fire in water,

---

4. From the text it would seem that Iamblichus has carelessly transcribed something from his
source, perhaps Aristoxenus, relating stories told to him by the exiled Dionysius II of Syracuse.
Iamblichus returns to this at section 234 where he quotes Aristoxenus.

5. Diodorus Siculus tells the story of the abandonment, though without the edifying anecdotes given here (he reports 6000 mercenaries on the island (V, 12)), and relates it to the "great
wars between the Carthaginians and the Syracusans," which possibly dates the incident to the
480's B.C. Miltiades, however, is a strange name for a Carthaginian (as is Nausithous, above, for
an Etruscan).

6. Cf. sections 33-35 above. From the fact that a sentence in this section corresponds verbally
to one in sect 249 below, explicitly credited to Aristoxenus, one may attribute sections 129, and
the first half of 130, to that source.

7. Cf. Alexander Polyhistor's account of Pythagorean first principles in D.L. 8. 25-26.

ὅλως δὲ εὑρετὴν αὐτὸν γενέσθαι φασὶ καὶ τῆς πολιτικῆς
ὅλης παιδείας, εἰπόντα μηδὲν εἰλικρινὲς εἶναι τῶν ὄντων
πραγμάτων, ἀλλὰ μετέχειν καὶ γῆν πυρὸς καὶ πῦρ ὕδατος καὶ
πνεῦμα τούτων καὶ ταῦτα πνεύματος, ἔτι καλὸν αἰσχροῦ καὶ
δίκαιον ἀδίκου καὶ τἆλλα κατὰ λόγον τούτοις (ἐκ δὲ ταύτης
τῆς ὑποθέσεως λαβεῖν τὸν λόγον τὴν εἰς ἑκάτερον μέρος
ὁρμήν· δύο δὲ εἶναι κινήσεις καὶ τοῦ σώματος καὶ τῆς ψυχῆς,
τὴν μὲν ἄλογον, τὴν δὲ προαιρετικήν), πολιτειῶν δὲ
γραμμάς τινας τοιάσδε τρεῖς συστησάμενον, τοῖς ἄκροις
ἀλλήλων συμψαυούσας, μίαν ὀρθὴν γωνίαν ποιούσας, τὴν
μὲν ἐπίτριτον φύσιν ἔχουσαν, τὴν δὲ πέντε τοιαῦτα
δυναμένην, τὴν δὲ τούτων ἀμφοτέρων ἀνὰ μέσον.
[131] λογιζομένων δ' ἡμῶν τάς τε τῶν γραμμῶν πρὸς ἀλλήλας
συμπτώσεις καὶ τὰς τῶν χωρίων τῶν ἀπὸ τούτων, βελ-
τίστην ὑποτυποῦσθαι πολιτείας εἰκόνα. σφετερίσασθαι δὲ
τὴν δόξαν Πλάτωνα, λέγοντα φανερῶς ἐν τῇ Πολιτείᾳ τὸν
ἐπίτριτον ἐκεῖνον πυθμένα τὸν τῇ πεμπάδι συζευγνύμενον
καὶ τὰς δύο παρεχόμενον ἁρμονίας. ἀσκῆσαι δέ φασιν αὐτὸν
καὶ τὰς μετριοπαθείας καὶ τὰς μεσότητας καὶ τὸ σύν τινι
προηγουμένῳ τῶν ἀγαθῶν ἕκαστον εὐδαίμονα ποιεῖν τὸν
βίον, καὶ συλλήβδην προσευρεῖν τὴν αἵρεσιν τῶν ἡμετέρων
ἀγαθῶν καὶ προσηκόντων ἔργων.
[132]   ἀπαλλάξαι δὲ λέγεται τοὺς Κροτωνιάτας καὶ τῶν παλ-
λακίδων καὶ καθόλου τῆς πρὸς τὰς ἀνεγγύους γυναῖκας
ὁμιλίας. πρὸς Δεινὼ γὰρ τὴν Βροντίνου γυναῖκα, τῶν
Πυθαγορείων ἑνός, οὖσαν σοφήν τε καὶ περιττὴν τὴν
ψυχήν, ἧς ἐστὶ καὶ τὸ καλὸν καὶ περίβλεπτον ῥῆμα, τὸ τὴν
γυναῖκα δεῖν θύειν αὐθημερὸν ἀνισταμένην ἀπὸ τοῦ ἑαυτῆς
ἀνδρός, ὅ τινες εἰς Θεανὼ ἀναφέρουσι, πρὸς δὴ ταύτην
παρελθούσας τὰς τῶν Κροτωνιατῶν γυναῖκας παρακαλέσαι
περὶ τοῦ συμπεῖσαι τὸν Πυθαγόραν διαλεχθῆναι περὶ τῆς
πρὸς αὐτὰς σωφροσύνης τοῖς ἀνδράσιν αὐτῶν. ὃ δὴ καὶ
συμβῆναι, καὶ τῆς γυναικὸς ἐπαγγειλαμένης καὶ τοῦ
Πυθαγόρου διαλεχθέντος καὶ τῶν Κροτωνιατῶν πεισθέντων
ἀναιρεθῆναι παντάπασι τὴν τότε ἐπιπολάζουσαν ἀκολασίαν.

and air in these, and these in air; further, beautiful in ugly, and just in unjust, and other things in like fashion (in accordance with this assumption reason possesses an impulsion in either direction: there are two motions of the body and of the soul, one irrational, and the other purposive); and so he brought together three lines of civic constitutions such that they intersect one another at their extremities and produce a right angle:[8] one line standing to the other in the ratio of 4:3, while the other again was equivalent to five such units; and the third is in the middle of

[131] both these. When we calculate the relationships of these lines with one another, and of the figures resulting from these, the best likeness of a civic constitution is sketched out. Plato appropriated this opinion, saying clearly in the *Republic* that the first couple of numbers giving the ratio of 4:3, is paired with the number five and produces two harmonies.[9]

He is also said to have practiced moderation of the passions and the doctrine of the mean[10] and the concept of making a happy life for oneself by directing it in accordance with one dominant good. In sum, he discovered the concept of a choice of goods and deeds relative to them.

[132] He is said also to have freed the Crotoniates entirely from concubines and from intercourse with unwedded women. For to Deino, wife of Brontinus, one of the Pythagoreans, a woman of wise and exceptional spirit, to whom also belongs a saying noble and admired by all: "the wife ought to sacrifice on the very day she arose from sleep with her own husband" (which saying some ascribe to Theano);[11] to her, then, the wives of the Crotoniates came, and requested her to join them in persuading Pythagoras to talk about the chastity due them from their own husbands. This, in fact, came about: the woman passed on the message, Pythagoras spoke to the Crotoniates, and they were persuaded to abolish altogether the licentiousness then prevalent.[12]

---

8. The famous "Pythagorean Theorem" in its political application. Cf. E. L. Minar, *Early Pythagorean Politics in Practice and Theory* (Baltimore, 1942).

9. *R.* 546 c.

10. Thus assimilating Pythagoras to Peripatetic as opposed to Stoic doctrine. Both Plutarch, in *Virt. mor.* 441 E ff., and Nicomachus of Gerasa, *Intr. Arith.* 1.14.2, regard Pythagoreanism as siding with Aristotle in ethics, as does Pseudo-Archytas, among the *Pseudo-Pythagorica* (*De Educ.* 2, p. 41, 15-18 Thesleff, *Pythagorean Texts*).

11. Diogenes Laertius (8.42) reports two alternative traditions, that Theano was daughter of Bro(n)tinus, and wife of Pythagoras, and that she was the wife of Brotinus, pupil of Pythagoras. See Delatte, *La vie de Pythagore*, 246-249 for a lengthy discussion of the conflicting reports.

12. Cf. the relevant section (48) of his discourse to the Crotoniates reported above in chap. 9.

[133] ἔτι φασὶ Πυθαγόραν, ἀφικομένων εἰς τὴν πόλιν τῶν
Κροτωνιατῶν ἐκ τῆς Συβάριδος πρεσβευτῶν ἐπὶ τὴν
ἐξαίτησιν τῶν φυγάδων, θεασάμενόν τινα τῶν πρέσβεων
αὐτόχειρα γεγενημένον τῶν αὐτοῦ φίλων, μηδὲν ἀποκρίνα-
σθαι αὐτῷ. ἐπερομένου δὲ τοῦ ἀνθρώπου καὶ βουλομένου τῆς
ὁμιλίας αὐτοῦ μετέχειν, εἰπεῖν ὡς οὐ θεμιστεύοι τοῖς
⟨τοιούτοις⟩ ἀνθρώποις· ὅθεν δὴ καὶ παρά τισιν Ἀπόλλωνα
νομισθῆναι αὐτόν. ταῦτα δὴ πάντα καὶ ὅσα μικρὸν ἔμπροσθεν εἰρήκαμεν περὶ τῆς τῶν τυράννων καταλύσεως καὶ τῆς
τῶν πόλεων ἐλευθερώσεως τῶν ἐν Ἰταλίᾳ τε καὶ Σικελίᾳ καὶ
ἄλλων πλειόνων δείγματα ποιησώμεθα τῆς εἰς τὰ πολιτικὰ
ἀγαθὰ ὠφελείας αὐτοῦ, ἣν συνεβάλλετο τοῖς ἀνθρώποις.

[133]   Again,[13] they say that Pythagoras, when ambassadors from Sybaris arrived at the city of the Crotoniates demanding their fugitives for punishment, on seeing that one of the ambassadors had been a murderer of his own friends, made no reply to him. But when the man asked again, and wished to share his company, Pythagoras said that he would not deliver oracles to such men. Hence, he was believed by some to be Apollo.

All these things then, and what we have said a little before[14] about the overthrow of the tyrants, liberation of the cities both in Italy and Sicily, and many other things, let us take as examples of the good influence in public affairs which he contributed to human beings.

---

13. This story is also told, in different words, in section 177 below. These events seem to have occurred in 510 B.C., when a democratic revolution took place in Sybaris. Cf. Diodorus Siculus, XII 9, 2.

14. This was described, not "a little before," but back in chap. 7 (sections 33-34). Can it be that Iamblichus is copying this from his source?

[134]   Τὸ δὴ μετὰ τοῦτο μηκέθ' οὑτωσὶ κοινῶς, ἀλλὰ καὶ κατ' ἰδίαν ἀποτεμόμενοι τὰ τῶν ἀρετῶν ἔργα αὐτοῦ τῷ λόγῳ κοσμήσωμεν. ἀρξώμεθα δὲ πρῶτον ἀπὸ θεῶν, ὥσπερ καὶ νομίζεται, τήν τε ὁσιότητα αὐτοῦ πειραθῶμεν ἐπιδεῖξαι καὶ τὰ ἀπ' αὐτῆς θαυμαστὰ ἔργα ἐπιδείξωμεν ἑαυτοῖς καὶ τῷ λόγῳ κοσμήσωμεν. ἓν μὲν οὖν δεῖγμα αὐτῆς ἐκεῖνο ἔστω, οὗ καὶ πρότερον ἐμνημονεύσαμεν, ὅτι δὴ ἐγίνωσκε τὴν ἑαυτοῦ ψυχήν, τίς ἦν καὶ πόθεν εἰς τὸ σῶμα εἰσεληλύθει, τούς τε προτέρους αὐτῆς βίους, καὶ τούτων πρόδηλα τεκμήρια παρεῖχε. μετὰ τοῦτο τοίνυν ἐκεῖνο. Νέσσον ποτὲ τὸν ποταμὸν σὺν πολλοῖς τῶν ἑταίρων διαβαίνων προσεῖπε τῇ φωνῇ, καὶ ὁ ποταμὸς γεγωνόν τι καὶ τρανὸν ἀπεφθέγξατο πάντων ἀκουόντων· "χαῖρε, Πυθαγόρα". ἔτι μιᾷ καὶ τῇ αὐτῇ ἡμέρᾳ ἔν τε Μεταποντίῳ τῆς Ἰταλίας καὶ ἐν Ταυρομενίῳ τῆς Σικελίας συγγεγονέναι καὶ διειλέχθαι κοινῇ τοῖς ἑκατέρωθι ἑταίροις αὐτὸν διαβεβαιοῦνται σχεδὸν ἅπαντες, σταδίων ἐν μεσαιχμίῳ παμπόλλων καὶ κατὰ γῆν καὶ κατὰ θάλατταν
[135]   ὑπαρχόντων, οὐδ' ἡμέραις ἀνυσίμων πάνυ πολλαῖς. τὸ μὲν γὰρ ὅτι τὸν μηρὸν χρύσεον ἐπέδειξεν Ἀβάριδι τῷ Ὑπερβορέῳ, εἰκάσαντι αὐτὸν Ἀπόλλωνα εἶναι τὸν ⟨ἐν⟩ Ὑπερβορέοις, οὗπερ ἦν ἱερεὺς ὁ Ἄβαρις, βεβαιοῦντα ὡς τοῦτο ἀληθὲς ὑπολαμβάνοι καὶ οὐ διαψεύδοιτο, καὶ πάνυ τεθρύλληται. καὶ μυρία ἕτερα τούτων θειότερα καὶ θαυμαστότερα περὶ τἀνδρὸς ὁμαλῶς καὶ συμφώνως ἱστορεῖται, προρρήσεις τε σεισμῶν ἀπαράβατοι καὶ λοιμῶν ἀποτροπαὶ σὺν τάχει καὶ ἀνέμων βιαίων χαλαζῶν τε χύσεως παραυτίκα κατευνήσεις καὶ κυμάτων ποταμίων τε καὶ θαλασσίων ἀπευδιασμοὶ πρὸς εὐμαρῆ τῶν ἑταίρων διάβασιν. ὧν μεταλαβόντας Ἐμπεδοκλέα τε τὸν Ἀκραγαντῖνον καὶ Ἐπιμενίδην τὸν Κρῆτα καὶ Ἄβαριν τὸν Ὑπερβόρειον πολλαχῇ καὶ αὐτοὺς τοιαῦτά τινα ἐπιτετελεκέναι. δῆλα δ' αὐτῶν

CHAPTER TWENTY-EIGHT

*What divine and marvelous deeds were accomplished which aim
at piety, and by the goodwill of the gods provide the
greatest benefit to human beings deeds bestowed
on the human race by Pythagoras.*

[134] After this, then, let us celebrate in words his virtuous deeds no longer in general, but according to the individual virtues.[1] Let us begin first with the gods, as is the custom, and let us try to exhibit his piety, and display for ourselves his marvelous deeds resulting from it, and adorn them with a suitable account. Let this, then, be one example of it, which we also mentioned earlier:[2] that he recognized his own soul, who it had been, and whence it had entered his body, and his soul's former lives; and for these he provided clear proofs.

And then there is also the following example:[3] once when crossing the river Nessus with many of his disciples, he spoke to it, and the river replied loud and clear while all listened: "Greetings, Pythagoras." Again, nearly all authorities assert that on one and the same day he was present in Metapontium in Italy and in Tauromenium in Sicily, and conversed with his disciples in both places, although there is a distance of many stades both by land and sea between the two cities, and the journey takes a great many days.

[135] It is a matter of common knowledge that he showed his golden thigh to Abaris the Hyperborean, who guessed that he was the Hyperborean Apollo, whose priest Abaris was. He did this to confirm the truth of Abaris's supposition, and to show that he (Abaris) was not deceived.[4] And ten thousand other incidents more divine

---

1. There now begins a series of six chapters (28-33), dealing with individual virtues, which contain a considerable degree of repetition from earlier parts of the work where the same material is often presented in a different context.

2. Above, section 63.

3. This next section is virtually identical with Porph. *VP* 27-28 except that Porphyry calls the river "Caucasus." Diogenes Laertius (8.11) gives the river as Nessus (apparently drawing on Timaeus). See Delatte, *La vie de Pythagore*, 171. These legends seem ultimately to go back to Aristotle's lost work *On the Pythagoreans*, but are transmitted in various versions: the *Historia Mirabilium* of Apollonius, Diogenes Laertius, Aelian (in his *Varia historia*, 2.26 and 4.17), and Nicomachus (if Porphyry and Iamblichus are dependent on him). Aelian has the most nearly correct form of the river which is the Casas, near Metapontium. How Iamblichus comes up with a different name from Porphyry is a matter for conjecture.

4. Iamblichus here omits a story, present in Porph. *VP*, 28, about his discernment that a boat passing by was carrying a corpse. He gives it later, though, in section 142. The golden thigh story is otherwise told in connection with his appearance at Olympia.

[136] τὰ ποιήματα ὑπάρχει, ἄλλως τε καὶ ἀλεξανέμας μὲν ὂν τὸ ἐπώνυμον Ἐμπεδοκλέους, καθαρτὴς δὲ τὸ Ἐπιμενίδου, αἰθροβάτης δὲ τὸ Ἀβάριδος, ὅτι ἄρα οἰστῷ τοῦ ἐν Ὑπερβορέοις Ἀπόλλωνος δωρηθέντι αὐτῷ ἐποχούμενος ποταμούς τε καὶ πελάγη καὶ τὰ ἄβατα διέβαινεν, ἀεροβατῶν τρόπον τινά, ὅπερ ὑπενόησαν καὶ Πυθαγόραν τινὲς πεπονθέναι τότε, ἡνίκα καὶ ἐν Μεταποντίῳ καὶ ἐν Ταυρομενίῳ τοῖς ἑκατέρωθι ἑταίροις ὡμίλησε τῇ αὐτῇ ἡμέρᾳ. λέγεται δ' ὅτι καὶ σεισμὸν ἐσόμενον ἀπὸ φρέατος, οὗ ἐγεύσατο, προηγόρευσε, καὶ περὶ νεὼς οὐριοδρομούσης, ὅτι καταποντισθήσεται. καὶ ταῦτα μὲν [137] ἔστω τεκμήρια τῆς εὐσεβείας αὐτοῦ. βούλομαι δὲ ἄνωθεν τὰς ἀρχὰς ὑποδεῖξαι τῆς τῶν θεῶν θρησκείας, ἃς προεστήσατο Πυθαγόρας τε καὶ οἱ ἀπ' αὐτοῦ ἄνδρες.

ἄπαντα ὅσα περὶ τοῦ πράττειν ἢ μὴ πράττειν διορίζουσιν ἐστόχασται τῆς πρὸς τὸ θεῖον ὁμολογίας, καὶ ἀρχὴ αὕτη ἐστὶ καὶ βίος ἅπας συντέτακται πρὸς τὸ ἀκολουθεῖν τῷ θεῷ, καὶ ὁ λόγος οὗτος ταύτης ἐστὶ τῆς φιλοσοφίας, ὅτι γελοῖον ποιοῦσιν ἄνθρωποι ἄλλοθέν ποθεν ζητοῦντες τὸ εὖ ἢ παρὰ τῶν θεῶν, καὶ ὅμοιον ὥσπερ ἂν εἴ τις ἐν βασιλευομένῃ χώρᾳ τῶν πολιτῶν τινὰ ὕπαρχον θεραπεύσῃ, ἀμελήσας αὐτοῦ τοῦ πάντων ἄρχοντος καὶ βασιλεύοντος· τοιοῦτον γὰρ οἴονται ποιεῖν καὶ τοὺς ἀνθρώπους. ἐπεὶ γὰρ ἔστι τε θεὸς καὶ οὗτος πάντων κύριος, δεῖν δὲ ὡμολόγηται παρὰ τοῦ κυρίου τἀγαθὸν αἰτεῖν, πάντες τε, οὓς μὲν ἂν φιλῶσι καὶ οἷς ἂν χαίρωσι, τούτοις διδόασι τἀγαθά, πρὸς δὲ οὓς ἐναντίως [138] ἔχουσι, τἀναντία, δῆλον ὅτι ταῦτα πρακτέον, οἷς τυγχάνει ὁ θεὸς χαίρων. ταῦτα δὲ οὐ ῥᾴδιον εἰδέναι, ἂν μή τις ἢ θεοῦ ἀκηκοότος ἢ θεοῦ ἀκούσῃ ἢ διὰ τέχνης θείας πορίζηται. διὸ καὶ περὶ τὴν μαντικὴν σπουδάζουσι· μόνη γὰρ αὕτη ἑρμηνεία τῆς παρὰ τῶν θεῶν διανοίας ἐστί. καὶ ὅμως δὲ τὴν αὐτῶν πραγματείαν ἀξίαν (ἂν) τῳ δόξειεν εἶναι τῷ οἰομένῳ θεοὺς εἶναι, τοῖς δ' εὐήθειαν θάτερον τούτων καὶ ἀμφότερα. ἔστι δὲ καὶ τῶν ἀποταγμάτων τὰ πολλὰ ἐκ τελετῶν εἰσενηνεγμένα, διὰ τὸ οἴεσθαί τι εἶναι αὐτοὺς τὰ τοιαῦτα καὶ μὴ νομίζειν ἀλαζονείαν, ἀλλ' ἀπό τινος θεοῦ ἔχειν τὴν ἀρχήν. καὶ τοῦτό γε πάντες οἱ Πυθαγόρειοι ὅμως ἔχουσι πιστευτικῶς, οἷον περὶ Ἀριστέου τοῦ Προκοννησίου καὶ Ἀβάριδος τοῦ Ὑπερβορέου τὰ μυθολογούμενα καὶ ὅσα ἄλλα τοιαῦτα λέγεται. πᾶσι γὰρ πιστεύουσι τοῖς τοιούτοις, πολλὰ δὲ καὶ αὐτοὶ πειρῶνται, τῶν τοιούτων δέ, τῶν δοκούντων μυθικῶν,

and wonderful than these are related regularly and consistently about the man: infallible predictions of earthquakes, speedy preventions of plagues and violent winds, immediate cessations of hailstorms, and calmings of river and sea waves for easy passage of his disciples. These abilities Empedocles the Agrigentine, Epimenides the Cretan, and Abaris the Hyperborean shared in various degrees, and they themselves accomplished similar things. Their poems bear clear witness to

[136] this; in particular, Empedocles gained the epithet "wind averter," Epimenides "purifier," and Abaris "aether-treader" because, riding on the arrow given him by Apollo of the Hyperboreans, he crossed over rivers, seas, and impassable places, like "walking on air," something many suspect was the case with Pythagoras at that time when he met his disciples on the same day in Metapontium and Tauromenium.[5] It is also said that he foretold there would be an earthquake from a well from which he drank, and that a ship sailing before a fair wind would sink.

[137]   Let these, then, be proofs of his piety. But I wish to go over again the principles of religious worship of the gods which Pythagoras and his followers chose as guides.[6]

All such injunctions which define what is to be done or what is not to be done are directed at concordance with the divine, and this is a first principle, and their whole way of life is arranged for following the deity, and this is the rationale of their philosophy: human beings act ridiculously in seeking the good anywhere else than from the gods, just like someone who pays homage to some subordinate governor in a land ruled by a king, neglecting him who is the ruler of all; for just so they think men behave. For since there is a god, and he is in control of all, and it is agreed one ought to ask for the good from him who has control, and all give good things to those whom they cherish and with whom they are pleased, but to those whom they are oppositely disposed they give the opposite, it is clear that one must do those things in which God delights.

[138]   But it is not easy to know these things unless one learns them either from one who has heard a god, or by hearing a god oneself, or by a divine skill. Hence they take serious interest in divination, for this alone is the means of interpreting the gods' purpose. And this diligent study of theirs would seem equally worthwhile to one who believes there are gods, but to those who believe that either of these (i.e. divination or the gods' existence) is silliness, both are silliness.

Many of their prohibitions were taken from the mysteries because they take such things seriously, and do not believe that they are humbug, but that they have their origin from a god. And all Pythagoreans alike rely upon this (belief in the

---

5. Here ends the Porphyrian passage.

6. Iamblichus now repeats a short passage from earlier in the work, sections 86–87, with slight verbal amplifications; the whole passage down to section 140, which speaks of "Pythagoreans" in the present tense, may well go back to Aristoxenus.

[139] ἀπομνημονεύουσιν ὡς οὐδὲν ἀπιστοῦντες ὅ τι ἂν εἰς τὸ θεῖον
ἀνάγηται. ἔφη γοῦν Εὔρυτόν τις λέγειν ὅτι φαίη ποιμὴν
ἀκοῦσαί τινος ᾄδοντος, νέμων ἐπὶ τῷ τάφῳ τοῦ Φιλολάου,
καὶ τὸν οὐθὲν ἀπιστῆσαι, ἀλλ' ἐρέσθαι τίνα ἁρμονίαν. ἦσαν
δὲ οὗτοι ἀμφότεροι Πυθαγόρειοι, καὶ μαθητὴς Εὔρυτος
Φιλολάου. φασὶ δὲ καὶ τῷ Πυθαγόρᾳ τινά ποτε λέγειν ὅτι
δοκοίη ποτὲ ἐν τῷ ὕπνῳ τῷ πατρὶ διαλέγεσθαι τεθνεῶτι καὶ
ἐπερέσθαι· "τίνος τοῦτο [τὸ] σημεῖον;" τὸν δ' οὐθενὸς φάναι,
ἀλλ' ὡς διελέγετο αὐτῷ ἀληθῶς· "ὥσπερ οὖν οὐδὲ τὸ ἐμοὶ
νῦν σε διαλέγεσθαι σημαίνει οὐθέν, οὕτως οὐδὲ ἐκεῖνο".
ὥστε πρὸς πάντα τὰ τοιαῦτα οὐχὶ αὐτοὺς εὐήθεις
νομίζουσιν, ἀλλὰ τοὺς ἀπιστοῦντας· οὐ γὰρ εἶναι τὰ μὲν
δυνατὰ τῷ θεῷ, τὰ δὲ ἀδύνατα, ὥσπερ οἴεσθαι τοὺς
σοφιζομένους, ἀλλὰ πάντα δυνατά. καὶ ἡ ἀρχὴ ἡ αὐτή ἐστι
τῶν ἐπῶν, ἃ ἐκεῖνοί φασι μὲν εἶναι Λίνου, ἔστι μέντοι ἴσως
ἐκείνων·

ἔλπεσθαι χρὴ πάντ', ἐπεὶ οὐκ ἔστ' οὐδὲν ἄελπτον·
ῥᾴδια πάντα θεῷ τελέσαι, καὶ ἀνήνυτον οὐδέν.

[140]   τὴν δὲ πίστιν τῶν παρ' αὐτοῖς ὑπολήψεων ἡγοῦνται εἶναι
ταύτην, ὅτι ἦν ὁ πρῶτος εἰπὼν αὐτὰ οὐχ ὁ τυχών, ἀλλ' ὁ
θεός. καὶ ἓν τοῦτο τῶν ἀκουσμάτων ἐστί· "τίς εἶ, Πυθαγόρα;"
φασὶ γὰρ εἶναι Ἀπόλλωνα Ὑπερβόρεον· τούτου δὲ τεκμήρια
ἔχεσθαι ὅτι ἐν τῷ ἀγῶνι ἐξανιστάμενος τὸν μηρὸν παρέφηνε
χρυσοῦν καὶ ὅτι Ἄβαριν τὸν Ὑπερβόρεον εἱστία καὶ τὴν
ὀιστὸν αὐτοῦ ἀφείλετο, ᾗ ἐκυβερνᾶτο. λέγεται δὲ ὁ Ἄβαρις
[141] ἐλθεῖν ἐξ Ὑπερβορέων, ἀγείρων χρυσὸν εἰς τὸν νεὼν καὶ
προλέγων λοιμόν. κατέλυε δὲ ἐν τοῖς ἱεροῖς, καὶ οὔτε πίνων
οὔτε ἐσθίων ὤφθη ποτὲ οὐθέν. λέγεται δὲ καὶ ἐν
Λακεδαιμονίοις θῦσαι τὰ κωλυτήρια, καὶ διὰ τοῦτο
οὐδεπώποτε ὕστερον ἐν Λακεδαίμονι λοιμὸν γενέσθαι.
τοῦτον οὖν τὸν Ἄβαριν παρελόμενος ἣν εἶχεν ὀιστὸν
χρυσῆν, ἧς ἄνευ οὐχ οἷός τ' ἦν τὰς ὁδοὺς ἐξευρίσκειν,

divine); as for instance, the stories told about Aristeas of Proconnesus[7] and Abaris the Hyperborean, and whatever other such stories are told. For they believe in all such things, and many they have experience of themselves, and stories which [139] seem mythical, they preserve the memory of, since they disbelieve nothing which leads up to the divine. For instance, the story is told that Eurytus declared that a shepherd said, that while tending his flock at the grave of Philolaus, that he heard someone chanting. Disbelieving nothing, Eurytus asked "in what mode?" Both were Pythagoreans, and Eurytus was a pupil of Philolaus.[8] They also say that someone once said to Pythagoras that he imagined in his sleep that he spoke with his dead father and asked: "Of what is this a sign?" Pythagoras replied "Of nothing," but that he really conversed with him: "Just as your conversation with me now signified nothing, so even that signified nothing."[9] Thus in regard to all such things they do not believe themselves simple-minded, but those who disbelieve are so. For it is not the case, they would claim, that some things are possible for God, and other things impossible, as those who reason subtly think, but all things are possible. And this is the beginning of the verses which they say are by Linus, but are probably by them (the Pythagoreans):

> We must expect all things, since nothing is beyond expectation.
> All things are easy for God to fulfill, and nothing is impossible of fulfillment.[10]

[140] They consider the guarantee of their beliefs to be this: that the one who first declared them was not just anyone, but the god. And one of their *acusmata* is this: "Who are you, Pythagoras?" For they say he is Hyperborean Apollo. And of this there are the following pieces of evidence: that rising up at the athletic contest,[11] he showed his golden thigh, and that he entertained Abaris the Hyperborean,[12] and took from him the arrow with which he piloted himself. Abaris is said to have [141] come from the Hyperboreans, collecting gold for the temple, and foretelling a plague. He used to stay in sacred precincts, and was never seen drinking or eating. It is related also that among the Lacedaemonians he made preventive sacrifices, and because of this there was never again a plague in Lacedaemon. He made this

---

7. On Aristeas, see Burkert, *Lore and Science*, 147-9 and J. D. P. Bolton, *Aristeas of Proconnesus*, Oxford, 1962. Herodotus (VI. 13-15) is the earliest ancient source, but doesn't make the connection with Pythagoras, though he represents him as appearing in Metapontium.

8. This story is told again below, section 148. Eurytus is mentioned by Aristotle (*Metaph.* 1092b 10 ff.) as propounding a rather simple-minded theory of numbers, or rather the proper "number" of given things.

9. Porphyry also tells this story in a fragment preserved by Stobaeus (1.49, 59).

10. Quoted by Stobaeus (4.46.1) who attributes them to Linus, on whom see the *OCD*, s.v. and M.L. West, *The Orphic Poems* (Oxford, 1983) 56-67 (including a collection of his 'fragments').

11. In Olympia, cf. Ael. *V.H.* 4.17; Plut. *Num.* 8.

12. Cf. section 91 above.

[142] ὁμολογοῦντα ἐποίησε. καὶ ἐν Μεταποντίῳ, εὐξαμένων τινῶν γενέσθαι αὐτοῖς τὰ ἐν τῷ προσπλέοντι πλοίῳ, "νεκρὸς τοίνυν ἂν ὑμῖν" ἔφη, καὶ ἐφάνη νεκρὸν ἄγον τὸ πλοῖον. καὶ ἐν Συβάρει τὸν ὄφιν τὸν ἀποκτείναντα τὸν δασὺν ἔλαβε καὶ ἀπεπέμψατο, ὁμοίως δὲ καὶ τὸν ἐν Τυρρηνίᾳ τὸν μικρὸν ὄφιν, ὃς ἀπέκτεινε δάκνων. ἐν Κρότωνι δὲ τὸν ἀετὸν τὸν λευκὸν κατέψησεν ὑπομείναντα, ὥς φασι. βουλομένου δέ τινος ἀκούειν οὐκ ἔφη πω λέξειν πρὶν ἢ σημεῖόν τι φανῇ, καὶ μετὰ ταῦτα ἐγένετο ἐν Καυλωνίᾳ ἡ λευκὴ ἄρκτος. καὶ [143] πρὸς τὸν μέλλοντα ἐξαγγέλλειν αὐτῷ τὸν τοῦ υἱοῦ θάνατον προεῖπεν αὐτός. καὶ Μυλλίαν τὸν Κροτωνιάτην ἀνέμνησεν, ὅτι ἦν Μίδας ὁ Γορδίου, καὶ ᾤχετο ὁ Μυλλίας εἰς τὴν ἤπειρον, ποιήσων ὅσα ἐπὶ τῷ τάφῳ ἐκέλευσε. λέγουσι δὲ καὶ ὅτι τὴν οἰκίαν αὐτοῦ ὁ πριάμενος καὶ ἀνορύξας, ἃ μὲν εἶδεν οὐδενὶ ἐτόλμησεν εἰπεῖν, ἀντὶ δὲ τῆς ἁμαρτίας ταύτης ἐν Κρότωνι ἱεροσυλῶν ἐλήφθη καὶ ἀπέθανε· τὸ γὰρ γένειον ἀποπεσὸν τοῦ ἀγάλματος τὸ χρυσοῦν ἐφωράθη λαβών. ταῦτά τε οὖν λέγουσι πρὸς πίστιν καὶ ἄλλα τοιαῦτα. ὡς δὲ τούτων τε ὁμολογουμένων καὶ ἀδυνάτου ὄντος περὶ ἄνθρωπον ἕνα ταῦτα συμβῆναι, ἤδη οἴονται σαφὲς εἶναι ὅτι ὡς παρὰ κρείττονος ἀποδέχεσθαι χρὴ τὰ παρ' ἐκείνου λεχθέντα καὶ οὐχὶ ἀνθρώπου. ἀλλὰ καὶ τὸ ἀπορούμενον [144] τοῦτο σημαίνειν· ἔστι γὰρ παρ' αὐτοῖς λεγόμενον ὅτι

ἄνθρωπος δίπος ἐστὶ καὶ ὄρνις καὶ τρίτον ἄλλο.

τὸ γὰρ τρίτον Πυθαγόρας ἐστί. τοιοῦτος μὲν οὖν διὰ τὴν εὐσέβειαν ἦν καὶ ἐπὶ τῆς ἀληθείας ἐνομίζετο εἶναι. περὶ δὲ τοὺς ὅρκους εὐλαβῶς οὕτως διέκειντο πάντες οἱ Πυθαγόρειοι, μεμνημένοι τῆς Πυθαγόρου ὑποθήκης τῆς

ἀθανάτους μὲν πρῶτα θεούς, νόμῳ ὡς διάκειται,
τίμα καὶ σέβου ὅρκον, ἔπειθ' ἥρωας ἀγαυούς,

ὥστε ὑπὸ νόμου τις αὐτῶν ἀναγκαζόμενος ὀμόσαι, καίτοι εὐορκεῖν μέλλων, ὅμως ὑπὲρ τοῦ διαφυλάξαι τὸ δόγμα ὑπέμεινεν ἀντὶ τοῦ ὀμόσαι τρία μᾶλλον τάλαντα κατα-θέσθαι, ὅσουπερ τετίμητο τὸ τοιοῦτον τῷ δικασαμένῳ. ὅτι δ' οὐδὲν ᾤοντο ἐκ ταὐτομάτου συμβαίνειν καὶ ἀπὸ τύχης, ἀλλὰ

Abaris, then, a disciple, after taking away a golden arrow which he had, and without which he was not able to find his way.

[142] In Metapontium, also, when some people expressed the wish for the cargo of a ship sailing in to become theirs, he said "Then you will have a corpse," and the ship appeared carrying a corpse.[13] And in Sybaris he caught the thick, murderous snake and sent it away; and in like manner in Tyrrhenia he dealt with the small snake whose bite was fatal.[14] And in Croton, he stroked the white eagle while it remained still for him, so they say.[15] When someone wished to hear him speak, he said he would not speak until some sign appeared; and after this the white bear appeared in Caulonia.[16] And he himself foretold the death of his son to one who was about to announce it to him.

[143] Also he reminded Myllias the Crotoniate that he had been Midas, son of Gordius; and Myllias went to the mainland, in order to perform at the grave (of Midas) such rites as Pythagoras ordered.[17] They also say that the one who bought and dug up Pythagoras' house did not dare tell anyone what he saw, but because of this offense, he was arrested in Croton for committing sacrilege and put to death; for he was seen taking the golden beard which had fallen from the god's statue.[18]

They relate, then, these and other stories in order to inspire faith. On the assumption that these things are agreed upon, and that it is impossible that they happened to one who was a human being, the Pythagoreans now think it clear that it is necessary to accept the things said by him as issuing from a higher power, and not from a mortal. That is also the meaning of the following riddle, which they recite:

[144] "Two-footed is a human being, and a bird, and a third thing as well,"[19]

for the third thing is Pythagoras. Such he was, then, because of his piety, and truly was he believed to be such.

For oaths all Pythagoreans had such a great reverence, mindful of Pythagoras' counsel:

---

13. Cf. Apollon. *Mir.* 6, and Porph. *V.P.* 28.

14. Cf. Apollon. *Mir.* 6, who, however, tells of biting the snake to death!

15. Cf. section 62 above, where the story is fixed at Olympia, Porph. *VP* 25, and Ael., *V.H.*, 4.17.

16. Cf. Apoll. *Mir.* 6. Apparently different from the Daunian bear (see section 60 above).

17. Cf. Ael. *V. H.* 4.17. More about Myllias later. See sections 189-195.

18. Despite the definite article, it is not clear to whose statue reference is made. Probably that of the Hyperborean Apollo.

19. See A. Delatte, *Études sur la littérature pythagoricienne* (Paris, 1915) 16, for a brief discussion of the riddle.

[145] κατὰ θείαν πρόνοιαν, μάλιστα τοῖς ἀγαθοῖς καὶ εὐσεβέσι τῶν
ἀνθρώπων, βεβαιοῖ τὰ ὑπὸ Ἀνδροκύδου ἐν τῷ περὶ
Πυθαγορικῶν συμβόλων ἱστορούμενα περὶ Θυμαρίδου τοῦ
Ταραντίνου, Πυθαγορικοῦ. ἀποπλέοντι γὰρ αὐτῷ καὶ
χωριζομένῳ διά τινα περίστασιν περιέστησαν οἱ ἑταῖροι
ἀσπαζόμενοί τε καὶ προπεμπτικῶς ἀποτασσόμενοι. καί τις
ἤδη ἐπιβάντι τοῦ πλοίου εἶπεν· "ὅσα βούλει, παρὰ τῶν
θεῶν, ὦ Θυμαρίδα." καὶ ὃς "εὐφημεῖν" ἔφη, "ἀλλὰ
βουλοίμην μᾶλλον, ὅσ' ἄν μοι παρὰ τῶν θεῶν γένηται".
ἐπιστημονικὸν γὰρ τοῦτο ἡγεῖτο μᾶλλον καὶ εὔγνωμον, τὸ
μὴ ἀντιτείνειν καὶ προσαγανακτεῖν τῇ θείᾳ προνοίᾳ. πόθεν
δὴ οὖν τὴν τοσαύτην εὐσέβειαν παρέλαβον οὗτοι οἱ ἄνδρες,
εἴ τις βούλοιτο μαθεῖν, ῥητέον ὡς τῆς Πυθαγορικῆς κατ'
ἀριθμὸν θεολογίας παράδειγμα ἐναργὲς ἔκειτο παρὰ Ὀρφεῖ.

[146] οὐκέτι δὴ οὖν ἀμφίβολον γέγονε τὸ τὰς ἀφορμὰς παρὰ
Ὀρφέως λαβόντα Πυθαγόραν συντάξαι τὸν περὶ θεῶν
λόγον, ὃν καὶ ἱερὸν διὰ τοῦτο ἐπέγραψεν, ὡς ἂν ἐκ τοῦ
μυστικωτάτου ἀπηνθισμένον παρὰ Ὀρφεῖ τόπου, εἴτε ὄντως
τοῦ ἀνδρός, ὡς οἱ πλεῖστοι λέγουσι, σύγγραμμά ἐστιν, εἴτε
Τηλαύγους, ὡς ἔνιοι τοῦ διδασκαλείου ἐλλόγιμοι καὶ ἀξιό-
πιστοι διαβεβαιοῦνται ἐκ τῶν ὑπομνημάτων τῶν Δαμοῖ τῇ
θυγατρί, ἀδελφῇ δὲ Τηλαύγους, ἀπολειφθέντων ὑπ' αὐτοῦ
Πυθαγόρου, ἅπερ μετὰ θάνατον ἱστοροῦσι δοθῆναι Βιτάλῃ
τε τῇ Δαμοῦς θυγατρὶ καὶ Τηλαύγει ⟨ἐν⟩ ἡλικίᾳ γενομένῳ,
υἱῷ μὲν Πυθαγόρου, ἀνδρὶ δὲ τῆς Βιτάλης· κομιδῇ γὰρ νέος
ὑπὸ τὸν Πυθαγόρου θάνατον ἀπολελειμμένος ἦν παρὰ
Θεανοῖ τῇ μητρί. δηλοῦται δὴ διὰ τοῦ ἱεροῦ λόγου τούτου [ἢ
περὶ θεῶν λόγου, ἐπιγράφεται γὰρ ἀμφότερον] καὶ τίς ἦν ὁ
παραδεδωκὼς Πυθαγόρᾳ τὸν περὶ θεῶν λόγον. λέγει γάρ·
"⟨λόγος⟩ ὅδε περὶ θεῶν Πυθαγόρα τῷ Μνημάρχῳ, τὸν
ἐξέμαθον ὀργιασθεὶς ἐν Λιβήθροις τοῖς Θρᾳκίοις,
Ἀγλαοφάμῳ τελεστᾷ μεταδόντος, ὡς ἄρα Ὀρφεὺς ὁ Καλ-
λιόπας κατὰ τὸ Πάγγαιον ὄρος ὑπὸ τᾶς ματρὸς πινυσθεὶς
ἔφα, τὰν ἀριθμῶ οὐσίαν ἀίδιον ἔμμεν ἀρχὰν προμαθεστάταν
τῶ παντὸς ὠρανῶ καὶ γᾶς καὶ τᾶς μεταξὺ φύσιος, ἔτι δὲ καὶ
θείων ⟨ἀνθρώπων⟩ καὶ θεῶν καὶ δαιμόνων διαμονᾶς ῥίζαν." ἐκ

> First the immortal gods, as is fixed by law, do thou honor, and rever-
> ence oath; then the illustrious heroes.

One of them, when compelled by law to swear an oath, although he was about to
swear a true oath, nevertheless, for the sake of observing this prescription, was
prepared to pay three talents instead of swearing an oath (three talents was the
amount he was required to pay the man who had taken him to court.)[20]

[145] That they thought nothing happens spontaneously and by chance, but according to divine providence, especially to good and pious human beings, is confirmed by what is told by Androcydes in his work *On Pythagorean Symbols*, about the
Pythagorean Thymaridas of Tarentum.[21] For as he was about to sail away and leave
because of some matter of business, his companions stood about to see him off,
embracing and bidding him farewell. Someone said to him when he was already
on board: "Whatever things you wish, Thymaridas, may you get from the gods."
And he replied, "Hush"—"let me wish rather for whatever comes to me from the
gods." For he considered this a more wise and sensible attitude: not to strive
against and to be angry at divine providence.

If someone, then, wishes to learn from whence these men received such a degree of piety, it must be said that a clear model for Pythagorean theology according to number is found in (the writings of) Orpheus.[22] It is certainly no longer
[146] doubtful that Pythagoras took his inspiration from Orpheus when he organized
his treatise *On Gods*, which he also entitled *The Sacred Discourse*, since it sprang
from the most mystic part of the Orphic corpus. Either it is truly a treatise by the
man himself, as most authorities say, or rather a compilation by Telauges,[23] as
some famous and reliable members of his school strongly maintain, on the basis
of memoranda left by Pythagoras himself to Damo, his daughter, sister of Telauges. These memoranda, they record, were given after her death to Bitale, Damo's
daughter, and to Telauges, son of Pythagoras, who on reaching manhood became
Bitale's husband. For he was left behind quite young at the time of Pythagoras'
death, with his mother Theano. It is certainly clear from this *Sacred Discourse* (or
Discourse on the Gods, both titles exist)[24] who gave Pythagoras the discourse on

---

20. This story is told again in section 150, where the Pythagorean concerned is identified as
one Syllus of Croton.

21. On Androcydes, see Burkert, *Lore and Science*, 167. Androcydes may be the main authority
on the interpretation of the *symbola*, and is perhaps the source of sections 82-86 above Thymaridas contributed significantly to Pythagorean number-theory. His ἐπάνθημα ("efflorescence") is
mentioned by Iamb. *In Nic.* 62, 18 ff.

22. On the connection between Orphic and Pythagorean doctrine, see M. L. West, *The Orphic
Poems* (Oxford, 1983) 7-15. The tradition of the dependence of Pythagoras on Orphic writings
goes back at least to Ion of Chios in the mid-fifth century B. C. (*Triagmos*, D-K 36, B 2).

23. On Telauges, cf. D.L. 8. 43 and Thesleff, *Pythagorean Texts*, 188-9. Telauges seems to have
been accepted as Pythagoras' son rather late in the tradition. The source behind section 265 below (Timaeus?) does not know of him.

[147] δὴ τούτων φανερὸν γέγονεν ὅτι τὴν ἀριθμῷ ὡρισμένην οὐσίαν τῶν θεῶν παρὰ τῶν Ὀρφικῶν παρέλαβεν. ἐποιεῖτο δὲ διὰ τῶν αὐτῶν ἀριθμῶν καὶ θαυμαστὴν πρόγνωσιν καὶ θεραπείαν τῶν θεῶν κατὰ τοὺς ἀριθμοὺς ὅτι μάλιστα συγγενεστάτην. γνοίη δ᾿ ἄν τις τοῦτο ἐντεῦθεν· δεῖ γὰρ καὶ ἔργον τι παρασχέσθαι εἰς πίστιν τοῦ [δὲ] λεγομένου. ἐπειδὴ Ἄβαρις περὶ τὰ συνήθη ἑαυτῷ ἱερουργήματα διετέλει ὢν καὶ τὴν σπουδαζομένην παντὶ βαρβάρων γένει πρόγνωσιν διὰ θυμάτων ἐπορίζετο, μάλιστα τῶν ὀρνιθείων (τὰ γὰρ τῶν τοιούτων σπλάγχνα ἀκριβῆ πρὸς διάσκεψιν ἡγοῦνται), βουλόμενος ὁ Πυθαγόρας μὴ ἀφαιρεῖν μὲν αὐτοῦ τὴν εἰς τἀληθὲς σπουδήν, παρασχεῖν δὲ διά τινος ἀσφαλεστέρου καὶ χωρὶς αἵματος καὶ σφαγῆς, ἄλλως τε καὶ ὅτι ἱερὸν ἡγεῖτο εἶναι τὸν ἀλεκτρυόνα ἡλίῳ, τὸ λεγόμενον παναληθὲς ἀπετέλεσεν αὐτῷ, δι᾿ ἀριθμητικῆς ἐπιστήμης συντεταγ-
[148] μένον. ὑπῆρχε δ᾿ αὐτῷ ἀπὸ τῆς εὐσεβείας καὶ ἡ περὶ θεῶν πίστις· παρήγγελλε γὰρ ἀεὶ περὶ θεῶν μηδὲν θαυμαστὸν ἀπιστεῖν μηδὲ περὶ θείων δογμάτων, ὡς πάντα τῶν θεῶν δυναμένων. καὶ θεῖα δὲ τὰ δόγματα λέγειν (οἷς χρὴ πιστεύειν) ἃ Πυθαγόρας παρέδωκεν. οὕτως γοῦν ἐπίστευον καὶ παρειλήφεσαν περὶ ὧν δογματίζουσιν ὅτι οὐκ ἐψευδοδόξηται, ὥστε Εὔρυτος μὲν ὁ Κροτωνιάτης, Φιλολάου ἀκουστής, ποιμένος τινος ἀπαγγείλαντος αὐτῷ ὅτι μεσημβρίας ἀκούσειε Φιλολάου φωνῆς ἐκ τοῦ τάφου, καὶ ταῦτα πρὸ πολλῶν ἐτῶν τεθνηκότος, ὡσανεὶ ᾄδοντος, "καὶ τίνα, πρὸς θεῶν," εἶπεν "ἁρμονίαν;" Πυθαγόρας δ᾿ αὐτὸς ἐρωτηθεὶς ὑπό τινος τί σημαίνει τὸ ἰδεῖν ἑαυτοῦ πατέρα πάλαι τεθνηκότα καθ᾿ ὕπνους αὐτῷ προσδιαλεγόμενον, "οὐδέν" ἔφη· "οὐδὲ γὰρ ὅτι μοι ἄρτι λαλεῖς σημαίνει τι.᾿

gods, for it says: "This (discourse) is what I Pythagoras, son of Mnemarchus, learned on initiation in the Thracian Libethra, from Aglaophamus the initiator,[25] who communicated to me that Orpheus, son of Calliope, taught by his mother on Mt. Pangaeon, said: 'The eternal being of number is a most provident principle [147] of the whole heaven, earth, and of the intermediate nature; moreover it is a source of permanence for divine (men) and gods and daemons." From this, then, it is clear that he derived the idea of the essence of the gods as defined by number from the Orphics.[26] He created also, by means of the same numbers, both a marvelous degree of foreknowledge and a system of worship of the gods according to numbers, as much akin to their nature as possible. One may gather this from the following consideration (for one must also furnish an actual proof as guarantee of one's statements): since Abaris continued to be engaged in his usual sacrifices, and pursued the type of divination which is most valued by every race of barbarians, divination by means of animal sacrifices, and especially bird sacrifices (for the entrails of such are deemed to yield accurate predictions), Pythagoras, not wishing to deprive him of his zeal for truth, but to provide him with a more trusty means to it, free of blood and butchery (especially since he considered the cock sacred to the sun), produced for him that which is called "all-true,"[27] organized by means of arithmetical science.

[148]   It was from his piety that Pythagoras' belief in the gods also arose; for he always commanded that one should disbelieve nothing marvelous about the gods, or about divine teachings, since the gods are able to do all things. And the "divine teachings," which must be believed, mean those which Pythagoras handed down. To such an extent did they believe and hand down things about which they decreed that there was no false belief, that Eurytus the Crotoniate, disciple of Philolaus, when some shepherd reported to him that he had heard at noonday Philolaus' voice from the grave (and this after he had been dead for many years) as if singing, replied "And by heavens, in what mode?" And Pythagoras himself, when asked by someone what seeing his own father long since dead speaking with him in dreams signified, replied "nothing. . . any more than your speaking with me just now signifies anything."[28]

---

24. Bracketed as a gloss by Nauck, but it may be Iamblichus' amplification. On the *Sacred Discourse*, see Thesleff, *Pythagorean Texts*, 163-168.
    25. Libethra is an area in Pieria, near Mt. Olympus; on the Orphic Aglaophamus and connections between Orphism and Pythagoreanism, see Burkert, *Lore and Science*, esp. 128 ff.
    26. This is also attested by Proclus, *In Tim.* III. 161. 1 ff.
    27. Perhaps to be read as two words, cf. Syrianus, *In Met.* 106, 21, who seems to refer to it as the Decad. But how the Decad would help with divination is not clear.
    28. He has just told these two stories in section 139 above. Is he here using another source which discusses the same subject, perhaps Apollonius of Tyana?

[149] ἐσθῆτι δὲ ἐχρῆτο λευκῇ καὶ καθαρᾷ, ὡσαύτως δὲ καὶ
στρώμασι λευκοῖς καὶ καθαροῖς. εἶναι δὲ τὰ τοιαῦτα λινᾶ·
κωδίοις γὰρ οὐκ ἐχρῆτο. καὶ τοῖς ἀκροαταῖς δὲ τοῦτο τὸ ἔθος
παρέδωκεν. ἐχρῆτο δὲ καὶ εὐφημίᾳ πρὸς τοὺς κρείττονας καὶ
ἐν παντὶ καιρῷ μνήμην ἐποιεῖτο καὶ τιμὴν τῶν θεῶν, ὥστε
καὶ παρὰ τὸ δεῖπνον σπονδὰς ἐποιεῖτο τοῖς θεοῖς καὶ
παρήγγελλεν ἐφ' ἡμέρᾳ ἑκάστῃ ὑμνεῖν τοὺς κρείττονας.
[150] προσεῖχε δὲ καὶ φήμαις καὶ μαντείαις καὶ κληδόσιν, ὅλως
πᾶσι τοῖς αὐτομάτοις. ἐπέθυε δὲ θεοῖς λίβανον, κέγχρους,
πόπανα, κηρία, σμύρναν, τὰ ἄλλα θυμιάματα· ζῷα δὲ αὐτὸς
οὐκ ἔθυεν οὐδὲ τῶν θεωρητικῶν φιλοσόφων οὐδείς, τοῖς δὲ
ἄλλοις τοῖς ἀκουσματικοῖς ἢ τοῖς πολιτικοῖς προστέτακτο
σπανίως ἔμψυχα θύειν, ἤπου ἀλεκτρυόνα ἢ ἄρνα ἢ ἄλλο τι
τῶν νεογνῶν, βοῦς δὲ μὴ θύειν. κἀκεῖνο δὲ τῆς εἰς θεοὺς
τιμῆς αὐτοῦ τεκμήριον, τὸ παρηγγέλθαι μηδέποτε ὀμνύναι
θεῶν ὀνόμασι καταχρωμένους. διόπερ καὶ Σύλλος, εἷς τῶν ἐν
Κρότωνι Πυθαγορείων, ὑπὲρ τοῦ μὴ ὀμόσαι χρήματα
ἀπέτισε, καίτοι εὐορκήσειν μέλλων. ἀναφέρεταί γε μὴν εἰς
τοὺς Πυθαγορικοὺς καὶ τοιόσδε τις ὅρκος, αἰδῶ μὲν
ποιουμένων ὀνομάζειν Πυθαγόραν (ὥσπερ καὶ θεῶν ὀνόμασι
χρῆσθαι πολλὴν φειδὼ ἐποιοῦντο), διὰ δὲ τῆς εὑρέσεως τῆς
τετρακτύος δηλούντων τὸν ἄνδρα·

οὔ, μὰ τὸν ἀμετέρας σοφίας εὑρόντα τετρακτύν,
παγὰν ἀενάου φύσεως ῥιζώματ' ἔχουσαν.

[151] ὅλως δέ φασι Πυθαγόραν ζηλωτὴν γενέσθαι τῆς Ὀρφέως
ἑρμηνείας τε καὶ διαθέσεως καὶ τιμᾶν τοὺς θεοὺς Ὀρφεῖ
παραπλησίως, ἱσταμένους αὐτοὺς ἐν τοῖς ἀγάλμασι καὶ τῷ
χαλκῷ, οὐ ταῖς ἡμετέραις συνεζευγμένους μορφαῖς, ἀλλὰ
τοῖς ἱδρύμασι τοῖς θείοις, πάντα περιέχοντας καὶ πάντων
προνοοῦντας καὶ τῷ παντὶ τὴν φύσιν καὶ τὴν μορφὴν ὁμοίαν
ἔχοντας, ἀγγέλλειν δὲ αὐτῶν τοὺς καθαρμοὺς καὶ τὰς
λεγομένας τελετάς, τὴν ἀκριβεστάτην εἴδησιν αὐτῶν
ἔχοντα. ἔτι δέ φασι καὶ σύνθετον αὐτὸν ποιῆσαι τὴν θείαν
φιλοσοφίαν καὶ θεραπείαν, ἃ μὲν μαθόντα παρὰ τῶν
Ὀρφικῶν, ἃ δὲ παρὰ τῶν Αἰγυπτίων ἱερέων, ἃ δὲ παρὰ
Χαλδαίων καὶ μάγων, ἃ δὲ παρὰ τῆς τελετῆς τῆς ἐν
Ἐλευσῖνι γινομένης, ἐν Ἴμβρῳ τε καὶ Σαμοθρᾴκῃ καὶ
Λήμνῳ, καὶ εἴ τι παρὰ τοῖς κοινοῖς, καὶ περὶ τοὺς Κελτοὺς
δὲ καὶ τὴν Ἰβηρίαν. ἐν δὲ τοῖς Λατίνοις ἀναγινώσκεσθαι τοῦ

[149]   He wore white and clean clothing, and, in like manner, he used white and clean bedcoverings. All were of linen; for he did not use sheepskin,[29] and he handed down this custom to his disciples. He also used auspicious language toward the higher powers, and on every occasion he remembered and honored the gods, so that even at dinner he made libations to the gods, and gave orders to celebrate the higher powers in hymns every day. He paid attention to prophetic sayings, [150] oracular responses, and omens: in short, to all things without visible cause. He sacrificed to the gods frankincense, millet, *popana*,[30] honey-combs, myrrh, and other fragrant stuffs, but he himself did not sacrifice animals, nor did any of the contemplative philosophers. But the others, the *acusmatici* or the *politici*, were commanded to sacrifice animals sparingly, perhaps a cock or lamb or some other newborn animal, but never an ox. This is also a sign of his esteem for the gods: that he commanded never to swear an oath, (thus) misusing the gods' names. Hence, even Syllus, a Pythagorean in Croton, for the sake of not swearing an oath, paid a fine, even though he was about to take a true oath.[31] However, the following oath at least is ascribed to the Pythagoreans, who were reluctant out of respect to name Pythagoras (just as they were also very sparing about using the names of gods), but by mentioning the discovery of the tetraktys, they indicated the man:

> No, by him who discovered the tetraktys of our wisdom,
> a source having roots of ever-flowing nature.[32]

[151]   In general, they say Pythagoras was a zealous admirer of Orpheus' style and rhetorical art, and honored the gods in a manner nearly like Orpheus', setting them up, indeed, in the bronze of statues, not bound down with our human appearances, but with those divine rites of gods who comprehend and take thought for all things, and who have a substance and form similar to the All.[33] He proclaimed their purificatory rites and what are called "mystic initiations," and he had most accurate knowledge of these things. Moreover, they say that he made a synthesis of divine philosophy and worship of the gods, having learned some things from the Orphics, others from the Egyptian priests; some from the Chaldeans and the magi, others from the mystic rites in Eleusis, Imbros, Samothrace, and Lemnos, and whatever was to be learned from mystic associations;[34] and some from the Celts and Iberians.

---

29. These two lines are repeated verbatim from section 100 above.

30. Round cakes used especially for sacrifices.

31. This story is alluded to above, in section 144, but without Syllus being mentioned by name.

32. Quoted again in section 162. Much has been written on the *tetraktys*; see, for example, Burkert, *Lore and Science*, 72, *et passim*.

33. This is a very troublesome passage, and despite several grammatical problems, it may be best to take it as a reference to the theurgic "divinising" of statues, for which the technical term is ἵδρυσις We adopt Scaliger's emendation ἱστάμενον for ἱσταμένους.

34. If this is what τὰ κοινά or οἱ κοινοί are. An alternative is to read τυρρηνοῖς ("Etruscans") with Nauck; but see Poland, *Geschichte des griechischen Vereinswesens*, 163 ff.

[152] Πυθαγόρου τὸν ἱερὸν λόγον, οὐκ εἰς πάντας οὐδ᾽ ὑπὸ πάντων, ἀλλ᾽ ὑπὸ τῶν μετεχόντων ἑτοίμως πρὸς τὴν τῶν ἀγαθῶν διδασκαλίαν καὶ μηδὲν αἰσχρὸν ἐπιτηδευόντων. λέγειν δὲ αὐτὸν τρὶς σπένδειν τοὺς ἀνθρώπους καὶ μαντεύεσθαι τὸν Ἀπόλλωνα ἐκ τρίποδος διὰ τὸ κατὰ τὴν τριάδα πρῶτον φῦναι τὸν ἀριθμόν. Ἀφροδίτῃ δέ τι θυσιάζειν ἕκτῃ διὰ τὸ πρῶτον τοῦτον τὸν ἀριθμὸν πάσης μὲν ἀριθμοῦ φύσεως κοινωνῆσαι, κατὰ πάντα δὲ τρόπον μεριζόμενον ὅμοιον λαμβάνειν τήν τε τῶν ἀφαιρουμένων καὶ τὴν τῶν καταλειπομένων δύναμιν. Ἡρακλεῖ δὲ δεῖν θυσιάζειν ὀγδόῃ
[153] τοῦ μηνὸς ἱσταμένου σκοποῦντας τὴν ἑπτάμηνον αὐτοῦ γένεσιν. λέγει δὲ καὶ εἰς ἱερὸν εἰσιέναι δεῖν ⟨λευκὸν καὶ⟩ καθαρὸν ἱμάτιον ἔχοντα καὶ ἐν ᾧ μὴ ἐγκεκοίμηταί τις, τὸν μὲν ὕπνον τῆς ἀργίας καὶ τὸ μέλαν καὶ τὸ πυρρόν, τὴν δὲ καθαρειότητα τῆς περὶ τοὺς λογισμοὺς ἰσότητος καὶ δικαιοσύνης μαρτυρίαν ἀποδιδούς. παραγγέλλει δέ, ἐν ἱερῷ ἄν τι ἀκούσιον αἷμα γένηται, ἢ χρυσῷ ἢ θαλάττῃ περιρραίνεσθαι, τῷ πρώτῳ γενομένῳ καὶ ⟨τῷ⟩ καλλίστῳ τῶν ὄντων, σταθμωμένῳ τὴν τιμὴν τῶν ἁπάντων. λέγει δὲ καὶ μὴ τίκτειν ἐν ἱερῷ· οὐ γὰρ εἶναι ὅσιον ἐν ἱερῷ καταδεῖσθαι
[154] τὸ θεῖον τῆς ψυχῆς εἰς τὸ σῶμα. παραγγέλλει δὲ ἐν ἑορτῇ μήτε κείρεσθαι μήτε ὀνυχίζεσθαι, τὴν ἡμετέραν αὔξησιν τῶν ἀγαθῶν οὐχ ἡγούμενος δεῖν τὴν τῶν θεῶν ἀπολείπειν ἀρχήν. λέγει δὲ καὶ φθεῖρα ἐν ἱερῷ μὴ κτείνειν, οὐδενὸς τῶν περιττῶν καὶ φθαρτικῶν νομίζων δεῖν μεταλαμβάνειν τὸ δαιμόνιον. κέδρῳ δὲ λέγει καὶ δάφνῃ καὶ κυπαρίττῳ καὶ δρυΐ καὶ μυρρίνῃ τοὺς θεοὺς τιμᾶν, καὶ μηδὲν τούτοις ἀποκαθαίρεσθαι τοῦ σώματος μηδὲ σχινίζειν τοὺς ὀδόντας, ταύτην πρώτην γονὴν τῆς ὑγρᾶς φύσεως καὶ τροφὴν τῆς πρώτης καὶ κοινοτέρας ὕλης ὑπολαμβάνων. ἑφθὸν δὲ παραγγέλλει μὴ ὀπτᾶν, τὴν πραότητα λέγων μὴ προσδεῖσθαι τῆς ὀργῆς. κατακάειν δὲ οὐκ εἴα τὰ σώματα τῶν τελευτησάντων, μάγοις ἀκολούθως, μηδενὸς τῶν θείων τὸ θνητὸν μεταλαμβάνειν ἐθελήσας. τοὺς δὲ τελευτήσαντας ἐν
[155] λευκαῖς ἐσθῆσι προπέμπειν ὅσιον ἐνόμιζε, τὴν ἁπλῆν καὶ τὴν πρώτην αἰνιττόμενος φύσιν κατὰ τὸν ἀριθμὸν καὶ τὴν ἀρχὴν τῶν πάντων. εὐορκεῖν δὲ πάντων μάλιστα παραγγέλλει, ἐπεὶ μακρὸν τοὐπίσω, θεοῖς δ᾽ οὐδὲν μακρὸν εἶναι. πολλῷ δὲ μᾶλλον ἀδικεῖσθαι ὅσιον εἶναι λέγει ἢ

[152]   Among the Latins the sacred discourse of Pythagoras is read aloud, not to all or by all, but by those favorably disposed to the teaching of good things, and who indulge in no shameful practices.[35] He said that human beings should make libations three times, and that Apollo gave oracles from the tripod because the triad is the first number by nature; to sacrifice something to Aphrodite on the sixth day because this is the first number to share in the whole nature of number, and when divided in every way, yields the same product from the numbers subtracted as from those that remain.[36] One should sacrifice to Heracles on the eighth day from the beginning of the month, commemorating his birth in the seventh

[153] month,. He also said that one should enter a temple wearing a <white and>[37] clean cloak in which one has not slept, rendering testimony that sleep and the black and yellowish-red are signs of laziness, but cleanliness is a sign of impartiality and equity in reasonings. He ordered that if blood be involuntarily spilt in a temple, it be purified either with gold or sea water, calculating the value of all things with the first that came into being (the sea) and with the loveliest of all things (gold). He also forbade giving birth in a temple, for it was not holy to bind down in a temple the divine part of the soul with the body.

[154]   He forbade cutting hair or trimming nails in the course of a festival, thinking sovereignty of the gods ought not be abandoned for the increase of our own goods. He forbade also killing a louse in a temple, believing that the divine ought not share in superfluous and destructive things. He said: honor the gods with cedar, laurel, cypress, oak and myrtle; and cleanse neither the body nor teeth with these, but believe these are the first offspring of the moist nature, and nourishment for the first and more common matter. He forbade roasting the boiled, saying gentleness does not need anger. In accord with the Magi, he did not permit burning dead bodies, desiring that the mortal have no share in things divine.[38]

[155] He believed it holy to follow the dead to the grave in white garments, hinting by this at the simple and primary nature, both numerically and as the source of all things. He prescribed, above all, swearing a true oath, since the future is long, but for the gods nothing is long. He said that it is much more holy to be wronged than to kill a human being (for the judgment rests with Hades), if one reflects on the natures of the soul and its status as first of existing things. He decreed that a coffin ought not be made of cypress, because Zeus' sceptre was made of cypress, or for some other secret (mystic) reason. He required that libations be made before din-

---

35. All these *acusmata* have been collected and numbered by F. Boehm, *De Symbolis Pythagoreis*. In this form, with allegorizing explanation, they possibly go back to the book of Androcydes, *On the Pythagorean Symbols*. See Burkert, *Lore and Science*, 174-5.

36. That is, 6 is the first combination of odd and even; and both by subtraction and by division, one gets remainders of 1, 2, and 3.

37. Added by Wakefield, perhaps superfluously.

38. The Magi held fire to be divine.

κτείνειν ἄνθρωπον (ἐν ᾅδου γὰρ κεῖσθαι τὴν κρίσιν), ἐκλογιζόμενον τὰς περὶ τὴν ψυχὴν καὶ τὴν οὐσίαν αὐτῆς τὴν πρώτην τῶν ὄντων φύσεις. κυπαρισσίνην δὲ μὴ δεῖν κατασκευάζεσθαι σορὸν ὑπαγορεύει διὰ τὸ κυπαρίσσινον γεγονέναι τὸ τοῦ Διὸς σκῆπτρον ἢ δι' ἄλλον τινὰ μυστικὸν λόγον. σπένδειν δὲ πρὸ τραπέζης παρακαλεῖ Διὸς σωτῆρος καὶ Ἡρακλέους καὶ Διοσκόρων, τῆς τροφῆς ὑμνοῦντας τὸν ἀρχηγὸν καὶ τὸν ταύτης ἡγεμόνα Δία, καὶ τὸν Ἡρακλέα [καὶ] τὴν δύναμιν τῆς φύσεως, καὶ τοὺς Διοσκόρους τὴν [156] συμφωνίαν τῶν ἁπάντων. σπονδὴν δὲ μὴ καταμύοντα προσφέρεσθαι δεῖν φησί· οὐδὲν γὰρ τῶν καλῶν ἄξιον αἰσχύνης καὶ αἰδοῦς διελάμβανεν. ὅταν δὲ βροντήσῃ, τῆς γῆς ἅψασθαι παρήγγελλε, μνημονεύοντας τῆς γενέσεως τῶν ὄντων. εἰσιέναι δὲ εἰς τὰ ἱερὰ κατὰ τοὺς δεξιοὺς τόπους παραγγέλλει, ἐξιέναι κατὰ τοὺς ἀριστερούς, τὸ μὲν δεξιὸν ἀρχὴν τοῦ περιττοῦ λεγομένου τῶν ἀριθμῶν καὶ θεῖον τιθέμενος, τὸ δὲ ἀριστερὸν τοῦ ἀρτίου καὶ διαλυομένου σύμβολον τιθέμενος. τοιοῦτός τις ὁ τρόπος λέγεται αὐτοῦ γεγονέναι τῆς περὶ τὴν εὐσέβειαν ἐπιτηδεύσεως, καὶ τἆλλα δέ, ὅσα παραλείπομεν περὶ αὐτῆς, ἀπὸ τῶν εἰρημένων ἔνεστι τεκμαίρεσθαι, ὥστε περὶ μὲν τούτου παύομαι λέγων.

ing to Zeus the deliverer, and to Heracles and the Dioscuri, celebrating Zeus as the chief and leader of this nourishment, and Heracles as the power of nature, [156] and the Dioscuri as the harmony of all things. He said that one must not present a drink-offering with closed eyes, for he considered nothing noble to be worthy of shame and disgrace. Whenever it thundered, he ordered that the earth be touched to show our recognition of the origin of existing things. He ordered entering temples from the right, but departing from the left, postulating that the right is a principle of the numbers called "odd," and is divine; and that the left is a sign of the "even" and of what is subject to dissolution.

Such, then is said to have been the manner of his devotion to piety. All the other aspects of it which we omit can be conjectured from what has been said, so I may cease the discussion of this topic.

[157] Περὶ δὲ τῆς σοφίας αὐτοῦ, ὡς μὲν ἁπλῶς εἰπεῖν, μέγιστον ἔστω τεκμήριον τὰ γραφέντα ὑπὸ τῶν Πυθαγορείων ὑπομνήματα, περὶ πάντων ἔχοντα τὴν ἀλήθειαν, καὶ στρογγύλα μὲν παρὰ τὰ ἄλλα πάντα, ἀρχαιοτρόπου δὲ καὶ παλαιοῦ πίνου διαφερόντως ὥσπερ τινὸς ἀχειραπτήτου χνοῦ προσπνέοντα, μετ' ἐπιστήμης δὲ δαιμονίας ἄκρως συλλελογισμένα, ταῖς δὲ ἐννοίαις πλήρη τε καὶ πυκνότατα, ποικίλα τε ἄλλως καὶ πολύτροπα τοῖς εἴδεσι καὶ ταῖς ὕλαις, ἀπέρισσα δὲ ἐξαιρέτως ἅμα καὶ ἀνελλιπῆ τῇ φράσει καὶ πραγμάτων ἐναργῶν καὶ ἀναμφιλέκτων ὡς ὅτι μάλιστα μεστὰ μετὰ ἀποδείξεως ἐπιστημονικῆς καὶ πλήρους, τὸ λεγόμενον, συλλογισμοῦ, εἴ τις αἷς προσῆκεν ὁδοῖς κεχρημένος ἐπ' αὐτὰ ἴοι, μὴ παρέργως μηδὲ παρηκουσμένως ἀφοσιούμενος. ταῦτα τοίνυν ἄνωθεν τὴν περὶ τῶν νοητῶν καὶ τὴν περὶ θεῶν ἐπιστήμην παραδίδωσιν. ἔπειτα τὰ
[158] φυσικὰ πάντα ἀναδιδάσκει, τήν τε ἠθικὴν φιλοσοφίαν καὶ τὴν λογικὴν ἐτελειώσατο, μαθήματά τε παντοῖα παραδίδωσι καὶ ἐπιστήμας τὰς ἀρίστας, ὅλως τε οὐδὲν ἔστιν εἰς γνῶσιν ἐληλυθὸς περὶ ὁτουοῦν παρὰ ἀνθρώποις, ὃ μὴ ἐν τοῖς συγγράμμασι τούτοις διηκρίβωται. εἰ τοίνυν ὁμολογεῖται τὰ μὲν Πυθαγόρου εἶναι τῶν συγγραμμάτων τῶν νυνὶ φερομένων, τὰ δὲ ἀπὸ τῆς ἀκροάσεως αὐτοῦ συγγεγράφθαι, καὶ διὰ τοῦτο οὐδὲ ἑαυτῶν ἐπεφήμιζον αὐτά, ἀλλὰ εἰς Πυθαγόραν ἀνέφερον αὐτὰ ὡς ἐκείνου ὄντα, φανερὸν ἐκ πάντων τούτων ὅτι Πυθαγόρας πάσης σοφίας ἔμπειρος ἦν ἀποχρώντως. λέγουσι δὲ γεωμετρίας αὐτὸν ἐπὶ πλεῖον ἐπιμεληθῆναι· παρ' Αἰγυπτίοις γὰρ πολλὰ προβλήματα γεωμετρίας ἐστίν, ἐπείπερ ἐκ παλαιῶν ἔτι καὶ ἀπὸ θεῶν διὰ τὰς τοῦ Νείλου προσθέσεις τε καὶ ἀφαιρέσεις ἀνάγκην ἔχουσι πᾶσαν ἐπιμετρεῖν ἣν ἐνέμοντο γῆν Αἰγυπτίων οἱ λόγιοι, διὸ καὶ γεωμετρία ὠνόμασται. ἀλλ' οὐδ' ἡ τῶν οὐρανίων θεωρία παρέργως αὐτοῖς κατεζήτηται, ἧς καὶ αὐτῆς ἐμπείρως ὁ Πυθαγόρας εἶχε. πάντα δὴ τὰ περὶ τὰς γραμμὰς θεωρήματα ἐκεῖθεν ἐξηρτῆσθαι δοκεῖ· τὰ γὰρ περὶ λογισμοὺς καὶ ἀριθμοὺς ὑπὸ τῶν περὶ τὴν Φοινίκην φασὶν εὑρεθῆναι. τὰ γὰρ οὐράνια θεωρήματα κατὰ κοινόν τινες Αἰγυπτίοις καὶ

CHAPTER TWENTY-NINE

On Pythagoras' wisdom, what it was and into how many kinds and
forms it was divided, and how from the first to the last faculties
concerned with knowledge, Pythagoras established and handed down
to human beings correctness and accuracy (in understanding).

[157] On the subject of his wisdom, in a word, let the greatest proof be the commentaries written by the Pythagoreans, containing the truth about all things. They are well-rounded in all other respects, and encrusted with an old-fashioned and ancient style, exuding as it were a bloom not touched by hand. Composed perfectly with heaven-sent knowledge, they are full of most sagacious conceptions, and especially varied and versatile in form and content, remarkably simple and, at the same time, not lacking style, and filled to the utmost with clear and indisputable realities accompanied by scientific and full demonstration, what is called "deductive argument".[1] (All this) if someone goes through them making use of the proper methods, and is not content with a casual or careless perusal.

These commentaries, then, transmit knowledge about the intelligibles and about the gods beginning from first principles.

[158] Then they explain all physical matters, and give a complete account of both ethical and logical philosophy;[2] and they provide all sorts of mathematical learning and the best sciences. In short, there is nothing concerned with human knowledge about anything whatsoever, which has not been discussed minutely in these writings. If, then, it be agreed that some writings now circulated are by Pythagoras, but others were composed on the basis of his lectures, and on this account the authors did not give their own names, but attributed them to Pythagoras as his work, it is clear from all these treatises that Pythagoras was sufficiently experienced in all wisdom. They say he was particularly concerned with geometry: for among the Egyptians there is much geometrical theorising, ever since ancient times and by way of the gods. Because of the Nile's floodings and recedings, the learned among the Egyptians have been forced to measure out all the land which they inhabit;

---

1. Ἀπόδειξις and συλλογισμός or "demonstration" and "deductive argument" respectively, are very reminiscent of Aristotelian logic. See, for example, *A. Po.* 71b, 11-17 and *A. Pr.* 246, 18. The Stoics, however, used the same terminology; see I. Mueller, "An Introduction to Stoic Logic," in *The Stoics*, ed. J. Rist (Berkeley, 1978) 3 ff. on the syllogism.

2. Implying the order of subjects: physics, ethics, logic. This was the order followed by the Stoics, and attributed to Xenocrates (Sextus Empiricus, *AM* 7, 16-19), who may well have attributed it in turn to Pythagoras.

[159] Χαλδαίοις ἀναφέρουσι. ταῦτα δὴ πάντα φασὶ τὸν Πυθαγόραν παραλαβόντα καὶ συναυξήσαντα τὰς ἐπιστήμας
προαγαγεῖν τε καὶ ὁμοῦ σαφῶς καὶ ἐμμελῶς τοῖς αὑτοῦ
ἀκροωμένοις δεῖξαι.

φιλοσοφίαν μὲν οὖν πρῶτος αὐτὸς ὠνόμασε, καὶ ὄρεξιν
αὐτὴν εἶπεν εἶναι καὶ οἱονεὶ φιλίαν σοφίας, σοφίαν δὲ
ἐπιστήμην τῆς ἐν τοῖς οὖσιν ἀληθείας. ὄντα δὲ ᾔδει καὶ ἔλεγε
τὰ ἄυλα καὶ ἀίδια καὶ μόνα δραστικά, ὅπερ ἐστὶ τὰ ἀσώματα,
ὁμωνύμως δὲ λοιπὸν ὄντα κατὰ μετοχὴν αὐτῶν οὕτως
καλούμενα σωματικὰ εἴδη καὶ ὑλικά, γεννητά τε καὶ φθαρτὰ
καὶ ὄντως οὐδέποτε ὄντα. τὴν δὲ σοφίαν ἐπιστήμην εἶναι
τῶν κυρίως ὄντων, ἀλλ᾽ οὐχὶ τῶν ὁμωνύμως, ἐπειδήπερ οὐδὲ
ἐπιστητὰ ὑπάρχει τὰ σωματικὰ οὐδὲ ἐπιδέχεται γνῶσιν
βεβαίαν, ἄπειρά τε ὄντα καὶ ἐπιστήμῃ ἀπερίληπτα καὶ
οἱονεὶ μὴ ὄντα κατὰ διαστολὴν τῶν καθόλου καὶ οὐδὲ ὅρῳ
ὑποπεσεῖν εὐπεριγράφως δυνάμενα. τῶν δὲ φύσει μὴ
[160] ἐπιστητῶν οὐδὲ ἐπιστήμην οἷόν τε ἐπινοῆσαι· οὐκ ἄρα
ὄρεξιν τῆς μὴ ὑφεστώσης ἐπιστήμης εἰκὸς εἶναι, ἀλλὰ
μᾶλλον τῆς περὶ τὰ κυρίως ὄντα καὶ ἀεὶ κατὰ τὰ αὐτὰ καὶ
ὡσαύτως διαμένοντα καὶ τῇ "ὄντα" προσηγορίᾳ ἀεὶ
συνυπάρχοντα. καὶ γὰρ τῇ τούτων καταλήψει συμβέβηκε
καὶ τὴν τῶν ὁμωνύμως ὄντων παρομαρτεῖν, οὐδὲ
ἐπιτηδευθεῖσάν ποτε, οἷα δὴ τῇ καθόλου ἐπιστήμῃ ἢ τοῦ
κατὰ μέρος. "τοιγὰρ περὶ τῶν καθόλου" φησὶν Ἀρχύτας
"καλῶς διαγνόντες ἔμελλον καὶ περὶ τῶν κατὰ μέρος, οἷα
ἐντί, καλῶς ὀψεῖσθαι." διόπερ οὐ μόνα οὐδὲ μονογενῆ οὐδὲ
ἁπλᾶ ὑπάρχει τὰ ὄντα, ποικίλα δὲ ἤδη καὶ [τὰ] πολυειδῆ
θεωρεῖται, τά τε νοητὰ καὶ ἀσώματα, ὧν τὰ ὄντα ἡ κλῆσις,
καὶ τὰ σωματικὰ καὶ ὑπ᾽ αἴσθησιν πεπτωκότα, ἃ δὴ κατὰ
μετοχὴν κοινωνεῖ τοῦ ὄντως γενέσθαι. περὶ δὲ τούτων

hence (this science) is named "geo-metry" ("land- measurement"). But the theo-ry of heavenly bodies was also not cursorily researched by them, and in this study Pythagoras was very well experienced. Indeed, all theorems about lines seem to be derived from there (Egypt); while theorems about counting and numbers, they say, were discovered by the Phoenicians.[3] Theories about celestial bodies are re-ferred by some to the Egyptians and Chaldeans in common. They say, then, that Pythagoras took over and joined in promoting all these investigations, and so ad-vanced the sciences and explained them clearly and elegantly to his hearers.

[159]

He himself,[4] then, first named philosophy, and said it is a desire, indeed a love, as it were, of wisdom, and wisdom is knowledge of the truth in existing things. Ex-isting things he recognized and declared to be immaterial, eternal, and solely ac-tive, that is, things which are incorporeal. Other "existing things" are equivocally so called by sharing in existing things themselves, that is, corporeal and material forms, which are both generable and corruptible, and never truly existing. Wis-dom is knowledge of things truly existing, not of those equivocally existing, since corporeal things are neither knowable nor admit of firm knowledge, being devoid of limit and not comprehensible by knowledge. Virtually non-existent by compar-ison with the universals, they cannot even be easily defined. But it is impossible to conceive knowledge of things naturally not knowable. It is not likely, then, there is desire for non-existent knowledge, but rather for knowledge about things truly existing, always in the same state, and in like manner, permanent, and always co-existing with the appellation "existing things." For it is the case that apprehension of things equivocally existing accompanies the apprehension of these (things tru-ly existent), even when this apprehension is never pursued; just as knowledge of particulars accompanies knowledge of universals. "Therefore," says Archytas, "having well discerned the universals, they are also in a position to discern well the particulars, what sort of things they are."[5] Hence, the things existing are not single, homogeneous, or simple, but already are viewed as varied and multiform: both the intelligible and incorporeal things, for which the appellation is "the ex-isting things," and the corporeal things and things accessible to sensation, which, then, by participation share in that which truly is.

[160]

---

3. Iamblichus reported earlier in *VP* the tradition that Pythagoras studied in Egypt and Phoe-nicia (see sections 12-19 above). On the subject of Pythagoras and Greek mathematics, especially geometry, see Burkert, *Lore and Science*, 408 ff. Arithmetic is treated on pp. 427-447.

4. This passage, to the end of section 160, is reproduced virtually verbatim in Iamblichus' commentary on Nicomachus' *Introduction to Arithmetic*, (*In Nic.* 5, 27- 7, 2 Pistelli), which does not, however necessarily indicate that it is not by Iamblichus. It is actually redolent of his style.

5. This quotation is from the beginning of Archytas' *Harmonikos*, one of the few works attrib-uted to him thought to be authentic (fr. B1, D.-K.). On Archytas and his work, see Guthrie, *His-tory*, I, 333-336.

[161] ἀπάντων ἐπιστήμας παρέδωκε τὰς οἰκειοτάτας καὶ οὐδὲν παρέλιπεν ἀδιερεύνητον. καὶ τὰς κοινὰς δὲ ἐπιστήμας, ὥσπερ τὴν ἀποδεικτικὴν καὶ τὴν ὁριστικὴν καὶ τὴν διαιρετικήν, παρέδωκε τοῖς ἀνθρώποις, ὡς ἔστιν ἀπὸ τῶν Πυθαγορικῶν ὑπομνημάτων εἰδέναι. εἰώθει δὲ καὶ διὰ κομιδῇ βραχυτάτων φωνῶν μυρίαν καὶ πολυσχιδῆ ἔμφασιν συμβολικῷ τρόπῳ τοῖς γνωρίμοις ἀποφοιβάζειν, ὥσπερ διὰ χειροχρήστων τινῶν λόγων ἢ μικρῶν τοῖς ὄγκοις σπερμάτων ὁ Πύθιός τε καὶ αὐτὴ ἡ φύσις πλήθη ἀνήνυτα καὶ δυσεπινόητα ἐννοιῶν καὶ ἀποτελεσμάτων ὑποφαίνουσι. [162] τοιοῦτον δή ἐστι τὸ

ἀρχὴ δέ τοι ἥμισυ παντός,

ἀπόφθεγμα Πυθαγόρου αὐτοῦ. οὐ μόνον δὲ ἐν τῷ παρόντι ἡμιστιχίῳ, ἀλλὰ καὶ ἐν ἑτέροις παραπλησίοις ὁ θειότατος Πυθαγόρας τὰ τῆς ἀληθείας ἐνέκρυπτε ζώπυρα τοῖς δυναμένοις ἐναύσασθαι, βραχυλογίᾳ τινὶ ἐναποθησαυρίζων ἀπερίβλεπτον καὶ παμπληθῆ θεωρίας ἔκτασιν, οἷόνπερ καὶ ἐν τῷ

ἀριθμῷ δέ τε πάντ᾽ ἐπέοικεν,

ὃ δὴ πυκνότατα πρὸς ἅπαντας ἀπεφθέγγετο, ἢ πάλιν ἐν τῷ "φιλότης ἰσότης" [φιλότης], ἢ ἐν τῷ "κόσμος" ὀνόματι, ἢ νὴ Δία ἐν τῷ "φιλοσοφία", ἢ καὶ ἐν τῷ "ἐστώ", ἢ καὶ ἐν τῷ ··, ἢ [τὸ διαβοώμενον] ἐν τῷ "τετρακτύς". ταῦτα πάντα καὶ ἕτερα πλείω τοιαῦτα Πυθαγόρας πλάσματα καὶ ποιήματα εἰς ὠφέλειαν καὶ ἐπανόρθωσιν τῶν συνδιαγόντων ἐπενοεῖτο, καὶ οὕτως σεβαστὰ ἦν καὶ ἐξεθειάζετο ὑπὸ τῶν συνιέντων, ὥστε εἰς ὅρκου σχήματα περιίστατο τοῖς ὁμακόοις·

οὐ, μὰ τὸν ἁμετέρᾳ γενεᾷ παραδόντα τετρακτύν,
παγὰν ἀενάου φύσεως ῥιζώματ᾽ ἔχουσαν.

τοῦτο μὲν οὕτω θαυμαστὸν ἦν τὸ εἶδος αὐτοῦ τῆς σοφίας.

[161]   In regard to all these matters he provided the most appropriate sciences and left nothing uninvestigated. Also the general sciences, like the techniques of demonstration, definition, and division, he bestowed on human beings, as can be learned from the Pythagorean writings. He was also accustomed by means of very brief sayings to deliver with inspiration to his disciples immense and complex explanation in a symbolical fashion—just as, by means of certain handy sayings or seeds small in bulk, both Pythian Apollo and nature itself bring to light countless and complex multitudes of conceptions and created objects.

[162]   An example, then, is the apophthegm of Pythagoras himself:

"Beginning is half of all."[6]

Not only in the present half-verse, but also in others similar,[7] the most divine Pythagoras hid the embers of truth for those able to kindle them, storing up in brevity of speech, a limitless and vast extent for contemplation, even as in

"All things are like unto number,"[8]

an apophthegm which, indeed, he uttered very often to all his disciples; or again, "friendship is equality,"[9] or in the terms "cosmos," or, indeed "philosophy" or "being"[10] or . . . [11]or that celebrated term the "tetraktys." All these and many other poetical images and forms Pythagoras invented for the benefit and improvement of the community of his disciples, and they were so venerated and deified by those who understood them that they became forms of oath for the fellow-hearers:

No, by him who gave the tetraktys to our race,
a source having roots of everlasting nature.[12]

---

6. Iamblichus is probably thinking of "Archytas'" works on logic.

7. See Delatte, *Études*, 17, and cf. this saying with section 182.

8. Delatte, *Études*, 14 ff.

9. Cf. Aristotle, *E N* VIII 7, 1157b 36 and IX 8, 1168b 8, and D.L. 8. 10, quoting Timaeus.

10. The term ἐστώ is distinctively Pythagorean. Cf. Archytas, *On First Principles*, 19, 21 ff., cf Thesleff, *Pythagorean Texts*, 19-20, where it is the word for "matter." Nicomachus, in his *Theol. Ar.* (*ap.* Photius, *Bibl.* 143 a), gives it as an epithet of the Dyad.

11. A small corruption or lacuna here. Von Albrecht (trans. p. 164) suggests ἐόν, another term for 'being'.

12. Quoted also at section 150 above.

[163]   τῶν δ᾽ ἐπιστημῶν οὐχ ἥκιστά φασι τοὺς Πυθαγορείους
τιμᾶν μουσικήν τε καὶ ἰατρικὴν καὶ μαντικήν. σιωπηλοὺς δὲ
εἶναι καὶ ἀκουστικοὺς καὶ ἐπαινεῖσθαι παρ᾽ αὐτοῖς τὸν
δυνάμενον ἀκοῦσαι. τῆς δὲ ἰατρικῆς μάλιστα μὲν ἀποδέχεσθαι τὸ διαιτητικὸν εἶδος καὶ εἶναι ἀκριβεστάτους ἐν
τούτῳ, καὶ πειρᾶσθαι πρῶτον μὲν καταμανθάνειν σημεῖα
συμμετρίας πόνων τε καὶ σίτων καὶ ἀναπαύσεως, ἔπειτα
περὶ αὐτῆς τῆς κατασκευῆς τῶν προσφερομένων σχεδὸν
πρώτους ἐπιχειρῆσαί τε πραγματεύεσθαι καὶ διορίζειν.
ἅψασθαι δὲ [χρὴ] καὶ καταπλασμάτων ἐπὶ πλείω τοὺς
Πυθαγορείους τῶν ἔμπροσθεν, τὰ δὲ περὶ τὰς φαρμακείας
ἧττον δοκιμάζειν, αὐτῶν δὲ τούτων τοῖς πρὸς τὰς ἑλκώσεις
[164] μάλιστα χρῆσθαι, ⟨τὰ δὲ⟩ περὶ τὰς τομάς τε καὶ καύσεις
ἥκιστα πάντων ἀποδέχεσθαι. χρῆσθαι δὲ καὶ ταῖς ἐπῳδαῖς
πρὸς ἔνια τῶν ἀρρωστημάτων. ὑπελάμβανον δὲ καὶ τὴν
μουσικὴν μεγάλα συμβάλλεσθαι πρὸς ὑγείαν, ἄν τις αὐτῇ
χρῆται κατὰ τοὺς προσήκοντας τρόπους. ἐχρῶντο δὲ καὶ
Ὁμήρου καὶ Ἡσιόδου λέξεσι διειλεγμέναις πρὸς
ἐπανόρθωσιν ψυχῆς.

ᾤοντο δὲ δεῖν κατέχειν καὶ διασώζειν ἐν τῇ μνήμῃ πάντα
τὰ διδασκόμενά τε καὶ φραζόμενα, καὶ μέχρι τούτου
συσκευάζεσθαι τάς τε μαθήσεις καὶ τὰς ἀκροάσεις, μέχρι
ὅτου δύναται παραδέχεσθαι τὸ μανθάνον καὶ διαμνημονεύον,
ὅτι ἐκεῖνό ἐστιν ᾧ δεῖ γιγνώσκειν καὶ ἐν ᾧ γνώμην φυ-
λάσσειν. ἐτίμων γοῦν σφόδρα τὴν μνήμην καὶ πολλὴν αὐτῆς
ἐποιοῦντο γυμνασίαν τε καὶ ἐπιμέλειαν, ἔν τε τῷ μανθάνειν
οὐ πρότερον ἀφιέντες τὸ διδασκόμενον, ἕως περιλάβοιεν
βεβαίως τὰ ἐπὶ τῆς πρώτης μαθήσεως, καὶ καθ᾽ ἡμέραν
λεγομένων ἀνάμνησιν ⟨ποιούμενοι⟩ τόνδε τὸν τρόπον.
[165] Πυθαγόρειος ἀνὴρ οὐ πρότερον ἐκ τῆς κοίτης ἀνίστατο ἢ τὰ
χθὲς γενόμενα πρότερον ἀναμνησθείη. ἐποιεῖτο δὲ τὴν
ἀνάμνησιν τόνδε τὸν τρόπον. ἐπειρᾶτο ἀναλαμβάνειν τῇ
διανοίᾳ, τί πρῶτον εἶπεν ἢ ἤκουσεν ἢ προσέταξε τοῖς ἔνδον
ἀναστὰς καὶ τί δεύτερον καὶ τί τρίτον, καὶ περὶ τῶν
ἐσομένων ὁ αὐτὸς λόγος· καὶ πάλιν αὖ ἐξιὼν τίνι πρώτῳ
ἐνέτυχε καὶ τίνι δευτέρῳ, καὶ λόγοι τίνες ἐλέχθησαν πρῶτοι
καὶ δεύτεροι καὶ τρίτοι, καὶ περὶ τῶν ἄλλων δὲ ὁ αὐτὸς
λόγος. πάντα γὰρ ἐπειρᾶτο ἀναλαμβάνειν τῇ διανοίᾳ τὰ
συμβάντα ἐν ὅλῃ τῇ ἡμέρᾳ, οὕτω τῇ τάξει προθυμούμενος

[163] So marvelous, then, was this form of his wisdom. They say that of the sciences the Pythagoreans honored, music, medicine, and divination were among the foremost. They were much given to silence and ready to listen, and the one who was able to listen was praised by them. And of medicine[13] they especially approved the kind pertaining to diet, and in this they attained great precision, and first tried to discover signs of due proportion in work,[14] foods, and rest. Therefore they were more or less the first to attempt to treat systematically and to lay down rules about the preparation of foods. The Pythagoreans used unctions[15] and poultices more than their predecessors, but approved less of drugs and used these mostly for ul-
[164] cerations; they sanctioned surgery and cautery least of all. They also used incantations for some illnesses. And they believed that music contributed greatly to health if someone used it in proper ways. They also used selected verses of Homer and Hesiod for the improvement of the soul.[16]

They thought it necessary to hold fast and to preserve in the memory everything taught and said, and to prepare themselves accordingly in their lessons and lectures until the time when the faculty which learns and remembers is able to receive these; because (memory) is that through which one acquires knowledge, and in which one must preserve it. At any rate, they honored memory exceedingly, exercised it much, and paid great attention to it. And in learning, they did not leave off what was taught until they firmly comprehended the first rudiments of
[165] it. Also daily they made recall of things said in the following manner: a Pythagorean did not rise from his bed before he recalled what had happened the day before. He remembered as follows: he tried to recollect what he first said or heard, or after arising, what he ordered his servants to do; and what second, and what third, and about subsequent events on the same principles. And again, on going out, whom he first met and whom second; what words were first spoken and which second and which third, and about everything else the same reasoning. For he tried to recollect everything which happened in the entire day, exerting himself to remember in what order each event took place. And if he had more leisure on
[166] awakening, he would even try to recollect what happened on the day before that in the same manner. Even further they tried to train the memory, for with respect to knowledge, experience, and practical wisdom, there is nothing greater than the ability to remember.

By reason of these pursuits, then, all Italy was filled with philosophers and although it was formerly unknown, later, because of Pythagoras, it was named "Ma-

---

13. This passage, to the beginning of 164, is repeated almost verbatim in 244.

14. At the parallel passage in 244, the mss. read ποτῶν, "drinks." Either makes sense, but perhaps "work," is more appropriate. "Drinks" might have slipped in by analogy with "food."

15. Reading χρισμάτων with von Albrecht, for χρή of mss. χρή is omitted in 244, so perhaps it should simply be dropped here.

16. Cf. section 111 above, and the note ad. loc.

ἀναμιμνήσκεσθαι, ὥς ποτε συνέβη γενέσθαι ἕκαστον αὐτῶν. εἰ δὲ πλείω σχολὴν ἄγοι ἐν τῷ διεγείρεσθαι, καὶ τὰ τρίτην ἡμέραν συμβάντα τὸν αὐτὸν τρόπον ἐπειρᾶτο [166] ἀναλαμβάνειν. καὶ ἐπὶ πλέον ἐπειρῶντο τὴν μνήμην γυμνάζειν· οὐδὲν γὰρ μεῖζον πρὸς ἐπιστήμην καὶ ἐμπειρίαν καὶ φρόνησιν τοῦ δύνασθαι μνημονεύειν.

ἀπὸ δὴ τούτων τῶν ἐπιτηδευμάτων συνέβη τὴν Ἰταλίαν πᾶσαν φιλοσόφων ἀνδρῶν ἐμπλησθῆναι καί, πρότερον ἀγνοουμένης αὐτῆς, ὕστερον διὰ Πυθαγόραν Μεγάλην Ἑλλάδα κληθῆναι, καὶ πλείστους παρ' αὐτοῖς ἄνδρας φιλοσόφους καὶ ποιητὰς καὶ νομοθέτας γενέσθαι. τάς τε γὰρ τέχνας τὰς ῥητορικὰς καὶ τοὺς λόγους τοὺς ἐπιδεικτικοὺς καὶ τοὺς νόμους τοὺς γεγραμμένους παρ' ἐκείνων εἰς τὴν Ἑλλάδα συνέβη κομισθῆναι, καὶ περὶ τῶν φυσικῶν ὅσοι τινὰ μνείαν πεποίηνται, πρῶτον Ἐμπεδοκλέα καὶ Παρμενίδην τὸν Ἐλεάτην προφερόμενοι τυγχάνουσιν, οἵ τε γνωμολογῆσαί τι τῶν κατὰ τὸν βίον βουλόμενοι τὰς Ἐπιχάρμου διανοίας προφέρονται, καὶ σχεδὸν πάντες αὐτὰς οἱ φιλόσοφοι κατέχουσι. περὶ μὲν οὖν τῆς σοφίας αὐτοῦ καὶ πῶς ἅπαντας ἀνθρώπους ἐπὶ πλεῖστον εἰς αὐτὴν προεβίβασεν, ἐφ' ὅσον ἕκαστος οἷός τε ἦν μετέχειν αὐτῆς, καὶ ὡς παρέδωκεν αὐτὴν τελέως, διὰ τούτων ἡμῖν εἰρήσθω.

gna Graecia," and very many men there became philosophers, poets, and law-givers. For rhetorical skills, speeches for display, and laws written by them were brought into Hellas (from Italy). And all who have mentioned the physicists cite as authorities first Empedocles and Parmenides of Elea, while those who wish to propound maxims about the conduct of life cite as authority the wise sayings of Epicharmus; nearly all philosophers know these by heart.[17]

About his wisdom, then, and how to the greatest extent he led all human beings on to it, so far as each was able to share in it, and about the perfection of his teaching it, let this be a sufficient statement.

---

17. On Epicharmus, see *OCD*, s.v., 389-90, and A. Rostagni, *Il verbo di Pitagora*, (Turin, 1924), who tries to make special use of Epicharmus to reconstruct the doctrines of Pythagoras. The tradition that he was a Pythagorean first appears in Plutarch's *Numa* (ch. 8). Cf. also D.L. 8. 78.

[167] Περὶ δὲ δικαιοσύνης, ὅπως αὐτὴν ἐπετήδευσε καὶ παρέδωκε τοῖς ἀνθρώποις, ἄριστα ἂν καταμάθοιμεν, εἰ ἀπὸ τῆς πρώτης ἀρχῆς κατανοήσαιμεν αὐτὴν καὶ ἀφ' ὧν πρώτων αἰτίων φύεται, τήν τε τῆς ἀδικίας πρώτην αἰτίαν κατίδοιμεν· καὶ μετὰ τοῦτο ἂν εὕροιμέν τε, ὡς τὴν μὲν ἐφυλάξατο, τὴν δ' ὅπως καλῶς ἐγγένηται παρεσκεύασεν. ἀρχὴ τοίνυν ἐστὶ δικαιοσύνης μὲν τὸ κοινὸν καὶ ἴσον καὶ τὸ ἐγγυτάτω ἑνὸς σώματος καὶ μιᾶς ψυχῆς ὁμοπαθεῖν πάντας, καὶ ἐπὶ τὸ αὐτὸ τὸ ἐμὸν φθέγγεσθαι καὶ τὸ ἀλλότριον, ὥσπερ δὴ καὶ Πλάτων [168] μαθὼν παρὰ τῶν Πυθαγορείων συμμαρτυρεῖ. τοῦτο τοίνυν ἄριστα ἀνδρῶν κατεσκεύασεν, ἐν τοῖς ἤθεσι τὸ ἴδιον πᾶν ἐξορίσας, τὸ δὲ κοινὸν αὐξήσας μέχρι τῶν ἐσχάτων κτημάτων καὶ στάσεως αἰτίων ὄντων καὶ ταραχῆς· κοινὰ γὰρ πᾶσι πάντα καὶ ταὐτὰ ἦν, ἴδιον δὲ οὐδεὶς οὐδὲν ἐκέκτητο. καὶ εἰ μὲν ἠρέσκετο ⟨τις⟩ τῇ κοινωνίᾳ, ἐχρῆτο τοῖς κοινοῖς κατὰ τὸ δικαιότατον, εἰ δὲ μή, ἀπολαβὼν ἂν τὴν ἑαυτοῦ οὐσίαν καὶ πλείονα ἧς εἰσενηνόχει εἰς τὸ κοινὸν ἀπηλλάττετο. οὕτως ἐξ ἀρχῆς τῆς πρώτης τὴν δικαιοσύνην ἄριστα κατεστήσατο. μετὰ ταῦτα τοίνυν ἡ μὲν οἰκείωσις ἡ πρὸς τοὺς ἀνθρώπους εἰσάγει δικαιοσύνην, ἡ δὲ ἀλλοτρίωσις καὶ καταφρόνησις τοῦ κοινοῦ γένους ἀδικίαν ἐμποιεῖ. ταύτην τοίνυν πόρρωθεν τὴν οἰκείωσιν ἐνθεῖναι βουλόμενος τοῖς ἀνθρώποις καὶ πρὸς τὰ ὁμογενῆ ζῷα αὐτοὺς συνέστησε, παραγγέλλων οἰκεῖα νομίζειν αὐτοὺς ταῦτα καὶ φίλα, ὡς μήτε ἀδικεῖν μηδὲν αὐτῶν μήτε φονεύειν μήτε ἐσθίειν. ὁ [169] τοίνυν καὶ τοῖς ζῴοις, διότι ἀπὸ τῶν αὐτῶν στοιχείων ἡμῖν ὑφέστηκε καὶ τῆς κοινοτέρας ζωῆς ἡμῖν συμμετέχει, οἰκειώσας τοὺς ἀνθρώπους πόσῳ μᾶλλον τοῖς τῆς ὁμοειδοῦς ψυχῆς κεκοινωνηκόσι καὶ τῆς λογικῆς τὴν οἰκείωσιν ἐνεστήσατο. ἐκ δὲ ταύτης δῆλον ὅτι καὶ τὴν δικαιοσύνην εἰσῆγεν ἀπ' ἀρχῆς τῆς κυριωτάτης παραγομένην. ἐπεὶ δὲ πολλοὺς ἐνίοτε καὶ σπάνις χρημάτων συναναγκάζει παρὰ τὸ δίκαιόν τι ποιεῖν, καὶ τούτου καλῶς προενόησε, διὰ τῆς οἰκονομίας τὰ ἐλευθέρια δαπανήματα καὶ τὰ δίκαια ἱκανῶς ἑαυτῷ παρασκευάζων. καὶ γὰρ ἄλλως ἀρχή ἐστιν ἡ περὶ τὸν οἶκον δικαία διάθεσις τῆς ὅλης ἐν ταῖς πόλεσιν εὐταξίας· ἀπὸ γὰρ τῶν οἴκων αἱ πόλεις συνίστανται. φασὶ τοίνυν αὐτὸν

CHAPTER THIRTY

*What Pythagoras contributed to human beings in the area of
justice, and how from the beginning he practiced it from its
highest kinds to its most particular forms, and transmitted it to all.*

[167]   We can best understand how he practiced justice and taught it to human beings
if we consider it from its first principle and from which first causes it originates,
and if we discern the first cause of injustice. And after this, we will discover how
he avoided the one but provided for the proper origin of the other.

The first principle of justice, then, is the concept of the common and the equal,
and the idea that all should approximate as nearly as possible in their attitudes to
having one body and one soul in which all have the same experience, and should
call that which is mine and that which belongs to another by the same name, just
[168] as Plato, who learned from the Pythagoreans, also maintains.[1] This, then, he of
mortals best established, by having banished everything private in customs, and
by having increased what is common as far as the lowliest possessions, which are
causes of discord and tumult. For all things were common and the same for all,
and no one possessed anything privately. And if someone were satisfied with the
community, he used the things in common most justly; but if not, he got back his
own property, and indeed more than he had contributed to the common stock,
and so left. Thus from its first source, Pythagoras established justice in the best
manner.

Following on this, fellow-feeling[2] with human beings introduces justice, but es-
trangement and contempt for the common race produce injustice. Wishing,
then, to instill this fellow-feeling in human beings on a broader basis, he also
brought them together with animals, who are of the same kind,[3] exhorting them
to believe these related and friendly, so as neither to wrong, kill, nor eat any of
them. Seeing, then, that he made humans friends with animals because they con-
[169] sist of the same elements as we do, and share in the more basic level of life with
us, how much more did he thereby institute familiarity among those sharing the
same kind of soul, even the rational! From this it is evident that he also introduced
justice fully developed from its supreme source.

---

1. A reference to the provisions for the training of the guardians in the *Republic,* esp. 462 b ff.
We see here a very characteristic attempt to reclaim later doctrine for Pythagoras on the basis of
such a precept as "friends have all things in common."

2. A reference to the Stoic concept of οἰκείωσις, and another attempt to claim later doctrine
for Pythagoras.

3. That is, of the broader genus "living thing" (ζῷον).

[170] τὸν Πυθαγόραν κληρονομήσαντα τὸν Ἀλκαίου βίον, τοῦ μετὰ τὴν εἰς Λακεδαίμονα πρεσβείαν τὸν βίον καταλύσαντος, οὐδὲν ἧττον θαυμασθῆναι κατὰ τὴν οἰκονομίαν ἢ τὴν φιλοσοφίαν, γήμαντα δὲ τὴν γεννηθεῖσαν αὐτῷ θυγατέρα, μετὰ ταῦτα δὲ Μένωνι τῷ Κροτωνιάτῃ συνοικήσασαν, ἀγαγεῖν οὕτως, ὥστε παρθένον μὲν οὖσαν ἡγεῖσθαι τῶν χορῶν, γυναῖκα δὲ γενομένην πρώτην προσιέναι τοῖς βωμοῖς· τοὺς δὲ Μεταποντίνους, διὰ μνήμης ἔχοντας ἔτι τὸν Πυθαγόραν καὶ μετὰ τοὺς αὐτοῦ χρόνους,
[171] τὴν μὲν οἰκίαν αὐτοῦ Δήμητρος ἱερὸν τελέσαι, τὸν δὲ στενωπὸν Μουσεῖον. ἐπεὶ δὲ καὶ ὕβρις καὶ τρυφὴ πολλάκις καὶ νόμων ὑπεροψία ἐπαίρουσιν εἰς ἀδικίαν, διὰ ταῦτα ὀσημέραι παρήγγελλε νόμῳ βοηθεῖν καὶ ἀνομίᾳ πολεμεῖν. διὰ ταῦτα δὲ καὶ τὴν τοιαύτην διαίρεσιν ἐποιεῖτο, ὅτι τὸ πρῶτον τῶν κακῶν παραρρεῖν εἴωθεν εἴς τε τὰς οἰκίας καὶ τὰς πόλεις ἡ καλουμένη τρυφή, δεύτερον ὕβρις, τρίτον ὄλεθρος· ὅθεν ⟨παρήγγελλεν⟩ ἐκ παντὸς εἴργειν τε καὶ ἀπωθεῖσθαι τὴν τρυφὴν καὶ συνεθίζεσθαι ἀπὸ γενετῆς σώφρονί τε καὶ ἀνδρικῷ βίῳ, δυσφημίας δὲ πάσης καθαρεύειν τῆς τε σχετλιαστικῆς καὶ τῆς μαχίμου καὶ τῆς λοιδορητικῆς καὶ τῆς
[172] φορτικῆς καὶ γελωτοποιοῦ. πρὸς τούτοις ἄλλο εἶδος δικαιοσύνης κάλλιστον κατεστήσατο, τὸ νομοθετικόν, ὃ προστάττει μὲν ἃ δεῖ ποιεῖν, ἀπαγορεύει δὲ ἃ μὴ χρὴ πράττειν, κρεῖττον δέ ἐστι καὶ τοῦ δικαστικοῦ· τὸ μὲν γὰρ τῷ ἰατρικῷ προσέοικε καὶ νοσήσαντας θεραπεύει, τὸ δὲ τὴν ἀρχὴν οὐδὲ νοσεῖν ⟨ἐᾷ⟩, ἀλλὰ πόρρωθεν ἐπιμελεῖται τῆς ἐν τῇ ψυχῇ ὑγείας. τούτου δὲ οὕτως ἔχοντος νομοθέται πάντων ἄριστοι γεγόνασιν οἱ Πυθαγόρᾳ προσελθόντες, πρῶτον μὲν Χαρώνδας ὁ Καταναῖος, ἔπειτα Ζάλευκος καὶ Τιμάρατος οἱ Λοκροῖς γράψαντες τοὺς νόμους, πρὸς δὲ τούτοις Θεαίτητος καὶ Ἑλικάων καὶ Ἀριστοκράτης καὶ Φύτιος, οἱ Ῥηγίνων γενόμενοι νομοθέται. καὶ πάντες οὗτοι παρὰ τοῖς αὐτῶν πολίταις ἰσοθέων τιμῶν ἔτυχον. οὐ γὰρ καθάπερ
[173] Ἡράκλειτος γράψειν Ἐφεσίοις ἔφη τοὺς νόμους, ἀπάγξασθαι τοὺς πολίτας ἡβηδὸν κελεύσας, ἀλλὰ μετὰ πολλῆς ἐννοίας καὶ πολιτικῆς ἐπιστήμης νομοθετεῖν ἐπεχείρησαν. καὶ τί δεῖ τούτους θαυμάζειν, τοὺς ἀγωγῆς καὶ τροφῆς ἐλευθέρας μετασχόντας; Ζάμολξις γὰρ Θρᾷξ ὢν καὶ Πυθαγόρου δοῦλος γενόμενος καὶ τῶν λόγων τῶν Πυθαγόρου

Since lack of goods sometimes forces many to contravene what is just, even this he foresaw well, providing for himself by household management necessaries fit for a freeman, and sufficiently well-balanced. And besides, right management of the household is the source of all good order in communities; for it is from house-
[170] holds that cities arise.[4] They say, moreover, that Pythagoras himself having inherited the property of Alcaeus, who died after the embassy to Lacedaemon,[5] was no less admired for his household management than for his philosophy. After marrying, he educated the daughter born to him (who afterwards married Menon of Croton) in such a way that when she was a maiden she led the dances, and on becoming a wife, she was first to approach the altars. The Metapontines still remembered Pythagoras even after his time, and consecrated his house as a temple to Demeter, making the lane in which it stood a shrine of the Muses.

[171]   Since insolence, luxury, and disdain for laws also often stir up injustice, he exhorted his hearers daily to assist law and to war against lawlessness. Therefore he made the following division: the first of evils usually to slip unawares into households and cities is that called "luxury"; second, "insolence"; third "ruin."[6] Thus he ordered that one should by every means hinder and spurn luxury; become accustomed from birth to a temperate and manly way of life, and abstain from all evil talk, such as is expressive of anger, belligerent, abusive, vulgar and excites laugh-
[172] ter. In addition to this, he established another form of justice on an excellent footing: which commands the legislative, what ought to be done, and forbids what ought not to be done. It is superior to forensic justice, for the latter resembles medicine which heals those who are sick, while the former does not allow sickness to occur in the first place, but cares for the health of the soul in the longer term. Hence the best of all legislators are those who studied with Pythagoras: first, Charondas the Catanian, then Zaleucus and Timaratus who wrote laws for the Locrians; in addition to these, Theaetetus, Helicaon, Aristocrates, and Phytius, who became legislators of Rhegium.[7] And all these received from their own citizens honors equal to the gods.

[173]   For unlike Heraclitus, who declared he would legislate for the Ephesians, and then decreed that the citizens should be hanged as each attained manhood,[8] they set out to legislate with much good sense and political acumen. And why is it nec-

---

4. A doctrine propounded by Aristotle, *Pol.* I, 2.

5. Presumably an embassy of Croton. The story seems familiar to Iamblichus' hearers or readers since he says "*the* embassy." All the information in this section seems derived ultimately from Timaeus, as we can see from comparison with Porph. *VP*, 4.

6. The sequence "luxury," "insolence," "ruin," is found in the treatise of "Kallikratidas," *On Happiness in the Home*, 104, 27-105, 4 Thesleff, *Pythagorean Texts*.

7. All these were mentioned above in section 130.

8. See B 121, D.-K. This is not an accurate reference to Heraclitus who actually related his remark to the Ephesians' exiling his friend Hermodorus, and sees the Ephesians themselves operating by: "let no one be best among us."

διακούσας, ἀφεθεὶς ἐλεύθερος καὶ παραγενόμενος πρὸς τοὺς
Γέτας, τούς τε νόμους αὐτοῖς ἔθηκε, καθάπερ καὶ ἐν ἀρχῇ
δεδηλώκαμεν, καὶ πρὸς τὴν ἀνδρείαν τοὺς πολίτας
παρεκάλεσε, τὴν ψυχὴν ἀθάνατον εἶναι πείσας. ἔτι καὶ νῦν
οἱ Γαλάται πάντες καὶ οἱ Τράλλεις καὶ οἱ πολλοὶ τῶν
βαρβάρων τοὺς αὐτῶν υἱοὺς πείθουσιν, ὡς οὐκ ἔστι
φθαρῆναι τὴν ψυχήν, ἀλλὰ διαμένειν, τῶν ἀποθανόντων,
καὶ ὅτι τὸν θάνατον οὐ φοβητέον, ἀλλὰ πρὸς τοὺς κινδύνους
εὐρώστως ἑκτέον. καὶ ταῦτα παιδεύσας τοὺς Γέτας καὶ
γράψας αὐτοῖς τοὺς νόμους μέγιστος τῶν θεῶν ἐστι παρ'
[174] αὐτοῖς. ἔτι τοίνυν ἀνυσιμώτατον πρὸς τὴν τῆς δικαιοσύνης
κατάστασιν ὑπελάμβανεν εἶναι τὴν τῶν θεῶν ἀρχήν, ἄνωθέν
τε ἀπ' ἐκείνης πολιτείαν καὶ νόμους, δικαιοσύνην τε καὶ τὰ
δίκαια διέθηκεν. οὐ χεῖρον δὲ καὶ τὰ καθ' ἕκαστον ὅπως
διώρισε προσθεῖναι. τὸ διανοεῖσθαι περὶ τοῦ θείου, ὡς ἔστι
τε καὶ πρὸς τὸ ἀνθρώπινον γένος οὕτως ἔχει ὡς ἐπιβλέπειν
καὶ μὴ ὀλιγωρεῖν αὐτοῦ, χρήσιμον εἶναι ὑπελάμβανον οἱ
Πυθαγόρειοι παρ' ἐκείνου μαθόντες. δεῖσθαι γὰρ ἡμᾶς
ἐπιστατείας τοιαύτης, ᾗ κατὰ μηδὲν ἀνταίρειν ἀξιώσομεν·
τοιαύτην δ' εἶναι τὴν ὑπὸ τοῦ θείου γινομένην, εἴπερ ἐστὶ τὸ
θεῖον τοιοῦτον ⟨οἷον⟩ ἄξιον εἶναι τῆς τοῦ σύμπαντος ἀρχῆς.
ὑβριστικὸν γὰρ δὴ φύσει τὸ ζῷον ἔφασαν εἶναι, ὀρθῶς
λέγοντες, καὶ ποικίλον κατά τε τὰς ὁρμὰς καὶ κατὰ τὰς
ἐπιθυμίας καὶ κατὰ τὰ λοιπὰ τῶν παθῶν· δεῖσθαι οὖν
[175] τοιαύτης ὑπεροχῆς τε καὶ ἐπανατάσεως, ἀφ' ἧς ἐστι
σωφρονισμός τις καὶ τάξις. ᾤοντο δὴ δεῖν ἕκαστον αὐτῷ
συνειδότα τὴν τῆς φύσεως ποικιλίαν μηδέποτε λήθην ἔχειν
τῆς πρὸς τὸ θεῖον ὁσιότητός τε καὶ θεραπείας, ἀλλ' ἀεὶ
τίθεσθαι πρὸ τῆς διανοίας ὡς ἐπιβλέποντός τε καὶ
παραφυλάττοντος τὴν ἀνθρωπίνην ἀγωγήν. μετὰ δὲ τὸ θεῖόν
τε καὶ τὸ δαιμόνιον πλεῖστον ποιεῖσθαι λόγον γονέων τε καὶ
νόμου, καὶ τούτων ὑπήκοον αὐτὸν κατασκευάζειν, μὴ
πλαστῶς, ἀλλὰ πεπεισμένως. καθόλου δὲ ᾤοντο δεῖν
ὑπολαμβάνειν μηδὲν εἶναι μεῖζον κακὸν ἀναρχίας· οὐ γὰρ
πεφυκέναι τὸν ἄνθρωπον διασώζεσθαι μηδενὸς ἐπιστα-
[176] τοῦντος. τὸ μένειν ἐν τοῖς πατρίοις ἔθεσί τε καὶ νομίμοις
ἐδοκίμαζον οἱ ἄνδρες ἐκεῖνοι, κἂν ᾖ μικρῷ χείρω ἑτέρων· τὸ
γὰρ ῥᾳδίως ἀποπηδᾶν ἀπὸ τῶν ὑπαρχόντων νόμων καὶ
οἰκείους εἶναι καινοτομίας οὐδαμῶς εἶναι σύμφορον οὐδὲ

essary to marvel at these, since they shared in upbringing and education fit for freemen? For Zamolxis, a Thracian, and former slave of Pythagoras, who mastered the teachings of Pythagoras, when he was set free and returned to the Getae, established laws for them, just as we showed at the beginning;[9] he exhorted the citizens to courage, having persuaded them that the soul is immortal. Even now, all the Gauls and the Trallians, and many barbarians, still convince their own sons that the soul cannot be destroyed, but remains after they are dead; and that death is not to be feared, but one must behave stoutly before dangers. And having educated the Getae in these matters and having written laws for them, he (Zamolxis) is regarded as the greatest deity among them.

[174] Furthermore Pythagoras believed the gods' sovereignty most effectual for the establishment of justice, and on that sovereignty, as a first principle, he based the constitution and laws, justice and just acts. It is also well to add how he decided individual cases. To have the attitude to the divine that it exists and is so disposed to the human race that it looks attentively on it, and does not neglect it: this the Pythagoreans learned from him, and deemed to be useful. For we need supervision, of such a sort that we shall not at all dare to rebel against it; and such is the supervision which arises from the divinity, if indeed the divine is such as to be worthy of total sovereignty. For they declared, correctly, that the living being is by nature prone to insolence, and unstable in its impulses, desires, and the rest of its emotions. It needs, thus, such supremacy and threatening from which there de-

[175] rives some self-control and order. They thought, then, that every one, being conscious of the complexity of his own nature, must never be forgetful of piety toward and worship of the divine, but always put before his mind the fact that the divinity looks attentively at and watches over the conduct of human beings.

After the divine and daemonic they took most account of parents and law:[10] to make oneself obedient to these, not feignedly but from conviction. They thought it entirely necessary to believe there is no greater evil than anarchy, for by nature,

[176] the human being does not survive when no one is in charge. Those men sanctioned observance of ancestral customs and traditions even if they were somewhat[11] inferior to others. For easily turning away from existing customs to private

---

9. The beginning of what? Rohde notes this remark, *RhM* 27 (1872) 49, but suggests no solution, except mindless transcriptions by Iamblichus of an unidentifiable source. The mention of Gauls and Trallians (an Illyrian or Thracian people), "even now holding their beliefs," refers to a time when these peoples were not absorbed into the Roman Empire, and so a Hellenistic source, perhaps Aristoxenus or Timaeus. Zamolxis is mentioned in section 104.

10. From here to section 176 we can see, from passages preserved in Stobaeus (4, 24, 45 and 4, 1, 49) that Iamblichus makes verbatim use of Aristoxenus' *Pythagorean Sayings*, so that we may suspect the style here is not Iamblichean. Rohde would claim all of 174-6 for Aristoxenus, *RhM* 27 (1872) 49, with great probability.

11. Keeping μικρῷ of mss. which agrees with Aristoxenus, *ap.* Stobaeus. Deubner's emendation μακρῷ seems misguided.

σωτήριον. πολλὰ μὲν οὖν καὶ ἄλλα τῆς πρὸς θεοὺς ὁσίας
ἐχόμενα ἔργα διεπράξατο, σύμφωνον ἑαυτοῦ τὸν βίον τοῖς
λόγοις ἐπιδεικνύων· οὐ χεῖρον δ' ἑνὸς μνημονεῦσαι,
δυναμένου καὶ τὰ ἄλλα σαφῶς ἐμφαίνειν. ἐρῶ δὲ τὰ πρὸς τὴν
[177] πρεσβείαν τὴν ἐκ Συβάριδος εἰς Κρότωνα παραγενομένην
ἐπὶ τὴν ἐξαίτησιν τῶν φυγάδων ὑπὸ Πυθαγόρου ῥηθέντα καὶ
πραχθέντα. ἐκεῖνος γάρ, ἀνῃρημένων τινῶν τῶν μετ' αὐτοῦ
συνδιατριψάντων ὑπὸ τῶν ἡκόντων πρεσβευτῶν, ὧν ὃ μὲν
τῶν αὐτοχείρων, ὃ δ' υἱὸς τετελευτηκότος ὑπ' ἀρρωστίας
τῶν τῆς στάσεως μετεσχηκότων, ἔτι μὲν τῶν ἐν τῇ πόλει
διαπορούντων, ὅπως χρήσονται τοῖς πράγμασιν, εἶπε πρὸς
τοὺς ἑταίρους ὡς οὐκ ἂν βούλοιτο μεγάλα πρὸς αὐτὸν
διαφωνῆσαι τοὺς Κροτωνιάτας καί, δοκιμάζοντος αὐτοῦ μηδ'
ἱερεῖα τοῖς βωμοῖς προσάγειν, ἐκείνους καὶ τοὺς ἱκέτας ἀπὸ
τῶν βωμῶν ἀποσπᾶν. προσελθόντων δ' αὐτῷ τῶν
Συβαριτῶν καὶ μεμφομένων, τῷ μὲν αὐτόχειρι λόγον
ἀποδιδόντι τῶν ἐπιτιμωμένων οὐ θεμιστεύειν ἔφησεν· ὅθεν
ᾐτιῶντο αὐτὸν Ἀπόλλωνα φάσκειν εἶναι παρὰ τὸ καὶ
πρότερον ἐπί τινος ζητήσεως ἐρωτηθέντα "διὰ τί ταῦτ'
ἐστίν;" ἀντερωτῆσαι τὸν πυνθανόμενον, εἰ καὶ τὸν
Ἀπόλλωνα λέγοντα τοὺς χρησμοὺς ἀξιώσειεν ἂν τὴν αἰτίαν
[178] ἀποδοῦναι. πρὸς δὲ τὸν ἕτερον, ὡς ᾤετο, καταγελῶντα τῶν
διατριβῶν, ἐν αἷς ἀπεφαίνετο Πυθαγόρας ἐπάνοδον εἶναι
ταῖς ψυχαῖς, καὶ φάσκοντα πρὸς τὸν πατέρα δώσειν
ἐπιστολήν, ἐπειδὰν εἰς ᾅδου μέλλῃ καταβαίνειν, καὶ
κελεύοντα λαβεῖν ἑτέραν, ὅταν ἐπανίῃ παρὰ τοῦ πατρός, οὐκ
ἔφη μέλλειν εἰς τὸν τῶν ἀσεβῶν τόπον παραβάλλειν, ὅπου
σαφῶς οἶδε τοὺς σφαγεῖς κολαζομένους. λοιδορηθέντων δ'
αὐτῷ τῶν πρεσβευτῶν, κἀκείνου προάγοντος ἐπὶ τὴν
θάλατταν καὶ περιρρανομένου πολλῶν ἀκολουθούντων, εἶπέ
τις τῶν συμβουλευόντων τοῖς Κροτωνιάταις, ἐπειδὴ τὰ ἄλλα
τῶν ἡκόντων κατέδραμεν, ὅτι καὶ Πυθαγόρᾳ προσκόπτειν
ἀπενοήθησαν, ὑπὲρ οὗ, πάλιν ἐξ ἀρχῆς, ὥσπερ οἱ μῦθοι
παραδεδώκασιν, ἁπάντων ἐμψύχων τὴν αὐτὴν φωνὴν τοῖς
ἀνθρώποις ἀφιέντων, μηδὲ τῶν ἄλλων ζῴων μηδὲν ἂν
[179] τολμῆσαι βλασφημεῖν. καὶ ἄλλην δὲ μέθοδον ἀνεῦρε τοῦ
ἀναστέλλειν τοὺς ἀνθρώπους ἀπὸ τῆς ἀδικίας, διὰ τῆς
κρίσεως τῶν ψυχῶν, εἰδὼς μὲν ἀληθῶς ταύτην λεγομένην,
εἰδὼς δὲ καὶ χρησίμην οὖσαν εἰς τὸν φόβον τῆς ἀδικίας.

innovations is by no means beneficial or salutary. He also accomplished many other deeds of piety towards the gods, showing his own life harmonious with his words.

[177]   It is good to make mention of one deed which can reflect the others clearly: I will tell what was said and done by Pythagoras when the embassy came from Sybaris to Croton to demand punishment for the fugitives from their city. Some of his close associates had been killed by those who came as ambassadors (one of these belonged to the murderers, and another was a son of one who had participated in the rebellion, but had then died of sickness). While those in the city (the Crotoniates) were still at a loss as to what position they should adopt, he said to his disciples that he did not wish the Crotoniates to disagree greatly with him and, since he himself did not approve of leading sacrificial victims to altars, he also did not approve of those (the ambassadors) dragging away the suppliants (the fugitives) from the altars. When the Sybarites came to Pythagoras and complained, Pythagoras said to the murderer who was giving voice to their complaints, that he would not deliver precepts to him.[12] Hence, they accused him of claiming to be Apollo, since also before, when someone asked him in an inquiry "why these things are so," he asked the inquirer, in return, whether he would expect Apollo

[178] also, when speaking oracles, to give his reason. And another ambassador by way of poking fun, so he thought, at the discourses in which Pythagoras propounded the return of souls, said that he would give him a letter for his (departed) father when (Pythagoras) was ready to descend to Hades, and requested him to bring back another letter from his father on his return thence. To him Pythagoras said he was not about to approach the place of the impious where he knew clearly that murderers were punished. The ambassadors abused him, so he went with a great crowd of his followers to the sea and purified himself. A counselor of the Crotoniates then remarked, after he had criticized the ambassadors in all other respects, that they had lost all sense by taking offense at Pythagoras, whom no other living being would dare blaspheme, even if all living beings could once more speak the same language as humans, which, as the myths have taught, they did at the beginning of things.

[179]   He also discovered another method of restraining human beings from injustice, through belief in the judgment of souls. He knew that this story has a true meaning, and that it is also useful for instilling fear of committing injustice. He, then, proclaimed[13] that one ought much rather be wronged than kill a human being (for the judgment rests with Hades), if one reflects on the soul, its being, and the primary nature of existing things. Wishing to show that in things unequal, disproportionate, and indefinite justice is that which is definite, equal, and propor-

---

12. This story was told, in a slightly different form, in section 133 above.
13. Very similar lines are found also in section 155.

πολλῷ δὴ μᾶλλον ἀδικεῖσθαι δεῖν παρήγγελλεν ἢ κτείνειν
ἄνθρωπον (ἐν ἅδου γὰρ κεῖσθαι τὴν κρίσιν), ἐκλογιζόμενος
τὴν ψυχὴν καὶ τὴν οὐσίαν αὐτῆς καὶ τὴν πρώτην τῶν ὄντων
φύσιν. βουλόμενος δὲ τὴν ἐν τοῖς ἀνίσοις καὶ ἀσυμμέτροις
καὶ ἀπείροις πεπερασμένην καὶ ἴσην καὶ σύμμετρον
δικαιοσύνην παραδεῖξαι, ὅπως δεῖ αὐτὴν ἀσκεῖν
ὑφηγήσασθαι, τὴν δικαιοσύνην ἔφη προσεοικέναι τῷ
σχήματι ἐκείνῳ, ὅπερ μόνον τῶν ἐν γεωμετρίᾳ διαγραμ-
μάτων ἀπείρους μὲν ἔχει τὰς τῶν σχημάτων συστάσεις,
ἀνομοίως δὲ ἀλλήλοις διακειμένων ἴσας ἔχει τὰς τῆς
[180] δυνάμεως ἀποδείξεις. ἐπεὶ δὲ καὶ ἐν τῇ πρὸς ἕτερον χρείᾳ
ἔστι τις δικαιοσύνη, καὶ ταύτης τοιοῦτόν τινα τρόπον
λέγεται ὑπὸ τῶν Πυθαγορείων παραδίδοσθαι. εἶναι γὰρ κατὰ
τὰς ὁμιλίας τὸν μὲν εὔκαιρον, τὸν δὲ ἄκαιρον, διαιρεῖσθαι δὲ
ἡλικίας τε διαφορᾷ καὶ ἀξιώματος καὶ οἰκειότητος τῆς
συγγενικῆς καὶ εὐεργεσίας, καὶ εἴ τι ἄλλο τοιοῦτον ἐν ταῖς
πρὸς ἀλλήλους διαφοραῖς ὂν ὑπάρχει. ἔστι γάρ τι ὁμιλίας
εἶδος, ὃ φαίνεται νεωτέρῳ μὲν πρὸς νεώτερον οὐκ ἄκαιρον
εἶναι, πρὸς δὲ τὸν πρεσβύτερον ἄκαιρον· οὔτε γὰρ ὀργῆς
οὔτε ἀπειλῆς εἶδος πᾶν (ἄκαιρον) οὔτε θρασύτητος, ἀλλὰ
πᾶσαν τὴν τοιαύτην ἀκαιρίαν εὐλαβητέον εἶναι τῷ νεωτέρῳ
πρὸς τὸν πρεσβύτερον. παραπλήσιον δέ τινα εἶναι καὶ τὸν
[181] περὶ τοῦ ἀξιώματος λόγον· πρὸς γὰρ ἄνδρα ἐπὶ καλοκα-
γαθίας ἥκοντα ἀληθινὸν ἀξίωμα οὔτ' εὔσχημον οὔτ'
εὔκαιρον εἶναι προσφέρειν οὔτε παρρησίαν πάλιν οὔτε τὰ
λοιπὰ τῶν ἀρτίως εἰρημένων. παραπλήσια δὲ τούτοις καὶ
περὶ τῆς πρὸς τοὺς γονεῖς ὁμιλίας ἐλέγετο, ὡσαύτως δὲ καὶ
περὶ τῆς πρὸς τοὺς εὐεργέτας. εἶναι δὲ ποικίλην τινὰ καὶ
πολυειδῆ τὴν τοῦ καιροῦ χρείαν· καὶ γὰρ τῶν ὀργιζομένων τε
καὶ θυμουμένων τοὺς μὲν εὐκαίρως τοῦτο ποιεῖν, τοὺς δὲ
ἀκαίρως, καὶ πάλιν αὖ τῶν ὀρεγομένων τε καὶ ἐπιθυμούντων
καὶ ὁρμώντων ἐφ' ὁτιδήποτε τοῖς μὲν ἀκολουθεῖν καιρόν,
τοῖς δ' ἀκαιρίαν. τὸν αὐτὸν δ' εἶναι λόγον καὶ περὶ τῶν
ἄλλων παθῶν τε καὶ πράξεων καὶ διαθέσεων καὶ ὁμιλιῶν καὶ
[182] ἐντεύξεων. εἶναι δὲ τὸν καιρὸν μέχρι μέν τινος διδακτόν τε
καὶ ἀπαράλογον καὶ τεχνολογίαν ἐπιδεχόμενον, καθόλου δὲ
καὶ ἁπλῶς οὐδὲν αὐτῷ τούτων ὑπάρχειν. ἀκόλουθα δὲ εἶναι
καὶ σχεδὸν τοιαῦτα οἷα συμπαρέπεσθαι τῇ τοῦ καιροῦ φύσει
τήν τε ὀνομαζομένην ὥραν καὶ τὸ πρέπον καὶ τὸ ἁρμόττον,

tionate, and wishing to demonstrate how one should practice justice, he said that justice is like that figure which alone of geometrical figures contains an unlimited range of possible combinations of figures, but although these figures are unequal in proportion to one another, the relationship between their squares are equal.[14]

[180]   Since justice also consists in relationships with others, the following method of instruction is also said to have been handed down by the Pythagoreans.[15] In regard to associations with others, there is both appropriateness[16] and inappropriateness; these associations are distinguished from each other by difference of age, dignity, degrees of relationship, and good service done, and whatever else there may be of like kind in the differences between human beings. There is a form of association, then, which does not appear inappropriate for a young person with another young person; but it is inappropriate for a younger person with one older. For not every kind of anger, threat of punishment, or boldness is inappropriate, but one must beware of all such inappropriateness on the part of one younger

[181]   toward one older. The situation is similar in the case of dignity. For with a man who has attained the true dignity of perfect character, it is again neither decent nor suitable to use outspokenness, or the things just mentioned. Similar prescriptions were also made about relationships with parents, and in like manner about association with benefactors.

The use of the opportune time, then, is a complex and many-faceted art. For of those who become angry and furious, some do so appropriately, other inappropriately; and again, of those yearning for, desirous, and eager for whatever it may be, appropriateness accompanies some, but inappropriateness others. And the same goes for all other emotions, actions, dispositions, associations and conversa-

[182]   tion. Appropriateness is to some extent teachable and subject to calculation, and thus admits of systematic treatment, but when considered generally and simply, none of these exist for it. In accord with, and almost concomitant with the nature of the opportune time, are such things called "the right time," "the fitting," and "the appropriate," and anything else which may be akin to these. They asserted that a "first principle"[17] is in everything one of the things most honorable, equally in knowledge and experience, in generation, and also in a household, a city, an army, and in all such organizations. But the nature of "principle" is difficult to discern and survey in all the areas mentioned. For in the sciences, when looking at the parts of a study, it is a task for no ordinary intellect to understand and to form

---

14. A description of the famous Pythagorean theorem used also by Plato in *Republic* VIII for social purposes. Cf. Burkert, *Lore and Science*, 428-432.

15. For the next sections, 180-83, Iamblichus writes of Pythagoreans rather than of Pythagoras himself. This Rohde connects, reasonably, with Aristoxenus, *RhM* 27 (1872) 50.

16. Pythagorean reverence for καιρός is well known (See section 49). It was also a title of the number seven. Cf. (Iambl.) *Theol. Ar.* 54, 4; 70, 24; 71, 3 ff. De Falco, and Proclus, *In Alc.* 121, 1 ff.

17. Ἀρχή can, of course, mean either "beginning" or "ruling principle."

καὶ εἴ τι ἄλλο τυγχάνει τούτοις ὁμοιογενὲς ὄν. ἀρχὴν δὲ ἀπε-
φαίνοντο ἐν παντὶ ἕν τι τῶν τιμιωτάτων εἶναι ὁμοίως ἐν
ἐπιστήμῃ τε καὶ ἐμπειρίᾳ καὶ ἐν γενέσει, καὶ πάλιν αὖ ἐν
οἰκίᾳ τε καὶ πόλει καὶ στρατοπέδῳ καὶ πᾶσι τοῖς τοιούτοις
συστήμασι, δυσθεώρητον δ' εἶναι καὶ δυσσύνοπτον τὴν τῆς
ἀρχῆς φύσιν ἐν πᾶσι τοῖς εἰρημένοις. ἔν τε γὰρ ταῖς ἐπιστή-
μαις οὐ τῆς τυχούσης εἶναι διανοίας τὸ καταμαθεῖν τε καὶ
κρῖναι καλῶς βλέψαντας εἰς τὰ μέρη τῆς πραγματείας, ποῖον
[183] τούτων ἀρχή. μεγάλην δ' εἶναι διαφορὰν καὶ σχεδὸν περὶ
ὅλου τε καὶ παντὸς τὸν κίνδυνον γίνεσθαι μὴ ληφθείσης
ὀρθῶς τῆς ἀρχῆς· οὐδὲν γάρ, ὡς ἁπλῶς εἰπεῖν, ἔτι τῶν μετὰ
ταῦτα ὑγιὲς γίνεσθαι ἀγνοηθείσης τῆς ἀληθινῆς ἀρχῆς. τὸν
αὐτὸν δ' εἶναι λόγον καὶ περὶ τῆς ἑτέρας ἀρχῆς· οὔτε γὰρ
οἰκίαν οὔτε πόλιν εὖ ποτε ἂν οἰκηθῆναι μὴ ὑπάρξαντος
ἀληθινοῦ ἄρχοντος καὶ κυριεύοντος τῆς ἀρχῆς τε καὶ
ἐπιστασίας ἑκουσίως. ἀμφοτέρων γὰρ δεῖ βουλομένων τὴν
ἐπιστατείαν γίνεσθαι, ὁμοίως τοῦ τε ἄρχοντος καὶ τῶν
ἀρχομένων, ὥσπερ καὶ τὰς μαθήσεις τὰς ὀρθῶς γινομένας
ἑκουσίως δεῖν ἔφασαν γίνεσθαι, ἀμφοτέρων βουλομένων,
τοῦ τε διδάσκοντος καὶ τοῦ μανθάνοντος· ἀντιτείνοντος γὰρ
ὁποτέρου δήποτε τῶν εἰρημένων οὐκ ἂν ἐπιτελεσθῆναι κατὰ
τρόπον τὸ προκείμενον ἔργον. οὕτω μὲν οὖν τὸ πείθεσθαι
τοῖς ἄρχουσι καλὸν εἶναι ἐδοκίμαζε καὶ τὸ τοῖς διδασκάλοις
ὑπακούειν. τεκμήριον δὲ δι' ἔργων μέγιστον παρείχετο
[184] τοιοῦτον. πρὸς Φερεκύδην τὸν Σύριον, διδάσκαλον αὐτοῦ
γενόμενον, ἀπὸ τῆς Ἰταλίας εἰς Δῆλον ἐκομίσθη, νοσοκομήσων τε αὐτὸν περιπετῆ γενόμενον τῷ ἱστορουμένῳ τῆς
φθειριάσεως πάθει καὶ κηδεύσων αὐτόν· παρέμεινέ τε ἄχρι
τῆς τελευτῆς αὐτῷ καὶ τὴν ὁσίαν ἀπεπλήρωσε περὶ τὸν
αὐτοῦ καθηγεμόνα. οὕτω περὶ πολλοῦ τὴν περὶ τὸν
διδάσκαλον ἐποιεῖτο σπουδήν.
[185]   πρός γε μὴν συνταγὰς καὶ τὸ ἀψευδεῖν ἐν αὐταῖς οὕτως εὖ
παρεσκεύαζε τοὺς ὁμιλητὰς Πυθαγόρας, ὥστε φασί ποτε
Λῦσιν προσκυνήσαντα ἐν Ἥρας ἱερῷ καὶ ἐξιόντα συντυχεῖν
Εὐρυφάμῳ Συρακουσίῳ τῶν ἑταίρων τινὶ περὶ τὰ προπύλαια
τῆς θεοῦ εἰσιόντι. προστάξαντος δὲ τοῦ Εὐρυφάμου
προσμεῖναι αὐτόν, μέχρις ἂν καὶ αὐτὸς προσκυνήσας ἐξέλθῃ,
ἑδρασθῆναι ἐπί τινι λιθίνῳ θώκῳ ἱδρυμένῳ αὐτόθι. ὡς δὲ
προσκυνήσας ὁ Εὐρύφαμος καὶ ἔν τινι διανοήματι καὶ

[183] a right judgment as to what the "principle" of these is. And it makes a great difference, and is of almost crucial importance to the success of the whole enterprise to understand the "principle" correctly. For nothing, in a word, from there on comes out right when the true "principle" has not been recognized. The same goes for "principle" in its other sense (i.e. ruling principle): for neither a household nor a city is ever well managed when not voluntarily subject to the rule and authority of a genuine commander and master. For authority to arise it is necessary for both, the ruler and those ruled, to be equally willing. Just as they said that teaching is correctly imparted when it takes place voluntarily, and both the teacher and the student are willing. For if either of the two resists in any way, the proposed work can never be duly completed.

So then,[18] he approved of obedience to rulers as good, and also submission to teachers, and by his deeds he presented greatest proof of this, as follows. He trav-

[184] eled from Italy to Delos, in order to nurse his former teacher, Pherecydes of Syros, who had succumbed to the disease recorded as *morbus pedicularis*, and (finally) to bury him. He remained until his death and performed the funeral rites for his master. So greatly then did he value his teacher.

[185] In regard to agreements and honest observance of them, Pythagoras prepared his disciples so well, that they say that Lysis once worshipped in a temple of Hera, and on leaving met Euryphamus the Syracusan, one of his fellow disciples, entering the gateway of the goddess's temple. When Euryphamus asked him to wait until he himself came out after worshipping, he sat down on a stone seat set up there. As Euryphamus worshipped, he became absorbed in thought and deep reflection, and having quite forgotten the agreement, he left by another gate. But Lysis, without moving, stayed the rest of the day, the following night, and the greater part of the next day. And perhaps he would have been there longer if Euryphamus had not been at the Pythagorean school the next day, and remembered Lysis, when hearing that he was missed by his fellow disciples. He then went back and found him still waiting according to the agreement, and led him away, stating the cause of his forgetfulness and adding "one of the gods implanted this forgetfulness in me to be a means of testing your steadfastness about an agreement."

---

18. With this anecdote, Iamblichus no longer seems to use Aristoxenus, since the anecdote, which recurs in sections 251-52, is there attributed to Nicomachus of Gerasa.

βαθυτέρᾳ καθ᾽ ἑαυτὸν ἐννοίᾳ γενόμενος δι᾽ ἑτέρου πυλῶνος ἐκλαθόμενος ἀπηλλάγη, τό τε τῆς ἡμέρας λοιπὸν καὶ τὴν ἐπιοῦσαν νύκτα καὶ τὸ πλέον μέρος ἔτι τῆς ἄλλης ἡμέρας ὡς εἶχεν ἀτρέμας προσέμενεν ὁ Λῦσις. καὶ τάχα ἂν ἐπὶ πλείονα χρόνον αὐτοῦ ἦν, εἰ μή περ ἐν τῷ ὁμακοείῳ τῆς ἑξῆς ἡμέρας γενόμενος ὁ Εὐρύφαμος καὶ ἀκούσας ἐπιζητουμένου πρὸς τῶν ἑταίρων τοῦ Λύσιδος ἀνεμνήσθη. καὶ ἐλθὼν αὐτὸν ἔτι προσμένοντα κατὰ τὴν συνθήκην ἀπήγαγε, τὴν αἰτίαν εἰπὼν τῆς λήθης καὶ προσεπιθεὶς ὅτι "ταύτην δέ μοι θεῶν τις ἐνῆκε, δοκίμιον ἐσομένην τῆς σῆς περὶ συνθήκας εὐσταθείας."

[186]   καὶ τὸ ἐμψύχων δὲ ἀπέχεσθαι ἐνομοθέτησε διά τε ἄλλα πολλὰ καὶ ὡς εἰρηνοποιὸν τὸ ἐπιτήδευμα. ἐθιζόμενοι γὰρ μυσάττεσθαι φόνον ζῴων ὡς ἄνομον καὶ παρὰ φύσιν, πολὺ μᾶλλον ἀθεμιτώτερον τὸ ἄνθρωπον ἡγούμενοι κτείνειν οὐκέτ᾽ ἐπολέμουν. φόνων δὲ χορηγέτης καὶ νομοθέτης ὁ πόλεμος· τούτοις γὰρ καὶ σωματοποιεῖται. καὶ τὸ "ζυγὸν" δὲ "μὴ ὑπερβαίνειν" δικαιοσύνης ἐστὶ παρακέλευσμα, πάντα τὰ δίκαια παραγγέλλον ἀσκεῖν, ὡς ἐν τοῖς περὶ συμβόλων δειχθήσεται. πέφηνεν ἄρα διὰ πάντων τούτων μεγάλην σπουδὴν περὶ τὴν τῆς δικαιοσύνης ἄσκησιν καὶ παράδοσιν εἰς ἀνθρώπους πεποιημένος Πυθαγόρας ὡς ἐν τοῖς ἔργοις καὶ ἐν τοῖς λόγοις.

[186] And he (Pythagoras) ordered abstinence from living beings for many other reasons, but mainly because the practice tended to promote peace. For once human beings became accustomed to loathe the slaughter of animals as lawless and contrary to nature, they would no longer make war, thinking it even more unlawful to kill a human being. War is the leader and lawgiver of slaughters; for by these it is provided with sustenance. The injunction "not to step over the beam of a balance" is also an exhortation to justice, ordering the practice of all things just, as will be shown in the discussions on *symbola*.[19] It is apparent, then, through all these things, that Pythagoras took great pains about the practice and teaching of justice to human beings, both in his deeds and sayings.

---

19. Presumably a reference to Iamblichus' *Protrepticus,* s work composed after *VP,* and forming, like the latter, part of his *Compendium of Pythagorean Doctrine.,*

[187]　　"Επεται δὲ τῷ περὶ τούτων λόγῳ ὁ περὶ σωφροσύνης, ὥς τε αὐτὴν ἐπετήδευσε καὶ παρέδωκε τοῖς χρωμένοις. εἴρηται μὲν οὖν ἤδη τὰ κοινὰ παραγγέλματα περὶ αὐτῆς, ἐν οἷς πυρὶ καὶ σιδήρῳ τὰ ἀσύμμετρα πάντα ἀποκόπτειν διώρισται. τοῦ δὲ αὐτοῦ εἴδους ἐστὶν ἀποχὴ ἐμψύχων ἁπάντων καὶ προσέτι βρωμάτων τινῶν ἀκολάστων, καὶ τὸ παρατίθεσθαι μὲν ἐν ταῖς ἑστιάσεσι τὰ ἡδέα καὶ πολυτελῆ ἐδέσματα, ἀποπέμπεσθαι δὲ αὐτὰ τοῖς οἰκέταις, ἕνεκα τοῦ κολάσαι μόνον τὰς ἐπιθυμίας παρατιθέμενα, καὶ τὸ χρυσὸν ἐλευθέραν μηδεμίαν φορεῖν, μόνας δὲ τὰς ἑταίρας. καὶ αἱ ἐπεγρίαι δὲ αἱ
[188]　τοῦ λογισμοῦ καὶ αἱ εἰλικρίνειαι τῶν ἐμποδιζόντων τοῦ αὐτοῦ εἰσιν εἴδους. ἔτι δὲ ἐχεμυθία τε καὶ παντελὴς σιωπή, πρὸς τὸ γλώσσης κρατεῖν συνασκοῦσα, ἥ τε σύντονος καὶ ἀδιάπνευστος περὶ τὰ δυσληπτότατα τῶν θεωρημάτων ἀνάληψίς τε καὶ ἐξέτασις, διὰ τὰ αὐτὰ δὲ καὶ ἀνοινία καὶ ὀλιγοσιτία καὶ ὀλιγοϋπνία, δόξης τε καὶ πλούτου καὶ τῶν ὁμοίων ἀνεπιτήδευτος κατεξανάστασις, καὶ αἰδὼς μὲν ἀνυπόκριτος πρὸς τοὺς προήκοντας, πρὸς δὲ τοὺς ὁμήλικας ἄπλαστος ὁμοιότης καὶ φιλοφροσύνη, συνεπίτασις δὲ καὶ παρόρμησις πρὸς τοὺς νεωτέρους φθόνου χωρίς, καὶ πάντα
[189]　ὅσα τοιαῦτα, εἰς τὴν αὐτὴν ἀρετὴν ταχθήσεται. καὶ ἐξ ὧν δ' Ἱππόβοτος καὶ Νεάνθης περὶ Μυλλίου καὶ Τιμύχας τῶν Πυθαγορείων ἱστοροῦσι, μαθεῖν ἔνεστι τὴν ἐκείνων τῶν ἀνδρῶν σωφροσύνην καὶ ὅπως αὐτὴν Πυθαγόρας παρέδωκε. τὸν γὰρ Διονύσιον τὸν τύραννόν φασιν, ὡς πάντα ποιῶν οὐδενὸς αὐτῶν ἐπετύγχανε τῆς φιλίας, φυλαττομένων καὶ περιισταμένων τὸ μοναρχικὸν αὐτοῦ καὶ παράνομον, λόχον

CHAPTER THIRTY-ONE

*Concerning temperance, how Pythagoras practiced and taught
it to human beings by words and deeds, and by the whole nature
of his organization; how many forms of it there are
and which he established among human beings.*

[187]   Our account of justice is followed by that on temperance: how he practiced it and handed it down to his friends. The general precepts about it have already been mentioned,[1] in which it is prescribed to cut off everything ill-proportioned "with fire and sword." Precepts of the same kind are: abstinence from all living things, and also from certain foods which cause intemperance; serving at banquets delectable and very costly foods, but sending them back to the servants, since they are served only for the sake of punishing the desires; and no married woman to wear gold, but only courtesans. And practices designed to rouse the soul's reasoning power and to keep it pure from things hindering its exercise belong to the same kind of precepts.

[188]   Moreover, both reserve and absolute silence which help one to practice mastery of the tongue; intense and untiring repetition and close examination of theories about subjects most difficult to comprehend; and for the sake of these, abstinence from wine, moderation in food and sleep, an unaffected resistance to fame, wealth, and the like; sincere respect for those advanced in age; with those of the same age, a true affinity and friendliness; and joint exertion on and stimulation of those younger without ill-will; and all such things as these are assigned to
[189]   the same virtue. And from what Hippobotus and Neanthes report about the Pythagoreans,[2] Myllias and Timycha, it is possible to learn the temperance of those men, and how Pythagoras imparted it. For they say that Dionysius, the tyrant,[3] although doing everything possible, gained the friendship of none of them, since they avoided and shunned his monarchical and lawless rule. He sent against

---

1. Presumably in sections 68-69 above, most of which is repeated more or less here.

2. This story is from a different source, possibly Nicomachus, to judge from the parallel passage (unfortunately incomplete) from the end of Porph. *VP* 61, who cites Hippobotus and Neanthes. On Neanthes, see our introduction. Hippobotus (ca. 3rd century B.C.) wrote a philosophico-historical *On Sects* and *Record of Philosophers* used also by Diogenes Laertius.

3. Dionysius II of Syracuse. Dion who is mentioned shortly after in this section, was brother-in-law and son-in-law of Dionysius I, and later tried to liberate Syracuse from Dionysius II's rule after Plato failed to make him into a philosopher-king. This same Dion was commissioned by Plato (according to Satyrus *ap.* D.L. 3.9) to buy from Philolaus three "Pythagorean books." See Burkert, *Lore and Science*, 223 ff.

τινὰ τριάκοντα ἀνδρῶν, ἡγουμένου Εὐρυμένους Συρα-
κουσίου, Δίωνος ἀδελφοῦ, ἐπιπέμψαι τοῖς ἀνδράσι,
λοχήσοντα τὴν μετάβασιν αὐτῶν, τὴν ἀπὸ Τάραντος εἰς
Μεταπόντιον εἰωθυῖαν κατὰ καιρὸν γίνεσθαι· ἡρμόζοντο γὰρ
πρὸς τὰς τῶν ὡρῶν μεταβολὰς καὶ τόπους εἰς τὰ τοιάδε
ἐπελέγοντο ἐπιτηδείους. ἐν δὴ Φάναις, χωρίῳ τῆς Τάραντος
[190] φαραγγώδει, καθ᾽ ὃ συνέβαινεν αὐτοῖς ἀναγκαίως τὴν
ὁδοιπορίαν γενήσεσθαι, ἐλόχα κατακρύψας τὸ πλῆθος ὁ
Εὐρυμένης. ἐπειδὴ δὲ οὐδὲν προϊδόμενοι ἀφίκοντο οἱ ἄνδρες
περὶ μέσον ἡμέρας εἰς τὸν τόπον, ληστρικῶς αὐτοῖς
ἐπαλαλάξαντες ἐπέθεντο οἱ στρατιῶται. οἱ δὲ ἐκταραχθέντες
μετ᾽ εὐλαβείας ἅμα τε τὸ αἰφνίδιον καὶ αὐτὸ τὸ πλῆθος
(ἦσαν γὰρ αὐτοὶ σύμπαντες δέκα που τὸν ἀριθμόν), καὶ ὅτι
ἄνοπλοι πρὸς ποικίλως ὡπλισμένους διαγωνισάμενοι
ἔμελλον ἁλίσκεσθαι, δρόμῳ καὶ φυγῇ διασῴζειν αὐτοὺς
διέγνωσαν, οὐδὲ τοῦτο ἀλλότριον ἀρετῆς τιθέμενοι· τὴν γὰρ
ἀνδρείαν ᾔδεσαν φευκτέων τε καὶ ὑπομενετέων ἐπιστήμην,
ὡς ἂν ὁ ὀρθὸς ὑπαγορεύῃ λόγος. καὶ ἐπετύγχανον δὲ ἤδη
[191] τούτου (βαρούμενοι γὰρ τοῖς ὅπλοις ἀπελείποντο οἱ σὺν
Εὐρυμένει τοῦ διωγμοῦ), εἰ μή περ φεύγοντες ἐνέτυχον
πεδίῳ τινὶ κυάμοις ἐσπαρμένῳ καὶ τεθηλότι ἱκανῶς. καὶ μὴ
βουλόμενοι δόγμα παραβαίνειν τὸ κελεῦον κυάμων μὴ
θιγγάνειν ἔστησαν καὶ ὑπ᾽ ἀνάγκης λίθοις καὶ ξύλοις καὶ
τοῖς προστυχοῦσιν ἕκαστος μέχρι τοσούτου ἠμύνοντο τοὺς
διώκοντας, μέχρι τινὰς μὲν αὐτῶν ἀνῃρηκέναι, πολλοὺς δὲ
τετραυματικέναι. πάντας μὴν ὑπὸ τῶν δορυφόρων
ἀναιρεθῆναι καὶ μηδένα τὸ παράπαν ζωγρηθῆναι, ἀλλὰ πρὸ
[192] τούτων θάνατον ἀσμενίσαι κατὰ τὰς τῆς αἱρέσεως ἐντολάς.
ἐν συγχύσει δὴ πολλῇ τόν τε Εὐρυμένην καὶ τοὺς σὺν αὐτῷ
καὶ οὐ τῇ τυχούσῃ γενέσθαι, εἰ μηδὲ ἕνα ζῶντα ἀγάγοιεν τῷ
πέμψαντι Διονυσίῳ, εἰς αὐτὸ μόνον τοῦτο προτρεψαμένῳ
αὐτούς. γῆν οὖν ἐπαμήσαντες τοῖς πεσοῦσι καὶ ἡρῷον
πολυάνδριον ἐπιχώσαντες αὐτόθι ὑπέστρεφον. εἶτα αὐτοῖς
ἀπήντησε Μυλλίας Κροτωνιάτης καὶ Τιμύχα Λακεδαιμονία,
γυνὴ αὐτοῦ, ἀπολελειμμένοι τοῦ πλήθους, ὅτι ἔγκυος οὖσα
ἡ Τιμύχα τὸν δέκατον ἤδη μῆνα εἶχε καὶ σχολαίως διὰ τοῦτο
ἐβάδιζε. τούτους δὴ ζωγρήσαντες ἄσμενοι πρὸς τὸν τύραννον
ἤγαγον, μετὰ πάσης κομιδῆς καὶ ἐπιμελείας διασώσαντες. ὃ

these men an armed troop of thirty led by Eurymenes the Syracusan, a brother of Dion, to ambush them at an opportune time when their customary migration from Tarentum to Metapontium took place; for they adapted themselves to changes of the seasons, and selected suitable places for such.

[190]   In Phanae,[4] then, a district of Tarentum full of ravines, through which their journey necessarily went, Eurymenes concealed his troops and lay in wait. When the Pythagoreans, all unsuspecting, arrived at this place about mid-day, the soldiers raised the war cry and attacked them like pirates. They were thrown into confusion both by the sudden attack and the greater number of enemies (for they themselves were altogether perhaps ten in number). And since they, unarmed, were about to be captured in struggle against men variously armed, they resolved with discretion to save themselves by running and flight, not regarding this as foreign to virtue; for they knew courage is knowledge of what is to be avoided and endured, as right reason dictates.[5]

[191]   And they would have actually succeeded (for weighted down with heavy arms, those with Eurymenes were abandoning the pursuit) had they not encountered while fleeing a field planted and fully blooming with beans.[6] And not wishing to transgress the decree which ordered them not to touch beans, they stopped and by necessity defended themselves against those in pursuit. Each one (fought) with stones, sticks, and whatever else there was, until they had killed and wounded many. Nevertheless, all were destroyed by the tyrant's bodyguards and no one was taken alive, but rather than that, they gladly accepted death in accord with the commands of their school.

[192]   Eurymenes and his men, then, were in great confusion, since they could not bring back one alive to Dionysius, who had ordered and sent them for this purpose alone. Having, then, piled earth on those fallen and having made a common burial place there, they turned homeward. Then Myllias, of Croton, and his wife, Timycha, a Lacedaemonian, met them. The couple had been left behind the main body because Timycha, already ten months pregnant, was walking slowly. Pleased, then, at having captured these alive, the soldiers brought them to the tyrant, after guarding them with great care and attention.

---

4. Or Phalae. The place is uncertain. See H. Philipp, *RE*, s.v. Phalae.

5. The Platonic definition of courage (cf *Prt.* 360d, *R.* IV 429c), though couched in rather Stoic terminology (cf. *SVF* III 263, 286).

6. This aspect of the story is told about Pythagoras himself by Diogenes Laertius (8.39-40), who derives it from Hermippus. According to Hermippus, the incident, involving some Pythagoreans led by Pythagoras himself, occurred in the course of a battle between Syracuse and Acragas, with the Pythagoreans fighting for Acragas.

[193] δὲ περὶ τῶν γεγονότων διαπυθόμενος καὶ σφόδρα ἀθυμήσας ἐνέφαινεν. "ἀλλ' ὑμεῖς γε" εἶπεν "ὑπὲρ πάντων τῆς ἀξίας τεύξεσθε παρ' ἐμοῦ τιμῆς, εἴ μοι συμβασιλεῦσαι θελήσετε". τοῦ δὲ Μυλλίου καὶ τῆς Τιμύχας πρὸς πάντα ἃ ἐπηγγέλλετο ἀνανευόντων, "ἀλλὰ ἕν γέ με" ἔφη "διδάξαντες μετὰ τῆς ἐπιβαλλούσης προπομπῆς διασῴζεσθε". πυθομένου δὲ τοῦ Μυλλίου καὶ τί ποτ' ἐστίν, ὃ μαθεῖν προθυμεῖται, "ἐκεῖνο" εἶπεν ὁ Διονύσιος· "τίς ἡ αἰτία, δι' ἣν οἱ ἑταῖροί σου ἀποθανεῖν μᾶλλον εἵλαντο ἢ κυάμους πατῆσαι;" καὶ ὁ Μυλλίας εὐθὺς "ἀλλ' ἐκεῖνοι μὲν" εἶπεν "ὑπέμειναν, ἵνα μὴ κυάμους πατήσωσιν, ἀποθανεῖν, ἐγὼ δὲ αἱροῦμαι, ἵνα τούτου σοι τὴν αἰτίαν μὴ ἐξείπω, κυάμους μᾶλλον [194] πατῆσαι". καταπλαγέντος δὲ τοῦ Διονυσίου καὶ μεταστῆσαι κελεύσαντος αὐτὸν σὺν βίᾳ, βασάνους δὲ ἐπιφέρειν τῇ Τιμύχᾳ προστάττοντος (ἐνόμιζε γὰρ ἅτε γυναῖκά τε οὖσαν καὶ ἔπογκον ἐρήμην τε τοῦ ἀνδρὸς ῥᾳδίως τοῦτο ἐκλαλήσειν φόβῳ τῶν βασάνων), ἡ γενναία συμβρύξασα ἐπὶ τῆς γλώσσης τοὺς ὀδόντας καὶ ἀποκόψασα αὐτὴν προσέπτυσε τῷ τυράννῳ, ἐμφαίνουσα ὅτι, εἰ καὶ ὑπὸ τῶν βασάνων τὸ θῆλυ αὐτῆς νικηθὲν συναναγκασθείη τῶν ἐχεμυθουμένων τι ἀνακαλύψαι, τὸ μὴν ὑπηρετῆσον ἐκποδὼν ὑπ' αὐτῆς περικέκοπται. οὕτως δυσσυγκατάθετοι πρὸς τὰς ἐξωτερικὰς φιλίας ἦσαν, εἰ καὶ βασιλικαὶ τυγχάνοιεν. παραπλήσια δὲ [195] τούτοις καὶ τὰ περὶ τῆς σιωπῆς ἦν παραγγέλματα, φέροντα εἰς σωφροσύνης ἄσκησιν· πάντων γὰρ χαλεπώτατόν ἐστιν ἐγκρατευμάτων τὸ γλώσσης κρατεῖν. τῆς αὐτῆς δὲ ἀρετῆς ἐστι καὶ τὸ πεῖσαι Κροτωνιάτας ἀπέχεσθαι τῆς ἀθύτου καὶ νόθης πρὸς τὰς παλλακίδας συνουσίας, καὶ ἔτι ἡ διὰ τῆς μουσικῆς ἐπανόρθωσις, δι' ἧς καὶ τὸ οἰστρημένον μειράκιον ὑπὸ τοῦ ἔρωτος εἰς σωφροσύνην μετέστησε. καὶ ἡ τῆς ὕβρεως δὲ ἀπάγουσα παραίνεσις εἰς τὴν αὐτὴν ἀρετὴν ἀνήκει.

[196]   καὶ ταῦτα δὲ παρέδωκε τοῖς Πυθαγορείοις Πυθαγόρας, ὧν αἴτιος αὐτὸς ἦν. προσεῖχον γὰρ οὗτοι, τὰ σώματα ὡς ἂν ἐπὶ τῶν αὐτῶν ⟨ἀεὶ⟩ διακέηται, καὶ μὴ ποτὲ μὲν ῥικνά, ὁτὲ δὲ πολύσαρκα· ἀνωμάλου γὰρ βίου ᾤοντο εἶναι δεῖγμα. ἀλλὰ ὡσαύτως καὶ κατὰ τὴν διάνοιαν οὐχ ὁτὲ μὲν ἱλαροί, ὁτὲ δὲ κατηφεῖς, ἀλλὰ ἐφ' ὁμαλοῦ πρᾴως χαίροντες. διεκρούοντο δὲ ὀργάς, ἀθυμίας, ταραχάς, καὶ ἦν αὐτοῖς παράγγελμα, ὡς

[193] When he learned what had happened, Dionysius was plainly very despondent: "But you at least," he said, "on behalf of all, will obtain from me due honor, if you will consent to rule together with me." But when Myllias and Timycha refused everything he promised, he said, "Then teach me at least one thing, and you will be sent safely on your way with appropriate escort." When Myllias inquired what he was eager to learn, Dionysius said: "Just this: what was the reason your companions chose to die rather than tread on beans?" And Myllias immediately replied, "Those submitted to death in order that they not tread on beans, and I would choose rather to tread on beans than to tell you the reason for this." Dionysius was

[194] astounded, ordered him removed by force, and commanded infliction of tortures on Timycha (for he believed since she was a woman, both pregnant and deprived of her husband, she would readily divulge this for fear of the tortures). But the noble woman clamped her teeth on her tongue, cut it off and spat it at the tyrant, showing that, even if her female nature, conquered by tortures, were compelled to reveal something of the things kept secret, that which would serve that purpose would be removed by her. So slow were they to make friendships outside the school, even if they were friendships with kings.

[195] Similar to these also were the precepts about silence, leading to the practice of temperance. For mastery of the tongue is the most difficult of all instances of self-control. From this same virtue arose his persuasion of the Crotoniates to abstain from unholy and bastard cohabitation with concubines; also, correction through music, by which he (Pythagoras) even changed the youth driven mad by sexual desire to temperance. And exhortation which leads away from insolence is connected with the same virtue.

[196] And these things, for which he himself was instrumental, Pythagoras handed down to the Pythagoreans.[7] For they took heed that their bodies always be in the same condition: not sometimes skinny, and sometimes very fleshy, for they considered that evidence of an irregular way of life. In like manner, also, in regard to the intellect: they were not sometimes merry, and sometimes downcast, but observed an equitable and calm joy.[8] And they got rid of anger, despondency, and confusion, and their precept was that nothing of human mishaps ought to be unexpected by anyone possessed of intelligence—rather to expect all things, of which they themselves were not masters. But if anger, grief, or any other such emotion ever arose in them, they retired by themselves, and each on his own tried to quell and heal the emotion.

---

7. With the following passage, to the middle of 198, we seem to be back with material from Aristoxenus, who speaks of "the Pythagoreans" rather than of Pythagoras himself. Also included is a report of a saying of Aristoxenus' father, Spintharus, which seems orally transmitted.

8. Probably a reference to the Stoic state of χάρα.

οὐδὲν δεῖ τῶν ἀνθρωπίνων συμπτωμάτων ἀπροσδόκητον
εἶναι παρὰ τοῖς νοῦν ἔχουσιν, ἀλλὰ πάντα προσδοκᾶν, ὧν μὴ
τυγχάνουσιν αὐτοὶ κύριοι ὄντες. εἰ δέ ποτε αὐτοῖς συμβαίη
ἢ ὀργὴ ἢ λύπη ἢ ἄλλο τι τοιοῦτον, ἐκποδὼν ἀπηλλάττοντο,
[197] καὶ καθ' ἑαυτὸν ἕκαστος γενόμενος ἐπειρᾶτο καταπέττειν τε
καὶ ἰατρεύειν τὸ πάθος. λέγεται δὲ καὶ τάδε περὶ τῶν
Πυθαγορείων, ὡς οὔτε οἰκέτην ἐκόλασεν οὐθεὶς αὐτῶν ὑπὸ
ὀργῆς ἐχόμενος οὔτε τῶν ἐλευθέρων ἐνουθέτησέ τινα, ἀλλὰ
ἀνέμενεν ἕκαστος τὴν τῆς διανοίας ἀποκατάστασιν (ἐκάλουν
δὲ τὸ νουθετεῖν πεδαρτᾶν)· ἐποιοῦντο γὰρ τὴν ἀναμονὴν
σιωπῇ χρώμενοι καὶ ἡσυχίᾳ. Σπίνθαρος γοῦν διηγεῖτο
πολλάκις περὶ Ἀρχύτου ⟨τοῦ⟩ Ταραντίνου, ὅτι διὰ χρόνου
τινὸς εἰς ἀγρὸν ἀφικόμενος, ἐκ στρατιᾶς νεωστὶ παρα-
γεγονώς, ἣν ἐστρατεύσατο ἡ πόλις εἰς Μεσσαπίους, ὡς εἶδε
τόν τε ἐπίτροπον καὶ τοὺς ἄλλους οἰκέτας οὐκ εὖ τῶν περὶ
τὴν γεωργίαν ἐπιμελείας πεποιημένους, ἀλλὰ μεγάλῃ τινὶ
κεχρημένους ὀλιγωρίας ὑπερβολῇ, ὀργισθείς τε καὶ
ἀγανακτήσας οὕτως ὡς ἂν ἐκεῖνος, εἶπεν, ὡς ἔοικε, πρὸς τοὺς
οἰκέτας, ὅτι εὐτυχοῦσιν, ὅτι αὐτοῖς ὤργισται· εἰ γὰρ μὴ
τοῦτο συμβεβηκὸς ἦν, οὐκ ἄν ποτε αὐτοὺς ἀθῴους γενέσθαι
[198] τηλικαῦτα ἡμαρτηκότας. ἔφη δὲ λέγεσθαι καὶ περὶ Κλεινίου
τοιαῦτά τινα· καὶ γὰρ ἐκεῖνον ἀναβάλλεσθαι πάσας νουθετήσεις τε καὶ κολάσεις εἰς τὴν τῆς διανοίας ἀποκατάστασιν.
οἴκτων δὲ καὶ δακρύων καὶ πάντων τῶν τοιούτων εἴργεσθαι
τοὺς ἄνδρας, οὔτε δὲ κέρδος οὔτε ἐπιθυμίαν οὔτε ὀργὴν οὔτε
φιλοτιμίαν οὔτε ἄλλο οὐδὲν τῶν τοιούτων αἴτιον γίνεσθαι
διαφορᾶς, ἀλλὰ πάντας τοὺς Πυθαγορείους οὕτως ἔχειν πρὸς
ἀλλήλους, ὡς ἂν πατὴρ σπουδαῖος πρὸς τέκνα σχοίη.

καλὸν δὲ καὶ τὸ πάντα Πυθαγόρᾳ ἀνατιθέναι τε καὶ
ἀπονέμειν καὶ μηδεμίαν περιποιεῖσθαι δόξαν ἰδίαν ἀπὸ τῶν
εὑρισκομένων, εἰ μή πού τι σπάνιον· πάνυ γὰρ δή τινές εἰσιν
ὀλίγοι, ὧν ἴδια γνωρίζεται ὑπομνήματα. θαυμάζεται δὲ καὶ ἡ
[199] τῆς φυλακῆς ἀκρίβεια· ἐν γὰρ τοσαύταις γενεαῖς ἐτῶν οὐθεὶς
οὐθενὶ φαίνεται τῶν Πυθαγορείων ὑπομνημάτων περιτε-
τευχὼς πρὸ τῆς Φιλολάου ἡλικίας, ἀλλ' οὗτος πρῶτος
ἐξήνεγκε τὰ θρυλλούμενα ταῦτα τρία βιβλία, ἃ λέγεται
Δίων ὁ Συρακούσιος ἑκατὸν μνῶν πρίασθαι Πλάτωνος
κελεύσαντος, εἰς πενίαν τινὰ μεγάλην τε καὶ ἰσχυρὰν

[197]   The following things are also said about the Pythagoreans: none of them, while possessed by anger, punished a slave or admonished a freedman, but each waited for the restoration of his ability to think rationally (for they called admonition *pedartan*, "restoration"),[9] for they accomplished this delay by using silence and quiet. Spintharus, at any rate, often used to tell a story about Archytas the Tarantine: when he returned to his farm after a period of time, just back from a military expedition which his city had sent against the Messapians, he saw that his steward and other servants had not taken good care of its tillage, but had been exceedingly negligent. Though he was angry and annoyed as one like him could be, he said, it seems, to his servants, that they were fortunate that he was angry with them; for if this had not happened, they would never have gone unpunished for having failed so greatly (in their duty).[10]

[198]   He also said that a similar story was told about Cleinias;[11] for he also put off all admonitions and punishments until restoration of his ability to think rationally. And they (the Pythagoreans) kept aloof from lamentations, tears, and all such manifestations, nor did profit, desire, anger, ambition, or any such things become a cause of disagreement. But all Pythagoreans were so disposed to one another as a good father would be to his children.

       It was a fine custom of theirs also to ascribe and assign everything to Pythagoras, and only very seldom to claim personal fame for their discoveries, for there are very few of them indeed to whom works are ascribed personally.[12]

[199]   The strictness of the custody of their works is also remarkable: for over a very long span of years no one appears to have encountered any Pythagorean work before Philolaus' lifetime, but it was he who first published those three notorious books which Dion the Syracusan is said to have bought for a hundred minae at Plato's request, when Philolaus fell into great and severe poverty (since he himself had kindred ties with the Pythagoreans, he also got a share of their books).

---

9. Cf. D.L. 8. 20. See also Delatte, *La vie de Pythagore*, 191-192.

10. A similar story is told about Plato by many sources. See A. S. Riginos, *Platonica*, 155 (Anecdote no. 113 A). Since the Archytas story goes back to Spintharus (Aristoxenus' father), it may well be the original.

11. Cf. Chamaeleon of Pontus, *ap.* Ath. 14.624a, Chamaeleon says that Cleinias, whenever he felt overcome by anger, would take his lyre and play until restored to calmness. This is presumably Aristoxenus' version, since the next sentence is expressly attributed to him below, section 234. For Cleinias, see section 239.

12. This statement might have validity in Aristoxenus' time, but hardly makes much sense subsequent to the publication of the pseudo-Pythagorean writings (forty-three authors other than Pythagoras are represented in Thesleff's collection).

ἀφικομένου τοῦ Φιλολάου, ἐπειδὴ καὶ αὐτὸς ἦν ἀπὸ τῆς
συγγενείας τῶν Πυθαγορείων καὶ διὰ τοῦτο μετέλαβε τῶν
βιβλίων.

[200]   περὶ δὲ δόξης τάδε φασὶ λέγειν αὐτούς. ἀνόητον μὲν εἶναι
καὶ τὸ πάσῃ καὶ παντὸς δόξῃ προσέχειν, καὶ μάλιστα τὸ τῇ
παρὰ τῶν πολλῶν γινομένῃ· τὸ γὰρ καλῶς ὑπολαμβάνειν τε
καὶ δοξάζειν ὀλίγοις ὑπάρχειν. δῆλον γὰρ ὅτι περὶ τοὺς
εἰδότας τοῦτο γίνεσθαι· οὗτοι δέ εἰσιν ὀλίγοι. ὥστε δῆλον
ὅτι οὐκ ἂν διατείνοι εἰς τοὺς πολλοὺς ἡ τοιαύτη δύναμις.
ἀνόητον δ' εἶναι καὶ πάσης ὑπολήψεώς τε καὶ δόξης
καταφρονεῖν· συμβήσεται γὰρ ἀμαθῆ τε καὶ ἀνεπανόρθωτον
εἶναι τὸν οὕτω διακείμενον. ἀναγκαῖον δ' εἶναι τῷ μὲν
ἀνεπιστήμονι μανθάνειν ἃ τυγχάνει ἀγνοῶν τε καὶ οὐκ
ἐπιστάμενος, τῷ δὲ μανθάνοντι προσέχειν τῇ τοῦ
ἐπισταμένου τε καὶ διδάξαι δυναμένου ὑπολήψει τε καὶ
[201]   δόξῃ, καθόλου δ' εἰπεῖν ἀναγκαῖον εἶναι τοὺς σωθησομένους
τῶν νέων προσέχειν ταῖς τῶν πρεσβυτέρων τε καὶ καλῶς
βεβιωκότων ὑπολήψεσί τε καὶ δόξαις. ἐν δὲ τῷ ἀνθρωπίνῳ
βίῳ τῷ σύμπαντι εἶναί τινας ἡλικίας ἐνδεδασμένας (οὕτω
γὰρ καὶ λέγειν αὐτούς φασιν), ἃς οὐκ εἶναι τοῦ τυχόντος
πρὸς ἀλλήλας συνεῖραι· ἐκκρούεσθαι γὰρ αὐτὰς ὑπ'
ἀλλήλων, ἐάν τις μὴ καλῶς τε καὶ ὀρθῶς ἄγῃ τὸν ἄνθρωπον
ἐκ γενετῆς. δεῖν οὖν τῆς τοῦ παιδὸς ἀγωγῆς καλῆς τε καὶ
σώφρονος γινομένης καὶ ἀνδρικῆς πολὺ εἶναι μέρος τὸ
παραδιδόμενον εἰς τὴν τοῦ νεανίσκου ἡλικίαν, ὡσαύτως δὲ
καὶ τῆς τοῦ νεανίσκου ἐπιμελείας τε καὶ ἀγωγῆς καλῆς τε καὶ
ἀνδρικῆς καὶ σώφρονος γινομένης πολὺ εἶναι μέρος ⟨τὸ⟩
παραδιδόμενον εἰς τὴν τοῦ ἀνδρὸς ἡλικίαν, ἐπείπερ εἴς γε
[202]   τοὺς πολλοὺς ἄτοπόν τε καὶ γελοῖον εἶναι τὸ συμβαῖνον.
παῖδας μὲν γὰρ ὄντας οἴεσθαι δεῖν εὐτακτεῖν τε καὶ
σωφρονεῖν καὶ ἀπέχεσθαι πάντων τῶν φορτικῶν τε καὶ
ἀσχημόνων εἶναι δοκούντων, νεανίσκους δὲ γενομένους
ἀφεῖσθαι παρά γε δὴ τοῖς πολλοῖς ποιεῖν ὅ τι ἂν βούλωνται.
συρρεῖν δὲ σχεδὸν εἰς ταύτην τὴν ἡλικίαν ἀμφότερα τὰ γένη
τῶν ἁμαρτημάτων· καὶ γὰρ παιδαριώδη πολλὰ καὶ ἀνδρώδη
τοὺς νεανίσκους ἁμαρτάνειν. τὸ μὲν γὰρ φεύγειν ἅπαν τὸ τῆς
σπουδῆς τε καὶ τάξεως γένος, ὡς ἁπλῶς εἰπεῖν, διώκειν δὲ τὸ
τῆς παιγνίας τε καὶ ἀκολασίας καὶ ὕβρεως τῆς παιδικῆς
εἶδος, τῆς τοῦ παιδὸς ἡλικίας οἰκειότατον εἶναι· ἐκ ταύτης

[200]   About good opinion[13] it is reported they spoke as follows: it is foolish to seek
after every sort of good opinion on whatever basis, especially that proceeding
from the many. For correct supposition and opinion are achieved by few. It is clear
that these pertain to those who know, but they are few. So it is obvious that such
an ability would not extend to the many. But it is also foolish to despise every supposition and opinion; for it will be found that the one who is so disposed is ignorant and incorrigible. But it is necessary for the ignorant person to learn those
things of which he is ignorant and has no knowledge; and for the learner to give
heed to the supposition and opinion of the one who knows and is able to teach,
[201] and, generally speaking , it is necessary for those young men who are to be kept
safe to give heed to the suppositions and opinions of their elders, and to those
who have lived well. But in the whole of human life there are certain ages "divided
up" (such is said to be their term)[14] which the ordinary person finds difficult to
connect with one another; for these ages conflict with one another, if the human
being is not well and correctly guided from birth. It is necessary, then, that when
the training of the child is noble, temperate, and manly, a great part of it be transmitted to the age of his adolescence; and in like manner, when the care and training of an adolescent is noble, manly, and temperate, a great part of it be
transmitted to the age of manhood. For what happens in the case of the great ma-
[202] jority is absurd and ridiculous. They think children ought to be orderly and temperate, and to abstain from all things which appear coarse and unseemly. But
when they become adolescents, they are freed, at least in the judgment of the
many, to do whatever they wish. Roughly speaking, into this same age flow together both kinds of faults, for adolescents commit many errors both childish and
adult. Avoidance of every kind of serious effort and order, to speak simply, and
pursuance of every kind of game, intemperance, and boyish insolence, are most
conformable to the age of the child. Such a disposition as this, then, comes from
the age of the child into the age closely following. But the class of strong desires,
and in like manner, that of ambitions, and equally the remaining impulses and
dispositions which are of the difficult and turbulent kind, come from adulthood
[203] into adolescence. Thus, of all ages, adolescence needs greatest attention. And indeed, to speak generally, no man ought ever to be allowed to do whatever he wishes, but always some lawful and noble authority and rule ought to exist, to which
every citizen will be obedient; for, left alone and neglected, the living being quickly degenerates to badness and meanness. And they said they[15] frequently asked
and raised for discussion the question why we are accustomed to give nourishment

---

13. Δόξα can, of course, mean "opinion" or "fame," and so "good opinion" seems a suitable
compromise. We possibly return at this point to Aristoxenian material, until the end of the chapter.

14. This is the only occurrence of what is (if faithfully relayed from Aristoxenus) an old
Pythagorean locution (from ἐνδαίω).

οὖν εἰς τὴν ἐχομένην ἡλικίαν ἀφικνεῖσθαι τὴν τοιαύτην
διάθεσιν. τὸ δὲ τῶν ἐπιθυμιῶν τῶν ἰσχυρῶν, ὡσαύτως δὲ καὶ
τὸ τῶν φιλοτιμιῶν γένος, ὁμοίως δὲ καὶ τὰς λοιπὰς ὁρμάς τε
καὶ διαθέσεις, ὅσαι τυγχάνουσιν οὖσαι τοῦ χαλεποῦ τε καὶ
θορυβώδους γένους, ἐκ τῆς τοῦ ἀνδρὸς ἡλικίας εἰς τὴν τῶν
νεανίσκων ἀφικνεῖσθαι. διόπερ πασῶν δεῖσθαι τῶν ἡλικιῶν
ταύτην πλείστης ἐπιμελείας. καθόλου δ' εἰπεῖν οὐδέποτε τὸν
[203] ἄνθρωπον ἐατέον εἶναι ποιεῖν ὅ τι ἂν βούληται, ἀλλ' ἀεί
τινα ἐπιστατείαν ὑπάρχειν δεῖν καὶ ἀρχὴν νόμιμόν τε καὶ
εὐσχήμονα, ἧς ὑπήκοος ἔσται ἕκαστος τῶν πολιτῶν· ταχέως
γὰρ ἐξίστασθαι τὸ ζῷον ἐαθέν τε καὶ ὀλιγωρηθὲν εἰς κακίαν
τε καὶ φαυλότητα. ἐρωτᾶν τε καὶ διαπορεῖν πολλάκις αὐτοὺς
ἔφασαν, τίνος ἕνεκα τοὺς παῖδας συνεθίζομεν προσφέρεσθαι
τὴν τροφὴν τεταγμένως τε καὶ συμμέτρως, καὶ τὴν μὲν τάξιν
καὶ τὴν συμμετρίαν ἀποφαίνομεν αὐτοῖς καλά, τὰ δὲ τούτων
ἐναντία, τήν τε ἀταξίαν καὶ τὴν ἀσυμμετρίαν, αἰσχρά, ὃ καὶ
ἔστιν ὅ τε οἰνόφλυξ καὶ ἄπληστος ἐν μεγάλῳ ὀνείδει
κείμενος. εἰ γὰρ μηδὲν τούτων ἐστὶ χρήσιμον εἰς τὴν τοῦ
ἀνδρὸς ἡλικίαν ἀφικνουμένων ἡμῶν, μάταιον εἶναι τὸ
συνεθίζειν παῖδας ὄντας τῇ τοιαύτῃ τάξει· τὸν αὐτὸν δὲ
λόγον εἶναι καὶ περὶ τῶν ἄλλων ἐθῶν. οὐκ οὖν ἐπί γε τῶν
[204] λοιπῶν ζῴων τοῦτο ὁρᾶσθαι συμβαῖνον, ὅσα ὑπ' ἀνθρώπων
παιδεύεται, ἀλλ' εὐθὺς ἐξ ἀρχῆς τόν τε σκύλακα καὶ τὸν
πῶλον ταῦτα συνεθίζεσθαί τε καὶ μανθάνειν, ἃ δεήσει
πράττειν αὐτοὺς τελεωθέντας. καθόλου δὲ τοὺς Πυθαγορείους ἔφασαν παρακελεύεσθαι τοῖς ἐντυγχάνουσί τε καὶ
ἀφικνουμένοις εἰς συνήθειαν εὐλαβεῖσθαι τὴν ἡδονήν, εἴπερ
τι καὶ ἄλλο τῶν εὐλαβείας δεομένων· οὐθὲν γὰρ οὕτω
σφάλλειν ἡμᾶς οὐδ' ἐμβάλλειν εἰς ἁμαρτίαν ὡς τοῦτο τὸ
πάθος. καθόλου δέ, ὡς ἔοικε, διετείνοντο μηδέποτε μηδὲν
πράττειν ἡδονῆς στοχαζομένους (καὶ γὰρ ἀσχήμονα καὶ
βλαβερὸν ὡς ἐπὶ τὸ πολὺ τοῦτον εἶναι τὸν σκοπόν), ἀλλὰ
μάλιστα μὲν πρὸς τὸ καλόν τε καὶ εὐσχημον βλέποντας
πράττειν ὃ ἂν ᾖ πρακτέον, δεύτερον δὲ πρὸς τὸ συμφέρον τε
[205] καὶ ὠφέλιμον, δεῖσθαί τε ταῦτα κρίσεως οὐ τῆς τυχούσης.
περὶ δὲ τῆς σωματικῆς ὀνομαζομένης ἐπιθυμίας τοιαῦτα
λέγειν ἔφασαν τοὺς ἄνδρας ἐκείνους. αὐτὴν μὲν τὴν
ἐπιθυμίαν ἐπιφοράν τινα εἶναι τῆς ψυχῆς καὶ ὁρμὴν καὶ
ὄρεξιν ἤτοι πληρώσεώς τινος ἢ παρουσίας τινῶν αἰσθήσεως

to boys regularly and moderately, and why we declare regularity and due proportion "good" for them, but their opposites, lack of regularity and disproportion,
"disgraceful" (which is why both the drunkard and the glutton are held in great
disgrace). For if nothing of this is useful when we reach manhood, it is foolish to
[204] accustom us when boys to a regularity of this kind. And the same goes also for other habits. This, however, is not seen to happen at least to the other animals, such
as are trained by men, but immediately from the beginning, the puppy and the
colt are both accustomed to, and learn, what things they must do when they reach
maturity.

And in general, they said that the Pythagoreans exhorted those whom they encountered or who joined their fellowship to be cautious about pleasure, more
than anything else; for nothing so disconcerts us or causes us to err as this emotion. In general, so it seems, they made every effort never to do anything aiming
at pleasure (for this aim is, for the most part, indecorous and harmful), but looking, most of all, to the noble and decorous, to do whatever must be done; and in
second place, (they advised looking) to the useful and beneficial. And such choic-
es require no ordinary judgment.

[205] About so-called "bodily desire," they report that those men said the following:[16]
desire itself is a certain propensity of the soul, an impulse, and a desire either for
some gratification, or for the presence of a certain sensation, or for a disposition
based on sensation. And a desire for the opposites of these also arises: for instance, for depletion, absence of sensation, and not perceiving some things. This
emotion is complex, and perhaps the most complicated of those connected with
a human being. But the majority of human desires are acquired and developed by
human beings themselves; hence this emotion needs greatest care, watching, and
no ordinary bodily training. For when the body is empty, desire for nourishment
is natural; and again, when it is filled, desire for the proper evacuation is also natural. But desire for needless nourishment, needless and luxurious clothing and
bedding, or needless and very expensive and elaborate housing, is acquired. And
the same goes for furniture, drinking cups, servants, and animals which are raised

---

15. This sentence parallels part of an extract from Aristoxenus' *Pythagorean Sayings*, preserved
by Stobaeus (4. 1, 49).
16. The following four sentences correspond closely, but with some alterations and elaborations to Aristoxenus, *ap.* Stobaeus, 3. 10. 66 (the *Pyth. Apoph.*).

ἢ διαθέσεως αἰσθητικῆς. γίνεσθαι δὲ καὶ τῶν ἐναντίων
ἐπιθυμίαν, οἷον κενώσεώς τε καὶ ἀπουσίας καὶ τοῦ μὴ
αἰσθάνεσθαι ἐνίων. ποικίλον δ' εἶναι τὸ πάθος τοῦτο καὶ
σχεδὸν τῶν περὶ ἄνθρωπον πολυειδέστατον. εἶναι δὲ τὰς
πολλὰς τῶν ἀνθρωπίνων ἐπιθυμιῶν ἐπικτήτους τε καὶ
κατεσκευασμένας ὑπ' αὐτῶν τῶν ἀνθρώπων, διὸ δὴ καὶ
πλείστης ἐπιμελείας δεῖσθαι τὸ πάθος τοῦτο καὶ φυλακῆς τε
καὶ σωμασκίας οὐ τῆς τυχούσης. τὸ μὲν γὰρ κενωθέντος τοῦ
σώματος τῆς τροφῆς ἐπιθυμεῖν φυσικὸν εἶναι, καὶ τὸ πάλιν
ἀναπληρωθέντος κενώσεως ἐπιθυμεῖν τῆς προσηκούσης
φυσικὸν καὶ τοῦτ' εἶναι· τὸ δὲ ἐπιθυμεῖν περιέργου τροφῆς ἢ
περιέργου τε καὶ τρυφερᾶς ἐσθῆτός τε καὶ στρωμνῆς ἢ περιέργου τε καὶ πολυτελοῦς καὶ ποικίλης οἰκήσεως ἐπίκτητον
εἶναι. τὸν αὐτὸν δὴ λόγον εἶναι καὶ περὶ σκευῶν τε καὶ
ποτηρίων καὶ διακόνων καὶ θρεμμάτων τῶν εἰς τροφὴν
[206] ἀνηκόντων. καθόλου δὲ τῶν περὶ ἄνθρωπον παθῶν σχεδὸν
τοῦτο μάλιστα τοιοῦτον εἶναι οἷον μηδαμοῦ ἵστασθαι, ἀλλὰ
προάγειν εἰς ἄπειρον. διόπερ εὐθὺς ἐκ νεότητος ἐπιμελητέον
εἶναι τῶν ἀναφυομένων, ὅπως ἐπιθυμήσωσι μὲν ὧν δεῖ,
φυλάξωνται δὲ τῶν ματαίων τε καὶ περιέργων ἐπιθυμιῶν,
ἀτάρακτοί τε καὶ καθαροὶ τῶν τοιούτων ὀρέξεων ὄντες καὶ
καταφρονοῦντες αὐτῶν τε τῶν ἀξιοκαταφρονήτων καὶ τῶν
ἐνδεδεμένων ἐν ταῖς ἐπιθυμίαις. μάλιστα δ' εἶναι κατανοῆσαι
τάς τε ματαίους καὶ τὰς βλαβερὰς καὶ τὰς περιέργους καὶ τὰς
ὑβριστικὰς τῶν ἐπιθυμιῶν παρὰ τῶν ἐν ἐξουσίαις
ἀναστρεφομένων γινομένας· οὐδὲν γὰρ οὕτως ἄτοπον εἶναι,
ἐφ' ὃ τὴν ψυχὴν οὐχ ὁρμᾶν τῶν τοιούτων παίδων τε καὶ
[207] ἀνδρῶν καὶ γυναικῶν. καθόλου δὲ ποικιλώτατον εἶναι τὸ
ἀνθρώπινον γένος κατὰ τὸ τῶν ἐπιθυμιῶν πλῆθος. σημεῖον
δὲ ἐναργὲς εἶναι τὴν τῶν προσφερομένων ποικιλίαν·
ἀπέραντον μὲν γάρ τι πλῆθος εἶναι καρπῶν, ἀπέραντον δὲ
ριζῶν, ᾧ χρῆται τὸ ἀνθρώπινον γένος. ἔτι δὲ σαρκοφαγίᾳ
παντοδαπῇ χρῆσθαι, καὶ ἔργον εἶναι εὑρεῖν, τίνος οὐ γεύεται
τῶν τε χερσαίων καὶ τῶν πτηνῶν καὶ τῶν ἐνύδρων ζῴων. καὶ
δὴ σκευασίας παντοδαπὰς περὶ ταῦτα μεμηχανῆσθαι καὶ
χυμῶν παντοίας μίξεις. ὅθεν εἰκότως μανικόν τε καὶ
πολύμορφον εἶναι κατὰ τὴν τῆς ψυχῆς κίνησιν τὸ
[208] ἀνθρώπινον φῦλον· ἕκαστον γὰρ δὴ τῶν προσφερομένων
ἰδίου τινὸς διαθέσεως αἴτιον γίνεσθαι. ἀλλὰ τοὺς ἀνθρώπους

[206] for food. And generally, of the human emotions, desire stops almost nowhere, but goes on to infinity. Hence, immediately from youth, one must care for those growing up: that they desire what they need, and beware of vain and superfluous desires; that they be undisturbed by and free from such desires, and despise both what is intrinsically worthy of contempt and those who are entangled in desires. Most discernible are the vain, harmful, superfluous and insolent desires that issue from those in positions of power. For there is nothing too absurd to which the soul [207] of such boys, men, and women does not rush headlong.

In general, the human race has a diverse multitude of desires. And a clear sign is the many foods served; for there is a countless quantity of fruits and a countless quantity of roots which the human race consumes. Moreover, it eats every kind of flesh, and it would be difficult to find any flesh of animals terrestrial, winged and aquatic, which it does not enjoy. And then there are all kinds of dressings, and all sorts of mixtures of flavors prepared for these. Hence, the human race is naturally [208] prone to many forms of lunacy arising from the motions of the soul. For each of the foods served becomes a cause for a certain disposition. But human beings can see things which become, immediately, causes of great change, as for example, wine: when taken in excessive quantity up to a certain point, it makes them more merry, but then more mad and indecorous. But they are oblivious to things which do not display such a power. For everything taken into oneself becomes cause for a certain distinct disposition. Hence, it also takes great wisdom to understand and to see what kind and quantity of food one ought to use for nourishment. From the beginning, this knowledge belonged both to Apollo and Paean, and later to followers of Asclepius.[17]

---

17. Cf. section 126 above where one finds a prohibition against picking up anything falling to the floor in the temple of Asclepius.

τὰ μὲν παραχρῆμα μεγάλης ἀλλοιώσεως αἴτια γενόμενα
συνορᾶν, οἷον καὶ τὸν οἶνον, ὅτι πλείων προσενεχθεὶς μέχρι
μέν τινος ἱλαρωτέρους ποιεῖ, ἔπειτα μανικωτέρους καὶ
ἀσχημονεστέρους· τὰ δὲ μὴ τοιαύτην ἐνδεικνύμενα δύναμιν
ἀγνοεῖν. γίνεσθαι δὲ πᾶν τὸ προσενεχθὲν αἴτιόν τινος ἰδίου
διαθέσεως. διὸ δὴ καὶ μεγάλης σοφίας τὸ κατανοῆσαί τε καὶ
συνιδεῖν, ποίοις τε καὶ πόσοις δεῖ χρῆσθαι πρὸς τὴν τροφήν.
εἶναι δὲ ταύτην τὴν ἐπιστήμην τὸ μὲν ἐξ ἀρχῆς Ἀπόλλωνός
τε καὶ Παιῶνος, ὕστερον δὲ τῶν περὶ Ἀσκληπιόν. περὶ δὲ
[209] γεννήσεως τάδε λέγειν αὐτοὺς ἔφασαν. καθόλου μὲν ᾤοντο
δεῖν φυλάττεσθαι τὸ καλούμενον προφερές (οὔτε γὰρ τῶν
φυτῶν τὰ προφερῆ οὔτε τῶν ζῴων εὔκαρπα γίνεσθαι), ⟨ἀλλὰ
δεῖν γενέσθαι⟩ τινὰ χρόνον πρὸ τῆς καρποφορίας, ὅπως ἐξ
ἰσχυόντων τε καὶ τετελειωμένων τῶν σωμάτων τὰ σπέρματα
καὶ οἱ καρποὶ γίνωνται. δεῖν οὖν τούς τε παῖδας καὶ τὰς
παρθένους ἐν πόνοις τε καὶ γυμνασίοις καὶ καρτερίαις ταῖς
προσηκούσαις τρέφειν, τροφὴν προσφέροντας τὴν ἁρμότ-
τουσαν φιλοπόνῳ τε καὶ σώφρονι καὶ καρτερικῷ βίῳ. πολλὰ
δὲ τῶν κατὰ τὸν ἀνθρώπινον βίον τοιαῦτα εἶναι ἐν οἷς
βέλτιόν ἐστιν ἡ ὀψιμάθεια· ὧν εἶναι καὶ τὴν τῶν
[210] ἀφροδισίων χρείαν. δεῖν οὖν τὸν παῖδα οὕτως ἄγεσθαι, ὥστε
μὴ ζητεῖν ἐντὸς τῶν εἴκοσιν ἐτῶν τὴν τοιαύτην συνουσίαν.
ὅταν δ' εἰς τοῦτο ἀφίκηται, σπανίοις εἶναι χρηστέον τοῖς
ἀφροδισίοις. ἔσεσθαι δὲ τοῦτο, ἐὰν τίμιόν τε καὶ καλὸν εἶναι
νομίζηται ἡ εὐεξία· ἀκρασίαν γὰρ ἅμα καὶ εὐεξίαν οὐ πάνυ
γίνεσθαι περὶ τὸν αὐτόν. ἐπαινεῖσθαι δ' αὐτοῖς ἔφασαν καὶ
τὰ τοιάδε τῶν προϋπαρχόντων νομίμων ἐν ταῖς Ἑλληνικαῖς
πόλεσι, τὸ μήτε μητράσι συγγίνεσθαι μήτε θυγατρὶ μήτ'
ἀδελφῇ μήτ' ἐν ἱερῷ μήτ' ἐν τῷ φανερῷ· καλόν τε γὰρ εἶναι
καὶ σύμφορον τὸ ὡς πλεῖστα γίνεσθαι κωλύματα τῆς
ἐνεργείας ταύτης. ὑπελάμβανον δ', ὡς ἔοικεν, ἐκεῖνοι οἱ
ἄνδρες περιαιρεῖν μὲν δεῖν τάς τε παρὰ φύσιν γεννήσεις καὶ
τὰς μεθ' ὕβρεως γιγνομένας, καταλιμπάνειν δὲ τῶν κατὰ
φύσιν τε καὶ μετὰ σωφροσύνης γινομένων τὰς ἐπὶ
τεκνοποιίᾳ σώφρονί τε καὶ νομίμῳ γινομένας. ὑπελάμβανον

[209]   About generation[18] they report they said the following: generally they believed
it necessary to guard against that called "premature" (for neither premature
plants nor animals produce good fruit), <but it is necessary>[19] there be some time
before fruit-bearing in order that seeds and fruits arise from strong and perfect
bodies. It is necessary, then, to rear boys and girls with tasks, bodily exercises, and
fitting tests of endurance, and to give them nourishment appropriate to a labori-
ous, temperate, and patient way of life. But there are many things in human life
for which late-gotten learning is better; among these is sexual activity. It is neces-
[210] sary, then, for a boy to be so brought up that he not seek intercourse before his
twentieth year. And even when he arrives at this age, he must enjoy sexual pleasure seldom. This will happen if good physical condition is held to be honorable
and noble; for intemperance cannot arise in the same person together with good
physical condition.

Of customs which existed in Hellenic cities before their time, they said the
Pythagoreans praised the following: not to have intercourse with mothers or with
a daughter or sister, nor in a temple nor in a public place; for it is good and beneficial that there be as many hindrances as possible to this activity. And those men
apparently believed it necessary to prevent births which arise contrary to nature
and with violence. They allowed, however, those in accord with nature and temperance, which take place for the purpose of temperate and lawful begetting of
children.

---

18. Once again, this passage, until section 211, is a development of a section of Aristoxenus,
Pyth. Apoph. preserved by Stobaeus, 4. 37. 4. Another version is found in Ocellus Lucanus, *De
uniu. nat.* sections 52-57. Thesleff, *Pythagorean Texts* 137-138 (= Harder 23-24), but Iamblichus
seems dependent rather on Aristoxenus. Much material is represented only in Ocellus and Iamblichus, not in Stobaeus' extract.
19. A necessary addition of Westermann.

[211] δὲ δεῖν πολλὴν πρόνοιαν ποιεῖσθαι τοὺς τεκνοποιουμένους τῶν ἐσομένων ἐκγόνων. πρώτην μὲν οὖν εἶναι καὶ μεγίστην πρόνοιαν τὸ προσάγειν αὐτὸν πρὸς τὴν τεκνοποιίαν σωφρόνως τε καὶ ὑγιεινῶς βεβιωκότα τε καὶ ζῶντα καὶ μήτε πληρώσει χρώμενον τροφῆς ἀκαίρως μήτε προσφερόμενον τοιαῦτα ἀφ' ὧν χείρους αἱ τῶν σωμάτων ἕξεις γίνονται, μήτι δὴ μεθύοντά γε, ἀλλ' ἥκιστα πάντων· ᾤοντο γὰρ ἐκ φαύλης τε καὶ ἀσυμφώνου καὶ ταραχώδους κράσεως μοχθηρὰ [212] γίνεσθαι τὰ σπέρματα. καθόλου δὲ παντελῶς ᾤοντο ῥᾳθύμου τινὸς εἶναι καὶ ἀπροσκέπτου τὸν μέλλοντα ζῳοποιεῖν καὶ ἄγειν τινὰ εἰς γένεσίν τε καὶ οὐσίαν, τοῦτον μὴ μετὰ πάσης σπουδῆς προορᾶν, ὅπως ἔσται ὡς χαριεστάτη τῶν γινομένων ἡ εἰς τὸ εἶναί τε καὶ ζῆν ἄφιξις, ἀλλὰ τοὺς μὲν φιλόκυνας μετὰ πάσης σπουδῆς ἐπιμελεῖσθαι τῆς σκυλακείας, ὅπως ἐξ ὧν δεῖ καὶ ὅτε δεῖ καὶ ὡς δεῖ διακειμένων προσηνῆ γίνηται τὰ σκυλάκια, ὡσαύτως δὲ καὶ τοὺς φιλόρνιθας (δῆλον δ' ὅτι καὶ [213] τοὺς λοιποὺς τῶν ἐσπουδακότων περὶ τὰ γενναῖα τῶν ζῴων πᾶσαν ποιεῖσθαι σπουδὴν περὶ τοῦ μὴ εἰκῇ γίνεσθαι τὰς γεννήσεις αὐτῶν), τοὺς δ' ἀνθρώπους μηδένα λόγον ποιεῖσθαι τῶν ἰδίων ἐκγόνων, ἀλλ' ἅμα γεννᾶν εἰκῇ τε καὶ ὡς ἔτυχε σχεδιάζοντας πάντα τρόπον καὶ μετὰ ταῦτα τρέφειν τε καὶ παιδεύειν μετὰ πάσης ὀλιγωρίας. ταύτην γὰρ εἶναι τὴν ἰσχυροτάτην τε καὶ σαφεστάτην αἰτίαν τῆς τῶν πολλῶν ἀνθρώπων κακίας τε καὶ φαυλότητος· βοσκηματώδη γὰρ καὶ εἰκαίαν τινὰ γίνεσθαι τὴν τεκνοποιίαν παρὰ τοῖς πολλοῖς. τοιαῦτα τὰ ὑφηγήματα καὶ ἐπιτηδεύματα παρὰ τοῖς ἀνδράσιν ἐκείνοις διὰ λόγων τε καὶ ἔργων ἠσκεῖτο περὶ σωφροσύνης, ἄνωθεν παρειληφόσιν αὐτοῖς τὰ παραγγέλματα ὥσπερ τινὰ πυθόχρηστα λόγια παρ' αὐτοῦ Πυθαγόρου.

[211] They also believed it necessary for those begetting children to think much about their future offspring. A first and greatest precaution, then, is to engage in procreation after having lived and still living temperately and healthfully; neither to indulge in filling up with food in an untimely manner, nor to take such food and drink by which bodily conditions become worse; least of all to be intoxicated. For they believed that from a bad, discordant, and troubled temperament the seed produced was worthless.[20] And, in general, they thought it quite frivolous [212] and improvident for one about to procreate and to bring someone into existence and being not to provide for this with all seriousness, that the arrival of those born into existence and life be as favorable as possible. For dog-lovers attend to the breeding of dogs with all seriousness: that puppies be born gentle from the right parents, at the right time, and that the parents have the right dispositions; and in [213] like manner lovers of birds, (and it is clear that the rest of those, too, who are concerned with the good breeding of animals, make every effort that their engenderings not be random). But human beings take no account of their own offspring, and beget them both without plan and by chance, doing it wholly off-hand, and then rear and train them with total negligence. This is the most forceful and clearest cause of the vice and meanness of many human beings; for with the multitude, child-bearing becomes brutish and without purpose.

Such directions[21] and ways of living were practiced by those men in words and deeds in connection with temperance, after receiving their precepts from the beginning like oracles delivered by the Pythian god from Pythagoras himself.

---

20. This provision, at least, is Platonic, cf. *Lg.* 775b-e.
21. This final sentence is a summing up by Iamblichus.

[214]   Περὶ δὲ ἀνδρείας πολλὰ μὲν ἤδη καὶ τῶν εἰρημένων
οἰκείως καὶ πρὸς αὐτὴν ἔχει, οἷον τὰ περὶ Τιμύχαν θαυμαστὰ
ἔργα καὶ τὰ τῶν ἑλομένων ἀποθανεῖν πρὸ τοῦ τι παραβῆναι
τῶν ὁρισθέντων ὑπὸ Πυθαγόρου περὶ κυάμων καὶ ἄλλ' ἄττα
τῶν τοιούτων ἐπιτηδευμάτων ἐχόμενα, ὅσα τε Πυθαγόρας
αὐτὸς ἐπετέλεσε γενναίως, ἀποδημῶν πανταχοῦ μόνος καὶ
πρὸς πόνους καὶ κινδύνους ἀμηχάνους ὅσους παραβαλ-
λόμενος, ἑλόμενος δὲ καὶ τὴν πατρίδα ἀπολιπεῖν καὶ ἐπὶ τῆς
ἀλλοδαπῆς διατρίβων, τυραννίδας δὲ καταλύων καὶ
πολιτείας συγκεχυμένας διατάττων, ἐλευθερίαν τε ἀπὸ
δουλείας ταῖς πόλεσι παραδιδοὺς καὶ τὴν παρανομίαν
παύων, ὕβριν τε καταλύων καὶ τοὺς ὑβριστὰς καὶ τυραν-
νικοὺς κολούων, καὶ τοῖς μὲν δικαίοις καὶ ἡμέροις πρᾶον
ἑαυτὸν παρέχων καθηγεμόνα, τοὺς δὲ ἀγρίους ἄνδρας καὶ
ὑβριστὰς ἀπελαύνων τῆς συνουσίας καὶ μὴ θεμιστεύειν
τούτοις ἀπαγορεύων, καὶ τοῖς μὲν συναγωνιζόμενος προ-
[215]   θύμως, τοῖς δὲ παντὶ σθένει ἐνιστάμενος. πολλὰ μὲν οὖν
τούτων ἔχοι τις ἂν λέγειν τεκμήρια καὶ πολλάκις αὐτῷ
κατορθωθέντα, μέγιστα δὲ πάντων ἐστὶ τὰ πρὸς Φάλαριν
αὐτῷ μετὰ παρρησίας ἀνυποστάτου ῥηθέντα τε καὶ πραχθέντα. ὅτε γὰρ ὑπὸ Φαλάριδος τοῦ ὠμοτάτου τῶν τυράννων
κατείχετο, καὶ συνέμιξεν αὐτῷ σοφὸς ἀνήρ, Ὑπερβόρειος τὸ
γένος, Ἄβαρις τοὔνομα, αὐτοῦ τούτου ἕνεκα ἀφικόμενος
τοῦ συμβαλεῖν αὐτῷ, λόγους τε ἠρώτησε καὶ μάλα ἱερούς,
περὶ ἀγαλμάτων καὶ τῆς ὁσιωτάτης θεραπείας καὶ τῆς τῶν
θεῶν προνοίας, τῶν τε κατ' οὐρανὸν ὄντων καὶ τῶν περὶ τὴν
γῆν ἐπιστρεφομένων, ἄλλα τε πολλὰ τοιαῦτα ἐπύθετο, ὁ δὲ
[216]   Πυθαγόρας, οἷος ἦν, ἐνθέως σφόδρα καὶ μετ' ἀληθείας πάσης
ἀπεκρίνατο καὶ πειθοῦς, ὥστε προσαγαγέσθαι τοὺς
ἀκούοντας, τότε ὁ Φάλαρις ἀνεφλέχθη μὲν ὑπὸ ὀργῆς πρὸς
τὸν ἐπαινοῦντα Πυθαγόραν Ἄβαριν, ἠγρίαινε δὲ καὶ πρὸς
αὐτὸν Πυθαγόραν, ἐτόλμα δὲ πρὸς τοὺς θεοὺς αὐτοὺς
βλασφημίας δεινὰς προφέρειν καὶ τοιαύτας οἵας ἂν ἐκεῖνος

CHAPTER THIRTY-TWO

On courage: the precepts Pythagoras communicated to human beings, what sort they were, and what practices and noble works he himself practiced: and what he required his associates to practice.

[214] The subject of courage has already been touched on in many earlier parts of this book: for example, the admirable deeds of Timycha, and of those who chose death instead of trangressing anything laid down by Pythagoras about beans,[1] and other things belonging to such a way of life; also the noble deeds performed by Pythagoras himself: traveling everywhere alone, exposing himself to innumerable tasks and dangers, choosing even to leave his fatherland and to live his life on foreign soil, overthrowing despotic regimes and bringing order to governments in confusion, bestowing freedom from slavery on cities, stopping lawlessness, putting down insolence, and curbing those who were overbearing and despotic. He showed himself a gentle guide to those just and civilized, but expelled savage and insolent men from his society, refusing to deliver precepts to them. He helped the former readily, but resisted the latter with all his strength.

[215] One could, then, report many proofs of these deeds often accomplished successfully by him; but greatest of all is what he said and did with irresistible frankness to Phalaris.[2] For while he was detained by Phalaris, the most cruel of despots, he also came into contact with a wise man, Hyperborean by race, whose name was Abaris. Abaris came for the sake of conversing with him, and asked questions about very sacred matters: about statues in honor of the gods, and about things

[216] existing in heaven and on the earth; and he inquired about many other such matters. But Pythagoras, as was his nature, answered in a truly inspired manner, with complete truth and persuasiveness, so as to bring those listening over to his side. Then Phalaris, infuriated by Abaris' praise of Pythagoras, and angry at Pythagoras

---

1. Above, in sections 189-194. In general, the latter part of the chapter, sections 223-8, is composed largely of repetitions from other parts of the book.

2. The following passage, through section 219, seems like a summary of an edifying fictional dialogue. P. Boyancé, *REA* 36 (1934) 321 ff. suggested the *Abaris* of Heraclides. But the reference in 217 to *Il.* 22, 13 (see the next note), which Philostratus introduces also into his account of Apollonius of Tyana's trial before Domitian (*VA.* VIII, 5), led Rohde to suggest Apollonius as the source, *RhM* 27 (1872) 55. Much of the terminology is certainly Hellenistic, chiefly Stoic, and so Heraclides could only be an ultimate, and not a proximate source. Needless to say, the confrontation is quite unhistorical, since Phalaris ruled Acragas from 570-554 B. C., long before Pythagoras arrived in Italy.

εἶπεν. ὁ δ᾽ Ἄβαρις πρὸς ταῦτα ὡμολόγει μὲν χάριν Πυθαγόρᾳ, μετὰ δὲ τοῦτο ἐμάνθανε παρ᾽ αὐτοῦ περὶ τοῦ
οὐρανόθεν ἠρτῆσθαι καὶ οἰκονομεῖσθαι πάντα ἀπ᾽ ἄλλων τε
πλειόνων καὶ ἀπὸ τῆς ἐνεργείας τῶν ἱερῶν, πολλοῦ τε ἔδει
γόητα νομίζειν Πυθαγόραν τὸν ταῦτα παιδεύοντα, ὅς γε
αὐτὸν καὶ ἐθαύμαζεν ὡς ἂν θεὸν ὑπερφυῶς. πρὸς ταῦτα
Φάλαρις ἀνῄρει μὲν μαντείας, ἀνῄρει δὲ καὶ τὰ ἐν τοῖς ἱεροῖς
[217] δρώμενα περιφανῶς. ὁ δ᾽ Ἄβαρις μετῆγε τὸν λόγον ἀπὸ
τούτων ἐπὶ τὰ πᾶσι φαινόμενα ἐναργῶς, καὶ ἀπὸ τῶν ἐν
ἀμηχάνοις, ἤτοι πολέμοις ἀτλήτοις ἢ νόσοις ἀνιάτοις ἢ
καρπῶν φθοραῖς ἢ λοιμῶν φοραῖς ἢ ἄλλοις τισὶ τοιούτοις
παγχαλέποις καὶ ἀνηκέστοις παραγιγνομένων δαιμονίων
τινῶν καὶ θείων εὐεργετημάτων ἐπειρᾶτο συμπείθειν, ὡς
ἔστι θεία πρόνοια, πᾶσαν ἐλπίδα ἀνθρωπίνην καὶ δύναμιν
ὑπεραίρουσα. ὁ δὲ Φάλαρις καὶ πρὸς ταῦτα ἠναισχύντει τε
καὶ ἀπεθρασύνετο. αὖθις οὖν ὁ Πυθαγόρας, ὑποπτεύων μὲν
ὅτι Φάλαρις αὐτῷ ῥάπτοι θάνατον, ὅμως δὲ εἰδὼς ὡς οὐκ εἴη
Φαλάριδι μόρσιμος, ἐξουσιαστικῶς ἐπεχείρει λέγειν. ἀπιδὼν
γὰρ πρὸς τὸν Ἄβαριν ἔφη, ὅτι οὐρανόθεν ἡ διάβασις εἴς τε
[218] τὰ ἀέρια καὶ τὰ ἐπίγεια φέρεσθαι πέφυκε, καὶ ἔτι περὶ τῆς
πρὸς τὸν οὐρανὸν ἀκολουθίας πάντων διεξῆλθε γνωριμώτατα
τοῖς πᾶσι, περί τε τῆς ἐν τῇ ψυχῇ αὐτεξουσίου δυνάμεως
ἀναμφισβητήτως ἀπέδειξε, καὶ προϊὼν περὶ τῆς τοῦ λόγου
καὶ τοῦ νοῦ τελείας ἐνεργείας ἐπεξῆλθεν ἱκανῶς, κᾆθ᾽ οὕτω
μετὰ παρρησίας περὶ τυραννίδος τε καὶ τῶν κατὰ τύχην
πλεονεκτημάτων πάντων, ἀδικίας τε καὶ τῆς ἀνθρωπίνης
πλεονεξίας ὅλης, στερεῶς ἀνεδίδαξεν, ὅτι οὐδενός ἐστι
ταῦτα ἄξια. μετὰ δὲ ταῦτα θείαν παραίνεσιν ἐποιήσατο περὶ
τοῦ ἀρίστου βίου καὶ πρὸς τὸν κάκιστον ἀντιπαραβολὴν
αὐτοῦ προθύμως ἀντιπαρέτεινε, περὶ ψυχῆς τε καὶ τῶν
δυνάμεων αὐτῆς καὶ τῶν παθῶν, ὅπως ἔχει ταῦτα,
σαφέστατα ἀπεκάλυψε, καὶ τὸ κάλλιστον πάντων,
ἐπέδειξεν ὅτι οἱ θεοὶ τῶν κακῶν εἰσιν ἀναίτιοι, καὶ ὅτι νόσοι
καὶ ὅσα πάθη σώματος ἀκολασίας ἐστὶ σπέρματα· περί τε
τῶν κακῶς λεγομένων ἐν τοῖς μύθοις διήλεγξε τοὺς
λογοποιούς τε καὶ ποιητάς. τόν τε Φάλαριν μετ᾽ ἐλέγχων
ἐνουθέτει, καὶ τὴν τοῦ τυράννου δύναμιν, ὁποία τίς ἐστι καὶ
ὅση, δι᾽ ἔργων ἐπεδείκνυε, περί τε τῆς κατὰ νόμον
κολάσεως, ὡς εἰκότως γίνεται, τεκμήρια πολλὰ παρέθετο,

himself, dared to utter terrible blasphemies against the gods themselves, which only a man such as he would utter. But Abaris thanked Pythagoras for what he had learned, and then inquired from him about how everything is dependent on and governed from heaven, and about many other things, including the efficacy of sacrifices. Far from believing that Pythagoras who taught these things was a sorcerer, he admired him exceedingly as if a god.

[217]   For this reason, Phalaris openly argued against prophecy, and also against rites and ceremonies. But Abaris moved the discussion from these to things apparent to all, and argued from the presence of marvelous and divine kindness in hopeless circumstances, either insufferable wars, incurable illnesses, destructions of crops, occasions of plagues, or other such things most difficult to deal with and beyond remedy. He tried to persuade him that there is a divine providence transcending all human hope and power. But Phalaris shamelessly maintained his presumptious attitude. In turn, Pythagoras, suspecting that Phalaris planned his death, but knowing that he was not doomed[3] to die by Phalaris' hand, began to speak authoritatively. And looking at Abaris, he said that the transition from heav-

[218] en to things in the air and on the earth was appointed by nature. He also told in detail things well known to all about the conformity of everything with heaven, and he clearly demonstrated the power of free choice in the soul. He also amply discussed the perfect activity of reason and intellect, and then, with frankness, he spoke about despotism, and all successes in accord with chance, about injustice and all human greediness: he taught firmly that these are worth nothing.

After this, he made a divine exhortation about the best way of life, and vigorously contrasted it with the worst. He revealed most clearly the truth about the nature of the soul and its abilities and emotions. Noblest of all, he showed that the gods are blameless of evils, and that sicknesses and the whole gamut of bodily problems are seeds of licentiousness. He condemned both prose writers and poets for the errors in their versions of myths.[4] By cross-examinations, he admonished Phalaris and showed the nature and extent of the power of heaven[5] by its works. And in regard to punishment by law, he gave many proofs that it takes place reasonably; about the difference of human beings from other animals he made notable demonstrations; about the reason residing within and proceeding forth (in speech)[6] he spoke knowledgeably; the nature of the intellect and knowledge de-

---

3. The word μόρσιμος ("doomed" or "fated") recalls Apollo's word to Achilles in the *Iliad* (22, 13): "You will never kill me. I am not the one fated (μόρσιμος)," a line quoted to Domitian by Apollonius of Tyana, according to Philostratus (see previous note).

4. All this seems suspiciously like a précis of Plato's doctrines in the *Republic*. "Gods blameless of evils" (θεούς ἀναιτίους) is clearly a reference to *R.* X, 617e; perhaps the saying quoted by Plato is Orphic in origin. See W, K. C. Guthrie, *Orpheus and Greek Religion* (New York 1966) 167f., 183.

5. Rejecting Deubner's τυράννου for οὐρανοῦ of ms.

6. The Stoic distinction between λόγος ἐνδιάθετος and προφορικός seems indicated here.

περί τε τῆς διαφορᾶς ἀνθρώπων πρὸς τὰ ἄλλα ζῷα παρέδειξε
περιφανῶς, περί τε τοῦ ἐνδιαθέτου λόγου καὶ τοῦ ἔξω
προϊόντος ἐπιστημονικῶς διεξῆλθε, περί τε νοῦ καὶ τῆς ἀπ'
αὐτοῦ κατιούσης γνώσεως ἀπέδειξε τελείως, ἠθικά τε ἄλλα
πολλὰ ἐχόμενα τούτων δόγματα περὶ τῶν ἐν τῷ βίῳ
[219] χρηστῶν ὠφελιμώτατα ἐπαίδευσε, παραινέσεις τε συμφ-
ώνους τούτοις συνήρμοσεν ἐπιεικέστατα, ἀπαγορεύσεις τε
ὧν οὐ χρὴ ποιεῖν παρέθετο· καὶ τὸ μέγιστον, τῶν ⟨κατὰ
πεπρωμένην καὶ⟩ καθ' εἱμαρμένην καὶ κατὰ νοῦν δρωμένων
τὴν διάκρισιν ἐποιήσατο [καὶ τῶν κατὰ πεπρωμένην καὶ καθ'
εἱμαρμένην], περὶ δαιμόνων τε πολλὰ καὶ σοφὰ διελέχθη καὶ
περὶ ψυχῆς ἀθανασίας. ταῦτα μὲν οὖν ἄλλος ἂν εἴη τρόπος
λόγων· ἐκεῖνα δὲ καὶ μάλα τοῖς περὶ ἀνδρείας ἐπιτηδεύμασι
[220] προσήκει. εἰ γὰρ ἐν αὐτοῖς μέσοις ἐμβεβηκὼς τοῖς δεινοῖς
σταθερᾷ τῇ γνώμῃ φιλοσοφῶν ἐφαίνετο, παντάπασι
παρατεταγμένως καὶ καρτερούντως ἠμύνετο τὴν τύχην, καὶ
εἰ πρὸς αὐτὸν τὸν ἐπάγοντα τοὺς κινδύνους ἐξουσίᾳ καὶ
παρρησίᾳ χρώμενος ἔνδηλος ἦν, πάντως που καταφρο-
νητικῶς εἶχε τῶν νομιζομένων εἶναι δεινῶν ὡς οὐδενὸς ἀξίων
ὄντων. καὶ εἰ τοῦ θανάτου προσδοκωμένου, ὅσα γε δὴ τὰ
ἀνθρώπινα, ὠλιγώρει τούτου παντάπασι καὶ οὐκ ἦν
προσ⟨έχων⟩ τῇ παρούσῃ τότε προσδοκίᾳ, δῆλον δήπουθεν ὡς
εἰλικρινῶς ἀδεὴς ἦν πρὸς θάνατον. καὶ τούτων δὲ ἔτι
γενναιότερον διεπράξατο, τὴν κατάλυσιν τῆς τυραννίδος
ἀπεργασάμενος καὶ κατασχὼν μὲν τὸν τύραννον μέλλοντα
ἀνηκέστους συμφορὰς ἐπάγειν τοῖς ἀνθρώποις, ἐλευθερώσας
δὲ τῆς ὠμοτάτης τυραννίδος Σικελίαν. ὅτι δὲ αὐτὸς ἦν ὁ
[221] ταῦτα κατορθώσας, τεκμήριον μὲν καὶ ἀπὸ τῶν χρησμῶν τοῦ
Ἀπόλλωνος, τότε τὴν κατάλυσιν διασημαι-νόντων τῷ
Φαλάριδι γενήσεσθαι τῆς ἀρχῆς, ὅτε κρείττονες καὶ ὁμονοη-
τικώτεροι γένοιντο καὶ συνιστάμενοι μετ' ἀλλήλων οἱ
ἀρχόμενοι, οἷοι καὶ τότε ἐγένοντο Πυθαγόρου παρόντος διὰ
τὰς ὑφηγήσεις αὐτοῦ καὶ παιδεύσεις. τούτου δ' ἔτι μεῖζον
τεκμήριον ἦν ἀπὸ τοῦ χρόνου· ἐπὶ γὰρ τῆς αὐτῆς ἡμέρας
Πυθαγόρᾳ τε καὶ Ἀβάριδι Φάλαρις ἐπῆγε κίνδυνον περὶ
θανάτου καὶ αὐτὸς ὑπὸ τῶν ἐπιβουλευόντων ἀπεσφάγη. καὶ
τὸ κατ' Ἐπιμενίδην δὲ τῶν αὐτῶν τούτων ἔστω τεκμήριον.

[219] scending from it he demonstrated perfectly. And many other ethical doctrines dependent upon these, concerning the good things in life, he taught most beneficially, and most suitably joined with these compatible exhortations, and gave prohibitions for things which one ought not do. Most important of all, he made a distinction between things done <in accord with fate>[7] and according to intellect; and he also said many wise things about daemons and the immortality of the soul.

But these matters would require another mode of discourse.[8] What follows, however, is quite germane to his activities in regard to courage. For if when en-
[220] tered into the midst of fearful circumstances, he manifestly continued to philosophize with steadfast mind, with absolute self-possession, and stoutly defended himself against misfortune, and if toward the very author of his dangers he was found using authority and frankness, I suppose that he altogether despised those things generally held to be fearful as undeserving of notice. And if, when his death was in all human probability to be expected, he took absolutely no heed of this, and paid no attention to its present expectation, I suppose it is clear that he was wholly fearless toward death.

And he accomplished something still more noble than this by causing the overthrow of the tyranny, restraining the despot who was about to bring misfortunes beyond remedy on human beings, and freeing Sicily from the cruelest despotism.
[221] Proof that it was he himself who accomplished these things is given by the oracles of Apollo which signified that the overthrow of Phalaris' rule would occur when his subjects became more powerful, more in agreement, and united with one another. And such they became when Pythagoras was present, and were under the influence of his directions and instructions. A yet greater proof than this is given by the time in which it happened: for on the very day Phalaris threatened Pythagoras and Abaris with death, he himself was slain by those plotting against him.[9]

---

7. Accepting Deubner's reorganization of the text; the contrast, in any case, is between Fate and Intellect (of which, on the cosmic level) Providence is the expression.

8. This seems to signify the end of the "dialogue with Phalaris" section.

9. Since Phalaris was slain in 554 B.C., this is absurd.

[222] ὥσπερ γὰρ Ἐπιμενίδης ὁ Πυθαγόρου μαθητής, μέλλων ὑπό
τινων ἀναιρεῖσθαι, ἐπειδὴ τὰς ἐρινύας ἐπεκαλέσατο καὶ τοὺς
τιμωροὺς θεούς, ἐποίησε τοὺς ἐπιβουλεύοντας πάντας ἄρδην
περὶ ἑαυτοῖς ἀποσφαγῆναι, οὕτω δήπου καὶ Πυθαγόρας,
ἐπαμύνων τοῖς ἀνθρώποις κατὰ τὴν τοῦ Ἡρακλέους δίκην
καὶ ἀνδρείαν, τὸν ἐξυβρίζοντα καὶ πλημμελοῦντα εἰς τοὺς
ἀνθρώπους ἐπ᾽ ὠφελείᾳ τῶν ἀνθρώπων ἐκόλασε καὶ θανάτῳ
παρέδωκε δι᾽ αὐτῶν τῶν χρησμῶν τοῦ Ἀπόλλωνος, οἷς ἦν
αὐτοφυῶς συνηρτημένος ἀπὸ τῆς ἐξ ἀρχῆς γενέσεως. τοῦτο
μὲν οὖν τὸ θαυμαστὸν αὐτοῦ τῆς ἀνδρείας κατόρθωμα ἄχρι
τοσούτου μνήμης ἠξιώκαμεν. ἄλλο δὲ τεκμήριον αὐτῆς ποιη-
[223] σώμεθα τὴν σωτηρίαν τῆς ἐννόμου δόξης, δι᾽ ἣν αὐτός τε
μόνα τὰ δοκοῦντα ἑαυτῷ ἔπραττε καὶ τὰ ὑπὸ τοῦ ὀρθοῦ
λόγου ὑπαγορευόμενα, μήτε ὑπὸ ἡδονῆς μήτε ὑπὸ πόνου
μήτε ὑπ᾽ ἄλλου τινὸς πάθους ἢ κινδύνου μεθιστάμενος ἀπ᾽
αὐτῶν, οἵ τε ἑταῖροι αὐτοῦ πρὸ τοῦ τι παραβῆναι τῶν
ὁρισθέντων ὑπ᾽ αὐτοῦ ἡροῦντο ἀποθανεῖν, ἐν παντοδαπαῖς
τε τύχαις ἐξεταζόμενοι τὸ αὐτὸ ἦθος ἀδιάφθορον διεφύλαττον, ἐν μυρίαις τε συμφοραῖς γενόμενοι οὐδέποτε ὑπ᾽
αὐτῶν μετετράπησαν. ἦν δὲ καὶ ἀδιάλειπτος παρ᾽ αὐτοῖς
παράκ-λησις τὸ "νόμῳ βοηθεῖν ἀεὶ καὶ ἀνομίᾳ πολεμεῖν", καὶ
πρὸς τὸ εἴργειν καὶ ἀπωθεῖσθαι τὴν τρυφὴν καὶ συνεθίζεσθαι
ἀπὸ γενετῆς σώφρονι καὶ ἀνδρικῷ βίῳ. ἦν δέ τινα μέλη παρ᾽
[224] αὐτοῖς πρὸς τὰ ψυχῆς πάθη πεποιημένα, πρός τε ἀθυμίας καὶ
δηγμούς, ἃ δὴ βοηθητικώτατα ἐπινενόητο, καὶ πάλιν αὖ
ἕτερα πρός τε τὰς ὀργὰς καὶ πρὸς τοὺς θυμούς, δι᾽ ὧν
ἐπιτείνοντες αὐτὰ καὶ ἀνιέντες ἄχρι τοῦ μετρίου σύμμετρα
πρὸς ἀνδρείαν ἀπειργάζοντο. ἦν δὲ καὶ τοῦτο μέγιστον εἰς
γενναιότητα ἕρμα, τὸ πεπεῖσθαι ὡς οὐδὲν δεῖ τῶν
ἀνθρωπίνων συμπτωμάτων ἀπροσδόκητον εἶναι παρὰ τοῖς
νοῦν ἔχουσιν, ἀλλὰ πάντα προσδοκᾶν, ὧν μὴ τυγχάνουσιν
αὐτοὶ κύριοι ὄντες. οὐ μὴν ἀλλ᾽ εἴ ποτε συμβαίη αὐτοῖς ἢ
[225] ὀργὴ ἢ λύπη ἢ ἄλλο τι τῶν τοιούτων, ἐκποδὼν ἀπηλλάττοντο, καὶ καθ᾽ ἑαυτὸν ἕκαστος γενόμενος ἐπειρᾶτο
καταπέττειν τε καὶ ἰατρεύειν τὸ πάθος ἀνδρικῶς. ἦν δὲ
γεννικὸν αὐτῶν καὶ τὸ περὶ τὰ μαθήματα καὶ ἐπιτηδεύματα
ἐπίπονον καὶ αἱ τῆς ἐμφύτου πᾶσιν ἀκρασίας τε καὶ
πλεονεξίας βάσανοι, ποικιλώταταί τε κολάσεις καὶ ἀνακοπαὶ
πυρὶ καὶ σιδήρῳ συντελούμεναι ἀπαραιτήτως καὶ οὔτε πόνων

[222]   And let what happened in the case of Epimenides be proof of these same things. For just as Epimenides, the disciple of Pythagoras, when about to be killed by certain persons, invoked the Erinyes and the avenging gods, and caused those plotting against him to kill one another all at once, so, it would seem, Pythagoras also, coming to aid human beings after the fashion of Heracles' justice and courage,[10] punished and delivered up to death him who committed violence and crimes against humanity. (He did this) by means of Apollo's very oracles with which he was naturally joined together from his birth. This marvelous achievement of his courage, then, we have considered worthy of commemoration up to this point.

[223]   But let us give, as another proof of his courage, his maintenance of correctly-arrived-at opinion, by which he did only things which had won his assent and were dictated by right reason, diverted from these neither by pleasure, trouble, nor any other emotion or danger. Also his disciples chose to die rather than to transgress anything ordered by him. Tested in all sorts of misfortunes, they maintained the same incorruptible character, and although involved in countless calamities, they were never turned aside by them. And unceasing also was their summons "to assist law and to war with lawlessness,"[11] to prevent and to drive away luxury, and to become accustomed from birth to a temperate and manly way of life.

[224]   There were[12] also certain melodies created by them for the soul's emotions which, were in fact, devised to be most helpful against despondency and mental suffering; and again, other melodies against rages and angers, by means of which they intensified and relaxed the emotions as far as the mean and made them commensurate with courage. And the greatest foundation for nobility of character was this:[13] the conviction that nothing of human mishaps ought to be unexpected by anyone possessed of intelligence, but to expect all things of which they themselves
[225] were not masters. And if, in fact, anger, grief, or any other such emotion ever arose in them, they retired by themselves, and, each on his own, tried to quell and heal the emotion courageously.

Noble also[14] was the effort they put into studies and ascetic exercises, and their testing of the incontinence inborn in all and of greediness; varied punishments and restraints accomplished "by fire and sword" unmercifully, which spared of neither effort nor patient endurance. For abstinence from all animal flesh and also from certain foods was nobly practiced by them. Also[15] they were trained in

---

10. It is worth noting, perhaps, that Apollonius of Tyana was honored as Heracles Alexikakos ("Warder-off of Evil") by the Ephesians, according to Lactantius (*Div. Inst.* V. 3). Perhaps Apollonius represented Pythagoras in this same guise.

11. Cf. sections 100 and 171 above.

12. The first part of this section is repeated verbatim from section 111.

13. This and the next sentence are repeated from section 196.

14. The following section, to the beginning of section 226, is partly repeated from section 68.

οὔτε καρτερίας οὐδεμιᾶς φειδόμεναι. τοῦτο μὲν γὰρ ἀποχὴ
ἐμψύχων ἁπάντων καὶ προσέτι βρωμάτων τινῶν ἠσκεῖτο
γενναίως, τοῦτο δὲ ἐπεγρίαι τοῦ λογισμοῦ καὶ εἰλικρίνειαι
τῶν ἐμποδιζόντων ἐπετηδεύοντο, τοῦτο δὲ ἐχεμυθία τε καὶ
παντελὴς σιωπή, πρὸς τὸ γλώσσης κρατεῖν συνασκοῦσα ἐπὶ
ἔτη πολλά, τὴν ἀνδρείαν αὐτῶν ἐγύμναζεν, ἥ τε σύντονος
καὶ ἀδιάπνευστος περὶ τὰ δυσληπτότατα τῶν θεωρημάτων
ἐξέτασίς τε καὶ ἀνάληψις, διὰ ταὐτὰ δὲ ἀνοινία καὶ
ὀλιγοσιτία καὶ ὀλιγοϋπνία, δόξης τε καὶ πλούτου καὶ τῶν
[226] ὁμοίων ἀνεπιτήδευτος περιφρόνησις· καὶ ταῦτα πάντα εἰς
ἀνδρείαν αὐτοῖς συνέτεινεν. οἴκτων δὲ καὶ δακρύων καὶ
πάντων τῶν τοιούτων εἴργεσθαι τοὺς ἄνδρας ἐκείνους φασί.
ἀπείχοντο δὲ καὶ δεήσεων καὶ ἱκετειῶν καὶ πάσης τῆς
τοιαύτης ἀνελευθέρου θωπείας ὡς ἀνάνδρου καὶ ταπεινῆς
οὔσης. τῆς δὲ αὐτῆς ἰδέας τῶν ἠθῶν θετέον καὶ ὅτι τὰ
κυριώτατα καὶ συνεκτικώτατα τῶν ἑαυτῶν δογμάτων
ἀπόρρητα ἐν ἑαυτοῖς διεφύλαττον ἅπαντες ἀεί, μετὰ
ἀκριβοῦς ἐχεμυθίας πρὸς τοὺς ἐξωτερικοὺς ἀνέκφορα
διατηροῦντες ἀγράφως ἐν μνήμῃ, τοῖς διαδόχοις ἅπερ
μυστήρια θεῶν μεταπαραδιδόντες. διόπερ οὐδὲν ἐξεφοίτησε
[227] τῶν γε λόγου ἀξίων μέχρι πολλοῦ, διδασκόμενά τε καὶ
μανθανόμενα ἐντὸς τοίχων μόνον ἐγνωρίζετο. ἐπὶ δὲ τῶν
θυραίων καὶ ὡς εἰπεῖν βεβήλων, εἰ καί ποτε τύχοι, διὰ
συμβόλων ἀλλήλοις οἱ ἄνδρες ᾐνίττοντο, ὧν ἴχνος ἔτι νῦν
[ὧν] περιφέρονται τὰ θρυλλούμενα, οἷον "πῦρ μαχαίρῃ μὴ
σκάλευε" καὶ τὰ τοιαῦτα σύμβολα, ἅπερ ψιλῇ μὲν τῇ φράσει
γραώδεσιν ὑποθήκαις ἔοικε, διαπτυσσόμενα δὲ θαυμαστήν
τινα καὶ σεμνὴν ὠφέλειαν παρέχεται τοῖς μεταλαβοῦσι.
μέγιστον δὲ πάντων πρὸς ἀνδρείαν παράγγελμά ἐστι τὸ
σκοπὸν προθέσθαι τὸν κυριώτατον, ῥύσασθαι καὶ
[228] ἐλευθερῶσαι τῶν τοσούτων εἰργμῶν καὶ συνδέσεως τὸν
κατεχόμενον ἐκ βρεφῶν νοῦν, οὗ χωρὶς ὑγιὲς οὐδὲν ἄν τις
οὐδὲ ἀληθὲς τὸ παράπαν ἐκμάθοι οὐδ᾽ ἂν κατίδοι δι᾽ ἧστινος
οὖν ἐνεργῶν αἰσθήσεως. "νοῦς" γὰρ κατ᾽ αὐτοὺς "πάνθ᾽ ὁρῇ
καὶ πάντ᾽ ἀκούει, τἆλλα δὲ κωφὰ καὶ τυφλά". δεύτερον δὲ τὸ
ὑπερσπουδάζειν διακαθαρθέντι λοιπὸν αὐτῷ καὶ ποικίλως
ἐπιτηδειωθέντι διὰ τῶν μαθηματικῶν ὀργιασμῶν, τὸ
τηνικάδε τῶν ὀνησιφόρων τι καὶ θείων ἐντιθέναι καὶ
μεταδιδόναι, ὡς μήτε τῶν σωμάτων ἀφιστάμενον ἀπο-

keeping alert the rational part of the soul, and freeing it from hindrances. And reserve and absolute silence, helping them to practice mastery of the tongue for many years, trained them in courage. Also intense and untiring close examination and repetition of theories about subjects most difficult to comprehend (was prac[226] ticed), and for the sake of these abstinence from wine, moderation in food and sleep, and sincere contempt[16] of fame, wealth, and the like. All these directed them earnestly to courage.

They say these men also kept aloof from lamentations, tears, and all such manifestations of grief.[17] They also abstained from entreaties, supplications and all such servile flattery as being cowardly and base. To the same quality of character must also be attributed the fact that they all always kept secret among themselves their own principal and most essential beliefs. Maintaining strict reserve toward those outside their fellowship, they kept these hidden, unwritten, in their memo[227] ry, and handed them down to their successors as mysteries of the gods. Hence for a long time nothing worth mentioning spread abroad, and what was taught and learned was known only within their walls. But in the presence of those outside the doors and, so to speak, profane, if ever one were present, these men spoke obscurely to one another by means of "symbols," of which the ones now commonly quoted still bear a trace: for example, "do not poke a fire with a sword," and similar *symbola,* which on the literal level seem like old wives' precepts, but when explained provide a marvelous and grand benefit to those sharing them.

[228] But the greatest precept of all[18] in regard to courage is setting before oneself this principal aim: to rescue and to free the intellect, subdued from infancy, from so many imprisonments and constrictions. For apart from the intellect, no one would thoroughly learn anything sound or absolutely true, nor would he perceive through which sense-organ he was functioning. For according to them "intellect sees and hears all, but all other things are deaf and blind."[19]

The second greatest precept is: when the intellect has been purified and in various ways made fit for taking great pains by initiation into scientific rites, at this time to put into and give it some share of beneficial and divine teachings, so that it neither greatly fears removal from the body, nor when led to things incorporeal,

---

15. The rest of this report is found also at sections 187-88 above.

16. We note the single word change from κατεξανάστασις in section 188 (a word attested elsewhere only in "Longinus") to περιφρόνησις here.

17. This sentence is repeated from section 198.

18. This passage down to the quotation of Epicharmus, "intellect sees...," is perhaps taken from Porph. *VP* 46, with a looser borrowing in the sections following. Rohde *RhM* 27 (1872) 54, presumes this to be a common borrowing from Nicomachus, but without adequate reason. The definition of courage here is in accord with that propounded by Plotinus, in *Enn.* I. 2, 4-6, and Porphyry in *Sent.* 32. The virtue of courage at the cathartic, or "purified" level, is Neoplatonic doctrine (so far as we know).

19. Epicharmus, fr. 249, Kaibel.

δειλιᾶν, μήτε πρὸς τὰ ἀσώματα προσαγόμενον ὑπὸ τῆς λαμπροτάτης αὐτῶν μαρμαρυγῆς ἀποστρέφεσθαι τὰ ὄμματα, μήτε τῶν προσηλούντων τῷ σώματι τὴν ψυχὴν παθημάτων καὶ προσπερονώντων ἐπιστρέφεσθαι, ὅλως δὲ ἀδάμαστον εἶναι πρὸς πάντα γενεσιουργὰ καὶ καταγωγὰ παθήματα· ἡ γὰρ διὰ τούτων πάντων γυμνασία καὶ ἄνοδος τῆς τελειοτάτης ἀνδρείας ἦν ἐπιτήδευσις. τοσαῦτα καὶ περὶ τῆς ἀνδρείας ἡμῖν τεκμήρια κείσθω περὶ Πυθαγόρου τε καὶ τῶν Πυθαγορείων ἀνδρῶν.

has its eyes turned away because of their brilliant splendor, nor turns to those emotions "nailing and fastening"[20] the soul to the body. In short, that it be unconquered by emotions concerned with generation and which debase the soul. For the training and ascent through all these was the practice of perfect courage. Let so many things remain proofs for us of the courage of Pythagoras and the Pythagoreans.

20. A reference to Plato's language at *Phd.* 83d.

[229] Φιλίαν δὲ διαφανέστατα πάντων πρὸς ἅπαντας Πυθαγόρας παρέδωκε, θεῶν μὲν πρὸς ἀνθρώπους δι' εὐσεβείας καὶ ἐπιστημονικῆς θεραπείας, δογμάτων δὲ πρὸς ἄλληλα καὶ καθόλου ψυχῆς πρὸς σῶμα λογιστικοῦ τε πρὸς τὰ τοῦ ἀλόγου εἴδη διὰ φιλοσοφίας καὶ τῆς κατ' αὐτὴν θεωρίας, ἀνθρώπων δὲ πρὸς ἀλλήλους, πολιτῶν μὲν διὰ νομιμότητος ὑγιοῦς, ἑτεροφύλων δὲ διὰ φυσιολογίας ὀρθῆς, ἀνδρὸς δὲ πρὸς γυναῖκα ἢ τέκνα ἢ ἀδελφοὺς καὶ οἰκείους διὰ κοινωνίας ἀδιαστρόφου, συλλήβδην δὲ πάντων πρὸς ἅπαντας καὶ προσέτι τῶν ἀλόγων ζῴων τινὰ διὰ δικαιοσύνης καὶ φυσικῆς ἐπιπλοκῆς καὶ κοινότητος, σώματος δὲ καθ' ἑαυτὸ θνητοῦ τῶν ἐγκεκρυμμένων αὐτῷ ἐναντίων δυνάμεων εἰρήνευσίν τε καὶ συμβιβασμὸν δι' ὑγείας καὶ τῆς εἰς ταύτην διαίτης καὶ σωφροσύνης κατὰ μίμησιν τῆς ἐν τοῖς κοσμικοῖς στοιχείοις
[230] εὐετηρίας. ἐν πᾶσι δὴ τούτοις ἑνὸς καὶ τοῦ αὐτοῦ κατὰ σύλληψιν τοῦ τῆς φιλίας ὀνόματος ὄντος, εὑρετὴς καὶ νομοθέτης ὁμολογουμένως Πυθαγόρας ἐγένετο, καὶ οὕτω θαυμαστὴν φιλίαν παρέδωκε τοῖς χρωμένοις, ὥστε ἔτι καὶ νῦν τοὺς πολλοὺς λέγειν ἐπὶ τῶν σφοδρότερον εὐνοούντων ἑαυτοῖς ὅτι τῶν Πυθαγορείων εἰσί. δεῖ δὴ καὶ περὶ τούτων τὴν Πυθαγόρου παιδείαν παραθέσθαι καὶ τὰ παραγγέλματα, οἷς ἐχρῆτο πρὸς τοὺς αὐτοῦ γνωρίμους. παρεκελεύοντο οὖν οἱ ἄνδρες οὗτοι ἐκ φιλίας ἀληθινῆς ἐξαιρεῖν ἀγῶνά τε καὶ φιλονεικίαν, μάλιστα μὲν ἐκ πάσης, εἰ δυνατόν, εἰ δὲ μή, ἔκ γε τῆς πατρικῆς καὶ καθόλου ἐκ τῆς πρὸς τοὺς πρεσβυτέρους· ὡσαύτως δὲ καὶ ἐκ τῆς πρὸς τοὺς εὐεργέτας. τὸ γὰρ διαγωνίζεσθαι ἢ διαφιλονεικεῖν πρὸς τοὺς τοιούτους ἐμπεσούσης ὀργῆς ἢ ἄλλου τινὸς τοιούτου πάθους οὐ σωτήριον
[231] τῆς ὑπαρχούσης φιλίας. ἔφασαν δὲ δεῖν ὡς ἐλαχίστας ἀμυχάς τε καὶ ἑλκώσεις ἐν ταῖς φιλίαις ἐγγίνεσθαι· ⟨τοῦτο δὲ γίνεσθαι,⟩ ἐὰν ἐπίστωνται εἴκειν καὶ κρατεῖν ὀργῆς ἀμφότεροι μέν, μᾶλλον μέντοι ὁ νεώτερός τε καὶ τῶν εἰρημένων τάξεων ἔχων ἡνδήποτε. τὰς ἐπανορθώσεις τε καὶ

CHAPTER THIRTY-THREE

On Friendship, what its nature and extent were in the case
of Pythagoras himself, and how he extended it to all;
how many forms of it exist and what activities consonant
with their way of life the Pythagoreans practiced.

[229] Friendship of all with all,[1] Pythagoras taught in the clearest manner: of gods with human beings through piety and scientific worship; of doctrines with one another, and generally, of the soul with the body, and of the rational part of the soul with all forms of the irrational through philosophy and contemplation in accord with this; of human beings with one another: of citizens through sound observance of law and of those of another race through correct inquiry into natural laws; of a husband with a wife or children, brothers and relatives, through an unperverted spirit of community; in short, friendship of all with all, and furthermore, with certain irrational animals through justice and natural union and affability; and friendship of the mortal body with itself, by reconciliation and conciliation of the opposite powers concealed in it, accomplished through health and a way of life conducive to this and temperance conducive to this, in imitation of the efficient functioning of the cosmic elements.

[230] For all these instances taken together, then, there is one and the same word, that of "friendship," of which, by common consent, Pythagoras was the discoverer and legislator, and he taught such an admirable friendship to his friends, that even now many say of those who are unusually well-disposed to one another that they belong to the Pythagoreans. We must, then, provide Pythagoras' training and teaching about these matters also, and the precepts which he used for his disciples.

These men,[2] then, advised removal of competition and rivalry from true friendship especially, and from all friendship if possible; at least its removal from paternal friendship, and generally, from friendship with one's elders; and in like manner, from friendship with benefactors. For persistence in contention or disputation with such as these, when anger or some other such emotion occurs, is [231] not designed to preserve the existence of friendship. They said that as few wounds

---

1. This passage down to "legislator" (230) is repeated from sections 69-70.
2. This passage, down to "incorrigible vice" in section 232, is repeated from sections 101-02 above. It is probably to be attributed to Aristoxenus, as is thought of the rest of the chapter (cf. below, section 233).

νουθετήσεις, ἃς δὴ πεδαρτάσεις ἐκάλουν ἐκεῖνοι, μετὰ
πολλῆς εὐφημίας τε καὶ εὐλαβείας ᾤοντο δεῖν γενέσθαι παρὰ
τῶν πρεσβυτέρων τοῖς νεωτέροις, καὶ πολὺ ἐμφαίνεσθαι ἐν
τοῖς νουθετοῦσι τὸ κηδεμονικόν τε καὶ οἰκεῖον· οὕτω γὰρ
εὐσχήμονά τε γίνεσθαι καὶ ὠφέλιμον τὴν νουθέτησιν. ἐκ
[232] φιλίας μηδέποτε ἐξαιρεῖν πίστιν μήτε παίζοντας μήτε
σπουδάζοντας· οὐ γὰρ ἔτι ῥᾴδιον εἶναι διυγιᾶναι τὴν
ὑπάρχουσαν φιλίαν, ὅταν ἅπαξ παρεμπέσῃ τὸ ψεῦδος εἰς τὰ
τῶν φασκόντων φίλων εἶναι ἤθη. φιλίαν μὴ ἀπογιγνώσκειν
ἀτυχίας ἕνεκα ἢ ἄλλης τινὸς ἀδυναμίας τῶν εἰς τὸν βίον
ἐμπιπτουσῶν, ἀλλὰ μόνην εἶναι δόκιμον ἀπόγνωσιν φίλου
τε καὶ φιλίας τὴν γινομένην διὰ κακίαν μεγάλην τε καὶ
ἀνεπανόρθωτον. ἔχθραν ἑκόντα μὲν μηδέποτε αἴρεσθαι πρὸς
τοὺς μὴ τελείως κακούς, ἀράμενον δὲ μένειν εὐγενῶς ἐν τῷ
διαπολεμεῖν, ἂν μὴ μεταπέσῃ τὸ ἦθος τοῦ διαφερομένου καὶ
προσγένηται εὐγνωμοσύνη. πολεμεῖν δὲ μὴ λόγῳ, ἀλλὰ τοῖς
ἔργοις· νόμιμον δὲ εἶναι καὶ ὅσιον τὸν πολέμιον, εἰ ὡς
ἄνθρωπος ἀνθρώπῳ πολεμήσειεν. αἴτιον μηδέποτε γίνεσθαι
εἰς δύναμιν διαφορᾶς, εὐλαβεῖσθαι ⟨δὲ⟩ ταύτης τὴν ἀρχὴν ὡς
οἷόν τε μάλιστα. ἐν τῇ μελλούσῃ ἀληθινῇ ἔσεσθαι φιλίᾳ ὡς
[233] πλεῖστα δεῖν ἔφασαν εἶναι τὰ ὡρισμένα καὶ νενομισμένα,
καλῶς δὲ ταῦτ' εἶναι κεκριμένα καὶ μὴ εἰκῇ, καὶ δῆτα καὶ εἰς
ἔθος ἕκαστον κατακεχωρισμένον δεῖν εἶναι, ὅπως μήτε ὁμιλία
μηδεμία ὀλιγώρως τε καὶ εἰκῇ γίνηται, ἀλλὰ μετ' αἰδοῦς τε
καὶ συννοίας καὶ τάξεως ὀρθῆς, μήτε πάθος ἐγείρηται μηδὲν
εἰκῇ καὶ φαύλως καὶ ἡμαρτημένως, οἷον ἐπιθυμία ἢ ὀργή. ὁ
αὐτὸς δὲ λόγος καὶ κατὰ τῶν λειπομένων παθῶν τε καὶ
διαθέσεων. ἀλλὰ μὴν τεκμήραιτο ἄν τις καὶ περὶ τοῦ μὴ
παρέργως αὐτοὺς τὰς ἀλλοτρίας ἐκκλίνειν φιλίας, ἀλλὰ καὶ
πάνυ σπουδαίως περικάμπτειν αὐτὰς καὶ φυλάττεσθαι, καὶ
περὶ τοῦ δὲ μέχρι πολλῶν γενεῶν τὸ φιλικὸν πρὸς ἀλλήλους
ἀνένδοτον διατετηρηκέναι, ἔκ τε ὧν Ἀριστόξενος ἐν τῷ περὶ
Πυθαγορικοῦ βίου αὐτὸς διακηκοέναι φησὶ Διονυσίου τοῦ
Σικελίας τυράννου, ὅτε ἐκπεσὼν τῆς μοναρχίας γράμματα ἐν
Κορίνθῳ ἐδίδασκε. φησὶ γὰρ οὕτως ὁ Ἀριστόξενος· "οἴκτων
δὲ καὶ δακρύων καὶ πάντων τῶν τοιούτων εἴργεσθαι τοὺς
[234] ἄνδρας ἐκείνους ὡς ἐνδέχεται μάλιστα· ὁ αὐτὸς δὲ λόγος καὶ
περὶ θωπείας καὶ δεήσεως καὶ λιτανείας καὶ πάντων τῶν
τοιούτων. Διονύσιος οὖν ὁ ἐκπεσὼν τῆς τυραννίδος καὶ

and ulcerations as possible should occur in friendships; <this will happen>[3] if both know how to draw back from and master anger, especially the younger of the two and one in any of the afore-mentioned relationships. Corrections and admonitions, which they called "right tuning," they thought ought to be delivered with much caution and respect by elders to those younger; also much solicitude and fellowship should be shown in the admonitions, for thus the admonition is both [232] graceful and beneficial. Trust should never be removed from friendship, neither in jest nor in earnest; for it is no longer easy for friendship to remain healthy when falsehood once creeps into the characters of those who claim to be friends. Friendship is not to be rejected on account of misfortune or any other inability occurring in life, and the only acceptable reason for rejection of a friend and friendship is that which arises from a great and incorrigible vice.

One should never willingly choose enmity towards those not wholly bad. But having done so, one should stick nobly to carrying the battle through, if the character of the one quarrelling not change and become reasonable. One should not quarrel with words, but with deeds; it is legitimate and proper to be an enemy if one quarrels as a human being with a human being. One should never become a cause, so far as possible, of disagreement, and one should beware of being the source of this as much as possible.

[233] In a friendship which is going to be genuine, they said that most things must be definite and established, and these well chosen and not at random. Also, of course, everything must be related to the specific character, in order that no association arise carelessly and at random, but with respect, deep thought, and right order; that no emotion be aroused at random, thoughtlessly and erroneously, for example, desire or anger. And the same goes for the other emotions and dispositions.

Yet someone might truly conclude, from what Aristoxenus in his work *On the Pythagorean Way of Life*[4] says he learned from Dionysius, tyrant of Sicily, who, having lost his kingship, taught letters in Corinth: they not only incidentally avoided friendships with outsiders, but avoided and guarded against them very earnestly, [234] and firmly maintained friendships with one another for many years. To quote Aristoxenus: "Those men avoided lamentations, tears, and all such things as much as possible; and the same goes also for flattery, entreaty, supplication, and all such things.[5] At any rate, Dionysius, who lost his throne and came to settle in Corinth,

---

3. Supplied from the parallel passage in section 101.
4. Iamblichus has drawn extensively from this work, both in these chapters on the virtues and earlier, but it appears possible from a parallel passage in Porphy. *VP* 59-61, where Porphyry attributes this story not to Aristoxenus but to Nicomachus, that Nicomachus is the intermediary. Here may be a case where Iamblichus is not borrowing from Porphyry, but directly from Nicomachus. At the same time, Iamblichus seems to quote Aristoxenus extensively (from Nicomachus?).

ἀφικόμενος εἰς Κόρινθον πολλάκις ἡμῖν διηγεῖτο περὶ τῶν κατὰ Φιντίαν τε καὶ Δάμωνα τοὺς Πυθαγορείους. ἦν δὲ ταῦτα τὰ περὶ τὴν τοῦ θανάτου γενομένην ἐγγύην. ὁ δὲ τρόπος τῆς ἐγγυήσεως τοιόσδε τις ἦν. ⟨εἶναί⟩ τινας ἔφη τῶν περὶ αὐτὸν διατριβόντων, οἳ πολλάκις ἐποιοῦντο μνείαν τῶν Πυθαγορείων, διασύροντες καὶ διαμωκώμενοι καὶ ἀλαζόνας ἀποκαλοῦντες αὐτοὺς καὶ λέγοντες ὅτι ἐκκοπείη ἂν αὐτῶν ἥ τε σεμνότης αὕτη καὶ ἡ προσποίητος πίστις καὶ ἡ ἀπάθεια, εἴ τις περιστήσειεν εἰς φόβον ἀξιόχρεων. ἀντιλεγόντων δέ τινων καὶ γινομένης φιλονεικίας συνταχθῆναι ἐπὶ τοὺς περὶ [235] Φιντίαν δρᾶμα τοιόνδε. μεταπεμψάμενος ὁ Διονύσιος ἔφη τὸν Φιντίαν ἐναντίον τέ τινα τῶν κατηγόρων αὐτοῦ εἰπεῖν, ὅτι φανερὸς γέγονε μετά τινων ἐπιβουλεύων αὐτῷ, καὶ τοῦτο μαρτυρεῖσθαί τε ὑπὸ τῶν παρόντων ἐκείνων, καὶ τὴν ἀγανάκτησιν πιθανῶς πάνυ γενέσθαι. τὸν δὲ Φιντίαν θαυμάζειν τὸν λόγον. ὡς δὲ αὐτὸς διαρρήδην εἰπεῖν, ὅτι ἐξήτασται ταῦτα ἀκριβῶς καὶ δεῖ αὐτὸν ἀποθνήσκειν, εἰπεῖν τὸν Φιντίαν ὅτι, εἰ οὕτως αὐτῷ δέδοκται ταῦτα γενέσθαι, ἀξιῶσαι γε αὐτῷ δοθῆναι τὸ λοιπὸν τῆς ἡμέρας, ὅπως οἰκονομήσηται τά τε καθ' αὑτὸν καὶ τὰ κατὰ τὸν Δάμωνα· συνέζων γὰρ οἱ ἄνδρες οὗτοι καὶ ἐκοινώνουν ἁπάντων, πρεσβύτερος δ' ὢν ὁ Φιντίας τὰ πολλὰ τῶν περὶ οἰκονομίαν ἦν εἰς αὑτὸν ἀνειληφώς. ἠξίωσεν οὖν ἐπὶ ταῦτα ἀφεθῆναι ἐγγυητὴν καταστήσας τὸν Δάμωνα. ἔφη οὖν ὁ Διονύσιος [236] θαυμάσαι τε καὶ ἐρωτῆσαι, εἰ ἔστιν ὁ ἄνθρωπος οὗτος ὅστις ὑπομενεῖ θανάτου γενέσθαι ἐγγυητής. φήσαντος δὲ τοῦ Φιντίου μετάπεμπτον γενέσθαι τὸν Δάμωνα, καὶ διακούσαντα τὰ συμβεβηκότα φάσκειν ἐγγυήσεσθαί τε καὶ μενεῖν αὐτοῦ, ἕως ἂν ἐπανέλθῃ ὁ Φιντίας. αὐτὸς μὲν οὖν ἐπὶ τούτοις εὐθὺς ἐκπλαγῆναι ἔφη, ἐκείνους δὲ τοὺς ἐξ ἀρχῆς εἰσαγαγόντας τὴν διάπειραν τὸν Δάμωνα χλευάζειν ὡς ἐγκαταλειφθησόμενον καὶ σκώπτοντας ἔλαφον ἀντιδεδόσθαι λέγειν. ὄντος δ' οὖν ἤδη τοῦ ἡλίου περὶ δυσμὰς ἥκειν τὸν Φιντίαν ἀποθανούμενον, ἐφ' ᾧ πάντας ἐκπλαγῆναί τε καὶ δουλωθῆναι. αὐτὸς δ' οὖν ἔφη περιβαλών τε καὶ φιλήσας τοὺς ἄνδρας ἀξιῶσαι τρίτον αὐτὸν εἰς τὴν φιλίαν παραδέξασθαι, τοὺς δὲ μηδενὶ τρόπῳ, καίτοι λιπαροῦντος αὐτοῦ, συγκαθεῖναι εἰς τὸ τοιοῦτον." καὶ ταῦτα μὲν Ἀριστόξενος ὡς παρ' αὐτοῦ Διονυσίου πυθόμενός φησι.

often told us the story of the Pythagoreans, Phintias and Damon: this concerned one being a security for the other's death. The manner of this security was as follows: he said that some of his associates often mentioned the Pythagoreans, disparaging, mocking, and stigmatizing them as braggarts, claiming that their dignity, pretended trustworthiness, and freedom from emotion would collapse if one inflicted on them with any considerable degree of terror.

[235]   After some contradicted this and an argument broke out, the following action was taken against Phintias and his followers. Dionysius said that he summoned Phintias and told him, in the presence of one of his accusers, that he, Phintias, was obviously involved in a plot against him (Dionysius). This was confirmed by those present, and (Dionysius) himself showed very plausible displeasure. Phintias was astonished at the speech. And when Dionysius himself said firmly that these things had been investigated carefully, and that he must die, Phintias replied that, if this was his decision, he wanted from him at least the rest of the day to settle both his own affairs and those of Damon. For these men lived together and shared all things, but Phintias, being older, had taken on himself the main management
[236] of the household. He requested, then, to be released for this business, and appointed Damon as security. Dionysius then said he was amazed, and asked, 'Is there such a person as this, one who is prepared to become a security for death?' When Phintias said, 'Yes,' Damon was sent for, and on hearing what had happened, said he would pledge himself, and remain there until Phintias returned. Dionysius then said that he was naturally astonished at this, but those who had staged the test from the beginning jeered at Damon as one left in the lurch, and mockingly said that he had been offered as a substitute stag.[6] But then, just at sunset, when Phintias came to die, all were astonished and subdued. Dionysius then said that he embraced and kissed the men, and asked to be received as a third into their friendship, but they, although he persisted, were not at all ready to agree to such a proposal."

---

5. Cf. section 198 above and note *ad loc.*
6. Presumably the reference to the stag which Artemis substituted for Iphigeneia at Aulis.

[237] λέγεται δὲ ὡς καὶ ἀγνοοῦντες ἀλλήλους οἱ Πυθαγορικοὶ
ἐπειρῶντο φιλικὰ ἔργα διαπράττεσθαι ὑπὲρ τῶν εἰς ὄψιν
μηδέποτε ἀφιγμένων, ἡνίκα τεκμήριόν τι λάβοιεν τοῦ
μετέχειν τῶν αὐτῶν λόγων, ὥστ' ἐκ τῶν τοιῶνδε ἔργων μηδ'
ἐκεῖνον τὸν λόγον ἀπιστεῖσθαι, ὡς ἄρ' οἱ σπουδαῖοι ἄνδρες
καὶ προσωτάτω γῆς οἰκοῦντες φίλοι εἰσὶν ἀλλήλοις πρὶν ἢ
γνώριμοί τε καὶ προσήγοροι γενέσθαι. καταχθῆναι γοῦν
φασι τῶν Πυθαγορικῶν τινα μακρὰν καὶ ἐρήμην ὁδὸν
βαδίζοντα εἴς τι πανδοχεῖον, ὑπὸ κόπου δὲ καὶ ἄλλης
παντοδαπῆς αἰτίας εἰς νόσον μακράν τε καὶ βαρεῖαν
ἐμπεσεῖν, ὥστ' ἐπιλιπεῖν αὐτὸν τὰ ἐπιτήδεια. τὸν μέντοι
πανδοχέα, εἴτε οἴκτῳ τοῦ ἀνθρώπου εἴτε καὶ ἀποδοχῇ, πάντα
[238] παρασχέσθαι, μήτε ὑπουργίας τινὸς φεισάμενον μήτε
δαπάνης μηδεμιᾶς. ἐπειδὴ δὲ κρείττων ἦν ἡ νόσος, τὸν μὲν
ἀποθνήσκειν ἑλόμενον γράψαι τι σύμβολον ἐν πίνακι καὶ
ἐπιστεῖλαι, ὅπως, ἄν τι πάθοι, κριμνὰς τὴν δέλτον παρὰ τὴν
ὁδὸν ἐπισκοπῇ, εἴ τις τῶν παριόντων ἀναγνωριεῖ τὸ
σύμβολον· τοῦτον γὰρ ἔφη αὐτῷ ἀποδώσειν τὰ ἀναλώματα,
ἅπερ εἰς αὐτὸν ἐποιήσατο, καὶ χάριν ἐκτίσειν ὑπὲρ ἑαυτοῦ.
τὸν δὲ πανδοχέα μετὰ τὴν τελευτὴν θάψαι τε καὶ
ἐπιμεληθῆναι τοῦ σώματος αὐτοῦ, μὴ μέντοι γε ἐλπίδας
ἔχειν τοῦ κομίσασθαι τὰ δαπανήματα, μή τί γε καὶ πρὸς εὖ
παθεῖν πρός τινος τῶν ἀναγνωριούντων τὴν δέλτον. ὅμως
μέντοι διαπειρᾶσθαι ἐκπεπληγμένον τὰς ἐντολὰς ἐκτιθέναι
τε ἑκάστοτε εἰς τὸ μέσον τὸν πίνακα. χρόνῳ δὲ πολλῷ
ὕστερον τῶν Πυθαγορικῶν τινὰ παριόντα ἐπιστῆναί τε καὶ
μαθεῖν τὸν θέντα τὸ σύμβολον, ἐξετάσαι τε τὸ συμβὰν καὶ
τῷ πανδοχεῖ πολλῷ πλέον ἀργύριον ἐκτῖσαι τῶν
δεδαπανημένων. Κλεινίαν γε μὴν τὸν Ταραντῖνόν φασι
[239] πυθόμενον, ὡς Πρῶρος ὁ Κυρηναῖος, τῶν Πυθαγόρου λόγων
ζηλωτὴς ὤν, κινδυνεύοι περὶ πάσης τῆς οὐσίας, συλλεξάμενον χρήματα πλεῦσαι ἐπὶ Κυρήνης καὶ ἐπανορθώσασθαι
τὰ Πρώρου πράγματα, μὴ μόνον τοῦ μειῶσαι τὴν ἑαυτοῦ
οὐσίαν ὀλιγωρήσαντα, ἀλλὰ μηδὲ τὸν διὰ τοῦ πλοῦ κίνδυνον
περιστάντα. τὸν αὐτὸν δὲ τρόπον καὶ Θέστορα τὸν Ποσειδω-
νιάτην ἀκοῇ μόνον ἱστοροῦντα, ὅτι Θυμαρίδης εἴη ⟨ὁ⟩
Πάριος τῶν Πυθαγορείων, ἡνίκα συνέπεσεν εἰς ἀπορίαν
αὐτὸν καταστῆναι ἐκ πολλῆς περιουσίας, πλεῦσαί φασιν εἰς
τὴν Πάρον, ἀργύριον συχνὸν συλλεξάμενον, καὶ ἀνακτή-
σασθαι αὐτῷ τὰ ὑπάρξαντα. καλὰ μὲν οὖν ταῦτα καὶ

[237] All this Aristoxenus says he learned from Dionysius himself. And it is said that even when they did not know one another, the Pythagoreans tried to do friendly deeds on behalf of those they had never seen before, whenever they received some sure sign that they shared the same doctrines. Hence, from such deeds even that saying is worthy of belief that "good men, even dwelling in earth's farthest parts, are friends to one another even before they become acquainted and conversant." At any rate, they say that a Pythagorean turned in at an inn after walking a long and lonely road. Because of fatigue and many other reasons, he was afflicted by a persistent and grievous illness, which lasted until all his provisions were [238] gone. The innkeeper, however, whether out of pity for the man or out of hospitality, provided everything, sparing neither any service nor any expense. When the illness proved overwhelming, the dying man wrote a symbol on a writing tablet and ordered that if he should die, the innkeeper hang the writing tablet beside the road, and see if anyone passing by would recognize the symbol. For this one, he said, would repay him the expenses which he had expended upon him, and return thanks on his own behalf.

After his death, the innkeeper attended to and buried his guest's body, yet had no hope of recovering his expenses, and even less of receiving any benefits from someone recognizing the writing tablet. Nevertheless, he made the test, although astonished at the orders, and set the tablet out every day in a central place. A long time afterwards, a Pythagorean passing by stopped, and learned who placed the symbol (there). He then enquired into what had happened, and paid the innkeeper much more than his expenses.

[239] They say, furthermore, that Cleinias of Tarentum, on learning that Prorus of Cyrene,[7] a zealous admirer of Pythagoras' doctrines, was in danger of losing all his property, collected money to sail to Cyrene and to straighten out Prorus's affairs. He not only disregarded the consequent dimunition of his own property, but did not hesitate at the danger of the voyage.

In the same way, they say also that Thestor of Posidonia, on learning merely from hearsay that Thymaridas of Paros[8] was a Pythagorean, who fell into difficulties after having been wealthy, collected a large sum of money, sailed to Paros, and got back for him his possesions.

---

7. A treatise *On the Hebdomad* is attributed to Prorus by Nicomachus of Gerasa, *ap.* Ps. Iambl. *Theol. Ar.* 57, De Falco. From section 127 above, we know that this story also goes back to what Dionysius told Aristoxenus.

8. Another story about Thymaridas, originally from Tarentum, is told at section 145 above, on the authority of Androcydes (who *may* be a fourth century source; see Burkert, *Lore and Science*, 167).

[240] πρέποντα τῆς φιλίας τεκμήρια· πολὺ δὲ τούτων θαυμασ-
ιώτερα ἦν τὰ περὶ τῆς κοινωνίας τῶν θείων ἀγαθῶν καὶ τὰ
περὶ τῆς τοῦ νοῦ ὁμονοίας καὶ τὰ περὶ τῆς θείας ψυχῆς παρ'
αὐτοῖς ἀφορισθέντα. παρήγγελλον γὰρ θαμὰ ἀλλήλοις μὴ
διασπᾶν τὸν ἐν ἑαυτοῖς θεόν. οὐκοῦν εἰς θεοκρασίαν τινὰ καὶ
τὴν πρὸς τὸν θεὸν ἕνωσιν καὶ τὴν τοῦ νοῦ κοινωνίαν καὶ τὴν
τῆς θείας ψυχῆς ἀπέβλεπεν αὐτοῖς ἡ πᾶσα τῆς φιλίας
σπουδὴ δι' ἔργων τε καὶ λόγων. τούτου δὲ οὐκ ἂν ἔχοι τις
εὑρεῖν ἄλλο βέλτιον, οὔτε ἐν λόγοις λεγόμενον οὔτε ἐν
ἐπιτηδεύμασι πραττόμενον· οἶμαι δ' ὅτι καὶ πάντα τῆς
φιλίας ἀγαθὰ ἐν αὐτῷ περιέχεται. διόπερ καὶ ἡμεῖς ὥσπερ ἐν
κεφαλαίῳ τούτῳ τὰ πάντα περιλαβόντες τῆς Πυθαγορικῆς
φιλίας πλεονεκτήματα παυόμεθα τοῦ πλείω περὶ αὐτῆς
λέγειν.

[240]   These, then, are noble and fitting proofs of their friendship.[9] Much more wonderful than these, however, were what they established about partnership in divine goods, and about unity of intellect and the divine soul. For they often
encouraged one another not to disperse the god within themselves. At any rate,
all their zeal for friendship, both in words and deeds, aimed at some kind of min-
gling[10] and union with God, and at communion with intellect[11] and with the divine soul. For no one could find anything better, either in words spoken or in ways
of life practiced, than this kind of friendship. For I think that all the goods of
friendship are embraced by it. Hence, having included all excellences of
Pythagorean friendship in this summation, as it were, we need say no more about
it.

---

9. This final passage seems much like a summary by Iamblichus himself.

10. This term, θεοκρασία, recurs only in Damascius' *Life of Isidore* (5). The τινά here may indicate that it is a coinage of Iamblichus.

11. Or perhaps "communion of minds."

[241] Ἐπεὶ δὲ κατὰ γένη τεταγμένως οὕτω διήλθομεν περὶ Πυθαγόρου τε καὶ τῶν Πυθαγορείων, ἴθι δὴ τὸ μετὰ τοῦτο καὶ τὰς σποράδην ἀφηγήσεις εἰωθυίας λέγεσθαι ⟨τεκμήρια⟩ ποιησώμεθα, ὅσαι οὐχ ὑποπίπτουσιν ὑπὸ τὴν προειρημένην τάξιν. λέγεται τοίνυν ὡς φωνῇ χρῆσθαι τῇ πατρῴᾳ ἑκάστοις παρήγγελλον, ὅσοι τῶν Ἑλλήνων προσῆλθον πρὸς τὴν κοινωνίαν ταύτην· τὸ γὰρ ξενίζειν οὐκ ἐδοκίμαζον. προσῆλθον δὲ καὶ ξένοι τῇ Πυθαγορείῳ αἱρέσει καὶ Μεσσαπίων καὶ Λευκανῶν καὶ Πευκετίων καὶ Ῥωμαίων. Μητρόδωρός τε ὁ Θύρσου ⟨ἀδελφός, τῆς⟩ τοῦ πατρὸς Ἐπιχάρμου καὶ τῆς ἐκείνου διδασκαλίας τὰ πλείονα πρὸς τὴν ἰατρικὴν μετενέγκας, ἐξηγούμενος τοὺς τοῦ πατρὸς λόγους πρὸς τὸν ἀδελφόν φησι τὸν Ἐπίχαρμον καὶ πρὸ τούτου τὸν Πυθαγόραν τῶν διαλέκτων ἀρίστην λαμβάνειν τὴν Δωρίδα, καθάπερ καὶ τὴν ἁρμονίαν τῆς μουσικῆς. καὶ τὴν μὲν Ἰάδα καὶ τὴν Αἰολίδα μετεσχηκέναι τῆς ἐπὶ χρώματος προσῳδίας, Ἀτθίδα δὲ κατακορέστερον μετεσχηκέναι τοῦ χρώματος, τὴν [242] δὲ Δώριον διάλεκτον ἐναρμόνιον εἶναι, συνεστηκυῖαν ἐκ τῶν φωναέντων γραμμάτων. τῇ δὲ Δωρικῇ διαλέκτῳ μαρτυρεῖν τὴν ἀρχαιότητα καὶ τὸν μῦθον. Νηρέα γὰρ γῆμαι Δωρίδα τὴν Ὠκεανοῦ, τούτῳ δὲ μυθεύεσθαι γενέσθαι τὰς πεντήκοντα θυγατέρας, ὧν εἶναι καὶ τὴν Ἀχιλλέως μητέρα. λέγειν δέ τινάς φησι Δευκαλίωνος τοῦ Προμηθέως καὶ Πύρρας τῆς Ἐπιμηθέως γενέσθαι Δῶρον, τοῦ δὲ Ἕλληνα, τοῦ δὲ Αἴολον. ἐν δὲ τοῖς Βαβυλωνίων ἀκούειν ἱεροῖς Ἕλληνα γεγονέναι Διός, τοῦ δὲ Δῶρον καὶ Ξοῦθον καὶ Αἴολον, αἷς ὑφηγήσεσιν ἀκολουθῆσαι καὶ αὐτὸν Ἡσίοδον. ὁποτέρως μὲν οὖν ἔχει, περὶ τῶν ἀρχαίων οὐκ εὐμαρὲς [243] δέχεσθαι τἀκριβὲς τοῖς νεωτέροις ἢ καταμαθεῖν, ὁμολογούμενον δὲ δι᾽ ἑκατέρας τῶν ἱστοριῶν συνάγεσθαι τὸ πρεσβυτάτην εἶναι τῶν διαλέκτων τὴν Δωρίδα, μετὰ δὲ

CHAPTER THIRTY-FOUR

Some miscellaneous stories of what was said and done either
by Pythagoras himself or by those who inherited
his philosophy, such as were not told in the
series of chapters about the virtues.

[241]   Thus far we have treated of Pythagoras and the Pythagoreans in orderly fashion, according to topics. After this, let us take into evidence the scattered reports which are customarily related, as many as do not fall under the previously stated arrangement.

It is said, then, that the Pythagoreans commanded all Hellenes who came into this fellowship to use their native dialect, for they did not approve of speaking foreign dialects.[1] And foreigners came to the Pythagorean school, Messapians and Leukanians, Picentines and Romans.[2] Metrodorus, brother of Thyrsus, who adapted[3] the greater part of the teaching of his father, Epicharmus, and of Pythagoras to medicine, explaining his father's doctrines to his brother, says that Epicharmus, and Pythagoras before him, believed Doric the best of dialects, just as the best musical harmony is Doric. Ionic and Aeolic partake of chromatic variation in pitch, and the Attic partakes more intensely of the chromatic, but the Doric dia-
[242] lect is enharmonic since it is organized by vowels.[4] The following myth testifies to the antiquity of the Doric dialect. For Nereus married Doris, daughter of Oceanus, and it is told that fifty daughters were born to him, of whom one was mother of Achilles. Metrodorus reports that some say Dorus was born from Deucalion, son of Prometheus, and Pyrrha, daughter of Epimetheus; from Dorus, Hellen, and from Hellen, Aeolus. In the shrines of Babylon he heard that Hellen was born from Zeus, and from Hellen were born Dorus and Xuthus and Aeolus, and this
[243] version even Hesiod himself follows.[5] Which of these stories, then, is correct, it is

---

1. By φωνῇ τῇ πατρῴᾳ is probably meant the dialect of the Italiote Pythagoreans (i.e. Doric), though this is ambiguously expressed. The context demands this interpretation, and Pythagorean treatises were invariably composed in Doric.

2. Just these foreigners are mentioned by Aristoxenus (quoted by Porph. *VP* 22 and D.L. 8. 14) as belonging to the school, so these reports may perhaps be attributed to him.

3. Precisely what was involved in this adaptation or "translation"? Perhaps since medical writings were normally in Ionic, transferral into that dialect, but some other kind of adaptation may be meant. On the connexion of Epicharmus with Pythagoreanism, see Burkert, *Lore and Science*, p. 289, n. 58, but he makes no mention of Metrodorus.

4. Presumably this refers to the broad *a*'s in Doric.

5. Fr. 7.1 Rzach; fr. 9 Merkelbach-West, from the *Catalogue of Women*.

ταύτην γενέσθαι τὴν Αἰολίδα, λαχοῦσαν ἀπὸ Αἰόλου τοὔνομα, τρίτην δὲ τὴν Ἀτθίδα, κληθεῖσαν ἀπὸ Ἀτθίδος τῆς
Κραναοῦ, τετάρτην δὲ τὴν Ἰάδα, λεγομένην ἀπὸ Ἴωνος τοῦ
Ξούθου καὶ Κρεούσης τῆς Ἐρεχθέως, τεθειμένην δὲ τρισὶ
γενεαῖς ὕστερον τῶν πρότερον κατὰ Θρᾷκας καὶ τὴν
Ὠρειθυίας ἁρπαγήν, ὡς οἱ πλείους τῶν ἱστορικῶν
ἀποφαίνουσι. κεχρῆσθαι δὲ τῇ Δωρικῇ διαλέκτῳ καὶ τὸν
Ὀρφέα, πρεσβύτατον ὄντα τῶν ποιητῶν. τῆς δὲ ἰατρικῆς
[244] μάλιστά φασιν αὐτοὺς ἀποδέχεσθαι τὸ διαιτητικὸν εἶδος καὶ
εἶναι ἀκριβεστάτους ἐν τούτῳ, καὶ πειρᾶσθαι πρῶτον μὲν
καταμανθάνειν σημεῖα συμμετρίας ποτῶν τε καὶ σίτων καὶ
ἀναπαύσεως, ἔπειτα περὶ αὐτῆς τῆς κατασκευῆς τῶν
προσφερομένων σχεδὸν πρώτους ἐπιχειρῆσαί τε πραγματεύεσθαι καὶ διορίζειν. ἅψασθαι δὲ καὶ καταπλασμάτων
ἐπὶ πλεῖον τοὺς Πυθαγορείους τῶν ἔμπροσθεν, τὰ δὲ περὶ
τὰς φαρμακείας ἧττον δοκιμάζειν, αὐτῶν δὲ τούτων ⟨τοῖς⟩
πρὸς τὰς ἑλκώσεις μάλιστα χρῆσθαι, τὰ δὲ περὶ τὰς τομάς τε
καὶ καύσεις ἥκιστα πάντων ἀποδέχεσθαι. χρῆσθαι δὲ καὶ ταῖς
ἐπῳδαῖς πρὸς ἔνια τῶν ἀρρωστημάτων. παραιτήσασθαι δὲ
λέγονται τοὺς τὰ μαθήματα καπηλεύοντας καὶ τὰς ψυχὰς ὡς
[245] πανδοχείου θύρας ἀνοίγοντας παντὶ τῷ προσιόντι τῶν
ἀνθρώπων, ἂν δὲ μηδ' οὕτως ὠνηταὶ εὑρεθῶσιν, αὐτοὺς
ἐπιχεομένους εἰς τὰς πόλεις καὶ συλλήβδην ἐργολαβοῦντας
τὰ γυμνάσια καὶ τοὺς νέους καὶ μισθὸν τῶν ἀτιμήτων
πράττοντας. αὐτὸν δὲ συνεπικρύπτεσθαι πολὺ τῶν
λεγομένων, ὅπως οἱ μὲν καθαρῶς παιδευόμενοι σαφῶς αὐτῶν
μεταλαμβάνωσιν, οἳ δ', ὥσπερ Ὅμηρός φησι τὸν
Τάνταλον, λυπῶνται παρόντων αὐτῶν ἐν μέσῳ τῶν
ἀκουσμάτων μηδὲν ἀπολαύοντες. λέγειν δ' αὐτοὺς οἶμαι καὶ
περὶ τοῦ μὴ μισθοῦ διδάσκειν τοὺς προσιόντας, οὓς καὶ
χείρους τῶν ἑρμογλύφων καὶ ἐπιδιφρίων τεχνιτῶν
ἀποφαίνουσι· τοὺς μὲν γὰρ ἐκδομένου τινὸς ἑρμῆν ζητεῖν εἰς
τὴν διάθεσιν τῆς μορφῆς ξύλον ἐπιτήδειον, τοὺς δὲ
προχείρως ἐκ πάσης φύσεως ἐργάζεσθαι τὴν ἀρετῆς ἐπι-
τήδευσιν. προνοεῖν δὲ δεῖν μᾶλλον λέγουσι φιλοσοφίας ἢ
[246] γονέων καὶ γεωργίας· τοὺς μὲν γὰρ γονέας καὶ τοὺς γεωργοὺς
αἰτίους εἶναι τοῦ ζῆν ἡμᾶς, τοὺς δὲ φιλοσόφους καὶ
παιδευτὰς ⟨τοῦ⟩ καὶ εὖ ζῆν καὶ φρονῆσαι, τὴν ὀρθὴν
οἰκονομίαν εὑρόντας. οὔτε δὲ λέγειν οὔτε συγγράφειν οὕτως

not easy, on account of their antiquity, for those of more recent times to understand or to learn precisely. Yet there is agreement that from each of these stories
it can be concluded that Doric is the oldest dialect. After this, the Aeolic dialect
came into being, having gotten this name from Aeolus. Third, the Attic dialect,
named after Atthis daughter of Cranaus. Fourth, Ionic, said to be from Ion, son
of Xuthus and Creusa, daughter of Erechtheus, and placed three generations later than the previous dialects, at the time of the Thracians and the seizure of Orei-
thyia, as most historians declare. Orpheus, oldest of poets, also used the Doric
dialect.

[244]   Of medicine[6] they say that they (the Pythagoreans) especially approved the
kind pertaining to diet, and in this they attained great precision, and first tried to
discover signs of due proportion in drinks, foods, and rest; therefore they were
more or less the first to attempt to treat systematically and to lay down rules about
the preparation of foods. The Pythagoreans used poultices more than their predecessors, but approved less of using drugs, and used these mostly for ulcerations;
they approved of surgery and cautery least of all. They also used incantations for
some illnesses.

[245]   They are said to have deprecated those who peddle learning, and who have
opened their souls, like doors of an inn, to every human entering; and who, if no
buyers thus be found, pour like a stream over the cities and, in short, make profit
out of gymnasia and youths, demanding a wage for things on which no price
should be put.[7] But he (Pythagoras) strove to conceal the meaning of much that
was said, in order that those who were educated on pure principles might clearly
share in it; but that the rest, as Homer says of Tantalus,[8] might be pained when
present in the midst of oral instructions and enjoy nothing.

I think the Pythagoreans also spoke about not teaching for pay anyone who
comes forward for instruction. Those who teach for pay they declared worse than
carvers of Herms, and craftsmen at their workbenches; for these, when someone
has contracted for a Herm, seek wood suitable for the representation of the
246] form.[9] But those teachers work rashly at the cultivation of virtue out of every temperament. They say one should give more regard to philosophy than to parents
and farming; for parents and farmers are responsible for our life, but philosophers and teachers are responsible for our living well and being wise, since they
have discovered the right management of affairs. He thought it proper neither to

6. This paragraph is repeated from sections 163-64 above, and probably derives from Aristoxenus.

7. A very Socratic/Platonic sentiment. Cf. *Prt.* 313 D, *Soph.* 231 D. The verb καπηλεύω ("peddle") is used in the *Protagoras* passage, the noun κάπηλος ("peddler") in the *Sophist.*

8. Cf. *Od.* 11, 582 ff.

9. A reference probably to the proverbial expression attributed by Apuleius, *Apol.* ch. 43, to
Pythagoras: "not out of every wood should one carve a Herm."

ἠξίου, ὡς πᾶσι τοῖς ἐπιτυχοῦσι κατάδηλα εἶναι τὰ νοήματα, ἀλλ' αὐτὸ δὴ τοῦτο πρῶτον διδάξαι λέγεται Πυθαγόρας τοὺς αὐτῷ προσφοιτῶντας, ὅπως ἀκρασίας ἁπάσης καθαρεύοντες ἐν ἐχερρημοσύνῃ φυλάττωσιν οὓς ἂν ἀκροάσωνται λόγους. τὸν γοῦν πρῶτον ἐκφάναντα τὴν τῆς συμμετρίας καὶ ἀσυμμετρίας φύσιν τοῖς ἀναξίοις μετέχειν τῶν λόγων οὕτως φασὶν ἀποστυγηθῆναι, ὡς μὴ μόνον ἐκ τῆς κοινῆς συνουσίας καὶ διαίτης ἐξορισθῆναι, ἀλλὰ καὶ τάφον αὐτοῦ κατασ-κευασθῆναι, ὡς δῆτα ἀποιχομένου ἐκ τοῦ μετ' ἀνθρώπων βίου τοῦ ποτε ἑταίρου γενομένου. οἳ δέ φασι καὶ τὸ [247] δαιμόνιον νεμεσῆσαι τοῖς ἐξώφορα τὰ Πυθαγόρου ποιησ-αμένοις. φθαρῆναι γὰρ ὡς ἀσεβήσαντα ἐν θαλάσσῃ τὸν δηλώσαντα τὴν τοῦ εἰκοσαγώνου σύστασιν· τοῦτο δ' ἦν δωδεκάεδρον, ἓν τῶν πέντε λεγομένων στερεῶν σχημάτων, εἰς σφαῖραν ἐκτείνεσθαι. ἔνιοι δὲ τὸν περὶ τῆς ἀλογίας καὶ τῆς ἀσυμμετρίας ἐξειπόντα τοῦτο παθεῖν ἔλεξαν. ἰδιότροπός τε μὴν καὶ συμβολικὴ ἦν ἡ σύμπασα Πυθαγόρειος ἀγωγή, [ἐν] αἰνίγμασί τισι καὶ γρίφοις ἔκ γε τῶν ἀποφθεγμάτων ἐοικυῖα διὰ τὸ ἀρχαΐζειν τῷ χαρακτῆρι, καθάπερ καὶ τὰ θεῖα τῷ ὄντι καὶ πυθόχρηστα λόγια δυσπαρακολούθητά πως καὶ δυσερμήνευτα φαίνεται τοῖς ἐκ παρέργου χρηστηριαζομένοις. τοσαῦτα ἄν τις καὶ ἀπὸ τῶν σποράδην λεγομένων τεκμήρια ἂν παράθοιτο περὶ Πυθαγόρου τε καὶ τῶν Πυθαγορείων.

speak nor to compose a treatise so that the thoughts be quite obvious to all ordinary persons. And Pythagoras is said to have taught first this very thing to those associating with him: that, free from all incontinence of will, they should guard in silence whatever discourse they heard. At any rate, he who first revealed the nature of commensurability and incommensurability to those unworthy to share in these doctrines was hated so violently, they say, that he was not only banished from their common association and way of life, but a tomb was even constructed for him. As one who had once been their companion, he had truly departed from life with human beings.

[247]   Others say that even the divine power was indignant with those who published Pythagoras' doctrines. For that man perished at sea as an offender against the gods who revealed the construction of a figure having twenty angles: this involved inscribing the dodecahedron, one of the five figures called "solid", within a sphere.[10] Some, however, maintained that the one who broke the news about the irrational and incommensurability suffered this fate.

Truly distinctive and enshrined in *symbola* was the entire Pythagorean system of education, resembling riddles and conundrums because of its apothegmatic and old-fashioned character, just as oracles truly divine and delivered by the Pythian god appear somehow hard to understand or follow for those consulting an oracle in a superficial manner.

So many sure pieces of evidence, on the basis of miscellaneous reports, might one provide about Pythagoras and the Pythagoreans.

---

10. Presumably Hippasus. See sections 75 and 88 above, and Burkert, *Lore and Science* 207 and 459. But Iamblichus and Clement have the letter (in section 75) addressed to a certain Hipparchus.

[248] Ἦσαν δέ τινες, οἳ προσεπολέμουν τοῖς ἀνδράσι τούτοις καὶ ἐπανέστησαν αὐτοῖς. ὅτι μὲν οὖν ἀπόντος Πυθαγόρου ἐγένετο ἡ ἐπιβουλή, πάντες συνομολογοῦσι, διαφέρονται δὲ περὶ τῆς τότε ἀποδημίας, οἳ μὲν πρὸς Φερεκύδην τὸν Σύριον, οἳ δὲ εἰς Μεταπόντιον λέγοντες ἀποδεδημηκέναι τὸν Πυθαγόραν. αἱ δὲ αἰτίαι τῆς ἐπιβουλῆς πλείονες λέγονται, μία μὲν ὑπὸ τῶν Κυλωνείων λεγομένων ἀνδρῶν τοιάδε γενομένη. Κύλων, ἀνὴρ Κροτωνιάτης, γένει μὲν καὶ δόξῃ καὶ πλούτῳ πρωτεύων τῶν πολιτῶν, ἄλλως δὲ χαλεπός τις καὶ βίαιος καὶ θορυβώδης καὶ τυραννικὸς τὸ ἦθος, πᾶσαν προθυμίαν παρασχόμενος πρὸς τὸ κοινωνῆσαι τοῦ Πυθαγορείου βίου καὶ προσελθὼν πρὸς αὐτὸν τὸν Πυθαγόραν ἤδη πρεσβύτην ὄντα, ἀπεδοκιμάσθη διὰ τὰς [249] προειρημένας αἰτίας. γενομένου δὲ τούτου πόλεμον ἰσχυρὸν ἤρατο καὶ αὐτὸς καὶ οἱ φίλοι αὐτοῦ πρὸς αὐτόν τε τὸν Πυθαγόραν καὶ τοὺς ἑταίρους, καὶ οὕτω σφοδρά τις ἐγένετο καὶ ἄκρατος ἡ φιλοτιμία αὐτοῦ τε τοῦ Κύλωνος καὶ τῶν μετ' ἐκείνου τεταγμένων, ὥστε διατεῖναι μέχρι τῶν τελευταίων Πυθαγορείων. ὁ μὲν οὖν Πυθαγόρας διὰ ταύτην τὴν αἰτίαν ἀπῆλθεν εἰς τὸ Μεταπόντιον, κἀκεῖ λέγεται καταστρέψαι τὸν βίον· οἱ δὲ Κυλώνειοι λεγόμενοι διετέλουν πρὸς Πυθαγορείους στασιάζοντες καὶ πᾶσαν ἐνδεικνύμενοι δυσμένειαν. ἀλλ' ὅμως ἐπεκράτει μέχρι τινὸς ἡ τῶν Πυθαγορείων καλοκαγαθία καὶ ἡ τῶν πόλεων αὐτῶν βούλησις, ὥστε ὑπ' ἐκείνων οἰκονομεῖσθαι βούλεσθαι τὰ περὶ τὰς πολιτείας. τέλος δὲ εἰς τοσοῦτον ἐπεβούλευσαν τοῖς ἀνδράσιν, ὥστε ἐν τῇ Μίλωνος οἰκίᾳ ἐν Κρότωνι συνεδρευόντων τῶν Πυθαγορείων καὶ βουλευομένων περὶ πολιτικῶν πραγμάτων ὑφάψαντες τὴν οἰκίαν κατέκαυσαν τοὺς ἄνδρας πλὴν δυεῖν, Ἀρχίππου τε καὶ Λύσιδος· οὗτοι δὲ νεώτατοι [250] ὄντες καὶ εὐρωστότατοι διεξεπαίσαντο ἔξω πως. γενομένου δὲ τούτου καὶ λόγον οὐδένα ποιησαμένων τῶν πόλεων περὶ τοῦ συμβάντος πάθους ἐπαύσαντο τῆς ἐπιμελείας οἱ Πυθαγόρειοι. συνέβη δὲ τοῦτο δι' ἀμφοτέρας τὰς αἰτίας, διά τε τὴν ὀλιγωρίαν τῶν πόλεων (τοῦ τοιούτου γὰρ καὶ τηλικούτου γενομένου πάθους οὐδεμίαν ἐπιστροφὴν ἐποιήσαντο), διά τε τὴν ἀπώλειαν τῶν ἡγεμονικωτάτων ἀνδρῶν. τῶν δὲ δύο τῶν περισωθέντων, ἀμφοτέρων Ταραντίνων ὄντων, ὁ μὲν Ἄρχιππος ἀνεχώρησεν εἰς Τάραντα, ὁ δὲ Λῦσις μισήσας τὴν ὀλιγωρίαν ἀπῆρεν εἰς τὴν Ἑλλάδα καὶ ἐν

CHAPTER THIRTY-FIVE

What the uprising was that took place against the Pythagoreans,
and where Pythagoras was at the time, and for what reasons
those tyrannical and sinful men rose up against them.

[248]   But there were some who fought against these men and rose up against them. All are in agreement that the plot took place in Pythagoras' absence, but there are differences about where he had gone at that time. For some say Pythagoras had gone to visit Pherecydes of Syros, others that he had gone to Metapontium. Further, many causes of the plot are reported. According to one account, the men called Cylonians were responsible, as follows:[1] Cylon, a Crotoniate, first among the citizens in family, reputation, and wealth, but otherwise ill-tempered, violent, turbulent, and despotic in character, showed great enthusiasm to share in the Pythagorean way of life, and approached Pythagoras, who was now an old man.

[249] But he was rejected as unfit for the aforementioned reasons. When this happened, both he and his friends began a violent struggle against Pythagoras and his disciples, and so excessive and intemperate was the ambitious rivalry of Cylon himself and those with him, that it extended to the very last Pythagoreans. Pythagoras, then, for this reason, departed to Metapontium, and there is said to have died. But those called Cylonians continued to quarrel with the Pythagoreans, and to show total enmity. Nevertheless, for some time the nobility of the Pythagoreans prevailed and the resolve of the cities themselves, so that they were willing to have their political affairs managed by them. Finally, however, they (the Cylonians) plotted against these men so that while the Pythagoreans were sitting in council in Milo's house in Croton and deliberating about civic affairs, they set fire to the house from below, burning all the men except two, Archippus and Lysis;[2] these,

[250] the youngest and strongest, somehow broke out. But when this happened and the cities paid no attention to the calamity which had occurred, the Pythagoreans

---

1. The chronology of this narrative is notoriously confused, and the confusion may go back to Aristoxenus, who is the source here (cf. below, section 251). Cylon seems, in fact, to date to 450 B.C., when the Pythagorean oligarchy in Croton was overthrown, rather than to ca. 510 B.C., when it was instituted. By Aristoxenus' time, the telescoping of these events seems already to have taken place. Cf. D.L. 8. 39, where the story is even more confused, and Plutarch, *De gen. Socr.* 583 A-C, where the conflagration is placed in Metapontium, and Philolaus and Lysis (rather than Archippus and Lysis) are given as the two youngest who survived. Olympiodorus, however, gives (*In Phaed.* 9,16, Norvin) the two survivors as Hipparchus and Lysis.

2. Since Lysis emigrated to Thebes, to become the teacher of Epaminondas (see below), this precludes a date of much before 450 B.C. for this event.

243

Ἀχαΐᾳ διέτριβε τῇ Πελοποννησιακῇ, ἔπειτα εἰς Θήβας μετῳκίσατο σπουδῆς τινος γενομένης· οὗπερ ἐγένετο Ἐπαμεινώνδας ἀκροατὴς καὶ πατέρα τὸν Λῦσιν ἐκάλεσεν. ὧδε καὶ τὸν βίον κατέστρεψεν. οἱ δὲ λοιποὶ τῶν Πυθαγορείων ἀπέστησαν τῆς Ἰταλίας πλὴν Ἀρχύτου τοῦ Ταραντίνου· ἀθροισθέντες δὲ εἰς τὸ Ῥήγιον ἐκεῖ διέτριβον μετ' ἀλλήλων. προϊόντος δὲ τοῦ χρόνου καὶ τῶν [251] πολιτευμάτων ἐπὶ τὸ χεῖρον προβαινόντων *** ἦσαν δὲ οἱ σπουδαιότατοι Φάντων τε καὶ Ἐχεκράτης καὶ Πολύμναστος καὶ Διοκλῆς Φλιάσιοι, Ξενόφιλος δὲ Χαλκιδεὺς τῶν ἀπὸ Θρᾴκης Χαλκιδέων. ἐφύλαξαν μὲν οὖν τὰ ἐξ ἀρχῆς ἤθη καὶ τὰ μαθήματα, καίτοι ἐκλειπούσης τῆς αἱρέσεως, ἕως εὐγενῶς ἠφανίσθησαν.

ταῦτα μὲν οὖν Ἀριστόξενος διηγεῖται· Νικόμαχος δὲ τὰ μὲν ἄλλα συνομολογεῖ τούτοις, παρὰ δὲ τὴν ἀποδημίαν Πυθαγόρου φησὶ γεγονέναι τὴν ἐπιβουλὴν ταύτην. ὡς γὰρ Φερεκύδη τὸν Σύριον, διδάσκαλον αὐτοῦ γενόμενον, εἰς [252] Δῆλον ἐπορεύθη, νοσοκομήσων τε αὐτὸν περιπετῆ γενόμενον τῷ ἱστορουμένῳ τῆς φθειριάσεως πάθει καὶ κηδεύσων. τότε δὴ οὖν οἱ ἀπογνωσθέντες ὑπ' αὐτῶν καὶ στηλιτευθέντες ἐπέθεντο αὐτοῖς καὶ πάντας πανταχῇ ἐνέπρησαν, αὐτοί τε ὑπὸ τῶν Ἰταλιωτῶν κατελεύσθησαν ἐπὶ τούτῳ καὶ ἐξερρίφησαν ἄταφοι. τότε δὴ οὖν συνεπιλιπεῖν συνέβαινε τὴν ἐπιστήμην τοῖς ἐπισταμένοις, ἅτε δὴ ἄρρητον ὑπ' αὐτῶν ἐν τοῖς στήθεσι διαφυλαχθεῖσαν μέχρι τότε, τὰ δὲ δυσσύνετα μόνα καὶ ἀδιάπτυκτα παρὰ τοῖς ἔξω διαμνημονεύεσθαι συνέβη, πλὴν ὀλίγων πάνυ, ὅσα τινὲς ἐν ἀλλοδημίαις τότε τυχόντες διέσωσαν ζώπυρα ἄττα πάνυ ἀμυδρὰ καὶ δυσθήρατα. καὶ οὗτοι γὰρ μονωθέντες καὶ ἐπὶ τῷ συμβάντι [253] οὐ μετρίως ἀθυμήσαντες διεσπάρησαν μὲν ἄλλος ἀλλαχῇ, καὶ οὐκέτι κοινωνεῖν ἀνθρώπῳ τινὶ λόγου τὸ παράπαν ὑπέμενον, μονάζοντες δ' ἐν ταῖς ἐρημίαις, ὅπου ἂν τύχῃ, καὶ κατάκλειστοι τὰ πολλὰ τὴν αὐτὸς ἑαυτοῦ ἕκαστος συνουσίαν ἀντὶ παντὸς ἠσμένιζον. διευλαβούμενοι δὲ μὴ παντελῶς ἐξ ἀνθρώπων ἀπόληται τὸ φιλοσοφίας ὄνομα καὶ θεοῖς αὐτοὶ διὰ τοῦτο ἀπεχθάνωνται, διολέσαντες ἄρδην τὸ τηλικοῦτον αὐτῶν δῶρον, ὑπομνήματά τινα κεφαλαιώδη καὶ συμβολικὰ συνταξάμενοι τά τε τῶν πρεσβυτέρων συγγράμματα καὶ ὧν διεμέμνηντο συναλίσαντες κατέλιπον ἕκαστος οὗπερ

ceased exercising their public charge. This happened for two reasons: because of the cities' negligence (for they paid no attention when such a great calamity took place), and because of the destruction of the men most fit to rule.

Of the two who escaped with their lives, both Tarentines, Archippus went back to Tarentum; Lysis, hating the contempt that had been shown them, departed for Hellas, and settled first in Peloponnesian Achaea, and then, when some enthusiasm for him was shown, moved to Thebes, where Epaminondas became his disciple and called Lysis his "father." And so he spent the rest of his life there.

[251] The rest of the Pythagoreans, except Archytas of Tarentum, left Italy. They gathered together in Rhegium, and maintained their society there. As time went on, and the governments steadily deteriorated . . . [3] the most important were Phanton, Echecrates, Polymnastus and Diocles the Phliasians, and Xenophilus the Chalcidean from the Chalcideans of Thrace. They, then, preserved their original customs and instructions, while their school dwindled, until, maintaining their nobility, they disappeared.

[252] This, then, is the account of Aristoxenus. Nicomachus[4] agrees with this in general, but says that the plot took place during the absence of Pythagoras. For he had journeyed to Delos to nurse Pherecydes of Syros, his teacher, who was afflicted by the disease called *morbus pedicularis*, and then to bury him. At that time, then, those who had been rejected by the Pythagoreans, and held up to public scorn,[5] attacked them, and burned them all everywhere. They themselves, in turn, were stoned to death by the Italians and cast out unburied. Then knowledge faded out together with those who knew, since it had been guarded closely until then in their hearts, never divulged, and only things hard to understand and unexplained were remembered by those outside the school: except for the very little which some Pythagoreans then in foreign lands preserved, some sparks very dim and hard to catch.

[253] These, being isolated and wholly disheartened at what had happened, scattered here and there, and absolutely could no longer bear to share conversation with any human being. Alone in solitary places, wherever they happened to be, and shut away for the most part, each took pleasure in his own company in preference to that of anyone else. And taking heed that the name of their philosophy not wholly perish among human beings and that they themselves consequently be hated by the gods, for destroying completely so great a gift as theirs, they put to-

---

3. A lacuna here, in which, presumably, it was stated that many of them emigrated to the mainland of Greece. A list then follows of their most distinguished disciples.

4. It is notable that for the first time in his work, Iamblichus explicitly sets out accounts of what seem to be his three principal sources: Aristoxenus, Nicomachus, and Apollonius (for the latter, see 254 below).

5. The Pythagorean custom of raising a funeral monument to those who left, or who were expelled from the community, is probably meant here.

ἐτύγχανε τελευτῶν, ἐπισκήψαντες υἱοῖς ἢ θυγατράσιν ἢ
γυναιξὶ μηδενὶ δόμεναι τῶν ἐκτὸς τᾶς οἰκίας. αἳ δὲ μέχρι
παμπόλλου χρόνου τοῦτο διετήρησαν, ἐκ διαδοχῆς τὴν
αὐτὴν ταύτην ἐντολὴν ἐπιστέλλουσαι τοῖς ἐπιγόνοις.

[254] ἐπεὶ δὲ καὶ Ἀπολλώνιος περὶ τῶν αὐτῶν ἔστιν ὅπου
διαφωνεῖ, πολλὰ δὲ καὶ προστίθησι τῶν μὴ εἰρημένων παρὰ
τούτοις, φέρε δὴ καὶ τὴν τούτου παραθώμεθα διήγησιν περὶ
τῆς εἰς τοὺς Πυθαγορείους ἐπιβουλῆς. λέγει τοίνυν ὡς
ἐκείνῳ παρηκολούθει μὲν εὐθὺς ἐκ παίδων ὁ φθόνος παρὰ
τῶν ἄλλων. οἱ γὰρ ἄνθρωποι, μέχρι μὲν διελέγετο πᾶσι τοῖς
προσιοῦσι Πυθαγόρας, ἡδέως εἶχον, ἐπεὶ δὲ μόνοις
ἐνετύγχανε τοῖς μαθηταῖς, ἠλαττοῦτο. καὶ τοῦ μὲν ἔξωθεν
ἥκοντος συνεχώρουν ἡττᾶσθαι, τοῖς δ' ἐγχωρίοις πλεῖον
φέρεσθαι δοκοῦσιν ἤχθοντο, καὶ καθ' αὑτῶν ὑπελάμβανον
γίνεσθαι τὴν σύνοδον. ἔπειτα καὶ τῶν νεανίσκων ὄντων ἐκ
τῶν ἐν τοῖς ἀξιώμασι καὶ ταῖς οὐσίαις προεχόντων,
συνέβαινε προαγούσης τῆς ἡλικίας μὴ μόνον αὐτοὺς ἐν τοῖς
ἰδίοις βίοις πρωτεύειν, ἀλλὰ τὸ κοινῇ τὴν πόλιν οἰκονομεῖν,
μεγάλην μὲν ἑταιρείαν συναγηοχόσιν (ἦσαν ⟨γὰρ⟩ ὑπὲρ
τριακοσίους), μικρὸν δὲ μέρος τῆς πόλεως οὖσι, τῆς οὐκ ἐν
τοῖς αὐτοῖς ἔθεσιν οὐδ' ἐπιτηδεύμασιν ἐκείνοις πολιτε-
νομένης. οὐ μὴν ἀλλὰ μέχρι μὲν οὖν τὴν ὑπάρχουσαν χώραν
[255] ἐκέκτηντο καὶ Πυθαγόρας ἐπεδήμει, διέμενεν ἡ μετὰ τὸν
συνοικισμὸν κεχρονισμένη κατάστασις, δυσαρεστουμένη καὶ
ζητοῦσα καιρὸν εὔρασθαι μεταβολῆς. ἐπεὶ δὲ Σύβαριν
ἐχειρώσαντο, κἀκεῖνος ἀπῆλθε, καὶ τὴν δορίκτητον
διωκήσαντο μὴ κατακληρουχηθῆναι κατὰ τὴν ἐπιθυμίαν τῶν
πολλῶν, ἐξερράγη τὸ σιωπώμενον μῖσος, καὶ διέστη πρὸς
αὐτοὺς τὸ πλῆθος. ἡγεμόνες δὲ ἐγένοντο τῆς διαφορᾶς οἱ ταῖς
συγγενείαις ⟨καὶ⟩ ταῖς οἰκειότησιν ἐγγύτατα καθεστηκότες
τῶν Πυθαγορείων. αἴτιον δ' ἦν, ⟨ὅτι⟩ τὰ μὲν πολλὰ αὐτοὺς
ἐλύπει τῶν πραττομένων, ὥσπερ καὶ τοὺς τυχόντας, ἐφ'
ὅσον ἰδιασμὸν εἶχε παρὰ τοὺς ἄλλους, ἐν δὲ τοῖς μεγίστοις
καθ' αὑτῶν μόνον ἐνόμιζον εἶναι τὴν ἀτιμίαν. ἐπὶ μὲν γὰρ
τῷ μηδένα τῶν Πυθαγορείων ὀνομάζειν Πυθαγόραν, ἀλλὰ
ζῶντα μέν, ὁπότε βούλοιντο δηλῶσαι, καλεῖν αὐτὸν θεῖον,
ἐπεὶ δὲ ἐτελεύτησεν, ἐκεῖνον τὸν ἄνδρα, καθάπερ Ὅμηρος
ἀποφαίνει τὸν Εὔμαιον ὑπὲρ Ὀδυσσέως μεμνημένον·

gether some works containing their teachings in summary and symbolic form. And they collected treatises of the older Pythagoreans and such sayings of theirs as they remembered. Each left these behind where he died, after strictly charging sons, daughters, or wives to give them to no one outside the household.[6] They kept this charge faithfully for a very long time, passing on in succession the same command to their offspring.

[254]   But since Apollonius differs in some places about the same events,[7] and adds many things not said by these authorities, let us also give his account of the plot against the Pythagoreans.[8] He says, accordingly, that immediately from childhood, the envy of others closely followed the Pythagoreans. For, so long as Pythagoras discoursed with all comers, men were pleased; but when he consorted with his disciples alone, he lost esteem. And they (sc. the Crotoniates) were prepared to give way to one coming from outside, but they were annoyed when natives of the land laid claim to precedence, and they assumed that the association was directed against them. Further, it also happened that, since the young men concerned were sons of those who were eminent in honors and possessions, as they advanced in age, they not only became pre-eminent in their private lives, but also in publicly managing the city: they formed a large political club (for they were more than three hundred); but they were still only a small part of the city, which was not governed by their customs and ways of living.

[255]   However, so long as they (the Crotoniates) possessed only their own land and Pythagoras remained among them, the constitution, continuing from the foundation of the city, stood firm, though there was displeasure with it, and opportunity to find change was sought. But when they conquered Sybaris,[9] and that one (Pythagoras) departed, and they (the Pythagoreans) administered the captured land, but did not divide it by lot according to the desire of the multitude, the people's silent hatred broke out, and they formed a faction against them. And those who stood closest to the Pythagoreans in ties of kinship and friendship became leaders of the dissension. The cause was this: many of the things done by them (the Pythagoreans) annoyed them (the leaders), as indeed they did the people as a whole, in so far as their way of life had something peculiar in it when compared with that of others. And in most important matters they believed that the loss of privileges was directed only against themselves. For instance, no Pythagorean

---

6. This is a close paraphrase of the end of the *Letter to Lysis* (p. 603, 5 Hercher, 114 Thesleff, *Pythagorean Texts*), even down to the archaic form δόμεναι.

7. Probably Apollonius of Tyana, who may have written extensively on Pythagoras, but of whose works little survives, See Lévy, *Récherches*, 104 ff. for a reasonable account of Apollonius as one of Iamblichus' main sources.

8. Read ἐκείνοις, with the ms. Kuster's ἐκείνῳ is misguided.

9. This is dated to 510 B.C. In general, Apollonius' account seems superior in accuracy to the other two (apart from the notion that these events occurred in Pythagoras' lifetime).

τὸν μὲν ἐγών, ὦ ξεῖνε, καὶ οὐ παρεόντ᾽ ὀνομάζειν
αἰδέομαι· πέρι γάρ μ᾽ ἐφίλει καὶ ἐκήδετο λίην,

[256] ὁμοτρόπως δὲ μηδ᾽ ἐκ τῆς κλίνης ἀνίστασθαι ὕστερον ἢ τὸν
ἥλιον ἀνίσχειν, μηδὲ δακτύλιον ἔχοντα θεοῦ σημεῖον φορεῖν,
ἀλλὰ τὸν μὲν παρατηρεῖν ὅπως ἀνιόντα προσεύξωνται, τὸν
δὲ μὴ περιτίθεσθαι, φυλαττομένους μὴ προσενέγκωσι πρὸς
ἐκφορὰν ἤ τινα τόπον οὐ καθαρόν, ὁμοίως δὲ μηδ᾽
ἀπροβούλευτον μηδ᾽ ἀνυπεύθυνον μηδὲν ποιεῖν, ἀλλὰ πρωὶ
μὲν προχειρίζεσθαι τί πρακτέον, εἰς δὲ τὴν νύκτα
ἀναλογίζεσθαι τί διῳκήκασιν, ἅμα τῷ σκοπεῖσθαι καὶ τὴν
μνήμην γυμναζομένους, παραπλησίως δ᾽, εἴ τις τῶν κοινω-
νούντων τῆς διατριβῆς ἀπαντῆσαι κελεύσειεν εἴς τινα
τόπον, ἐν ἐκείνῳ περιμένειν, ἕως ἔλθοι, δι᾽ ἡμέρας καὶ
νυκτός, πάλιν ἐν τούτῳ τῶν Πυθαγορείων συνεθιζόντων

[257] μεμνῆσθαι τὸ ῥηθὲν καὶ μηδὲν εἰκῆ λέγειν, ὅλως δ᾽ ἄχρι τῆς
τελευτῆς εἶναί τι προστεταγμένον· κατὰ τὸν ὕστατον ⟨γὰρ⟩
καιρὸν παρήγγελλε μὴ βλασφημεῖν, ἀλλ᾽ ὥσπερ ἐν ταῖς
ἀναγωγαῖς οἰωνίζεσθαι μετὰ τῆς εὐφημίας, ἥνπερ ἐποιοῦντο
διωθούμενοι τὸν Ἀδρίαν. τὰ μὲν τοιαῦτα, καθάπερ
προεῖπον, ἐπὶ τοσοῦτον ἐλύπει κοινῶς ἅπαντας, ἐφ᾽ ὅσον
ἔγνωσαν ἰδιάζοντας ἐν αὑτοῖς τοὺς συμπεπαιδευμένους. ἐπὶ
δὲ τῷ μόνοις τοῖς Πυθαγορείοις τὴν δεξιὰν ἐμβάλλειν, ἑτέρῳ
δὲ μηδενὶ τῶν οἰκείων πλὴν τῶν γονέων, καὶ τῷ τὰς οὐσίας
ἀλλήλων μὲν παρέχειν κοινάς, πρὸς ἐκείνους δὲ ἐξηλ-
λοτριωμένας, χαλεπώτερον καὶ βαρύτερον ἔφερον οἱ
συγγενεῖς. ἀρχόντων δὲ τούτων τῆς διαστάσεως ἑτοίμως οἱ
λοιποὶ προσέπιπτον εἰς τὴν ἔχθραν. καὶ λεγόντων ἐξ αὐτῶν
τῶν χιλίων Ἱππάσου καὶ Διοδώρου καὶ Θεάγους ὑπὲρ τοῦ
πάντας κοινωνεῖν τῶν ἀρχῶν καὶ τῆς ἐκκλησίας καὶ διδόναι
τὰς εὐθύνας τοὺς ἄρχοντας ἐν τοῖς ἐκ πάντων λαχοῦσιν,
ἐναντιουμένων δὲ τῶν Πυθαγορείων Ἀλκιμάχου καὶ Δει-
νάρχου καὶ Μέτωνος καὶ Δημοκήδους καὶ διακωλυόντων τὴν

[258] πάτριον πολιτείαν μὴ καταλύειν, ἐκράτησαν οἱ τῷ πλήθει
συνηγοροῦντες. μετὰ δὲ ταῦτα συνιόντων τῶν πολλῶν
διελόμενοι τὰς δημηγορίας κατηγόρουν τῶν αὐτῶν ἐκ τῶν
ῥητόρων Κύλων καὶ Νίνων. ἦν δ᾽ ὃ μὲν ἐκ τῶν εὐπόρων, ὃ
δὲ ἐκ τῶν δημοτικῶν. τοιούτων δὲ λόγων, μακροτέρων δὲ
παρὰ τοῦ Κύλωνος ῥηθέντων ἐπῆγεν ἅτερος, προσποι-

called Pythagoras by his name, but while alive, whenever they wished to mention him, they called him "the divine one" and when he died, they called him "that man,"[10] exactly as Homer shows Eumaeus making mention of Odysseus:

> that one, O stranger, I feel ashamed to name
> since he is not present; for he loved me
> greatly and cared for me exceedingly.[11]

[256]   In the same manner, they neither arose from their bed later than the sun's rising, nor wore a seal-ring having a god's image, but took care that they reverenced the sun's rising, and did not put on a ring (with a god's image), to guard against wearing it at a burial or in some impure place; likewise, not to do anything unpremeditated or that will not bear investigation, but early in the day, to determine what must be done; and at night, to reckon up what they had managed, at the same time, examining their conduct and exercising their memory; similarly, if someone sharing in their way of life commanded them to meet at a certain place,[12] they remained day and night in that place until he came; in this again, the Pythagoreans were accustomed to remember what was said to them, and to ut-
[257] ter nothing at random. In short, there were prescriptions lasting until death; for in this last moment, he ordered them not to blaspheme, but, as in departing by sea, to seek to obtain a good omen by restraining one's speech, as those sailing across the Adriatic do.

    Such things, as I said before, annoyed all alike, in so far as they perceived that those who had been educated in common were setting themselves apart. But their relatives were especially indignant because the Pythagoreans gave the right hand as a pledge of good faith only to Pythagoreans, and to no other relatives except parents; also because they offered their possessions in common to one another, but excluded their relatives. When these started the dissension, the rest readily fell in with their enmity. And when, from the council of the Thousand, Hippasus, Diodorus, and Theages spoke in behalf of all citizens having a share in the political offices and in the assembly, and of having public officials give accounts of their conduct to those who had been elected by lot from all citizens, the Pythagoreans Alcimachus, Deinarchus, Meton and Democedes opposed this proposal and sought to prevent the inherited constitution from being abolished. Those who
258] were champions of the common people prevailed. Thereupon, when the people assembled, the politicians Cylon and Ninon, apportioning between themselves the thrust of their speeches, launched an attack on the Pythagoreans. The former of these was from the wealthy class, the latter from the ordinary folk. When their

---

10. See section 88.
11. *Od.* 14.145 f.
12. Cf. the story of Lysis and Euryphamus above in section 185.

ούμενος μὲν ἐζητηκέναι τὰ τῶν Πυθαγορείων ἀπόρρητα,
πεπλακὼς δὲ καὶ γεγραφὼς ἐξ ὧν μάλιστα αὐτοὺς ἤμελλε
διαβάλλειν, καὶ δοὺς τῷ γραμματεῖ βιβλίον ἐκέλευσεν
[259] ἀναγιγνώσκειν. ἦν δ᾽ αὐτῷ ἐπιγραφὴ μὲν "λόγος ἱερός", ὁ δὲ
τύπος τοιοῦτος τῶν γεγραμμένων. τοὺς φίλους ὥσπερ τοὺς
θεοὺς σέβεσθαι, τοὺς δ᾽ ἄλλους ὥσπερ τὰ θηρία χειροῦσθαι.
τὴν αὐτὴν ταύτην γνώμην ὑπὲρ Πυθαγόρου μεμνημένους ἐν
μέτρῳ τοὺς μαθητὰς λέγειν·

τοὺς μὲν ἑταίρους ἦγεν ἴσον μακάρεσσι θεοῖσι,
τοὺς δ᾽ ἄλλους ἡγεῖτ᾽ οὔτ᾽ ἐν λόγῳ οὔτ᾽ ἐν ἀριθμῷ.

[260] τὸν Ὅμηρον μάλιστ᾽ ἐπαινεῖν ἐν οἷς εἴρηκε ποιμένα λαῶν·
ἐμφανίσκειν γὰρ βοσκήματα τοὺς ἄλλους ὄντας, ὀλιγαρχι-
κὸν ὄντα. τοῖς κυάμοις πολεμεῖν ὡς ἀρχηγοῖς γεγονόσι τοῦ
κλήρου καὶ τοῦ καθιστάναι τοὺς λαχόντας ἐπὶ τὰς
ἐπιμελείας. τυραννίδος ὀρέγεσθαι παρακαλοῦντας κρεῖττον
εἶναι φάσκειν γενέσθαι μίαν ἡμέραν ταῦρον ἢ πάντα τὸν
αἰῶνα βοῦν. ἐπαινεῖν τὰ τῶν ἄλλων νόμιμα, κελεύειν δὲ
χρῆσθαι τοῖς ὑφ᾽ αὑτῶν ἐγνωσμένοις. καθάπαξ τὴν φιλοσοφίαν αὐτῶν συνωμοσίαν ἀπέφαινε κατὰ τῶν πολλῶν καὶ
παρεκάλει μηδὲ τὴν φωνὴν ἀνέχεσθαι συμβουλευόντων,
ἀλλ᾽ ἐνθυμεῖσθαι διότι τὸ παράπαν οὐδ᾽ ἂν συνῆλθον εἰς τὴν
ἐκκλησίαν, εἰ τοὺς χιλίους ἔπεισαν ἐκεῖνοι κυρῶσαι τὴν
συμβουλήν. ὥστε τοῖς κατὰ τὴν ἐκείνων δύναμιν
κεκωλυμένοις τῶν ἄλλων ἀκούειν οὐ προσήκειν ἐᾶν αὐτοὺς
λέγειν, ἀλλὰ τὴν δεξιὰν τὴν ὑπ᾽ αὐτῶν ἀποδεδοκιμασμένην
πολεμίαν ἐκείνοις ἔχειν, ὅταν τὰς γνώμας χειροτονῶσιν ἢ
τὴν ψῆφον λάβωσιν, αἰσχρὸν εἶναι νομίζοντας, τοὺς
τριάκοντα μυριάδων περὶ τὸν Τετράεντα ποταμὸν περι-
γενομένους ὑπὸ τοῦ χιλιοστοῦ μέρους ἐκείνων ἐν αὐτῇ τῇ
[261] πόλει φανῆναι κατεστασιασμένους. τὸ δ᾽ ὅλον οὕτω τῇ
διαβολῇ τοὺς ἀκούοντας ἐξηγρίωσεν, ὥστε μετ᾽ ὀλίγας
ἡμέρας, μουσεῖα θυόντων αὐτῶν ἐν οἰκίᾳ παρὰ τὸ Πύθιον,
ἀθρόοι συνδραμόντες οἷοί τ᾽ ἦσαν τὴν ἐπίθεσιν ἐπ᾽ αὐτοὺς
ποιήσασθαι. οἳ δὲ προαισθόμενοι, οἳ μὲν εἰς πανδοκεῖον
ἔφυγον, Δημοκήδης δὲ μετὰ τῶν ἐφήβων εἰς Πλατέας
ἀπεχώρησεν. οἳ δὲ καταλύσαντες τοὺς νόμους ἐχρῶντο
ψηφίσμασιν, ἐν οἷς αἰτιασάμενοι τὸν Δημοκήδην συνεστα-
κέναι τοὺς νεωτέρους ἐπὶ τυραννίδι, τρία τάλαντα ἐκήρυξαν

speeches had been delivered (the longer being by Cylon), the other continued
further, pretending to have inquired into the Pythagoreans' secrets but employing fabrication. And writing out the things which he thought would bring them
[259] most into discredit, he handed a book to the recorder, and ordered him to read
it aloud. Its title was *The Sacred Discourse*,[13] and the following is an outline of its
contents: "One should reverence friends like the gods, but subdue others like
beasts. And this very opinion the disciples speak in verse in reference to Pythagoras:

> His companions he held equal to the blessed gods;
> the rest he considered worth neither mention nor account.

[260] Homer is to be commended especially for his verses in which he speaks of the
shepherd of the people.[14] For, being a supporter of oligarchy, he represented the
rest of men as cattle. They are to war against beans, since they are lords of the lot,
and established those chosen by lot in their public offices. They incite to tyranny,
saying that it is better to be a bull for one day than a cow for a whole lifetime. They
commend law-abiding behavior in others, but command the observance only of
what is decreed by themselves." In short, he declared their philosophy to be a con-
spiracy against the people, and exhorted them not even to tolerate expression of
their opinion, but to keep in mind that they would not have come together in assembly at all, if the Pythagoreans had persuaded the Thousand to adopt their policy. So it was not fitting to let those speak, who, as far as in them lay, prevented
them from hearing other points of view. But they should employ their right hand,
which had been rejected by them, as an instrument of enmity to them, whenever
they voted for resolutions or took pebbles for voting, and to consider it disgraceful
that they who had conquered three hundred thousand at the river Traeis,[15]
should appear overpowered by the Pythagoreans, who were a part of the city itself.
[261] In short, he (Ninon) made those listening so wild with his slander, that after a
few days when the Pythagoreans were celebrating the festival of the Muses in a
house near the Pythion, crowds gathered together and were ready to attack them.
But the Pythagoreans were forewarned of this, and some fled to an inn, while Democedes with the ephebes withdrew to Plateae. The citizens then annulled the

---

13. Two versions of a *Hieros Logos* of Pythagoras were, in fact, preserved to later times, one in
hexameters, the other in Doric prose (see Thesleff, *Pythagorean Texts*, 158-68), but it is improba-
ble that either of them can be traced back to the 5th century B.C. Delatte's attempt in *Études*,
191-230, to reconstruct a fifth century B.C. version of the hexameter *Logos* seems excessively op-
timistic. See also P.C. van der Horst, *Les Vers d'Or Pythagoriciens* (Leiden, 1932) who examines the
Golden Verses in more detail than did Delatte, and seems more cautious.

14. A phrase (or "formula") used no less than forty-four times (in the accus. and dative singular) in the *Iliad*.

15. Probably the correct form, rather than "Tetraeis" of ms. See Diod. Sic. XII. 22, 1. This battle is described by Diodorus in XII, 9-10.

δώσειν, ἐάν τις αὐτὸν ἀνέλῃ, καὶ γενομένης μάχης, κρατή-
σαντος αὐτοῦ τὸν κίνδυνον [ὑπὸ] Θεάγους, ἐκείνῳ τὰ τρία
[262] τάλαντα παρὰ τῆς πόλεως ἐμέρισαν. πολλῶν δὲ κακῶν κατὰ
τὴν πόλιν καὶ τὴν χώραν ὄντων, εἰς κρίσιν προβληθέντων
τῶν φυγάδων καὶ τρισὶ πόλεσι τῆς ἐπιτροπῆς παραδοθείσης,
Ταραντίνοις, Μεταποντίνοις, Καυλωνιάταις, ἔδοξε τοῖς
πεμφθεῖσιν ἐπὶ τὴν γνώμην ἀργύριον λαβοῦσιν, ὡς ἐν τοῖς
τῶν Κροτωνιατῶν ὑπομνήμασιν ἀναγέγραπται, φεύγειν τοὺς
αἰτίους. προσεξέβαλον δὲ τῇ κρίσει κρατήσαντες ἅπαντας
τοὺς τοῖς καθεστῶσι δυσχεραίνοντας καὶ συνεφυγάδευσαν
τὴν γενεάν, οὐ φάσκοντες δεῖν ἀσεβεῖν οὐδὲ τοὺς παῖδας ἀπὸ
τῶν γονέων διασπᾶν. καὶ τά τε χρέα ἀπέκοψαν καὶ τὴν γῆν
[263] ἀνάδαστον ἐποίησαν. ἐπιγενομένων δὲ πολλῶν ἐτῶν καὶ τῶν
περὶ τὸν Δείναρχον ἐν ἑτέρῳ κινδύνῳ τελευτησάντων,
ἀποθανόντος καὶ Λιτάτους, ὅσπερ ἦν ἡγεμονικώτατος τῶν
στασιασάντων, ἔλεός τις καὶ μετάνοια ἐνέπεσε, καὶ τοὺς
περιλειπομένους αὐτῶν ἠβουλήθησαν κατάγειν. μετα-
πεμπόμενοι δὲ πρεσβευτὰς ἐξ Ἀχαΐας δι’ ἐκείνων πρὸς τοὺς
ἐκπεπτωκότας διελύθησαν καὶ τοὺς ὅρκους εἰς Δελφοὺς
[264] ἀνέθηκαν. ἦσαν δὲ τῶν Πυθαγορικῶν καὶ περὶ ἑξήκοντα τὸν
ἀριθμὸν οἱ κατελθόντες ἄνευ τῶν πρεσβυτέρων, ἐν οἷς ἐπὶ
τὴν ἰατρικήν τινες κατενεχθέντες καὶ διαίτῃ τοὺς ἀρρώστους
ὄντας θεραπεύοντες ἡγεμόνες κατέστησαν τῆς εἰρημένης
καθόδου. συνέβη δὲ καὶ τοὺς σωθέντας, διαφερόντως παρὰ
τοῖς πολλοῖς εὐδοκιμοῦντας, κατὰ τὸν καιρόν, ἐν ᾧ
λεγομένου πρὸς τοὺς παρανομοῦντας "οὐ τάδε ἐστὶν ἐπὶ
Νίνωνος" γενέσθαι φασὶ ταύτην τὴν παροιμίαν, κατὰ τοῦτον
ἐμβαλόντων τῶν Θουρίων κατὰ χώραν ἐκβοηθήσαντας καὶ
μετ’ ἀλλήλων κινδυνεύσαντας ἀποθανεῖν, τὴν δὲ πόλιν
οὕτως εἰς τοὐναντίον μεταπεσεῖν, ὥστε χωρὶς τῶν ἐπαίνων,
ὧν ἐποιοῦντο περὶ τῶν ἀνδρῶν, ὑπολαβεῖν μᾶλλον ταῖς
Μούσαις κεχαρισμένην ἔσεσθαι τὴν ἑορτήν, ⟨εἰ⟩ κατὰ τὸ
Μουσεῖον τὴν δημοσίαν ποιοῖντο θυσίαν, ⟨ὃ⟩ κατ’ αὐτοὺς
ἐκείνους πρότερον ἱδρυσάμενοι τὰς θεὰς ἐτίμων. περὶ μὲν οὖν
τῆς κατὰ τῶν Πυθαγορείων γενομένης ἐπιθέσεως τοσαῦτα
εἰρήσθω.

laws, and issued decrees in which they accused Democedes of having brought the younger men together for the purpose of establishing a tyranny, and they proclaimed a reward of three talents if someone should kill him; a battle then took place, and Theages overcame the danger (posed by Democedes), whereat they allotted three talents to Theages on behalf of the city. Since many evils existed throughout the city and land, the fugitives were brought to trial, and the power to decide the case granted to three cities: Tarentum, Metapontium, and Caulonia. And it was decided by those who had been summoned for a verdict, after they were bribed, as is registered in the records of the Crotoniates, that those who were guilty should go into exile. Having thus won the trial, they banished all who were discontented with the existing state of affairs, and banished, at the same time, their families, claiming that one ought not be impious and separate children from their parents. And they abolished debts, and redistributed the land.

[262]

[263] After many years, when Deinarchus and his followers had perished in another battle, and Litates, the chief leader of the rebels, had died, some pity and repentance overcame the Crotoniates, and they resolved to recall the surviving Pythagoreans. Summoning ambassadors to come from Achaea, through these they became reconciled with the exiles, and they solemnly ratified their oaths by recording them at Delphi.

[264] There were in number about sixty Pythagoreans who returned, not counting those who were over age.[16] Among these some had applied themselves to medicine, treating those who were sick by means of diet, and they became leaders of the aforementioned return from exile. It also happened that those who survived were especially honored by the multitude, at the time when it used to be said to those acting lawlessly: "Things are not as they were under Ninon." They report that this saying arose at the time when the Thurians invaded the land,[17] and these same Pythagoreans marched out to defend the state, and died joining in the common danger. Thus the city changed its opinion to such an extent, that, besides the praises which they bestowed on these men, they considered that the festival would be more pleasing to the Muses if they made the public sacrifice at the shrine of the Muses, in which, erected formerly at the request of those men, they had reverenced the goddesses. Let so much, then, be said about the attack which took place against the Pythagoreans.

---

16. Presumably this means "too old to take part in administration."
17. This must be appreciably later than 443 B.C. when Thurii was founded, perhaps in the early 430's.

[265] Διάδοχος δὲ πρὸς πάντων ὁμολογεῖται Πυθαγόρου γεγονέναι Ἀρισταῖος Δαμοφῶντος ὁ Κροτωνιάτης, κατ᾽ αὐτὸν
Πυθαγόραν τοῖς χρόνοις γενόμενος, ἑπτὰ γενεαῖς ἔγγιστα
πρὸ Πλάτωνος· καὶ οὐ μόνον τῆς σχολῆς, ἀλλὰ καὶ τῆς
παιδοτροφίας καὶ τοῦ Θεανοῦς γάμου κατηξιώθη διὰ τὸ
ἐξαιρέτως περικεκρατηκέναι τῶν δογμάτων. αὐτὸν μὲν γὰρ
Πυθαγόραν ἀφηγήσασθαι λέγεται ἑνὸς δέοντος ἔτη τεσ-
σαράκοντα, τὰ πάντα βιώσαντα ἔτη ἐγγὺς τῶν ἑκατόν,
παραδοῦναι δὲ Ἀρισταίῳ τὴν σχολὴν πρεσβυτάτῳ ὄντι.
μεθ᾽ ὃν ἡγήσασθαι Μνήμαρχον τὸν Πυθαγόρου, τοῦτον δὲ
Βουλαγόρᾳ παραδοῦναι, ἐφ᾽ οὗ διαρπασθῆναι συνέβη τὴν
Κροτωνιατῶν πόλιν. μεθ᾽ ὃν Γαρτύδαν τὸν Κροτωνιάτην
διάδοχον γενέσθαι, ἐπανελθόντα ἐκ τῆς ἀποδημίας, ἣν
ἐποιήσατο πρὸ τοῦ πολέμου· διὰ μέντοι τὴν συμφορὰν τῆς
πατρίδος ἐκλιπεῖν τὸν βίον. ἕνα δὴ μόνον γενέσθαι τοῦτον,
[266] ὃς ὑπὸ λύπης προύλιπε τὸν βίον· τοῖς δ᾽ ἄλλοις ἔθος εἶναι
γηραιοῖς σφόδρα γενομένοις ὥσπερ ἐκ δεσμῶν τοῦ σώματος
ἀπαλλάττεσθαι. χρόνῳ μέντοι γε ὕστερον Ἀρεσᾶν ἐκ τῶν
Λευκανῶν, σωθέντα διά τινων ξένων, ἀφηγήσασθαι τῆς
σχολῆς· πρὸς ὃν ἀφικέσθαι Διόδωρον τὸν Ἀσπένδιον, ὃν
παραδεχθῆναι διὰ τὴν σπάνιν τῶν ἐν τῷ συστήματι ἀνδρῶν.
οὗτος δὲ εἰς τὴν Ἑλλάδα ἐπανελθὼν διέδωκε τὰς
Πυθαγορείους φωνάς. ζηλωτὰς δὲ γράφειν γενέσθαι τῶν
ἀνδρῶν περὶ μὲν Ἡράκλειαν Κλεινίαν καὶ Φιλόλαον, ⟨ἐν⟩
Μεταποντίῳ δὲ Θεωρίδην ⟨καὶ⟩ Εὔρυτον, ἐν Τάραντι δὲ
Ἀρχύταν. τῶν δ᾽ ἔξωθεν ἀκροατῶν γενέσθαι καὶ
Ἐπίχαρμον, ἀλλ᾽ οὐκ ἐκ τοῦ συστήματος τῶν ἀνδρῶν·
ἀφικόμενον δὲ εἰς Συρακούσας διὰ τὴν Ἱέρωνος τυραννίδα
τοῦ μὲν φανερῶς φιλοσοφεῖν ἀποσχέσθαι, εἰς μέτρον δ᾽
ἐντεῖναι τὰς διανοίας τῶν ἀνδρῶν, μετὰ παιδιᾶς κρύφα
ἐκφέροντα τὰ Πυθαγόρου δόγματα.

CHAPTER THIRTY-SIX

On the succession to Pythagoras and on its end, and the
names of men and women who inherited philosophy from him.

The successor of Pythagoras is agreed by all[1] to have been Aristaeus, son of Damophon of Croton, who lived at the same time as Pythagoras, approximately seven generations before Plato. And because he especially had full command of their doctrines, he was thought worthy not only of leading the school, but also of rearing Pythagoras' children and of marrying Theano. For Pythagoras himself is said to have led the school for thirty-nine years, having lived nearly a total of one hundred years, and to have handed the school to Aristaeus as being the oldest. After him Mnemarchus, son of Pythagoras, was leader; and he in turn handed the school over to Boulagoras, in whose time the city of Croton was plundered. After him Gartydas of Croton became successor, when he returned from his travels abroad before the war; however, his country's misfortune caused his death[2]. He was the only one to die of grief; for the others it was a custom, when they became very old, to depart from the body as if from chains. Sometime later, however, Aresas from Lucania, saved by some strangers, led the school;[3] to him came Diodorus of Aspendus,[4] whom he received because of the scarcity of men in the community. This man, on returning to Hellas, spread abroad the Pythagorean sayings. In Heracleia, Cleinias and Philolaus devoted themselves to writing about these men; in Metapontium Theorides and Eurytus, and in Tarentum, Archytas. And Epicharmus became one of the disciples outside the school, but he was not from the inner circle of these men. When he arrived at Syracuse, he abstained from philosophizing openly because of Hieron's despotism, but he put the thoughts of the Pythagoreans in metre, and under the guise of foolery, published the secret teachings of Pythagoras.

---

1. This is certainly not agreed by all. Diogenes Laertius (8.43), gives Pythagoras' son Telauges as his successor, as does *Anon. Phot.* 438 b 29, and the Suda, s.v. *Pythagoras.*

2. Is this a reference to the anti-Pythagorean uprisings ca. 450 B.C.? If so, it is curiously phrased.

3. The meaning of this is also obscure. Aresas is attested as a Lucanian by Stobaeus, who preserves an extract from a treatise attributed to him on *The Nature of Man (Anth.* I. 49, 27).

4. Diodorus can be dated fairly securely to the early 4th century (and thus Aresas to the late 5th). Cf. Ath. 4.163d-f, and Burkert, *Lore and Science*, 202-4. Aresas is probably to be identified with the Arcesus of Plut. *De gen. Socr.* 583 B, to whom Gorgias (probably after his visit to Athens as an ambassador from Leontini in 427 B.C.) brought word of Lysis' whereabouts (De Lacy and Einarson in the Loeb Plutarch edition actually read Aresas here for Arcesus of the mss. which seems somewhat rash).

[267]
τῶν δὲ συμπάντων Πυθαγορείων τοὺς μὲν ἀγνῶτάς τε καὶ ἀνωνύμους τινὰς πολλοὺς εἰκὸς γεγονέναι, τῶν δὲ γνωριζομένων ἐστὶ τάδε τὰ ὀνόματα·

Κροτωνιᾶται Ἱππόστρατος, Δύμας, Αἴγων, Αἵμων, Σύλλος, Κλεοσθένης, Ἀγέλας, Ἐπίσυλος, Φυκιάδας, Ἔκφαντος, Τίμαιος, Βοῦθος, Ἔρατος, Ἰταναῖος, Ῥόδιππος, Βρύας, Εὔανδρος, Μυλλίας, Ἀντιμέδων, Ἀγέας, Λεόφρων, Ἀγύλος, Ὀνάτας, Ἱπποσθένης, Κλεόφρων, Ἀλκμαίων, Δαμοκλῆς, Μίλων, Μένων

Μεταποντῖνοι Βροντῖνος, Παρμίσκος, Ὀρεστάδας, Λέων, Δαμάρμενος, Αἰνέας, Χειλᾶς, Μελησίας, Ἀριστέας, Λαφάων, Εὔανδρος, Ἀγησίδαμος, Ξενοκάδης, Εὐρύφημος, Ἀριστομένης, Ἀγήσαρχος, Ἀλκίας, Ξενοφάντης, Θρασέας, Εὔρυτος, Ἐπίφρων, Εἰρίσκος, Μεγιστίας, Λεωκύδης, Θρασυμήδης, Εὔφημος, Προκλῆς, Ἀντιμένης, Λάκριτος, Δαμοτάγης, Πύρρων, Ῥηξίβιος, Ἀλώπεκος, Ἀστύλος, Λακύδας, Ἀνίοχος, Λακράτης, Γλυκῖνος

Ἀκραγαντῖνος Ἐμπεδοκλῆς

Ἐλεάτης Παρμενίδης

Ταραντῖνοι Φιλόλαος, Εὔρυτος, Ἀρχύτας, Θεόδωρος, Ἀρίστιππος, Λύκων, Ἑστιαῖος, Πολέμαρχος, Ἀστέας, Καινίας, Κλέων, Εὐρυμέδων, Ἀρκέας, Κλειναγόρας, Ἄρχιππος, Ζώπυρος, Εὔθυνος, Δικαίαρχος, Φιλωνίδης, Φροντίδας, Λῦσις, Λυσίβιος, Δεινοκράτης, Ἐχεκράτης, Πακτίων, Ἀκουσιλάδας, Ἴκκος, Πεισικράτης, Κλέαρατος, Λεοντεύς, Φρύνιχος, Σιμιχίας, Ἀριστοκλείδας, Κλεινίας, Ἁβροτέλης, Πεισίρροδος, Βρύας, Ἔλανδρος, Ἀρχέμαχος, Μιμνόμαχος, Ἀκμονίδας, Δικᾶς, Καροφαντίδας

Συβαρῖται Μέτωπος, Ἵππασος, Πρόξενος, Εὐάνωρ, Λεάναξ, Μενέστωρ, Διοκλῆς, Ἔμπεδος, Τιμάσιος, Πολεμαῖος, Ἔνδιος, Τυρσηνός

Καρχηδόνιοι Μιλτιάδης, Ἄνθης, Ὁδίος, Λεώκριτος

Πάριοι Αἰήτιος, Φαινεκλῆς, Δεξίθεος, Ἀλκίμαχος, Δείναρχος, Μέτων, Τίμαιος, Τιμησιάναξ, Εὔμοιρος, Θυμαρίδας

Λοκροὶ Γύττιος, Ξένων, Φιλόδαμος, Εὐέτης, Εὔδικος, Σθενωνίδας, Σωσίστρατος, Εὐθύνους, Ζάλευκος, Τιμάρης

Ποσειδωνιᾶται Ἀθάμας, Σῖμος, Πρόξενος, Κραναός, Μύης, Βαθύλαος, Φαίδων

[267]   Of all the Pythagoreans, it is likely that many are unknown and nameless, but of those who are known these are the names:[5]

From Croton: Hippostratus, Dymas, Aegon, Haemon, Syllus, Cleosthenes, Agelas, Episylus, Phyciadas, Ecphantus, Timaeus, Buthus, Eratus, Itanaeus, Rhodippus, Bryas, Euandrus, Myllias, Antimedon, Ageas, Leophron, Agylus, Onatas, Hipposthenes, Cleophron, Alcmaion, Damocles, Milon, Menon.

From Metapontium: Brontinus,[6] Parmiscus, Orestadas, Leon, Damarmenus, Aeneas, Cheilas, Melesias, Aristeas, Laphaon, Euandrus, Agesidamus, Xenocades, Euryphemus, Aristomenes, Agesarchus, Alcias, Xenophantes, Thraseas, Eurytus, Epiphron, Eiriscus, Megistias, Leocydes, Thrasymedes, Euphemus, Procles, Antimenes, Lacritus, Damotages, Pyrrhon, Rhexibius, Alopecus, Astylos, Lacydas, Haniochus, Lacrates, Glycinus.

From Acragas: Empedocles.

From Elea: Parmenides.

From Tarentum: Philolaus,[7] Eurytus, Archytas, Theodorus, Aristippus, Lycon, Hestiaeus, Polemarchus, Asteas, Caenias, Cleon, Eurymedon, Arceas, Cleinagoras, Archippus, Zopyrus, Euthynus, Dicaearchus, Philonides, Phrontidas, Lysis, Lysibius, Deinocrates, Echecrates, Paction, Acusiladas, Iccus, Peisicrates, Clearatus, Leonteus, Phrynichus, Simichias, Aristocleidas, Cleinias, Habroteles, Peisirrhodus, Bryas, Helandrus, Archemachus, Mimnomachus, Acmonidas, Dicas, Carophantidas.

From Sybaris: Metopus, Hippasus,[8] Proxenus, Euanor, Leanax, Menestor, Diocles, Empedus, Timasius, Polemaeus, Endius, Tyrsenus.

From Carthage: Miltiades, Anthes, Hodius, Leocritus.

From Paros: Aeetius, Phainecles, Dexitheus, Alcimachus, Deinarchus, Meton, Timaeus, Timesianax, Eumoerus, Thymaridas.

From Locri: Gyttius, Xenon, Philodamus, Euetes, Eudicus, Sthenonidas, Sosistratus, Euthynous, Zaleucus, Timares.

From Poseidonia:[9] Athamas, Simus, Proxenus, Cranaus, Myes, Bathylaus, Phaedon.

From Lucania: Occelus and Occilus (brothers), Aresandrus, Cerambus.

From Dardania: Malion.

From Argos: Hippomedon, Timosthenes, Euelthon, Thrasydamus,[10] Criton, Polyctor.

----

5. On the catalogue of Pythagoreans, see esp. Burkert, *Lore and Science,* 105. Of its 235 names, 145 occur only here.

6. He comes from Croton, (see D.L. 8. 42), but in section 132 above his origin is left vague.

7. Diogenes Laertius (8. 84) presents him as being from Croton.

8. In section 181 above, Iamblichus presents "some" as saying he is from Croton, "others" from Metapontium.

9. Or Paestum, coastal town of Lucania.

10. In section 145, he is presented as a Tarentine, but he emigrated to Paros (section 239).

Λευκανοὶ Ὄκκελος καὶ Ὄκκιλος ἀδελφοί, Ἀρέσανδρος, Κέραμβος

Δαρδανεὺς Μαλίων

Ἀργεῖοι Ἱππομέδων, Τιμοσθένης, Εὐέλθων, Θρασύδαμος, Κρίτων, Πολύκτωρ

Λάκωνες Αὐτοχαρίδας, Κλεάνωρ, Εὐρυκράτης

Ὑπερβόρειος Ἄβαρις

Ῥηγῖνοι Ἀριστείδης, Δημοσθένης, Ἀριστοκράτης, Φύτιος, Ἑλικάων, Μνησίβουλος, Ἱππαρχίδης, Εὐθοσίων, Εὐθυκλῆς, Ὄψιμος, Κάλαϊς, Σελινούντιος

Συρακούσιοι Λεπτίνης, Φιντίας, Δάμων

Σάμιοι Μέλισσος, Λάκων, Ἄρχιππος, Ἑλώριππος, Ἕλωρις, Ἵππων

Καυλωνιᾶται Καλλίμβροτος, Δίκων, Νάστας, Δρύμων, Ξενέας

Φλιάσιοι Διοκλῆς, Ἐχεκράτης, Πολύμναστος, Φάντων

Σικυώνιοι Πολιάδης, Δήμων, Στράτιος, Σωσθένης

Κυρηναῖοι Πρῶρος, Μελάνιππος, Ἀριστάγγελος, Θεόδωρος

Κυζικηνοὶ Πυθόδωρος, Ἱπποσθένης, Βούθηρος, Ξενόφιλος

Καταναῖοι Χαρώνδας, Λυσιάδης

Κορίνθιος Χρύσιππος

Τυρρηνὸς Ναυσίθοος

Ἀθηναῖος Νεόκριτος

Ποντικὸς Λύραμνος. οἱ πάντες σιη´.

Πυθαγορίδες δὲ γυναῖκες αἱ ἐπιφανέσταται· Τιμύχα γυνὴ [ἡ] Μυλλία τοῦ Κροτωνιάτου, Φιλτὺς θυγάτηρ Θεόφριος τοῦ Κροτωνιάτου, Βυνδάκου ἀδελφή, Ὀκκελὼ καὶ Ἐκκελὼ ⟨ἀδελφαὶ Ὀκκέλω καὶ Ὀκκίλω⟩ τῶν Λευκανῶν, Χειλωνὶς θυγάτηρ Χείλωνος τοῦ Λακεδαιμονίου, Κρατησίκλεια Λάκαινα γυνὴ Κλεάνορος τοῦ Λακεδαιμονίου, Θεανὼ γυνὴ τοῦ Μεταποντίνου Βροτίνου, Μυῖα γυνὴ Μίλωνος τοῦ Κροτωνιάτου, Λασθένεια Ἀρκάδισσα, Ἁβροτέλεια Ἁβροτέλους θυγάτηρ τοῦ Ταραντίνου, Ἐχεκράτεια Φλιασία, Τυρσηνὶς Συβαρῖτις, Πεισιρρόδη Ταραντινίς, Θεάδουσα Λάκαινα, Βοιὼ Ἀργεία, Βαβελύκα Ἀργεία, Κλεαίχμα ἀδελφὴ Αὐτοχαρίδα τοῦ Λάκωνος. αἱ πᾶσαι ιζ´.

From Laconia: Autocharidas, Cleanor, Eurycrates.

From Hyperborea: Abaris.

From Rhegium: Aristeides, Demosthenes, Aristocrates, Phytius, Helicaon, Mnesibulus, Hipparchides, Euthosion, Euthycles, Opsimus, Calais, Selinuntius.[11]

From Syracuse: Leptines, Phintias, Damon.

From Samos: Melissus, Lacon, Archippus, Helorippus, Heloris, Hippon.

From Caulonia: Callimbrotus, Dicon, Nastas, Drymon, Xeneas.

From Phlius: Diocles, Echecrates, Polymnastus, Phanton.

From Sicyon: Poliades, Demon, Stratius, Sosthenes.

From Cyrene: Prorus, Melanippus, Aristangelus, Theodorus.

From Cyzicus: Pythodorus, Hipposthenes, Butherus, Xenophilus.

From Catane: Charondas, Lysiades.

From Corinth: Chrysippus.

From Etruria: Nausithous.

From Athens: Neocritus.

From Pontus: Lyramnus

Total: 218.

The most famous Pythagorean women are: Timycha, wife of Myllias of Croton, Philtys, daughter of Theophris of Croton, sister of Byndacus, Occelo and Eccelo, sisters of the Lucanians Occelus and Occilus; Cheilonis, daugher of Cheilon the Lacedaimonian; Cratesicleia, the Laconian, wife of Cleanor, the Lacedaemonian; Theano, wife of the Metapontian Brotinus;[12] Myia, wife of Milon of Croton, Lastheneia from Arcadia, Habroteleia, daughter of Habroteles of Tarentum, Echecrateia of Phlius, Tyrsenis from Sybaris, Peisirrhode from Tarentum; Theadusa from Lacedaemon, Boeo from Argos, Babelyca from Argos, Cleaechma, sister of the Lacedaemonian Autocharidas.

Total: 17.

---

11. Or perhaps, Calais the Selinuntian.

12. The other form of his name, Brontinus, appears in section 132, and in the list of Metapontines above.

SELECT BIBLIOGRAPHY

Texts and Translations of De vita Pythagorica

von Albrecht, M., ed. and tr. *Iamblichos. Pythagoras. Legende, Lehre, Lebensgestaltung.* Zürich/Stuttgart: Artemis, 1963.

Clark, G., tr. *Iamblichus: On the Pythagorean Life.* Liverpool: Liverpool University Press, 1989.

Deubner, L., ed. *Iamblichus. De vita Pythagorica.* Leipzig: Teubner, 1937, ed. corr. cur. U. Klein, Stuttgart: Teubner, 1975.

Nauck, A., ed. *Iamblichi De vita Pythagorica; accedit epimetrum De Pythagorae Aureo carmine.* St. Petersburg, 1884, repr. Amsterdam: Hakkert, 1965.

Taylor, T., tr. *Iamblichus' Life of Pythagoras, or Pythagoric Life. Accompanied by Fragments of the Ethical Writings ... and a Collection of Pythagoric Sentences from Stobaeus and Others ....* London, 1818, repr. London: J. M. Watkins, 1965.

Secondary Literature

von Albrecht, M. "Das Menschenbild in Iamblichs Darstellung der pythagoreischen Lebensformen," *Antike und Abendland* 12 (1966) 51-63.

Barnes, T. D., "A Correspondent of Iamblichus," *Greek, Roman, and Byzantine Studies* 19 (1978) 99-106.

Bertermann, G. *De Iamblichi Vitae Pythagoricae fontibus.* Diss. Königsberg: Hartung, 1913.

Betz, H.D. "Gottmensch II (Griechisch-römische Antike und Urchristentum)," *Reallexicon für Antike und Christentum* XII (1983) 234-312.

Bidez, J. "Le philosophe Jamblique et son école," *Revue des études grecques* 32 (1919) 29-40.

Bidez, J. and Cumont, F. *Les mages héllenisés.* Paris: Les Belles Lettres, 1938.

Boehm, F. *De symbolis Pythagoreis.* Diss. Berlin, 1905.

Boyancé, P. "Sur l'*Abaris* d'Héraclide le Pontique," *Revue des études anciennes* 36 (1934) 321-352.

Boyancé, P. "Sur la vie pythagoricienne." *Revue des études grecques* 52 (1939) 36-50.

Burkert, W. "Platon oder Pythagoras? Zum Ursprung des Wortes 'Philosophie,'" *Hermes* 88 (1960) 159-177.

Burkert, W. "Hellenistische Pseudopythagorica," *Philologus* 105 (1961) 16-43, 226-246.

Burkert, W. *Weisheit und Wissenschaft: Studien zu Pythagoras, Philolaos, und Platon.* Nürnberg: H. Carl, 1962. Revised and trans. by E. L. Minar, Jr. as *Lore and Science in Ancient Pythagoreanism.* Cambridge, Mass.: Harvard Univ. Pr., 1972.

Cameron, A. "The Date of Iamblichus' Birth," *Hermes* 96 (1968) 374-376.

Corssen, P. "Zum Abaris des Heraklides Ponticus," *Rheinisches Museum* 67 (1912) 20-47.

Delatte, A. *Études sur la littérature pythagoricienne.* Paris: Champion, 1915.

Delatte, A., ed. and comm. *La Vie de Pythagore de Diogène Laërce.* Brussels: Lamertin, 1922.

Demand, N. "Pythagoras, Son of Mnesarchos," *Phronesis* 18 (1973) 91-96.

Detienne, M. *Homère, Hésiode, et Pythagore. Poésie et philosophie dans le pythagorisme ancien.* Brussells: Coll. *Latomus,* 57, 1962.

Detienne, M. *La notion de daïmon dans le pythagorisme ancien.* (Bibl. de la fac. de philos. et lettr. de l'univ. de Liège, 165). Paris: Société d'édition "Les belles lettres," 1963.

Deubner, L. "Bemerkungen zum Text der *Vita Pythagorae* des Iamblichos," *Sitzungsberichte der Preussischen Akademie der Wissenschaften zu Berlin,* phil.-hist. Kl. (1935) 612-690, 824-827.

Diels, H. *Die Fragmente der Vorsokratiker,* ed. W. Kranz, I, 8th ed. Berlin: Weidmann, 1956.

Dillon, J. "Iamblichus of Chalcis," *Aufstieg und Niedergang der römischen Welt,* pt. II, vol. 36:2 (1987) 863-909.

Dillon, J. *Iamblichi Chalcidensis in Platonis Dialogos Commentariorum Fragmenta.* Leiden: Brill, 1973.

Dillon, J. *The Middle Platonists.* London: Duckworth, 1977.

Ferrero, L. *Storia del pitagorismo nel mondo Romano.* Turin: Univ. di Torino, 1955.

Festugière, A.-J. "Les mémoires pythagoriques cités par Alexandre Polyhistor," *Revue des études grecques* 58 (1945) 1-65.

Festugière, A.-J. *La révélation d'Hermès Trismégiste* I (2nd ed. 1950), II-IV 1954. Paris: Société d'édition "Les belles lettres," repr. 1981.

Festugière, A.-J. "Sur une nouvelle édition du *De vita pythagorica* de Jamblique," *Revue des études grecques* 50 (1937) 470-494.

von Fritz, K. *Pythagorean Politics in Southern Italy: An Analysis of the Sources*. New York: Columbia Univ. Pr., 1940.

von Fritz, K. *et al.*, *Realencyclopädie der classischen Altertumswissenschaft* "Pythagoras" in *RE* 24 (Stuttgart 1963) 171-300, including: K. von Fritz, "Pythagoras von Samos," 171-209, and "Pythagoreer, Pythagoreismus bis zum Ende des 4. Jhdts. v. Chr.," 209-268; H. Dörrie, "Der nachklassische Pythagoreismus," 268-277; B. L. van der Waerden, "Zum Art. Pythagoras: Die Schriften und Fragmente des Pythagoras," *RE*. Supp. 10 (1965) 843-864.

von Fritz, F. "Mathematiker und Akusmatiker bei den alten Pythagoreern," *Sitzungsberichte der bayerischen Akademie der Wissenschaften*, philos.-hist. Kl. 11 Munich (1960).

Gottschalk, H. B. *Heraclides of Pontus*. Oxford: Oxford Univ. Pr., 1980.

Guthrie, W. K. C. *A History of Greek Philosophy* I-II. Cambridge: Cambridge Univ. Pr. 1962-1965.

Hershbell, J. P. "Plutarch's Pythagorean Friends," *Classical Bulletin* 60 (1984) 73-78.

Hölk, C. *De acusmatis sive symbolis Pythagoricis*. Diss. Kiel, 1894.

Larsen, B. D. *Jamblique de Chalcis. Exégète et philosophe*. Diss. Aarhus, 1972.

Leo, F. *Die griechisch-römische Biographie nach ihrer litterarischen Form*. Leipzig: Teubner, 1901.

Lévy, I. *La légende de Pythagore de Grèce en Palestine*. Paris: Champion, 1927.

Lévy, I. *Recherches sur les sources de la légende de Pythagore*. Paris: Leroux, 1926.

Méautis, G. *Recherches sur le pythagorisme*. Neuchâtel: Fac. de Lettres, 1922.

Merlan, P. *From Platonism to Neoplatonism*. The Hague: Nijhoff, 1953.

Mejer, J. *Diogenes Laertius and his Hellenistic Background. Hermes* Einzelschriften 40. Wiesbaden, 1978.

North, H. *Sophrosyne. Self-Knowledge and Self-Restraint in Greek Literature* (Ithaca: 1966).

O'Meara, D. J. *Pythagoras Revived. Mathematics and Philosophy in Late Antiquity*. Oxford: Oxford Univ. Pr., 1989.

Philip, J. A. "Aristotle's Monograph on the Pythagoreans," *Transactions of the American Philological Association* 94 (1963) 185-198.

Philip, J. A. "The Biographical Tradition-Pythagoras," *Transactions of the American Philological Association* 90 (1959) 185-194.

Philip, J. A. *Pythagoras and Early Pythagoreanism.* Toronto: Univ. Toronto Pr., 1966.

Rohde, E. "Die Quellen des Iamblichus in seiner Biographie des Pythagoras," *Rheinisches Museum* 26 (1871) 554-576, 27 (1872) 23-61, reprinted in his *Kleine Schriften* II: Tübingen: Mohr, 1901, 102-172.

Rostagni, A. *Il verbo di Pitagora.* Turin, 1924.

Thesleff, H. *An Introduction to the Pythagorean Writings of the Hellenistic Period.* Abo, 1961: Acta Academiae Aboensis, Humaniora 24.3.

Thesleff, H., ed. *The Pythagorean Texts of the Hellenistic Period.* Abo, 1965: Acta Academiae Aboensis, Humaniora 30.1.

Vanderspoel, J. "Themistios and the Origin of Iamblichus," *Hermes* 116 (1988), 125-133.

De Vogel, C. J. *Pythagoras and Early Pythagoreanism. An Interpretation of Neglected Evidence on the Philosopher Pythagoras.* Assen: van Gorcum, 1966.

van der Waerden, B. L. *Die Pythagoreer. Religiöse Bruderschaft und Schule der Wissenschaft.* Zurich and Munich: Artemis, 1979.

Wallis, R. T. *Neo-Platonism.* London: Duckworth, 1972.

Wehrli, F., ed. *Die Schule des Aristoteles.* Basel: Schwabe, 1944-1960, esp. I. *Dikaiarchos* (1944), II. *Aristoxenos* (1945), III. *Klearchos* (1948), VII. *Herakleides Pontikos* (1953), and VIII. *Eudemos von Rhodos* (1955).

Zeller, E. *Die Philosophie der Griechen in ihrer geschichtlichen Entwicklung* Leipzig: Riesland, I, ed. W. Nestle, 1923; II.1, 1922; II.2, 1921; III.1, 1923; III.2, 1923; repr. Darmstadt: Wissenschaftliche Buchgesellschaft 1963.

INDEX OF ANCIENT AUTHORS
AND PASSAGES CITED

When the author is explicitly alluded to in Iamblichus's text, the reference is obelised thus +; quotations in Iamblichus's text have the reference asterisked thus *.

INDEX OF MODERN AUTHORS CITED

Standard works (*LSJ*, *RAC*, *RE* etc.) are not cited, though the authors of individual articles are. Editors are mentioned when the reference is to a specific emendation or to a comment, but not just when the work they are editing is alluded to. Translators of modern works and the editors of such collections of essays as the *Entretiens Hardt* are omitted. The alphabetisation has followed that in the bibliography. Mentions in the bibliography are omitted.

INDEX OF NAMES

All references to writers are incorporated in the index of authors and are not repeated in this index. In case of doubt the index of authors should be consulted first. This index covers both text and notes and the introduction. Names of cities mentioned merely as the patria of a person are not included, nor are the names of those people who are mentioned merely for their relationship to others. The names of cities in the final section of the life have been indexed, but not those of people.

CPSIA information can be obtained
at www.ICGtesting.com
Printed in the USA
BVHW050725251122
652652BV00010B/216